W9-BAN-462

The French Revolution and the Birth of Modernity

EDITED BY

Ferenc Fehér

UNIVERSITY OF CALIFORNIA PRESS

Berkeley   Los Angeles   Oxford

University of California Press
Berkeley and Los Angeles, California

University of California Press
Oxford, England

Copyright © 1990 by The Regents of the University of California

Library of Congress Cataloging-in-Publication Data

The French Revolution and the birth of modernity / edited by Ferenc
Fehér.
    p. cm.
  ISBN 0-520-06879-3 (alk. paper).—ISBN 0-520-07120-4 (pbk.:
alk. paper)
    1. France—History—Revolution, 1789–1799—Influence.
2. Civilization, Modern. 3. Political science—History. I. Fehér.
Ferenc. 1933– .
DC148.F722   1990
944.04—dc20   90-10819
                                                                  CIP

Printed in the United States of America
1   2   3   4   5   6   7   8   9

The paper used in this publication meets the minimum requirements
of American National Standard for Information Sciences—Permanence
of Paper for Printed Library Materials, ANSI Z39.48-1984 ⊗

The French Revolution and the Birth of Modernity

158-168

Contents

v

Acknowledgment

The majority of the contributions to this volume have been originally published in the special issue of *Social Research*, the theoretical journal of the Graduate Faculty of the New School for Social Research, vol. 56, no. 1, Spring 1989. Editor and publisher would like to thank Professor Arien Mack, the editor of *Social Research* for her permission to use the material previously published in the journal.

Introduction

Ferenc Fehér

I

The historiography of the French Revolution has been traditionally and rightly regarded as the major yield and the ultimate confirmation of the golden age of historicism, a success story in which every representative paradigm of writing history has had its own share. From Jaurès to Lefebvre and Soboul, the Marxist chronicles transpired as proof positive of the validity of their master's paradigm. The liberal partisans of the thesis of "limited but infinite progress" thrived on an apparently inexhaustible treasure trove of the hagiography of the "Republic." In their accounts, an indestructible and constantly resurrected republicanism signaled "progress," and the surreptitiously surviving and occasionally reemerging "ultramontanism" or "royalism" meant "regression." The advocates of historical decay, from Bonald and De Maistre to Maurras, found their explanatory principle continually confirmed by their nation's intermittent loss of *gloire* and its incessant internecine strife. Prior to Nietzsche, the mythology of the superman demonstrated its seductive power through the exploitation of the material of the French Revolution in Carlyle's celebrated work. And the particularly French branch of "skeptical liberalism," initiated by Tocqueville, continued by Cochin, and inherited by Furet, felt itself confirmed by every new disastrous turn of a permanently shaky French democracy.

And yet, in the postwar domestic research of the French Revolution, unmistakable symptoms of the decline of the traditional interpretations have been emerging for decades, the sole exception being Soboul's classic on the sans-culottes of Year II and the direct democracy of the Paris districts. Put bluntly, the domestic narrative became tediously self-repetitive. Until the publication of Furet's *Thinking the French Revolution* in the second half of the

1

1970s, which has become a turning point for friend and foe alike, innovating impetus came exclusively from outside. The Anglo-American "revisionism" successfully questioned the relevance of the major explanatory devices of the Marxist school, at least in the actual form in which they had been used. Via the accumulated experience of sociological research, the new American "social history" or "historical sociology," whose paradigmatic works were Tilly's *The Vendée* and Skocpol's *States and Social Revolutions*, gave an important stimulus to that particular style of writing history, which had been captive too long to a dubious method of "typology." In her celebrated, as well as hotly debated, *On Revolution*, Hannah Arendt has drawn such a sharp contrast between the "American" and "French" models of revolution that the after-effects of her challenge or provocation have been reverberating ever since in historical consciousness. Of the contributors to the present volume, Higonnet with his most recent *Sister Republics* is thoroughly indebted to Arendt's provocative gesture. English and Scandinavian New Leftist historians were the only worthy sucessors to Guérin's and Soboul's pioneering explorations into a hitherto unknown continent of anonymous militants (I have in mind the works by Cobb and Tönnesson). *The French Revolution and the Birth of Modernity*, emerging from a special bicentennial issue of *Social Research* (the theoretical journal of the Graduate Faculty of the New School for Social Research) and with a majority of its contributors coming from outside of French research, tries to live up to the already very high standards of the new tradition.

A very serious trend, at once historical and philosophical, lurks behind the decline of the French domestic narrative. The end of World War II marked the simultaneous collapse of the great paradigms of nineteenth-century historicism, which, without public recognition, had been philosophically eroded already for a long time. The Hegelian–Marxian paradigm of a progressive conclusion of (pre)history was hard, later outright impossible, to maintain in the face of the Holocaust and the Gulag. Paradigms of historical decay had profoundly compromised themselves by their often close association with the "heroic" efforts of Fascism and Nazism to "overcome decadence." The paradigms of limited (mostly technological) progress, which had for a while fared best, ran into the insurmountable hurdle of the apparently ineliminable poverty of the postcolonial world and the skeptical "ecological consciousness." Although on the academic scene of "mass society" historical research has expanded to an incredible extent; although its methodological self-awareness has been immensely refined and its tools sharpened; although the walls of national segregation have been pulled down within the global institution of academe, historians have been increasingly at a loss concerning the *extra muros* relevance of their research.

In the meantime, however, a beneficial change has begun to develop in the professional–historical consciousness under the impact of the widespread acceptance of hermeneutics in the social sciences. This acceptance has influenced the historian, whether or not the historian was consciously preoccupied with philosophy. The nineteenth-century paradigms of history operated with the concept of an objective, uniform, homogeneous and coherent process comprising its "meaning" (which was to be "scientifically" deciphered by historians). They often used the hypothesis of objective historical laws, and they ascribed an unambiguous (although divergingly explicated) direction to the integral process. True enough, several constituents of these theories, above all its "objectivity," had already been profoundly questioned in the nineteenth century, primarily by Nietzsche. The methodological consequences of this challenge, however, dawned on the historian with excessive delay. But now we are living in an age of "hermeneutical consciousness," the spirit of which, transpiring in the present volume, can be summed up in a term that none of the participants uses and some of them would object to: *posthistoire.*

Posthistoire, a term coined in the process of exploring "postmodernity," seems to be a particularly inept category for the use of historians if it is meant in the facile and misleading sense of "history having come to a standstill." But there are other possible interpretations of the term. If "postmodernity" is understood not as an epoch subsequent to modernity, but as a position and attitude *within* modernity which confirms modernity's "arrival," its final settling-in, while at the same time making inquiries into modernity's credentials and efforts to render meaning to it, the concept *posthistoire* will emerge from a taboo and a barrier for the historian into a stimulus. In this understanding, history will transpire as a text that we read together, but each of us in his or her own individual way. This collective, at the same time personal, reading does not recognize any "distinguished" reader. (Such a position could only be achieved by the absolute transcendence of our common world: modernity.) But although there are only myths of and arrogant claims to a "distinguished position" and "absolute transcendence," there is indeed a shared core in the reading of the same story by every community of readers.

Despite the conspicuous—theoretical, methodological, and political— differences between the contributors to *The French Revolution and the Birth of Modernity,* the "shared core" of the story read and recounted by them, individually and collectively, is palpably present. It is comprised in the title of the volume, and it provides this collection of papers with a strong internal cohesion. The shared core is the authors' recognition that after several crucial antecedents and preludes, modernity has been born out of the French Revolution; further, that modernity "is here," it has arrived; and, finally, that it has to be given a meaning. It is at this point that the often heated debate between the seemingly isolated papers in the volume begins.

II

The first complex issue, about which there is a considerable degree of dis-agreement among the authors, but discussed in the "subtext" rather than in the text itself, is the question of whether the process of birth of modernity had actually come to an end or whether it is still a delivery-in-progress. This "merely" subtextual issue is of crucial significance. Its evaluation will ulti-mately decide the tone, the method, and the style of the contributions, the distance that has been taken in them to the collectively recounted story. Put briefly, this will define whether the subject matter of the narrative, to use a wise category that Agnes Heller coined in her *A Theory of History*, is "the past of the present" or past pure and simple, which, as such, is dead.

As is well known, Furet holds the view that the French Revolution has already come to an end and therefore has to be treated as a "cold issue" by the historian. In this context, it will suffice to assert about this regularly misread aperçu that it is not a hostile statement against the Revolution and that the thesis of the fait-accompli character of the Revolution is not an obstacle to Furet in participating in the "shared core" of the story, in "rendering meaning to modernity." On the contrary: it is precisely on this basis that he can formulate what he regards as the main message of our age. For my part, I have insisted in *The Frozen Revolution* that at least in one re-spect, concerning its inexhaustible and still active energy of generating Jaco-bin and neo-Jacobin blueprints, the revolutionary process *should* come to a halt (which by definition means that as yet it has not). In my contributions to this volume, I have repeated this warning. Higonnet has also been thinking along similar lines. His paper reconsiders the historical–cultural causes of the threat of what he calls "the universalist illusion" of French radical rev-olutionaries, which is for him evidently still topical. Other contributors to the volume clearly understand the French Revolution as a process still active, at least in its aftereffects, and, as such, uncompleted. Both in Tilly's and Skocpol's understanding, the Revolution was about the immense reinforce-ment of the nation-state, a process that, as Tilly stresses and proves in his paper, had been underway since the mideighteenth century. Moreover, the process has just commenced in certain areas of the world, as Skocpol pin-points with regard to Iran. The alternative views of our present, as either a dead or a merely extinguished volcano—that is, in a less metaphoric lan-guage, as either the consolidated end result of revolutions no longer in need of major change or of the aftereffects of a still lively revolutionary dynamic generating constant change—are undoubtedly crucial with regard to what kind of meaning is rendered to modernity.

The second major issue of controversy among the contributors concerns the terms of interpretation. Of them, Hobsbawm is the only eloquent cham-pion of the traditional understanding in terms of "class," whereas the relevant parts of Furet's paper serve as the most articulate refutation of the traditional position. Without rehashing their arguments, it has to be stated that, first, the "revisionist" thesis set forth primarily by Cobban decades ago seems to have broken through and now stands uncontested. Marc Richir's aperçu concerning the French bourgeoisie as the result, rather than the cause, of the Revolution, has in this volume been accepted by Furet and Wallerstein alike, although they hold widely divergent political views. Furthermore, the precise class identification of the actor has in the meantime lost a considerable degree of its topicality, unless someone regards the present as a mere prelude to the real drama. The major term of explanation can equally be "the nation–state," which is Tilly's option, "the world system" (this is Wallerstein's explanatory device, whereas Skocpol picks a bit of both), or the capability of a revolution to generate "master narratives" that, in turn, trigger the generalized learning processes of modernity. (The latter is the framework in terms of which both Higonnet and this writer understand the afterlife of the Revolution as well as its lasting impact on the present.) It goes without saying that the different key concepts imply different readings of the "text of history" and thus different meanings rendered to modernity. But in each case, they are selected and used with a view to the "shared core" of the readings.

The genuine clash among the authors, one which sheds a dramatic light on the nature of modernity, is the conflict between the "purely political" and the "social" interpretation of the Revolution. The latter is represented in several different versions in the volume and is in turn criticized both by Higonnet and Furet. Without claiming the position of umpire, it is this writer's conviction that only a combined interpretation, in which neither the political nor the economic (the "class") factor plays the role of *primus movens*, would uncover the unique achievement of the French Revolution, namely, the creation of a universal framework of political action in result of which the French Revolution has remained the master narrative of modernity. The lasting character of this achievement was for a long time covered by the bloody confusion of the revolutionary decades, the actual collapse of the French Revolution, and the complicity of a long line of history-writing that generated and circulated narratives of the great event not less one-sided and blindfolded than the actors' own accounts had been. But now, in the process of "rendering meaning to modernity," the framework resurfaces from under the debris of history. And the various contributions to *The French Revolution and the Birth of Modernity*, taken in their entirety, provide sufficient clues to the understanding of the framework.

The initial steps of the French actors were characterized by a surprising degree of both political naiveté and arbitrariness. They were naive insofar as they innocently believed that the sole, albeit gigantic, task awaiting them was the deed of a merely political reconstruction. Once the "fact" (more properly:

their revolutionary projection) that "every man is born free" had been recognized; once *la nation*, the new universal which is preexistent with regard to both individuals and corporations, had been established; once the state is "free" insofar as it proclaimed a new type of (collective) sovereign; once everyone was recognized as equal before the law, their task was done and completed. Like the American Cincinnati, they thought they could return to their homes. This belief in the cure-all character of the primary act of emancipation was extended by them to the economic domain as well. One of the as-yet-unwritten stories of the Revolution is the initial *volte-face* of even those economists who had been brought up in the school of an enlightened but firm state regulation of the markets during the last decades of the monarchy. This turnabout appears in light of Tilly's account of the increase in the direct rule of the state, accelerated by the Revolution, as sheer illusion. But in the early atmosphere of general enthusiasm, even the former *étatistes* became partisans of the complete deregulation of the markets.

The revolutionaries were also excessively arbitrary. On certain counts, in particular concerning the victims of religious prejudice, their generosity seemed to have no bounds. Gary Kates tells here the story of Jews having been turned into Frenchmen almost overnight. If slowly and inconsistently, they still did incomparably more for the emancipation of the slaves than the American founding fathers, exalted to high heavens by Arendt, had ever considered to do. On other counts, their record was appalling from the start. Their electoral system was drafted in the spirit of a patronizing and authoritarian Enlightenment; as a result, a considerable part of the poorer strata of the populace was excluded from it. The women's issue, as a problem to be addressed, was never put on their agenda. And in a pathbreaking study, Richard Andrews has shown quite recently that their first penal code contained such limitations on the freedom of speech that the government during the Reign of Terror needed very little imagination to amplify its rigor.

Naiveté could have been overcome and arbitrariness rectified, however, had it not been for the monumental and bitter surprise caused by the unruly behavior of the newly emancipated crowd. Both Singer's analysis of the centrality of the crowd's violence with its specific claim to popular justice and Skocpol's emphasis on mass mobilization make the crucial role of this "unruly behavior" of the crowd in the whole process sufficiently clear. Once recognized as citizens, the crowd seemed to be exclusively preoccupied, above all on the urban scene, with such vulgar issues as the price of bread. And at a well-known, crucial point, the urban poor proposed and imposed the total abandonment of both political and economic freedom in "putting the terror on the agenda" and forcing the introduction of *le maximum général.*

With this, the initial naive harmony of the first days exploded, never to return again. The Revolution embarked on the fateful course of navigating between the Scyllae of a strong, often terroristic state whose actual socioeconomic policies varied (hence the legitimate stress on the state in Tilly and Skocpol) and the Charybdis of the wish to return to the self-regulatory mechanisms of a market system (which has remained a pious or impious wish of French politics for a long time but which has never regained the position it had enjoyed and abused in the early days of the Revolution). And it is thus that the framework of modern politics, the extremes between which it has been moving for two centuries and the space between them wherein modernity worked itself out, have been created.

However, the "homecoming of modernity"—the historical moment in which "the rendering of meaning" can be undertaken—is to be achieved only if the two inherent trends of this cycle, political freedom and the management of the "social question," were reconciled at least to the degree of a peaceful cohabitation. For this, two requirements had to be met. First, the primacy of political freedom, the principle of the free state, had to be maintained. Neither the dialectical idea of a "tyranny of freedom" nor a streamlined form of tyranny pure and simple can solve "the social question," or, for that matter, any social issue. But they can eventually destroy modernity. It belongs to the greatness of the French Revolution, as long as it had remained a revolution and had not yet been turned into an autocratic–charismatic rule, that *at least the principle* of freedom and popular sovereignty was never abandoned by any of its representative statesmen. Robespierre gave a short symbolic expression of this reluctance to transcend the threshold in the famous question of *Au nom de qui?* on the last night of his life. And Saint-Just, before being silenced by the Convention for good, emphasized that two-thirds of the legislative work of the Assembly during the most lunatic days of the Reign of Terror had been aimed at strengthening, instead of extinguishing, civil society. This hesitation before the fateful threshold elevates the story of the French Revolution to the rank of modernity's master narrative over the Bolshevik "second and expanded edition."

The second requirement of "the homecoming of modernity" has been formulated by Furet in a paradoxical manner. In a lecture given at New York University in October 1988, he set forth the postulate of democracy "forgetting its origins." The prosaic meaning of this dictum reads as follows: the bitter struggles, which had torn asunder the initial harmony of the great Revolution and had propelled its actors as well as its successors onto a cycle of permanent civil wars, must come to a halt in an act of reconciliation, or else modernity will be destroyed. I am in complete agreement with Furet's postulate, but I deem it feasible only on the basis of creating a legitimate space for the constant renegotiation of "the social question" on the basis of political freedom as an absolute precondition.

Three major issues of the political culture of the Revolution have been discussed in the volume, each in turn contributing considerably to the present physiognomy and "meaning" of modernity. The first is the problem of "the republican legacy," dealt with in the papers by Smith, Furet, and this writer. The issue at stake is far more than purely terminological in nature. Whether democracy would tendentially move toward the Kantian *res publica noumenon* or remain the rule of the majority pure and simple (or even, as Sieyès feared, a facade for a new oligarchy) was perhaps the most crucial alternative the Revolution had to face. The "terminological hairsplitting" aiming at the definition of the new state formed an organic part of the bitter internal struggles of the epoch. The second issue, the "resacralizing" of the political sphere after it had been thoroughly secularized and rationalized, as recounted by this writer, has been joined and complemented by Miguel Abensour's analysis of the "cult of heroism" in the Revolution. On the surface, it transpires as a purely French story having no continuation in the political history of the continent. In fact, both the resacralizing of the political sphere and the cult of heroism, separately and conjointly, were the prelude to that major nightmare haunting modernity ever since: charismatic rule. Finally, the issue with which revolutions have never ceased to be associated since the French drama, namely the violence of the crowd as a constitutive part of political action, is, in its whole complexity, the subject matter of Singer's paper.

This political culture was "domestic," intrinsically and often chauvinistically French. At the same time, it was universalized in the (intentional as well as unintentional) efforts of the Revolution to impose itself on what it understood as the modern world. To regard the Napoleonic *Grande Armée* as the exclusive vehicle of this conquest would be an error and a simplification. From a certain aspect, modernity can be viewed as an aggregate of representative narratives that, as a rule, spread far beyond national borders and served as blueprints for, and thus implicitly conquered, other nations and national imaginations.

III

The cultural legacy of the French Revolution is heavily represented in this book, but once again exclusively with regard to its impact on the future culture of modernity. This impact is twofold. On the one hand, the Revolution gave the strongest possible impetus to the rise of the golden age of philosophy of history. On the other hand, it triggered the birth of the "objective" science of society. Both issues have been dealt with in this volume by the contributions of Furet, Mitchell, Smith, and this writer.

The impetus given by the Great Revolution to the grand narratives of the philosophy of history was direct. There was nothing pragmatic in the representative actors on the Paris scene. From the fall of the Bastille till Thermidor and even after, the most liberal as well as the most illiberal ones among them shared the conviction, albeit in different orchestrations and varying interpretations, that the Revolution had not only grown out of philosophy but that it had been assigned the task, as Robespierre put it most poignantly, to fulfill the promises of philosophy, to conclude the prehistory of humankind and complement the revolutions in the physical world by a moral world revolution.

But the watershed event was too close to the body of its actors for them to cast a glance at it from the distance necessary for philosophical speculation. No wonder, then, that the representative philosophies of history, whose specific content can be regarded as a response to the dilemmas posed by the French Revolution, were born outside the French context, primarily in Germany. (This is why the analyses of Kant and Hegel play such a central role in this volume.) Nor was this external fruition of the cultural yields of the Revolution restricted to philosophy. The immortal music of revolutionary enthusiasm—an emotion crucial for both Kant and Robespierre—found its ultimate expression in Beethoven's singular combination of an endless harmonic material with the titanic melody of "fraternity" and the emergence of the motif of the Hero. The single great historical drama written on the Revolution is Büchner's *Danton's Death*. Only revolutionary painting came of age on the domestic scene through the brush of that bizarre combination of an artist, as genius and individualist, and a security police chief, namely Jacques-Louis David.

Revolutionary (and immediate postrevolutionary) France's own contribution to this great intellectual transformation was the "science" of the new society, which immediately split and went in two different directions. With Saint-Simon, it concentrated on the critique of the society born out of the turbulences of a quarter of a century. Socialism was born as the critical science of the society created by the Revolution, one which applied revolutionary principles to the end result of the revolutionary process. With Comte, social science accepted the new society as an incontrovertible fact and went about the understanding of its mechanics with great equanimity.

Philosophy of history, growing out of the "philosophical revolution," focused on such issues as were, without exception, painful and ultimately unresolvable dilemmas for the revolutionaries themselves. What is the "meaning" of a revolution? Does it imply a complete break with the past, a total tabula rasa as the actors themselves had believed, or does it have a continuity with the past that had remained hidden for the actors in the fever of enthusiasm? Is the revolution a "solemn" act, a moral "surplus" the generated energy of which has to be preserved for the republic to survive? Or is it rather a "relapse into the state of nature" or perhaps the combination of this relapse and a signal of "progress in nature"? Should revolution be continued permanently, or should it come to a halt at some point while building its results in the body of the new society? What is the character of history created by this cataclysm? Is history from now on "determined" and predictable, operating according to moral or scientific laws? Or is it precisely its unpredictable and "chaotic," that is, indeterminate, character that had opened up in the great event? These and similar questions were asked by the philosophy of history under the direct impact of the French Revolution. And the questions themselves, together with the answers given to them then and there, (both being sufficiently analyzed in the contributions to this book, primarily in that of Harvey Mitchell), have never left us.

Posthistoire, under the aegis of which the present book was born, is not distinguished by having the "ultimate" answer to these old dilemmas. Rather, it is distinguished by recognizing the (obviously not identical) relevance of the varying answers given to the dilemmas, that is, by the spirit of hermeneutics. The book concludes on a seemingly modest note in Furet's rereading of the paradigms in terms of which historiography, in other words, every new present, tried to cope with its past: the Revolution. However, the yield of this hermeneutical voyage is important. For in the carefully worded questions addressed to the text, in the tentative answers the text and the reader together supply to the questions, a major turn has been negotiated. In the historical hour of the crisis of Bolshevik self-identity, the French Revolution, by removing layers of "the Russian interpretation" imposed on its text by generations of interpreters, reclaims its primogeniture as the authentic master narrative of modernity.

PART ONE

State, Nation, and Class in the French Revolution

ONE

Mars Unshackled: The French Revolution in World-Historical Perspective[1]

Theda Skocpol and Meyer Kestnbaum

Only with the French Revolution did the concept of "revolution" take on its modern meaning.[2] This etymological fact signals a larger truth about the grouping of events in world history. For many centuries prior to the 1500s, "revolution" referred to astronomical cycles. During the period of the English upheavals from 1640 to 1688, "revolution" was used to refer to fundamental political changes, yet still retained the sense of cycling back to a previous state of affairs. By the time of the French Revolution, however, "revolution" came to connote a sudden, fundamental, and *innovative* departure in a nation's social and political life—and the term has retained this connotation down to the present day. Since 1789–1799 in France, such massive *social revolutions* have punctuated modern world history. In part fueled by widespread revolts from below, social revolutions have recurrently brought basic changes in class relations, state structures, and hegemonic ideologies to particular countries. And they have transformed power balances and ideological models within the international system of nations.

Modern social revolutions have been tied together in both practical politics and academic scholarship. In practical politics, the actors in the social revolutions that followed the French Revolution often understood their own roles by reference back to what had happened in France; the obsession of the Bolsheviks with preventing a "Thermidorian reaction" in Russia is a case in point. Similarly, the French Revolution has served as a prototype for the academic analysis of succeeding revolutions. Yet later revolutions have also changed scholars' sense of what was interesting about the French case. Periodic reinterpretations of the French upheavals have been inspired not only by political or academic shifts within France; they have also depended on scholars' sense of how subsequent revolutions compare to, or build on, the great French precedent. As François Furet has correctly (if acerbically)

13

pointed out, the Russian Revolution cast a glaring light backward onto earlier French events, encouraging left-leaning scholars to probe ever more
deeply into "class conflicts" in revolutionary France, and shifting the central
focus from the period 1789–1791 toward 1792–1794 as the radical highpoint
of the French Revolution, the moment when Jacobin rule allegedly foreshadowed the later triumphs and tribulations of the Russian Bolsheviks.[3]

But for many years now, the "social interpretation of the French Revolution" (as Alfred Cobban called the Marxist account) has been under scholarly assault. In an era of anti-Stalinism and the international Cold War,
many scholars became critical of the theory that the French Revolution was
a "bourgeois revolution" punctuated by moments of greater class-based
radicalism from below. They reacted against Marxian concepts of class
struggle and Leninist readings of history. Some of these opponents of
Marxian interpretations have rested content with substituting alternative
social interpretations—for example Cobban's own reading of the French
Revolution as the falling out and recomposition of a noncapitalist landed
elite.[4] Others, such as Richard Cobb, have asked us to drop all efforts to give
the Revolution a macroscopic interpretation.[5] Still others, however—especially comparative–historical social scientists referring back to Alexis de
Tocqueville and Max Weber rather than Karl Marx—have put forward
"political" or "state-centered" readings of the French Revolution as alternatives to the Marxist schema.

It is not incidental that such political and comparative–historical readings of the French case proliferated just as dozens of "new nations" were
emerging on the world scene after the 1950s, and just as social scientists
became fascinated with problems of "modernization," including "political
development." Social revolutions since the midtwentieth century have
obviously been explosive dramas of national definition and assertion, with
their "class struggles" centered on peasants and landlords as much or more
than on proletarians and bourgeois. Arguably resonating with such patterns
on the contemporary world stage, Barrington Moore Jr.'s 1966 opus, *Social
Origins of Dictatorship and Democracy*, treated both historical and recent revolutions as steps toward one or another kind of modern political regime—
democracy, fascism, or communism—and attributed the 1789 French
Revolution to a political alliance of peasants and the bourgeoisie, arrayed
against the monarchy and a landed aristocracy.[6] Departing still further from
Marxian ideas, Samuel P. Huntington's 1968 book, *Political Order in Changing
Society*, also brought together European and Third World revolutions.[7] Huntington treated the French Revolution along with all other social revolutions
as an "explosion" of political participation giving rise to strengthened new
political institutions capable of channeling peasant and urban-middle-class
demands into national politics. Finally, Theda Skocpol's *States and Social Revolutions*, published in 1979, reanalyzed both the French and Russian Revolu-

tions in terms originally inspired by her sense of the intertwining of agrarian changes, international power shifts, and transformations in state structures during the Chinese Revolution of 1911 through 1949.[8] Like Samuel Huntington, Skocpol argued that the transformations wrought by social revolutions were, principally, the enhanced centralization and bureaucratization of the state, accompanied by the mobilization of formerly excluded popular groups into national political life.

AN "INTERNALIST" INTERPRETATION OF THE FRENCH REVOLUTION?

Interpretations of the French Revolution may always have been intimately intertwined with the significance attached to subsequent social revolutions in world history, yet many historians surely will agree with Lynn Hunt in her effort to set aside all such ways of situating the French Revolution in cross-national perspective. In Hunt's view, comparativist approaches (ranging from the Marxian to the political modernization views) offer overly "externalist" theories that treat the French "Revolution merely . . . as the vehicle of transportation between long-term causes and effects."[9] Hunt proposes to substitute for previous accounts of the French Revolution a radically "internalist" interpretation. She focuses strictly on the actors and symbols of revolutionary dramas between 1789 and 1794 and argues that the "chief accomplishment of the French Revolution was the institution of a dramatically new political culture."[10] This new political culture was inspired but not caused by the Enlightenment. The new political culture, along with the new political leaders who came to the fore in the midst of the conflicts of 1789–1794 to espouse and be shaped by the emergent political culture, advocated the recreation of the French people along universal, national, and rationalistic lines through "the mobilizing potential of democratic republicanism."[11]

Indeed, Hunt's provocative book, *Politics, Culture, and Class in the French Revolution*, represents a strong challenge to any crossnational, structuralist reading of the logic of revolutions, for it argues that the French Revolution's "origins, outcomes, and nature of experience were distinctively French."[12] Hunt unabashedly draws us away from looking for uniformities across social revolutions in modern world history, and into probing the meanings-for-the-participants of a few pivotal years in the singular history of a unique French nation. At the same time, however, Hunt wishes to retain a certain claim that the French Revolution had world–historical significance. This she does by asserting that the "Revolution . . . gave birth to so many essential characteristics of modern politics"[13]—characteristics such as ideological contention, democratic participation, and political party organization. "Once revolutionaries acted on Rousseau's belief that government could form a new people," Hunt claims, "the West was never again the same."[14] But by this she does not mean that the French Revolution could, or should, be understood as parallel to other revolutions. She means that new possibilities for democratic politics were loosed on the world, to be interpreted in many alternative ways ranging from socialist to authoritarian, but not in the future to be ignored.

Admirable as Lynn Hunt's tour-de-force of an interpretation may be, it can be questioned from various standpoints. Most problematic from our point of view is Hunt's attempt to decouple the French Revolution's "internal" political processes from what Alexis de Tocqueville correctly identified as its most striking and enduring structural accomplishment: the rationalization, bureaucratization, and further centralization of state power in France.[15] Furthermore, going beyond Tocqueville, we see many powerful links between the "internal" patterns of political mobilization during the revolutionary years in France and a set of "external" dynamics. These external dynamics were not constituted by the "emergence of capitalism" or the abstract march of "political modernization." They were very concrete challenges of international warfare faced by France in the late eighteenth century.

Let us briefly suggest how patterns of "internal" French revolutionary politics—including the revolutionary rhetoric so effectively dissected by Hunt—can be linked to the "external" geopolitical challenges France faced from the beginning to the end of the Revolution. Geopolitical challenges contributed fundamentally to the outbreak and the distinctive rhetoric of the French Revolution in 1787–1789, to its radical crescendo in the Year II (1793–1794), and to its culmination in the peculiar Napoleonic dictatorship that emerged after 1799. In resonant response to these geopolitical challenges, the Revolution unshackled the French state's capacities to wage war. The Revolution completed and infused new popular energy into organizational transformations in the French military, changes that were launched under the Old Regime but not brought to successful fruition until the advent of the Republic and the subsequent extension of the Republic's armies and martial achievements by Napoleon.

GEOPOLITICAL DECLINE AND THE OUTBREAK OF THE REVOLUTION

As is well known, the Old Regime's descent into the maelstrom started when the monarchy exhausted its ability to raise loans for military purposes, called without success on an Assembly of Notables for help, and then backed down in the face of demands by the *parlements* for the convening of the long-defunct Estates-General. Yet culturally oriented scholars are certainly right to pinpoint the subsequent emergence of demands for a National Assembly, a body that was challenger and alternative to the Estates, as the originating moment of revolution (rather than of reforms within the basic structure of the Old Regime).

More was involved here than contending groups of privileged Frenchmen vying for the best framework of representation in which to press their particular status interests against the king and one another. New political practices and a *rhetoric of national regeneration* came suddenly to the fore, just as Lynn Hunt would have it. In the search for a unifying political charisma to replace sacred absolute monarchy, Hunt tells us, successive leadership groups in the Revolution devised oaths and staged symbolic festivals. They also invoked "certain key words . . . as revolutionary incantations," including "*patrie*, constitution, law, and, more specific to the radicals, regeneration, virtue, and vigilance."[16] Among the key words of the Revolution, "nation was perhaps the most universally sacred" right from the start in 1789[17]—just as the bid of certain urban-based leaders to create the unified National Assembly was at the heart of the early revolutionary challenge to the Old Regime's monarchical and corporatist system of authority.[18]

To be sure, certain aspects of the innovative political practices and rhetoric of 1789 were inspired by certain readings of Enlightenment literatures, understandings that had gestated for some years in discussions by certain educated critics of the Old Regime, urban Third Estate and aristocratic critics alike. But the Enlightenment did not *cause* the new politics of 1789, for its many texts and ideals had been equally well invoked by defenders of monarchy or by coporatist critics of royal initiatives such as the parlements. To understand the revolutionary urge for uniformly national representation, we must understand how badly many French elites wanted to find a road to national regeneration in the late eighteenth century.

During the course of the eighteenth century, the French Old Regime, with its hodgepodge of monarchy and corporatist privilege, had proved recurrently unable to sustain the glory of France in the face of rising, newly efficient rivals and military enemies, especially Prussia on the continent of Europe and Britain on the high seas.[19] The French monarchy lost all of the intra-European wars of the eighteenth century in which it became involved, achieving a victory of sorts only in the far-flung conflict over American independence. The humiliation of martial defeats, along with the strain of raising revenues for wars, rendered credible critics' arguments that the country's institutions were in need of basic overhaul. "Nothing did more to fuel . . . [the] surge of public discussion than the Seven Years' War" of 1756–1763. "Undertaken with no clear aims, in alliance with Austria, a traditional enemy of centuries standing, it led to humiliating defeats on land and sea at what seemed like enormous economic cost. Taxes and state borrowing had soared, but there was nothing to show for such efforts. In these circumstances an inquest began which spared no aspect of French society or institutions, and was encouraged . . . by the government itself."[20]

Indeed, in the wake of the embarrassing French defeats at the hand of smaller Prussian armies in the Seven Years' War, major organizational changes in the army were devised by a succession of activist ministers, among the most influential of whom were Étienne François de Choiseul and Claude Louis de Saint-Germain. These changes, which laid the basis for later accomplishments under the Republic and Napoleon, featured the organization of infantry, cavalry, artillery, and support troops into self-sufficient divisions and corps; the subordination of individual regiments and companies to unified division and corps commands; and the unification of military supply operations, which were henceforth nominally directed by the monarchy rather than by private military contractors, thus taking them out of the hands of "enterprising" colonels and captains.[21] France's next major martial involvement did not, however, allow the effectiveness of these reforms to be fully tested; nor did it bring political payoffs to the monarchy. French victories in the War of American Independence were gained at sea against Britain. And even though France prevailed in this conflict, the Old Regime's longstanding fiscal inefficiencies—which had hampered earlier war efforts as well—reached an apogee in the war's immediate aftermath. In the words of Simon Schama,

> [T]he pleasures of witnessing British imperial disarray and the belated satisfaction for the defeats of the Seven Years' War carried an expensive price tag. . . . [T]he ballooning of the deficit so weakened the *nerfs*—the sinews—of state that by 1787, its foreign policy was robbed of real freedom of action. For in that year sheer financial exigency prevented France from intervening decisively in the civil war in the Dutch Republic to support its own partisans, themselves going by the name of "Patriots." Paradoxically, then, the war that had been intended to restore the imperial power of France ended up compromising it so badly that king and *patrie* seemed to be two different, and before long irreconcilable, entities. It was not much longer before this process was taken even further, so that the court itself seemed a foreign parasite feeding off the body of the "true" Nation.[22]

Institutional transformations, statesmen and elites understood, would have to encompass the king's fundamental political relationship to tax-paying Frenchmen as well as the inner workings of the military machine. By 1787–1789 French elites were not just worried about who might have to pay more taxes than whom to solve a temporary monarchical financial crisis. Inspired by the British example of parliamentarism, as well as by the achievements of the American Revolution, many of them believed that the monarchy could not restore French international prestige without somehow consulting and involving them in fundamental decisions for the future.[23] In this context of a crisis of legitimacy in the state's basic mission and structure, the door was opened for certain elite elements to make a radical argument: that the entire nation, not just separate privileged sectors, needed to be "represented" together with the king in the great work of political regeneration that was at hand.

We are suggesting, in short, that without the prior decades of geopolitical stress and relative decline for a great power that was facing escalating simultaneous challenges from land and sea, the national–moralistic dimension of the crisis of 1787–1789 might have been absent. Had this dimension been absent, the ensuing intraelite struggles might have resembled the decentralizing and particularistic conflicts of the Fronde over a century earlier, rather than leading into a politics of national regeneration, which was triggered by the calling of the Estates-General in 1789. The French elites who assembled to argue in—and about—the representative institutions of a constitutional monarchy were, despite their many differences, jointly concerned about how to strengthen the French nation through expanded political participation. Although in the early years of the Revolution declarations of war were far from the minds of most elites with contending constitutionalist visions, it was surely crucial that all French elites took for granted'the past and potential future glory of the French state and nation. They argued within and about the central political and administrative institutions of a great power struggling against relative international decline, and the rhetoric of national regeneration resonated with this context.

WAR AND POLITICAL RADICALIZATION

When we move on to examine the political radicalization of the French Revolution after the early years of attempts at constitutional monarchy, it becomes even easier to demonstrate the links between the geopolitics and the domestic politics of the French Revolution. Lynn Hunt is ambiguous on the matter of whether the French Revolution brought "democracy," but surely it is safe to conclude that there was, during the Revolution, no stable democratization of national politics in the modern Western sense of that term. Democratic politics was *not* part of revolutionary practice or rhetoric right at the start, for national representation at first meant only the direct participation of all active citizens—that is, in practice, the propertied and educated elites of French society. Moreover, in later years, as popular involvement in revolutionary politics deepened in Paris and the provinces alike, "democracy" never came to mean orderly, predictably institutionalized electoral participation, as it would come to mean in the post-1820s United States, for example. Calculable and predictable rules for a liberal-democratic political "game" never stabilized amidst the dizzy succession of regimes that ruled revolutionary France.

What "democracy" did come to mean, however, especially under the aegis of the Montagnard Jacobins, was *popular political mobilization* to secure the virtuous defense of the Revolution against its treasonous, conspiratorial enemies at home and abroad. As François Furet has argued, "Jacobinism laid down the model and the working of direct democracy by dictating opinion in the first organized group to appropriate the Revolution's discourse on itself."[24] But this did not happen all at once. It took an emergency context of national mobilization for war to bring out the full mass-mobilizing potential of Jacobinism.

The Jacobin clubs operated all along in some tension with the readings of national interest embodied in the representative Assemblies sitting in Paris, since they agitated on behalf of an "elect" understanding of the nation's and the Revolution's interests, namely their own understanding. Even so, in the early years when they were dominated by better-off middle-class elements, the Jacobin clubs operated as genuine forums for broad public discussion of all the major political issues of the day.[25] Arguably, the early Jacobin clubs embodied civic republicanism at its best. And they could hardly dictate to the national representative assemblies; they could only petition and lobby.

All of this changed after France went to war in 1792, and especially once the Montagnard Jacobins undertook the most intense efforts during 1793 and 1794 to defend their version of the Revolution against multiple revolts at home and invasions from abroad. After 1792, Isser Woloch tells us, the Jacobin clubs became more congenial places for political participation by the "common people," formerly passive citizens such as "master craftsmen, journeymen, artisans, small shopkeepers, minor clerks and functionaries, and common soldiers."[26] But during the same period the "clubs were markedly transformed. Having started as educational and propagandistic associations of middle-class reformers, they had gradually evolved into socially heterogeneous political action groups. Finally, in the Year II (1793–94), the *sociétés populaires* became the arms of a triumphant Montagnard government."[27] The clubs accepted central discipline from Paris, served as recruitment agencies for national administrative and military efforts, and became "unpaid bureaucratic agents" of local political surveillance and repression.

Exactly as both François Furet and Lynn Hunt would maintain, there was a powerful logic of political culture at work in all of this, not just the "force of circumstances." Because French revolutionary rhetoric did not leave room for institutionalized contention over *alternative* ways to further the national interest, and because "virtue" in revolutionary discourse was consistently defined in opposition to the treason of "aristocratic conspirators," those who mobilized more and more of "the people" into national politics found it easiest to do so in the context of unlimited wars against what were perceived as overwhelmingly threatening enemies at home and abroad. War and terror went hand in hand, and in an important sense fulfilled revolutionary rhetoric.

Yet surely it would be a mistake to overlook how well the Montagnard Jacobin practices and rhetoric of centrally directed popular mobilization also served the very real military needs of the Revolution—and, ironically, simultaneously brought to fruition the military reforms that had been attempted under the Old Regime.

Desperate to stop the invading armies of foreign monarchies and French emigrés, the Montagnard representatives on mission frequently cashiered officers who failed on the battlefield and immediately replaced them with other soldiers or officers who, regardless of previous social status, had demonstrated battlefield valor and excellence in the immediate cause of defending the Revolution. As has often been emphasized, this gave reality to the Revolution's theme of "careers open to talent." But, equally important, the surviving parts of the line armies of France were actually reinvigorated under the Jacobins.[28] After voluntary enlistments failed to bring in sufficient troops to meet foreign and domestic military threats, the Montagnard Committee on Public Safety decreed the *levée en masse* on 23 August 1793, subjecting to conscription for war all national resources, human and material. This measure not only enormously expanded French forces, it also reinforced the amalgamation of regular line forces and revolutionary militias which had been decreed by the Convention in February 1792. Together, the amalgamation and the levée en masse married the army of the Old Regime to the forces and principles of the Revolution.

In the officer corps, regular-army noncommissioned officers—those retaining their old positions and those newly promoted after the flight of French officers following the king's capture at Varennes in 1791—remained dominant in the expanding armies, ensuring continuity between the old and new armies. And there was not only continuity for many personnel, there was also continuity in the organization of military command structures.[29] The division of the army into independent commands, a reform made under the Old Regime, was lauded for its democratic character just as the Terror was emerging in full force![30]

Meanwhile, of course, the rank and file of the French armies was transformed as well as invigorated by national conscription into the amalgamated forces. As military historian John Lynn has argued, "from the first days of the Revolution its leaders insisted that 'every citizen ought to be a soldier and every soldier a citizen' . . . [and the] outbreak of war in 1792 gave substance to theories and ideals expressed during the preceding three years."[31] Specifically, Lynn further explains:

> Expansion of the army to the gargantuan size it attained in the summer of 1794 meant that young Frenchmen from all walks of life were called upon to serve. . . . Volunteers and conscripts made the army [as never before in French history] a representative cross-section of the French population. The troops

were now composed of the respectable and hard-working sons of its peasantry, artisans, and bourgeoisie. This change in composition alone . . . had immense significance. In the past those who suffered economic hardship, social inequity, or plain hard luck marched behind the regimental flags; they had reason to be reluctant or dispirited; they were certainly alienated. But by 1792–94 those young men who possessed full talent, confidence, and élan of the French people rallied around the banners of the revolutionary battalions. . . . It is impossible to read their letters without being struck by the intense pride of these soldiers who fought in defense of their homes and families and who expressed enthusiastic support for the revolutionary social and political order. . . . [And, in turn, the] soldiers of the Republic were honored by a grateful people. In hundreds of songs that so typified the Revolution, they were lauded as the heroes who protected their people and their revolution.[32]

Together, the amalgamation and the levée en masse created the first national army Europe had ever seen, fundamentally transforming the nature of war. As Carl von Clausewitz would later write, "a force appeared that beggared all imagination. Suddenly war became the business of the people— a people of thirty millions. . . . Instead of governments and armies as heretofore, the full weight of the nation was thrown into the balance. The resources and efforts now available for use surpassed all conventional limits: nothing now impeded the vigor with which war could be waged."[33] The armies of revolutionary France were able to adopt new, rapid, and flexible battlefield tactics involving the enhanced use not only of artillery, but also of aggressive drives by highly motivated citizen soldiers. Such tactics allowed France to defeat the forces of even those countries, Prussia and Britain, that were the most modern and efficient representatives of the monarchical coalition arrayed against the Revolution.

Thus, when Lynn Hunt suggests that French revolutionary politics was not distinctly "modernizing" because parallel achievements could be made under monarchies, she is simply wrong. She focuses on domestic politics alone and overlooks the real-world advantages of a mobilized, highly motivated citizen soldiery—a chief product of the French Revolution's radical phase of democratic mobilization. Prussia's Frederick the Great, we are told by Gunther Rothenberg, used administrative discipline to create a relatively efficient, albeit rigidly rank-ordered, officer corps, along with an efficient system of supply for his armies. But the Prussian monarch, Rothenberg also points out, never understood the value of native rank-and-file soldiers.[34] And why should he, sitting atop a regime where such soldiers were reluctantly impressed subjects rather than citizens fighting for "their" nation?

THE NAPOLEONIC DENOUEMENT

Lynn Hunt's failure to make much of the connection between revolutionary democratization and the Montagnard mobilization for war carries over into her reluctance to accept Napoleon's rule as a logical culmination of the politics of the French Revolution. She treats Napoleon's triumph as an "authoritarian" and "conservative" solution "made possible by the weaknesses in revolutionary political culture."[35] Focusing strictly on domestic politics, she points to Napoleon's abrogation of liberal representative politics and, eventually, of elections, along with the basis of his regime among "disenchanted republicans who preferred a stabilizing modernization to the upheavals and uncertainties of widespread political participation."[36] It is almost as if Hunt wishes to preserve the old notion of the French Revolution as, in its soul, liberal-democratic, even if, in the end, that essence survived only as a set of ideals and practices to be revived later.

What this overlooks is well stated by François Furet: "The concept 'bourgeois revolution' is simply not suited to account for the. . . revolutionary dynamic, for the political and cultural tidal wave unleashed by Jacobinism and the revolutionary war. Henceforth, the war conducted the Revolution far more than the Revolution conducted the war." "Nationalist feeling was no longer limited to the new France; it became an ideological model, the banner of a crusade. . . . [T]he French people did not exactly discover a miraculously exemplary form of human community; but surely they were the first to integrate the masses into the State and to form a modern democratic nation." "The price of that historical experience was open-ended war."[37]

Indeed, the final account of the French Revolution as a great drama of integrating "the masses into the State" was drawn up under Napoleon's regimes. The Consulate and the Empire were not simply exercises in domestic political stabilization under authoritarian "modernizing" rule. Institutionally speaking, Napoleon's regimes furthered the fusion of the political and the military, and the subordination of domestic policy to foreign policy, that had begun under the Jacobins and progressed through the Directory. This reached a climax after Napoleon's coronation, when the offices of chief of state and commander and chief were joined and a massive Imperial Headquarters was constructed, through whose staffs much of the business of state was conducted.[38]

Meanwhile, in the structure and operations of his *Grande Armée*, Napoleon fully exploited the meritocratic and democratic possibilities of the Revolution. As Gunther Rothenberg tells us, "from the Revolution, Napoleon inherited huge conscript armies, led by young and ambitious commanders, accustomed to a mobile, offensive, and ruthless way of war."[39] The Grande Armée's officer corps maintained the principle of careers opened to talent, both in military schools and on the battlefields, where Napoleon often personally rewarded daring soldiers and junior officers with on-the-spot advancement. "Opportunities for advancement in Napoleon's forces were far greater than those in any other contemporary army and served as a potent morale booster."[40] Advancement for many officers was, of course, also due to the fact that Napoleon vastly expanded his armies, enforcing revolutionary draft laws to bring in some two million men between 1804 and 1813. The avowed values of the rank-and-file soldiery may have changed, as John Lynn has argued, from republican "virtue" to a more professional sense of military "honor."[41] But French citizens were, more than ever, called in huge numbers to serve their nation through military valor. Especially on the field of battle, Napoleonic France was truly a mass-mobilizing regime. Certainly the leaders and peoples of other European nations were convinced that Napoleon had succeeded in channeling outward the new democratic energies unleashed by the French Revolution.

If Napoleon's regimes were devoted to perpetual, expansionist warfare, there were several reasons rooted in the overall French revolutionary process. Many Frenchmen, not to mention foreign rebels against their own old regimes, wanted French ideals to be carried as far as possible across the face of continental Europe. What is more, for Napoleon as for earlier rulers during the Revolution, perpetuation of personal rule, the "defense" of the nation, and aggression against foreign powers tended to fuse into a single impulse. French military successes inevitably alarmed and mobilized foreign enemies, who then had to be engaged again in the virtually unending conflicts of this period; and any failure in war would certainly embolden political enemies at home. Yet, perhaps most important, the very logic of the French military innovations first crystallized under the Republic called forth exactly the perpetual military expansionism that became the hallmark of Napoleon's regimes.

From the Republic onward, the enormous size of French armies freed them from the logistical constraints of the prior century—provided that they kept moving. Large French armies could bypass fortresses without beseiging them, as Old Regime armies normally did.[42] Moreover, without stopping to lay siege, the huge Republican, and later Imperial, armies could be provisioned not just by reserves and supply convoys, but above all by collecting supplies from the area and levying contributions with which supplies were later purchased. If they kept on the move, the French armies would not exhaust the supply potential of a given area; and if they fought on enemy territories, they would alleviate the burden on France. In short, the French armies could externalize their supply needs, imposing them upon conquered opponents or recently "liberated" allies, thus diminishing the need to supply French forces from a fixed base or from the rear. By fighting and living on the move, French armies avoided the logistical perils of feeding a huge force confined to one place which had previously plagued European armies.[43]

As the French armies built through the Revolution were freed from the logistical constraints of the prior century, they became highly mobile and effective. The "nation in arms" made fast-moving field armies rather than sieges the centerpiece of war and these armies, in turn, made war the means by which whole nations could be tamed. Napoleonic expansionism was made possible because the speed and mobility of the huge French armies expanded the range of what could be done by military might in the field. French armies massed to destroy the main field forces of their enemies could inflict extensive, even catastrophic losses, breaking the morale of opposing governments and stripping them of their military protection. This forced enemy governments into negotiations under highly unfavorable terms.[44] Eventually, of course, this spurred other Europeans to rebel against French conquests and encouraged rival governments to imitate French military innovations— further perpetuating warfare. Yet, initially the military innovations crystallized during the radical phase of the French Revolution, and perpetuated in the military during the Directory, made it easy for Napoleon to lead massive French forces in triumphant campaigns of conquest across Europe.

Not only military strategies and tactics, therefore, but also the foreign policy objectives that these new strategies facilitated, were remade by the French revolutionary "nation in arms." In war without end (until he was broken and exiled), Napoleon as the "Emperor of the French" truly realized the inherent possibilities for fusing nationalist politics and mass-mobilizing warfare unleashed in the modern world by the French Revolution.[45]

IN CONCLUSION: RETAINING A COMPARATIVE PERSPECTIVE ON THE FRENCH REVOLUTION

To sum up our commentary on Lynn Hunt's analysis of the political culture of the French Revolution, we see no reason why most of what she so vividly describes about political symbols and practices cannot be integrated into a state-centered and geopolitically situated "structural" analysis of the overall causes and outcomes of the French Revolution. It is surprising that Hunt herself did not see the possibilities for such an integration. The reason may lie in her quite proper reservations about a purely "Tocquevillian" account of domestic state-building. Alexis de Tocqueville *did* go too far in portraying the French Revolution primarily as a fulfillment of the Old Regime's teleology of administrative centralization. His interpretation overlooks the Revolution's burst of democratic participation in efforts for National Regeneration. It also overlooks that democratic participation was subsequently channeled far more into the military affairs of the French nation than into its patterns of domestic politics and administration.

All of this was argued in Theda Skocpol's 1979 book, *States and Social Revolutions*, yet that work did not stress the connections between social revolutions and mass military mobilization as strongly as it might have done. The reason for now highlighting those connections more vividly takes us back to a point we made at the start of this chapter. We suggested that later social revolutions in modern world history inevitably cast new light on our understandings of earlier social revolutions, including the pioneering French Revolution. A massive, new social revolution burst on the world in 1979, just as *States and Social Revolutions* was published. That revolution, of course, was the Iranian Revolution. Although this conflict has yet to fully run its course, the Iranian Revolution has unmistakably fused national political regeneration with mass mobilization for international warfare.

From Lynn Hunt's strictly "internalist" cultural perspective, the Iranian Revolution could hardly be more different from the great French Revolution of 1789. French revolutionary political culture was a secularist alternative to divine-right monarchy, because the French revolutionaries fought the prerogatives and symbols of Catholicism as well as monarchy and aristocratic privilege. The Iranian Revolution, by contrast, has opposed a secularist, "modernizing" absolutist monarchy in the name of an Islamic theocratic regime. Iran's revolutionary political culture is a militantly antisecularist and antimodernizing version of Shi'a Islam.[46] These contrasts are understandable in structural terms. Old-Regime France was a Great Power in which monarchy and a bureaucratic Catholic church were allied, thus encouraging critics of the Old Regime to elaborate secularist ideals. In contrast, Old-Regime Iran was a minor power facing cultural and economic penetration from the secular West. The Shah had curbed the privileges of Shi'a clerics, many of whom were fiercely critical of him for his pro-Western, anti-Islamic policies of modernization. Militant–traditionalist clerics in Iran were ultimately able to claim ideological and organizational leadership of the forces that undermined and overthrew the Shah, putting themselves in a position to build the New Regime, not oppose it.

Despite the obvious cultural and structural contrasts between France and Iran, however, notice the remarkable similarities in the overall political and geopolitical dynamics of these revolutions. Just as the French Revolution did, the Iranian Revolution brought to power an ideological leadership more obsessed with virtue and national regeneration than with economic struggles or modernizing efficiency. Similarly, the Iranian Revolution mobilized masses of formerly excluded people into national politics and excelled at motivating the new citizens, through ideology and exemplary leadership, to participate in protracted and humanly costly international warfare. Like revolutionary France, moreover, revolutionary Iran amalgamated urban militias and the remnants of royal line armies to produce military forces capable of hurling huge numbers of citizen soldiers into costly battles. From a comparative-historical and structuralist perspective, therefore, the Iranian Revolution and the French Revolution are remarkably parallel transformative events, and social analysts have much to gain by examining them in comparison to each other.[47] Both the parallels and the contrasts of these social revolutions can be better understood through comparative study.

All of this is by way of arguing that the French Revolution *was* in certain basic ways a prototype for later social-revolutionary transformations in very different times and places within the modern world. Try as they may, historians of France will never be able to reappropriate the French Revolution for French history alone—not even for European or Western history alone. The French Revolution was, is—and ever will be, as interpretations of it change from new vantage points—a truly world-historical event. The French Revolution is the property of all those who would understand the patterns and meanings of politics in our global era of democracy, bureaucracy, national state formation, and the still-burning passions of international warfare.

NOTES

1. "Mars Unshackled" is a phrase borrowed from Martin van Creveld, *Command in War* (Cambridge: Harvard University Press, 1985), p. 96. This article originated as a keynote address, "Reconsidering the French Revolution in World-Historical Perspective," delivered by Theda Skocpol at the Eighteenth Consortium on Revolutionary Europe, 1750–1850, held in Birmingham, Alabama, 25–27 February 1988. That address was subsequently published in pp. 3–22 of the 1988 Consortium's *Proceedings* (Athens: Department of History, University of Georgia, 1988); and a slightly expanded version appeared in *Social Research* 56, 1 (Spring 1989): 53–70. Meyer Kestnbaum has contributed further research on changes in the French military to this substantially revised version of the essay. Changes were also made in response to comments by anonymous reviewers for the University of California Press.

2. Karl Griewank, "Emergence of the Concept of Revolution," in *Revolution: A Reader*, eds. Bruce Mazlish, Arthur Kaledin, and David B. Ralston (New York: Macmillan, 1971), pp. 13–17; and Arthur Hatto, "'Revolution': An Inquiry into the Usefulness of an Historical Term," *Mind* 58 (1949): 495–517.

3. François Furet, *Interpreting the French Revolution*, trans. Elborg Forster (Cambridge and New York: Cambridge University Press, 1981), pt. 2, sec. 1.

4. Alfred Cobban, *The Social Interpretation of the French Revolution* (Cambridge and New York: Cambridge University Press, 1968).

5. Richard C. Cobb, *The Police and the People: French Popular Protest, 1789–1820* (London: Oxford University Press, 1970).

6. Barrington Moore, Jr., *Social Origins of Dictatorship and Democracy: Lord and Peasant in the Making of the Modern World* (Boston: Beacon Press, 1966).

7. Samuel P. Huntington, *Political Order in Changing Societies* (New Haven, Conn.: Yale University Press, 1968).

8. Theda Skocpol, *States and Social Revolutions: A Comparative Analysis of France, Russia, and China* (Cambridge and New York: Cambridge University Press, 1979).

9. Lynn Hunt, *Politics, Culture, and Class in the French Revolution* (Berkeley, Los Angeles, London: University of California Press, 1984), p. 3.

10. Ibid., p. 15.

11. Ibid.

12. Ibid., p. 235.

13. Ibid., p. 236.

14. Ibid., p. 16.

15. Alexis de Tocqueville, *The Old Regime and the French Revolution*, trans. Stuart Gilbert (Garden City, N.Y.: Doubleday Anchor Books, 1955; originally 1858).

16. Hunt, *Politics, Culture, and Class*, p. 21.

17. Ibid., emphasis added.

18. See George V. Taylor, "Revolutionary and Nonrevolutionary Content in the *Cahiers* of 1789: An Interim Report," *French Historical Studies* 7 (1972): 479–502.

19. One of the best overviews of the final decades of the Old Regime, stressing the interaction of geopolitics and domestic politics, remains C. B. A. Behrens, *The Ançien Régime* (New York: Harcourt, Brace, and World, 1967). A more recent discussion along the same lines is Bailey Stone, "The Geopolitical Origins of the French Revolution Reconsidered," *Proceedings of the 1988 Consortium on Revolutionary Europe, 1750–1850*, ed. David M. Vess (Athens: Department of History, University of Georgia, 1988), pp. 250–262.

20. William Doyle, *The Oxford History of the French Revolution* (Oxford: Oxford University Press, 1989), p. 57.

21. Geoffrey Best, *War and Society in Revolutionary Europe, 1770–1870* (Suffolk, England: Fontana Paperbacks, 1982), pp. 50–52; van Creveld, *Command in War*, pp. 60–62; Peter Paret, "Napoleon and the Revolution in War," in *Makers of Modern Strategy from Machiavelli to the Modern Age*, ed. Peter Paret (Princeton: Princeton University Press, 1986), pp. 127–128; and John R. Elting, *Swords Around a Throne: Napoleon's Grand Armée* (New York: Free Press, 1988), pp. 6–22.

22. Simon Schama, *Citizens: A Chronicle of the French Revolution* (New York: Knopf, 1989), pp. 61–63. Schama opposes any explanation of the Old Regime's demise which stresses structural contradictions, preferring to highlight instead the policy choices of royal ministers. But this poses a false opposition between structural and policy-based accounts. As Schama himself points out, "the ministers of Louis XVI were painfully impaled on the horns of a dilemma" (p. 62). This is what "structural contradictions" translate into in human terms: constrained choices where no options are really likely to resolve the problems the policies are meant to address.

23. Doyle, *Oxford History*, pp. 51, 63–65.

24. Furet, *Interpreting the French Revolution*, p. 52.

25. See Michael L. Kennedy, *The Jacobin Clubs in the French Revolution: The First Years* (Princeton: Princeton University Press, 1982); and Isser Woloch, *Jacobin Legacy* (Princeton: Princeton University Press, 1970), chap. 1.

26. Woloch, *Jacobin Legacy*, p. 6.

27. Ibid., p. 7.

28. See especially Samuel F. Scott, *The Response of the Royal Army to the French Revolution: The Role and Development of the Line Army, 1787–93* (Oxford: Oxford University Press, 1978); John A. Lynn, *The Bayonets of the Republic: Motivation and Tactics in the Army of Revolutionary France, 1791–94* (Urbana and Chicago: University of Illinois Press, 1984); and Gunther Rothenberg, *The Art of Warfare in the Age of Napoleon* (London: B. T. Batsford, 1977), chap. 4; William H. McNeill, *The Pursuit of Power: Technology, Armed Force, and Society since A.D. 1000* (Chicago: University of Chicago Press, 1982), chap. 6, esp. p. 192; and Elting, *Swords Around a Throne*, chap. 3.

29. McNeill, *Pursuit of Power*, p. 192; van Creveld, *Command in War*, chap. 3; and Elting, *Swords Around a Throne*, chap. 3.

30. Best, *War and Society in Revolutionary Europe*, chaps. 4–5; Paret, "Napoleon and Revolution in War," p. 127 and passim.

31. Lynn, *Bayonets of the Republic*, p. 64.

32. Ibid., pp. 64–65.

33. Carl von Clausewitz, *On War*, trans. and ed. Michael Howard and Peter Paret (Princeton: Princeton University Press, 1976), p. 592. For additional parts of von Clausewitz's analysis of the scale of war during the Revolution, see pp. 585–594 and 609–610.

34. Rothenberg, *Art of Warfare*, pp. 16–19.

35. Hunt, *Politics, Culture, and Class*, p. 227.

36. Ibid., p. 233.

37. Furet, *Interpreting the French Revolution*, pp. 126–127.

38. Van Creveld, *Command in War*, chap. 3, esp. pp. 96–102; Paret, "Napoleon and Revolution in War," pp. 127–130, 136–138; and Elting, *Swords Around a Throne*, chaps. 4, 5, and 20.

39. Rothenberg, *Art of Warfare*, p. 126, and chap. 5. This paragraph also draws on the text and references of Skocpol, *States and Social Revolutions*, pp. 196–198.

40. Rothenberg, *Art of Warfare*, p. 132.

41. John Lynn, "A Conflict of Principles: The Army of the Revolution and the Army of the Empire." *Proceedings of the 1988 Consortium on Revolutionary Europe, 1750–1850*, ed. David M. Vess (Athens: Department of History, University of Georgia, 1988), pp. 507–519.

42. Martin van Creveld, *Supplying War: Logistics from Wallenstein to Patton* (Cambridge and New York: Cambridge University Press, 1977), pp. 40–42, 73–74.

43. Ibid., chap. 2; and Elting, *Swords Around a Throne*, chaps. 27–28.

44. Best, *War and Society in Revolutionary Europe*, chap. 9; Paret, "Napoleon and Revolution in War," pp. 129–133; Elting, *Swords Around a Throne*, chap. 26; and Gunther Rothenberg, "The Origins, Causes, and Extension of the Wars of the French Revolution and Napoleon," *The Journal of Interdisciplinary History* 28, 4 (1988): 771–793.

45. For discussion of the ways French military innovations compelled competitor nations to implement similar transformations, see Best, *War and Society in Revolutionary Europe*, chaps. 5, 10–14; and Paret, "Napoleon and Revolution in War." Thus, revolutionary France not only loosed "democracy" on the modern world, it also launched new modes of warfare that were also imitated and reworked by other nations.

46. Shaul Bakhash, *The Reign of the Ayatollahs: Iran and the Islamic Revolution* (New York: Basic Books, 1984).

47. For further exploration of the Iranian Revolution in comparative perspective, see Theda Skocpol's "Rentier State and Shi'a Islam in the Iranian Revolution," *Theory and Society* 11 (1982): 265–284; and "Social Revolutions and Mass Military Mobilization," *World Politics* 40 (1988): 147–168.

TWO

The Making of a "Bourgeois Revolution"

Eric Hobsbawm

"To entertain any theory about revolution," writes John Dunn[1]—"and it is not even possible to identify just what events do constitute revolutions without assuming *some* theory about the meaning of revolution—is to assume a political posture. . . . The value-free study of revolutions is a logical impossibility for those who live in the real world." For the student of revolutions the problem is complicated by the fact that the political postures assumed spontaneously by those who write or speak about them, and, if not careful, by the student him- or herself, are not necessarily coherent or consistent. We live in an era when rapid and fundamental change has become the norm in everyday life, so that the terms *revolution* and *revolutionary* extend far beyond the field of political science. Moreover, common discourse identifies them, much in the eighteenth-century manner, with progress and the improvement of life, so that, as advertising agencies understand only too well, the word *revolutionary*, when attached to a new microwave oven as distinct from a political regime, will sell the product more effectively, even among those most passionately committed to the defense of the status quo against subversion.

Nevertheless, the primary political meaning of "revolution" remains profoundly controversial, as the historiography of the subject demonstrates, and the debates surrounding the bicentenary of the French Revolution of 1789 demonstrate even more unmistakably. What usually happens to revolutions sufficiently distant from the present—and two centuries are, by the news-agency standards which dominate our information, almost beyond the range of the remembered past—is that they are either transformed into nonrevolutions, that is, integrated into historical continuity or excluded from it as insignificant temporary interruptions, or else they are celebrated by public rites of passage suitable to the occasions that mark the birth of nations and regimes. They remain controversial only among historians. Thus the English

revolution or revolutions of the seventeenth century have been tacitly eliminated from political discourse: even in the tercentenary year of what used to be
called the Glorious Revolution of 1688 and the constituting event of British
parliamentary sovereignty, its presence in public rhetoric has been subdued
and marginal. In contrast, a celebratory consensus has marked the various
bicentenaries connected with the American Revolution, and even opponents
of those aspects of it which are still—or again—highly controversial, such as
its deliberate refusal to give public recognition to religion, would not dream
of using this as an argument against it. Its public face, jubilees and cen-
tenaries apart, is that of a rite of passage in the life of the nation, Independence (celebrated on the Fourth of July) taking its place after first settlement
(celebrated on Thanksgiving).

Attempts to apply these two techniques of eliminating the controversial
aspects of the French Revolution have been made—by republicans and the
political right respectively—and the contention that it achieved little or
nothing other than what would have happened without it, and thus constitutes not a major transforming set of events but only a sort of stumble on the
long path of French history, is one of the main weapons in the intellectual
war against those who wish to celebrate its bicentenary. Yet these attempts
have failed. On the one hand, the Revolution never gained the general retrospective consensus without which such events cannot become harmless
national birthdays, not even after World War II briefly eliminated from the
political scene that French right which defined itself by its rejection of
1789. On the contrary, since the Revolution inspired not only the left of
the relatively remote past but also the contemporary left, it could not but
remain contentious. As is quite evident from the prebicentenary debates
in France, the traditional opponents of 1789 have been reinforced by the
opponents of 1917—reactionaries who would not disclaim that label, by
liberals who certainly would. On the other hand, the antirevolutionary
attempt to demote the Revolution or shunt it onto a sidetrack of French
historical development has also failed, since, if it had succeeded, it would no
longer need to be seriously argued. Indeed, the mere project of trying to
prove that the French Revolution is *not* an altogether major event in modern
history must strike non-Frenchmen as brave and quixotic, that is, as absurd.

Historians can no more escape taking a political posture about revolutions
than anybody else. However, they can at least avoid seeing and judging them
unhistorically, that is to say teleologically. Revolutions, or at all events such
major sociopolitical upheavals as the French Revolution, belong to the class
of historical phenomena whose significance is not to be judged by the intentions or expectations of those who make them, or even those that could be
imputed to them by subsequent analysis. Such intentions are not, of course,
irrelevant to the study of the phenomenon. However, they cannot determine
it, because uncontrollability of process and outcome is its essential character-

istic. Since such phenomena—modern great wars are other members of this class—are usually associated with declarations of intent before, during, and after the event, the temptation to judge them accordingly is great, all the more so since those who occupy the main parts in these dramas are usually rational, goal-oriented, problem-solving decision makers, "engineers of men's [bodies and] souls," to adapt the phrase of one of them (Stalin). This temptation must be resisted. The French Revolution cannot be adequately discussed in terms of its, or its makers', success or failure to achieve actual or ascribed objects. Consequently, however tempting, it is also pointless to indulge in the ex post facto cost-benefit analysis which asks such questions as "Was it all worth while?" and "Could the results have been achieved at less cost?" For we are not dealing with phenomena to which the criteria of social problem-solving apply more than peripherally: where human agencies can effectively choose between correct and incorrect solutions, alternative strategies, or more or less wasteful or elegant methods of achieving ends specifiable in advance. Such ends are not absent, but they are dwarfed by what is uncontrolled and unintended. Even if we suppose that the Constitution of 1791 was exactly what the leaders of the National Assembly of 1789 had intended to achieve and that it represented what turned out to be the lasting achievements of the Revolution, it cannot be seriously supposed that at the time of its promulgation it was in anyone's power to declare the Revolution over. The subsequent events prove the contrary.

But this raises precisely the dual problem of the (or any) revolution's aims and its results or consequences. And in the case of the French Revolution this is particularly thorny, because it produced different, and, it has been widely held, mutually incompatible consequences—for example, the heritage of the Constituent Assembly and the Jacobin Republic—and because in France "the passage from the feudal and aristocratic forms of society to the industrial and democratic was attended by convulsions,"[2] unlike in "other nations" (Britain), whereas the results were, in broad historical terms, not all that dissimilar.

Was the Revolution therefore avoidable? Did it produce results which could only have been achieved through revolution and not in other ways? Did it pursue a logical line of development which then "skidded off course"[3] and, if so, was this also inevitable? These are, of course, primarily political rather than historical questions, and the answers tend to fit political preconceptions. Yet if we start with the assumption that in great revolutions, as in the great mass wars of modern times, the unintended consequences are almost certainly more important than the intended ones, though not independent of these, then historians may find emancipation from their politics a little easier. So long as these do not actually prevent them from recognizing the historical specificity of their own timebound point of view, and the historical *dimensions* of their topic.

What, then, were the historical consequences of the French Revolution? If we compare the judgment of both educated opinion and professional historiography on the eve of the bicentenary with that on the occasion of the centenary, we shall be struck by the curious attempts to minimize what, a century ago, was regarded as, beyond question, let alone dispute, a historical phenomenon of extraordinary, nay of unique, importance. "The French Revolution," wrote a respected British historian and expert on the period,

> the most terrible and momentous series of events in all history, is the real starting-point for the history of the nineteenth century; for that great upheaval has profoundly affected the political and, still more, the social life of the Continent of Europe.[4]

Hardly any observer in 1889 would have disagreed.

Nor would many observers today take a different view about the Revolution's impact on world history in the nineteenth century. Only the curious retreat of French intellectual debate into a hexagonal provincialism can explain why the impact of the French Revolution on the non-French world has had so modest a place in the passionate historiographical and ideological debates that preceded the bicentenary. On the other hand, it is surprising that the economic effects of the Revolution, which are today viewed with generally skeptical or critical eyes, were seen as so patently positive by nineteenth-century observers. "Men of the highest social positions in France," wrote Richard Cobden in 1853,

> admit that to the measures of 1789 . . . which have elevated the millions of their countrymen, from a condition hardly superior to that of the Russian serf, to the rank of citizens and proprietors of the soil, France is indebted for a more rapid advance in civilization, wealth and happiness, than was ever previously made by any community of a similar extent, within the same period of time.[5]

Cobden, the apostle of free trade, was a Radical Liberal by British standards and a politician, and not one disinclined to underestimate the economic progress of his own country since 1789. However, his contemporary Heinrich von Sybel, the first (non-French) academic historian to bring the heavy artillery of archival scholarship to bear on the subject, was both more cautious and more moderate in his liberalism. Yet he estimated that since 1789 French industry had grown fourfold, French agriculture threefold, and French commerce more than threefold, a growth which he clearly linked to the Revolution.[6] I cite these opinions not because they carry any historical authority—they plainly do not—but as evidence that intelligent and informed observers took it for granted that the effects of the Revolution on nineteenth-century France had been as striking as they were, on balance, beneficent. Whether these beliefs were adequately founded, is a matter for historical investigation. But so also is the fact that such beliefs were widely and, probably among men and women of even a very moderate liberal persuasion, almost universally held for long stretches of the nineteenth century. For how people read the past, especially the past within, or almost within, living memory, is part of history. And what it is that makes them read (or misread) it in a particular way, is a matter of moment, not only because even myths and misunderstandings can become historical forces if widely enough accepted, but also because there may be something about the original event that encourages one particular reading rather than another.

This is particularly relevant to one aspect of the historical revisionism that has dominated the scholarly debate on the French Revolution for some decades and has discouraged excessively triumphalist celebrations of its bicentenary. The "orthodox" interpretation of the Revolution, which had dominated both institutions and scholarship for decades and which revisionism attacked—and, it must be said, has made largely untenable in its conventional versions—had become increasingly identified with a, or rather "the," Marxist interpretation. Indeed, at the time when the main assault on this position was launched in France by Furet and Richet in 1970,[7] the holder of the prestigious Chair in the History of the French Revolution at the Sorbonne, and thus the chief guardian of the Revolution's reputation, was a devoted member of the French Communist party. Revisionism about the French Revolution was part of the general process by which French intellectuals in the 1970s and 1980s distanced themselves from their radical and Marxist past, or—depending on their personal history—took their revenge upon those who had dominated intellectual fashion for so long. And the core of the Marxist interpretation of the Revolution appeared to be the claim, (1) that it was a class struggle and (2) a "bourgeois revolution" which overthrew feudalism in order to establish a bourgeois and capitalist France.

The interesting thing about both these claims is that—as Marx himself freely acknowledged—they were not his. He derived them from the French liberal historians of the Restoration. The French Revolution may not have been the "bourgeois revolution" whose nature or existence historians are today debating, but it was certainly read as one by the generation that immediately succeeded it. A recent study sees "les historiens bourgeois de la Restauration, tout à leur célébration de l'epopée des classes moyennes"[8] ("the bourgeois historians of the Restoration busy celebrating the epic of the middle classes"). A German historian of the *Vormärz*—and no one took to the concept of the bourgeois revolution more enthusiastically than German liberals of the pre-1848 era—presented the case for it in its classic if "idealist" form. The "institutions of the Middle Ages" had had their day. New ideas had arisen, and these had affected all ways of thinking about the world, but "above all the relations of the ranks of society [Stände] in human society." The "bourgeois rank" (Bürgerstand) became everyday more important, by virtue of the visibly growing mass of intellect and education (geistige Bildung) it represented. And so "men began to speak and write about the Rights of Man, and to investigate the rights of those who based their claims on so-called privileges."[9] That is how the French Revolution came about.

More concretely F. A. Mignet (1796–1884) who published his History of the French Revolution—the first on the subject written by a professional historian—as early as 1824, argued that in the Old Regime men were divided into rival classes, the nobles and "the people" or Third Estate, "whose power, wealth, stability and intelligence were growing daily," and which formulated the Constitution of 1791. "This constitution was the work of the middle class, at that time the strongest; for, as everyone knows, the dominant power always seizes control of institutions." Unfortunately, caught between the aristocracy and "the multitude," the liberal middle class "was attacked by the one and invaded by the other." The common people would never have become sovereign "if the civil war and the foreign coalition had not required its intervention and its help." As "the multitude" was needed to defend the country, "it required to govern it; so it made its own revolution just as the middle class had done." Nevertheless, the aim of the Revolution was achieved: despite "anarchy and despotism; the old society was destroyed during the revolution, and the new one established under the empire."[10]

If those who reflected on the history of their childhood or their parents' maturity took a view so different from that of today's historians, it was in seeing the revolution not only as bourgeois but also as a class struggle of the laboring masses against the ruling classes, in short as a social revolution. The current view that the bulk of Frenchmen were "attentistes ou indifférents" (except when the revolution's religious policy turned them into counterrevolutionaries), while even in the cities "participation in the revolutionary movement concerned only a narrow minority of militants,"[11] was clearly not shared by Tocqueville[12] or by François Guizot (1787–1874), the quintessence (and prime minister) of the July monarchy, which he certainly regarded as a bourgeois regime; and an exceedingly able historian whose insight remains impressive even today. For Guizot all of French history was a secular class struggle between landlords and peasants, nobles and commoners, which, in the language popularized by his contemporary Augustin Thierry (1795–1856)—who echoes the discourse of Walter Scott, as Guizot himself echoes that of the English Revolution of which he made himself the historian[13]—he saw as a war of races: as English feudalism was a Norman Conquest of the Anglo-Saxons, so French feudalism was the conquest of Franks over native Gauls.[14] Yet thirteen centuries had never fused rulers and ruled into a single people. 1789 gave the Gauls their chance. "The result of the revolution was not in doubt. The former vanquished became the victors. They had conquered France in their turn."[15]

For the historians who looked back on it after a generation, and pretty certainly for the average French "bourgeois" or notable after 1815, three things about the Revolution seemed clear. It had overthrown an old regime and instituted a new one, whatever the continuities with France before 1789. (It must have been as clear to contemporaries as it is to us that the world of Balzac was not that of Beaumarchais.) This new regime, bourgeois and liberal, found its most appropriate institutional form in something like the 1791 Constitution. Yet moderate bourgeois liberalism could not have been established against the resistance of court and nobility without mobilizing the common people (or the politically effective parts of it), nor could France have resisted counterrevolution and foreign invasion, or, for that matter, conquered most of Europe, without mobilizing forces that were neither bourgeois nor liberal.

Of course, Restoration historians, living in the memory of the Revolution, had no difficulty in seeing that it was pointless to suggest historical alternatives that had not been available. To quote Mignet again:

> Perhaps it would be bold to assert that things could not have turned out differently; but what is certain is that, taking account of the causes that led to it and the passions that it used and aroused, the revolution was bound to take this course and lead to this result. . . . I shall hope to show that it was no longer possible either to prevent it or to guide it.[16]

Even if one regarded the results of the Revolution as decisive and beneficent, as Mignet did, there was no denying that these results had been achieved by a process that was at odds with middle-class liberalism and, in important ways, incompatible with its objectives. And the obscure dialectic of this interaction between the first and the second Revolutions, between 1791 and 1794, liberals and Jacobins, haunted analytical observers, of whom Marx is an excellent example,[17] if only because the second seemed essential to the success of the first, perhaps even because both were, in different ways, essential to each other. For, as virtually all Marxist revolutionaries agreed up to and including the overthrow of tsarism, where would proletarian revolution be without the infrastructure of bourgeois revolution on which it would arise?

In any case, it was only too evident that the history of the nineteenth century would continue to be dominated by the relationships between the heirs of 1791 and the heirs of Year II. What moderate Liberals like Guizot liked about the 1814 Restoration (and even more in the July monarchy) was that it legitimized the France of 1791—"revolution and legitimacy today have in common the fact that both are seeking to preserve themselves and to preserve the *status quo*"—and in doing so to establish that "frank cooperation" by means of which "kings and nations [sc. England] have extinguished those internal wars which are denominated revolutions."[18] What he blamed the reactionaries for was not so much the intention of restoring an old regime which was beyond effective revival, but for bringing the masses back into a perhaps necessary but always dangerous and unpredictable action. For bourgeois France could only flourish under "free government." But "for the house of Bourbon and its supporters, absolute power is [now EJH] impossible; under them France must be free." Conversely, "Absolute power, amongst us, can only belong to the Revolution and its representatives, for they alone can (I do not say how long) retain the masses in their interest."

From the point of view of "the people," it was equally clear that the status quo needed to be changed and not preserved. For if the bourgeoisie had—I follow the socialist Louis Blanc's 1847 history of the French Revolution[19]— achieved *its* freedom, "the people" was only nominally free. Its revolution still had to be made, and the Jacobin Republic provided its obvious precedent and model.

How are we to explain this dramatic divergence between nineteenth-century assessments of the Revolution—including those of men within whose generation's memory it lay—and those of late-twentieth-century historians. Tempting though it is, it will not do to ascribe the downbeat accounts of modern "revisionist" scholars entirely to a political hostility to the French Revolution, or rather to it as ancestor and inspirer of modern Marxist revolutions. That such hostility plays an important part in shaping the attitude of several leading historians in France is not in doubt, even when they do not go as far as those reactionary publicists who have argued that the main thing for the bicentenary to commemorate is the counterrevolutionary rebellion of the Vendée, ancestor of *gulag* and genocide, if not the first of that grim species.[20] Even in the nineteenth century those who feared the revolutions of the masses were apt to play down their historic achievements of the Revolution, even when (like de Tocqueville) they welcomed the liberal part of its achievements—if only "this revolution, instead of being carried out by the masses on behalf of the sovereignty of the people, [had] been the work of an enlightened autocrat."[21] Those who feared and disliked democracy were apt to criticize the historic consequences of the Revolution, not so much because, given the terrible human and economic costs, they were so modest and could have been achieved with so much less disruption—retrospective cost-benefit calculations are characteristic of our own era—but because the effects of the Revolution were so negative and so great. As Goldwin Smith put it in an article of exceptional ill temper, it was a catastrophe, the greatest calamity to befall the human race, because it gave rise to "universal suffrage without intelligence" and created Jacobinism, which "is now as established a disease as the smallpox," whose infection "is beginning to cross the Channel."[22] However, it is worth recalling that even antirevolutionaries generally accepted much of the orthodox positive interpretation. For Tocqueville, our history from 1789 to 1830, viewed from a distance and as a whole, affords, as it were, the picture of a struggle to the death between the Ancien Régime, its traditions, memories, hopes and men, as represented by the aristocracy, and the New France, led by the Middle Class.[23]

And even Goldwin Smith accepted that "the one great achievement of the Revolution, in the way of construction, is the peasant proprietory of France."

Nevertheless, leaving political *parti pris* aside, it must be accepted that many of the "revisionist" criticisms of the orthodox interpretation are both factually and conceptually legitimate. There was not, in 1789, a self-conscious bourgeois class representing the new realities of economic power, ready to take into its own hands the destinies of the state, eliminating the declining feudal aristocracy; and insofar as there was such a class in the 1780s, a social revolution was not its object, but rather a reform of the institutions of the kingdom; and in any case its conscious objective was not the construction of an industrial capitalist economy. Nor was this the result of the Revolution which, almost certainly, had a negative effect on the French economy, both because it severely disrupted it for several years and because it created a large bloc of politically significant citizens—peasants and petty-bourgeois—whose interest it was to slow down economic growth. In any case the years of revolution and war gave the British industrial revolution an advantage over France which it did not lose until after World War II. And so on. That some of these observations were not new but part of traditional and orthodox historiography does not make the incompatibility between them and what became the orthodox concept of a "bourgeois revolution" any less. Nor can we dismiss factual criticisms by assimilating them to the counter-factual speculations or tacit historiographical preconceptions which have always inundated the debate on the Revolution. Could it have been avoided? Was the radicalization of the Revolution from 1791 on the result of the emergence of a bunch of Jacobin ideologues or a new type of revolutionary rhetoric or "discourse" rather than due to the logic of the Revolution's internal and external development? Was it all Rousseau's fault?

And yet, the gap between historical skepticism and contemporary conviction that an old era had ended and a new one had overthrown it, needs to be explained, for that belief itself became, with the French Revolution, a powerful historical phenomenon in its own right. Without it, how are we to understand the revolutions of the nineteenth century, and German liberals like the scholar Gervinus who declared on the eve of 1848:

Must a great people, seeking to break through to independent political life, to freedom and power, necessarily pass through the crisis of revolution? The double example of England and France comes close to compelling us to accept this proposition.[24]

There are, it may be suggested, two reasons why late-twentieth-century historians find it so hard to accept the reactions of nineteenth-century observers. One is that twentieth-century definitions of social classes do not seem to fit nineteenth-century realities, and for this the influence of Marxism is probably in large part responsible. If by *bourgeoisie* we understand essentially a class of profit-making business people, or even of industrial entrepreneurs employing hired wage-labor, then we shall certainly not rate their social importance and economic wealth in 1789 highly, especially if we insist on excluding entrepreneurs sprung from or absorbed into the aristocracy. If we suppose a *proletariat* to consist essentially of propertyless wage-workers in factory, mine, railroad, or similar establishments, we shall come to the correct conclusion, long used in argument by anti-Marxists, that most early "labor movements" contained very few proletarians, though this did not stop their members from assimilating themselves to "proletarians," even as modest German *Bürger* assimilated themselves to French and British *bourgeois*. The second reason is that, even insofar as such descriptions applied, subsequent development has been so much more massive and striking as to lead us to underestimate the contemporary impact of the relevant phenomena. Thus it seems evident to us that around the 1830s there had not yet been much industrialization anywhere. Britain was as yet far from being "an industry state," as (Sir) John Clapham pointed out long ago in the first volume of his monumental *Economic History of Modern Britain*.[25] Historians have argued that it is absurd to speak of the "Industrial Revolution" at this period. And yet it is undeniable that sometime in the 1820s intelligent men, sometimes with practical experiences of manufacturers, began to compare the changes in industry with the most dramatic transformation they could think of, namely the French Revolution; that words like *industrialist* and *industrialism* were coined to complement this concept of an "industrial revolution," and that predictions of the total transformation of society by means of this revolution began to be confidently made from a variety of ideological points of view. Rather than supposing that Robert Owen, Saint-Simon, the young Engels, or the ideologically very different Dr. Andrew Ure, Karl Marx's *bête noire*, were fantasizing, it seems more reasonable to see them as recognizing both the dramatic novelty of the industrial developments taking place, the high social "visibility," attested to by relays of continental visitors, of places like Manchester, and, above all, the unlimited *potential* of the revolution they embodied. Both skeptical historians and prophetic contemporaries were or are right, but both focus(ed) on a different aspect of the reality they record(ed). All the same, if we do not recognize what the contemporaries saw in that reality, we shall be unable to explain a great many important things about the period, as for instance why from 1840 on "a spectre was haunting Europe, the spectre of communism"—a statement for which there is ample evidence outside the Communist Manifesto, or the presence of activists representing the "proletariat" in the Provisional Government of France in 1848, which, it will be recalled, considered for a moment whether the flag of the new French Republic should be tricolour—or red.

It is even more essential to recapture the contemporary perspective if we wish to understand how the French Revolution became a bourgeois revolution, and indeed *the* bourgeois revolution. Let us return to Mignet who summarized its achievements in 1824:

> It replaced arbitrary power by law, privilege by equality; it freed men from class distinctions, the land from provincial barriers, industry from the handicaps of corporations and guilds, agriculture from feudal servitude and the oppression of tithes, property from the constraints of entail; and it brought everything together under a single state, a single law, a single people.[26]

On paper this tribute to social liberation, economic liberation, and institutional unification would have been acceptable to the prerevolutionary monarchy and elites and would certainly not have suggested to anyone that dominance of the middle class to which, as we have seen, Mignet himself ascribed the transformation.

Yet the "privilege" which the Revolution replaced was that of (noble) birth. The visible marks of class difference ("class distinctions") which it abolished were those which singled out aristocrats over members of the Third Estate. That enlightened nobles and rulers might themselves see such privileges and distinctions as unsustainable or undesirable cannot make the struggle against them socially neutral. Freemasonry, in spite of its attraction for enlightened aristocrats, could not be essentially an organization of landed nobles and gentlemen like, say, the Jockey Club, since its basis was precisely the absence of class distinctions within the craft. Moreover, while the decision to call the States-General in a particular manner certainly helped to turn 1789 politics into a struggle of nonnobles against aristocrats, this class struggle was already in being, as witness Beaumarchais's *Marriage of Figaro*, which, incidentally, and not fortuitously, turns on a specifically *feudal* privilege of lords, thus linking the case against "privilege" with the case for economic development, which in Mignet's view was benefited by its abolition.

Conversely, the "equality" achieved by the Revolution was, as we know, specifically *not* intended to be egalitarian or democratic. The Abbé Sieyès was not, in his famous pamphlet on the Third Estate, "pressing the social and political claims of all commoners," but only those of the group he called "the available classes of the Third Estate," that is, "the solid and unified group of professional men"[27] who were the only ones to get themselves elected as its representatives. The electorate of 1791, in Mignet's own words, was "restricted to the enlightened," who thereby "controlled all the force and power in the state," being "at the time alone qualified to control them because they alone had the intelligence necessary for the conduct of government."[28] It constituted an open elite selected for talent, irrespective of birth (except inasmuch as physical and psychological constitution was believed to exclude all women from such talents), the talent being demonstrated by property and education. It did not discriminate against individuals from the aristocracy, but only insofar as they fulfilled the criteria of membership independently of their hereditary status. It excluded individuals from the lower orders but only insofar as they failed to make their way into its ranks. Indeed its object was, in Mignet's words, to "let all share in [rights] *when they are capable of gaining them*" (emphasis added). That most of them could not or would not make their way out of the "pays réel" into the "pays légal" did not invalidate the argument that "true equality" had as its "real hallmark admissibility, as that of inequality is exclusion" (Mignet).

But a stratum of people who owed their position in the social order not to birth or privilege but to individual worth, open to all suitable recruits, *was* what was then understood by a "middle rank," "middle class," "Bürgertum," or whatever name was given to the ensemble of indigenous[29] (urban) adults situated, by status and income, between the nobility above and the (manually) laboring classes below. Insofar as they distinguished themselves, or were distinguished, as a group—and this does not seem to have happened anywhere before the eighteenth century—it was precisely by the implicitly antiaristocratic but negative characteristic of individuality as distinct from membership of social group or ascribed community. The ideology of eighteenth-century Enlightenment formulated this as a program for a humanity progressing out of the darkness of the past. I doubt whether men of this kind saw themselves as a social class. They were rather a human *type* that was more frequently found in certain social contexts, and perhaps in certain family settings, for instance, in the German lands, in families of Lutheran clergy. They certainly did not see this social zone of individual merit as specifically identified with entrepreneurs in commerce and manufactures, even though most of these would probably be found in this zone or entered it once they were sufficiently successful. Still less did they conceive of economy transformed by industrial revolution. We seek in vain for such a perspective in Adam Smith's *Wealth of Nations*. And there is no sign at all that members of such middle strata, however devoted to the ideal of a civil society of equal rights and chances for all[30] saw themselves as a ruling class or as challenging the political structure of old regimes. Indeed, one of the ideologically conscious strata of this kind, the German Bürgertum, consisted, until the mid-nineteenth century, largely of a body of men "bound by multiple links to the state of enlightened absolutism and of monarchical–bureaucratic constitutionalism"[31] and were, with all their liberalism, mostly loyal functionaries of their governments.

What the French Revolution did was to transform bodies of such people into self-conscious "classes" with the ambition to reshape society as "ruling classes." In France this happened because in the course of events, which certainly nobody had intended to produce this result, three discoveries were made. First, it became clear that the program of enlightened reform and progress would not be carried out through the old monarchy but through a new regime, that is, not by reform from above, as men of goodwill had hoped, but by revolution. Second, it became clear that this program required a collective struggle of "the people" or Third Estate against the aristocracy, and that, for practical purposes those who represented the Third Estate and spoke for it—and hence who shaped the new France—were the *classes disponibles* of that Estate, men of the middle ranks of society. Finally, it became clear in the course of the revolution that within the former Third Estate "the people" and the middle stratum had seriously conflicting interests. The makers of the new regime needed protection against the old and the new threats— the nobles and the masses. It is not surprising that they should learn to recognize themselves retrospectively as a middle class and the events of 1789–1799 as a class struggle. Outside France it was merely necessary to learn the French lessons and apply them with the required local modifications to make a bourgeois revolution. It may be pointed out in passing that Marx himself used the term quite infrequently in his writings.

What is not in doubt is that this is how Liberals saw the Revolution after 1815. It is quite beside the point to show in the abstract, however convincingly, that nothing much had changed in the distribution of property, and that "in the end the Revolution benefited the same landed elite that had started it, though it had torn itself to pieces in the course of the upheaval." It is entirely misleading to suggest that the new rising bourgeois continued to "s'inserer dans une volonté d'identification à l'aristocratie," unless this merely means that *arriviste* French businessmen in France were as snobbish as that species was in practically all countries.[32] That is not how a De Tocqueville saw matters at the time. For him the 1830 Revolution was a triumph of the middle class so

> definite and so thorough that all political power, every prerogative, and the whole government was confined and, as it were, heaped up within the narrow limits of this one class. . . . Not only did it thus rule society, but it may be said to have formed it.[33]

Who would have described France on the eve of the Revolution, or even in 1791, in such class terms? Would such a form of discourse have even been conceivable? The Revolution not only made it conceivable but logical.

This is all the more striking, since a specific sense of the middle strata as a single social group was neither natural—they are notoriously harder to define than other social strata, except in terms of vertical location—nor was it, as we have seen, part of the prerevolutionary political vocabulary of the middle ranks. They were *individuals*, collectively united precisely by not being institutionalized "orders of society," high or low, communities or corporations, and separated from those above by rejecting privilege, from those below by personal merit, and by emancipation from ignorance and backwardness, that is, by the use of reason. To abolish all institutions intermediate between the citizen as an individual and Mignet's "single state, single law and single people" was an essential part of the Revolution's political transformations.

Consequently their essential mode of public action was the association of individuals freely joining together for whatever purpose, and the term *association* was to become one of the key words in the political vocabulary of nineteenth-century bourgeois society. How else were the members of the elites of reason and worth, or for that matter the enthusiasts for music or statistics, to discover one another or act together? This characteristic mode of organization of the men of middle rank, especially for purposes of social and cultural interchange and mutual moral and intellectual improvement, has been misinterpreted as something separate from the social selection of the membership of lodge, club, or "circle" and seen as a sort of independent theater of cultural and ideological discourse, in which Jacobin agitators and zealots could rehearse their fanatical dramas, prior to diverting the reform of France from its otherwise more moderate course.[34] But the political culture of club or lodge life was not necessarily radical or, even before the Revolution, particularly political—though the Revolution naturally made it more obviously so. Moreover, what made the radical ideologists into a political force was not the existence of forms of sociability favoring cultural revolution as such but the events of the Revolution itself. Before it they were not of much importance: "Many of those whom one might claim as heralding the Revolution [before 1789] turn out to be a rather mangy collection of intellectual drop-outs, cranks, and failures."[35] Still, individualism was not class organization.

And yet, a body of men defining themselves thus as the opposite of a social "class," namely as an assembly of individuals, found itself welcoming the new collective label.

But how far was this new self-conscious middle class a class of bourgeois in the capitalist sense? In the view of foreign, and certainly of German observers, as well as of Balzac, postrevolutionary France was a society in which, more than in any other, wealth was power and men were dedicated to the accumulation of it. Lorenz von Stein even devised a historical explanation for this. Under Napoleon, the crucial question of the Revolution, namely "the right of every individual to rise, by his own ability, to the highest position in civil society and state," was inevitably narrowed down to the right to accumulate property, or to make a success in the army, since despotism excluded other forms of competition for public distinction. And so France became rich (once again, contemporaries seem less skeptical than historians)

> because, precisely through falling under the despotism of the Empire, it entered the epoch when *wealth* constitutes *power* for each individual.

Of course this class had no independent share in power, and thus could not be—in the somewhat old-fashioned terminology of pre-1848 Germans—an "estate of the realm [ein Stand]," since it had accepted the Napoleonic dictatorship as the only protection against social revolution. But sooner or later it would naturally demand its share of power, and after 1815 it did so.[36]

Of course, as a class this new bourgeoisie was plainly not primarily concerned with the industrial development of the national economy. But only a taste for teleology would lead us to expect this. The object of businessmen is not industrialization. It is to make money, and when industrial progress or tecnological innovation occur, they are the by-products of this process and not its purpose. As we now know, even in the Britain of the Industrial Revolution, the best way to become a millionaire was not to run a cotton mill but to be a risk-averse banker or merchant. Nor does the triumph of a liberal middle class guarantee the economic success of its country's national economy, except in circumstances that may be independent of its presence.

Nevertheless, it would be absurd to deny that the ideology of the Enlightenment inevitably made economic progress into a central aim of society, if only as a special aspect of human progress in general. And it was surely evident to followers—indeed even to opponents—of Adam Smith, that the best way to maximize economic progress was by means of an economy of private enterprise. As the liberal philosopher Victor Cousin wrote in 1828:

> The destiny of man . . . is to assimilate nature as much as possible to himself, to plant in it, and in it to make appear, unceasingly, the triumph of man over nature, whose tendency was to encroach upon and destroy him, but which retreats before him, and is metamorphosed in his hands; this is truly nothing less than the creation of a new world by man. Political economy explains the secret, or rather the detail of all this; it follows the achievements of industry, which are themselves connected with those of the mathematical and physical sciences.[37]

At a time when (to quote Tocqueville again) "the particular spirit of the middle class" was about to "become the general spirit of government" in France, would this tribute to the power of political economy not have been naturally read as a manifesto for capitalist development?

It has not been the purpose of this chapter to challenge recent "revisionist" tendencies in the historiography of the French Revolution, except insofar as they represent not new research but ideological reinterpretation. Nor, obviously, does it wish to defend the political or prophetic inferences that were drawn from the concept of the Revolution elaborated by its early nineteenth-century analysts; for instance, that all peoples "seeking to break through to independent political life, freedom and power" had to pass through such a revolution (Gervinus), that countries which did not do so could not become properly bourgeois or capitalist, that the proletarian revolution would follow the earlier supposed model, inasmuch as it would be also made by a class grown to maturity within the old system and demanding to break through its integument and take over power in its turn, or a variety of others. Such beliefs, derived at secondhand from the revolutionary experience, themselves were or became part of history, but they are not my concern here.

What this chapter has tried to show is that something which plainly forms the foundation of the classical view of the French Revolution as a social revolution, a "bourgeois revolution," and a central and decisive step in the evolution of modern society, emerged in the first postrevolutionary generation, and that this reading of the French Revolution and its consequences seemed more logical and realistic than the modern revisionist view that it was "haphazard in its origins and ineffectual in its outcome."[38] It seemed realistic to French liberals in three respects. First, because in 1830 it seemed evident that a middle class actually came to power. Second, the nineteenth century, moreover, seemed clearly to perpetuate and even to institutionalize the conflict between middle class and "people" or "masses" (later specified by some as "the proletariat"), which had not existed before 1789, but emerged between "1791" and "1794." Finally, above all, it seemed realistic because, as Tocqueville put it elegantly and eloquently, the Revolution

has entirely destroyed, or is in the process of destroying...everything in ancient society that was derived from aristocratic and feudal institutions, everything that was in any way connected with them, everything that had the least impress of them.[39]

And the canyon which the earthquake of the Revolution had opened between the old regime and the new society was evidently impassable, its profundity and width demonstrated, in France at least, beyond any doubt by the repeated failure to restore that old regime.

This was not a Sorelian "myth," even though the Revolution also generated and turned into such a mobilizing "myth" or set of "myths." It was an empirical generalization, based on how contemporary observers and analysts saw the history of France from 1789 to 1830, just as the concept of the "Industrial Revolution" which emerged during the same generation seemed to contemporaries an empirical generalization based on the observation of British cotton mills and ironworks. Both, of course, extrapolated the future from the past, since they were not concerned with historical analysis for its own sake. Both therefore tended to emphasize what they saw as new and dynamic, rather than what they regarded as relics of the past due to move to the margins of social reality. Both are, for that reason, easily criticized. And yet, if we have to choose between modern revisionist historiography as a guide to nineteenth-century history, including French history, and the liberal analysts of the Restoration, is it so certain that Furet is more illuminating than Guizot, Mignet, and De Tocqueville?

NOTES

1. John Dunn, *Modern Revolutions: An Introduction to the Analysis of a Political Phenomenon* (Cambridge, 1972), pp. 1–2.

2. Lord Acton, *Lectures on the French Revolution* (London, 1910), p. 2. The lectures were originally given by him in 1895.

3. I owe this translation of the term *dérapage*, a key concept in the work of François Furet, to George C. Comninel, *Rethinking the French Revolution: Marxism and the Revisionist Challenge* (London, 1987), p. 21.

4. J. Holland Rose, *A Century of Continental History, 1780–1880* (London, 1895), p. 1.

5. Richard Cobden, *1793 and 1853 in Three Letters* (London, 1853), pp. 51–52.

6. H. Sybel, *Geschichte der Revolutionszeit von 1795 bis 1800* (Duesseldorf, 1870).

7. François Furet and Denis Richet, *La Révolution française* (Paris, 1965). The British historian Alfred Cobban had launched the first attack in 1955, but Anglo-Saxon skepticism was only discovered in France ex post facto.

8. M. Gauchet, "Les lettres sur l'Histoire de France de Augustin Thierry," in *Les Lieux de Mémoire*, Vol. II*, *La Nation*, ed. Pierre Nora, p. 271.

9. Dr. Wilhelm Friedrich Volger, *Handbuch der allgemeinen Weltgeschichte*, II, ii: *Neueste Geschichte* (Hanover, 1839), p. 240.

10. I cite the translation, presumably by the editor, in Walter Simon, ed., *French Liberalism 1789–1848* (New York, 1972), pp. 139–143.

11. Jacques Solé, *La révolution en questions* (Paris, 1988), p. 337.

12. Alexis de Tocqueville, *L'Ancien Régime*, tr. M. W. Patterson (Oxford, 1947), p. 217.

13. Gauchet, "Les lettres," p. 273.

14. The greater radicalism of the French Revolution, compared to the English, he ascribed to the fact that the Normans, faced with Anglo-Saxon resistance on the basis of their own institutions, enjoyed a less absolute domination than the Frankish conquerors. Thus one might say that British compromise was to prevail because structured resistance to "the Norman Yoke" had never ceased.

15. Simon, ed., *French Liberalism*, p. 108.

16. Ibid., pp. 140–141.

17. Cf. E. J. Hobsbawm, "Revolution in the Theory of Karl Marx," in Bernard Chavance, ed., *Marx en perspective* (Paris, 1985), pp. 557–570.

18. Guizot in Simon, ed., *French Liberalism*, pp. 110, 112–113.

19. Louis Blanc, *Histoire de la Révolution Française* (Paris, 1847), 1: 121.

20. "Pierre Chaunu, a conservative historian, a decade ago denounced the Terror as 'a French–French genocide' that anticipated the mass killings of the 20th century."

New York Times, 15 September 1988, p. A4: "For Lovers of Turmoil, Here Comes 1789 Again."

21. De Tocqueville, *L'Ancien Régime*, trans. M. W. Patterson (Oxford, 1947), p. 176.

22. Goldwin Smith, "The Invitation to Celebrate the French Revolution," *The Living Age* 178 (1888): 602–612.

23. De Tocqueville, *Recollections*, ed. J. P. Mayer (New York, 1949), p. 2. The author's phrase is "la classe moyenne."

24. "Dass ein grosses Volk bei seinem Durchbruch zu selbständigen politischen Leben, zu Freiheit und Macht, notwendig die Krise der Revolution durchzumachen habe, ist durch das doppelte Beispiel von England und Frankreich...ungemein nahegelegt." Cited by R. Koselleck, "Revolution," in *Geschichtliche Grundbegriffe* (Stuttgart, 1984), 5: 747.

25. John Clapham, *Economic History of Modern Britain*, vol. 1 (Cambridge, 1926).

26. F. A. Mignet, *Histoire de la Révolution Française*, vol. 1, 18th ed. (Paris, 1898), p. 2.

27. Colin Lucas, "Nobles, Bourgeois and the French Revolution," in *French Society and the Revolution*, ed. D. Johnson (Cambridge, 1976), p. 1. Lucas is among the rare specialists who sees clearly that the problem of "bourgeois revolution" does not go away when we have shown that there were no distinct and antagonistic classes of bourgeois and nobles in 1789. For "in that case we have to decide why, in 1788–9, groups which can be identified as non-noble combatted and defeated groups which can be identified as noble, thereby laying the foundations of the political system of the nineteenth-century bourgeoisie; and why they attacked and destroyed privilege in 1789, thereby destroying the formal organization of eighteenth-century French society and thereby preparing a structure within which the socioeconomic developments of the nineteenth century might blossom" (p. 90).

28. Simon, ed., *French Liberalism*, p. 142.

29. Where such a stratum consisted of foreigners or strangers, its relation to the indigenous social structure was much more complicated, as nineteenth-century Jews discovered in Central and Eastern Europe.

30. The implicit link between such a *civil society* and *bourgeois society* is clear, for linguistic reasons, in German, where both are "buergerliche Gesellschaft." Even here we must not read the meanings of the nineteenth century into the words of the eighteenth.

31. Rudolf Vierhaus, "Gegenstand nachtrauernder Erinnerung: Ueber das bürgerliche Deutschland im europäischen Vergleich," *Süddeutsche Zeitung*, 5 October 1988. This is a review of Jürgen Kocka, ed., *Bürgertum im 19. Jahrhundert. Deutschland im europäischen Vergleich*, 3 vols. (Munich, 1988), which contains the best discussion of these topics.

32. Solé, *La Révolution*, pp. 273, 275.

33. Alexis de Tocqueville, *Recollections*, p. 2.

34. This seems to be the line taken by the antirevolutionary historian Cochin, whose views have been rediscovered and taken up by the head of the "revisionist" school, François Furet. The argument fitted in well with the fashion for analyzing changes in discourse as autonomous events in history, not requiring any further explanation. Cf. François Furet, *Interpreting the French Revolution* (Cambridge, 1981).

35. "Nobles, Bourgeois and the French Revolution," p. 123.

36. Lorenz Stein, *Der Socialismus und Communismus des heutigen Frankreich: Ein Beitrag zur Zeitgeschichte*, 2d ed. (Leipzig, 1848) pp. 126–131.

37. Victor Cousin, *Cours de Philosophie: Introduction à l'Histoire de la Philosophie* (Paris, 1828), Première Leçou, p. 12.

38. W. G. Runciman, "Unnecessary Revolution: The Case of France," *European Journal of Sociology* 23 (1982): 318.

39. Tocqueville, *L'Ancien Régime*, p. 23.

THREE

State and Counterrevolution in France

Charles Tilly

Tocqueville almost got it right. In one of his most famous arguments, Alexis de Tocqueville asserted that the administrative centralization most observers attributed to the Revolution of 1789 actually occurred under the Old Regime. The Intendants and other royal officers installed by Louis XIII and his successors had, he thought, almost imperceptibly supplanted a once-dominant aristocracy. They had adroitly erected an effective, centralized structure while edging great lords and parlements out of administration and into mere politics. "If I am asked," wrote Tocqueville,

> how it was possible for this part of the old régime to be taken over en bloc and integrated into the constitution of modern France, my answer is that the reason why the principle of the centralization of power did not perish in the Revolution is that this very centralization was at once the Revolution's starting-off point and one of its guiding principles. Indeed, I would go so far as to say that whenever a nation destroys its aristocracy, it almost automatically tends toward a centralization of power; a greater effort is then needed to hold it back than to encourage it to move in this direction. All the authorities existing within it are affected by this instinctive urge to coalesce, and much skill is needed to keep them separate. Thus the democratic revolution, though it did away with so many institutions of the past, was led inevitably to consolidate this one; centralization fitted in so well with the program of the new social order that the common error of believing it to have been a creation of the Revolution is easily accounted for.[1]

Almost right. At the top, French ministers and kings from Louis XIII onward cowed the haughty *gouverneurs* and grandees who had once administered much of provincial France and had frequently raised the standard of rebellion; great aristocrats became decorative adjuncts of royal officialdom.[2] The crown created a whole class of political entrepreneurs who organized finances, raised revenues, supplied armies, manipulated royal justice, and controlled access to the sovereign but lacked a base of power separate from their own attachment to the monarchy. The accelerated sale of offices brought into being a tax-dodging rentier nobility that depended for its revenues on the credit and credibility of the state, as the state's exchange of corporate or municipal privilege for loans and grants formed and coopted monopolists.

The Intendants who made the transition from roving troubleshooters to fixed regional administrators under Richelieu and Mazarin spearheaded the process of centralization. In important ways, as Tocqueville thought, that centralized structure provided models and precedents for revolutionary changes. Yet Tocqueville misperceived, or misrepresented, the Old Regime system in two significant ways. First, the aristocracy did not abdicate; nobles old and new occupied dominant positions in the royal apparatus and control; they differed from their predecessors chiefly in suffering much greater supervision by the king's ministers, and in lacking private armies, fortified castles, and large clienteles.

Second, contrary to Tocqueville's monolithic portrayal, the prerevolutionary system remained incomplete; direct royal control generally ceased at the level of the urban region, the administrative, judicial, and fiscal territory assigned to a major city. The *généralité, subdélégation,* and *élection* belonged to the royal apparatus, but their officers had only limited power to penetrate communities and households.[3] They had even less in the *pays d'Etat*, where oligarchic assemblies had survived the royal assault on regional magnates. From that level downward the king's agents had to contend with landlords, priests, monks, municipal oligarchies, parlements, courts, and Estates that wielded considerable power to block royal will.

Indeed, the monarchy's practice of establishing or confirming privileges, monopolies, and offices in return for loans had strengthened the barriers between ordinary individuals and royal policy.[4] Despite hectoring by Intendants and the occasional dispatch of armed force in support of ignored decrees, privileged intermediaries executed—or deliberately failed to execute—royal directives in the light of their own interests. Only during the Revolution did these last barriers fall. With the Revolution's bold supplanting of privileged, chartered, and partly autonomous local authorities, France again led Europe in administrative transformation.

Yet Tocqueville's problem persists: To what extent, how, and with what political consequences, did the revolutionaries of 1789–1799 forward the centralizing effort of the Old Regime monarchy? In pursuing that question, this chapter (1) examines relations between the French Revolution and the long-term mutation of the French state, (2) underscores the critical part played by revolutionary and Napoleonic France in the transformation of European states (especially the transition from indirect to direct rule), and (3) emphasizes the connection between resistance to the Revolution and efforts of revolutionary leaders to improvise new forms of government in place of the ones they and their supporters had destroyed. In the process, it also (4) gives reasons for thinking that in the sphere of the state something like a bourgeois revolution did, despite all recent doubts, actually occur.

Between 1750 and 1850 most European states shifted from indirect to direct rule. Up to the eighteenth century, all but the smallest states generally relied on privileged intermediaries—nobles, priests, municipal oligarchies, officeholders licensed but no more than loosely controlled by the crown—to collect taxes, contract loans, recruit soldiers, administer justice, and carry on the rest of royal business at the local level. Citizens dealt rarely and reluctantly with supervised full-time employees of the national state. Indirect rule included a wide range of social arrangements: the tribute-taking relation of the sultan's court to local headmen in the Ottoman Empire, the holding of judicial, economic, and military power by great landlords in Poland, reliance on a faithful clergy in Sweden, concession of an enormous role in parish and county administration to English gentry and clergy Justices of the Peace, and survival of the Dutch Republic as a federation of fiercely competitive municipalities and their dependencies.[5]

By 1850 most such systems of indirect rule had disappeared from Europe. States had substituted their own officials for the patrons of old, tax farming and similar practices had almost vanished, elected legislatures connected the more substantial citizens to the national government, and census-takers brought royal inquiries to individual households, as national bureaucracies attempted to monitor and regulate whole countries and all their residents. To be sure, landlords and tycoons still wielded disproportionate power and bent the state apparatus to their own ends.[6] But now they used their considerable influence to intervene in an organizationally distinct national state instead of constituting one of its chief components.

More than anything else, the exigencies of war, preparation for war, and payment for war drove the transition from indirect to direct rule. War made the greatest difference because it expanded not only armies and navies but also fiscal administration, supply services, support for veterans, and national debt; those expansions, in turn, inflated the state's demands on its subject populations.[7] As rulers sought to man large national armies and navies by means of conscripts or volunteers from their own populations, and to pay for those armies and navies through domestic taxation, they encountered resistance not only from ordinary people but also from the intermediaries who had been rulers' sometime allies. In striving to overcome both kinds of resistance, monarchs built new administrative hierarchies that bypassed the old and reached into local communities, bargained out agreements that gave ordinary people rewards and rights the state had not previously conceded to them, and established means of monitoring and repression that drew them willy-nilly into the administration of local life. In Great Britain, for example, the immense effort of the American, French, and Napoleonic wars produced a decisive enlargement of Parliament's powers, and thus indirectly of massed commoners' capacity to lay claims on the national government.[8]

French actions from 1789 to 1815 forwarded the general European transition from indirect to direct rule in two ways: by providing a model of centralized government that other states emulated, and by imposing variants of that model wherever France conquered. Even though many of the period's innovations in French government emerged from desperate improvisations in response to threats of rebellion and bankruptcy, their battle-tested forms endured beyond the Revolution and Empire.

What happened to France's system of rule during the revolutionary years? Before 1789 the French state, like almost all other states, ruled indirectly at the local level, relying especially on priests and nobles for mediation. From the end of the American war, the government's efforts to collect money to cover its war debts crystallized an antigovernmental coalition that initially included the parlements and other powerholders but changed toward a more popular composition as the confrontation between the regime and its opponents sharpened.[9] The state's visible vulnerability in 1788–1789 encouraged any group that had a stifled claim or grievance against the state, its agents, or its allies to articulate its demands and join others in calling for change.[10] The rural revolts—Great Fear, grain seizures, tax rebellions, attacks on landlords, and so on—of spring and summer 1789 occurred disproportionately in regions with large towns, commercialized agriculture, and many roads.[11] Their geography reflected a composite but largely bourgeois-led settling of scores. At the same time, those whose social survival depended most directly on the Old Regime state—nobles, officeholders, and higher clergy are the obvious examples—generally aligned themselves with the king.[12] Thus a revolutionary situation began to form: two distinct blocs both claimed power and both received support from some significant part of the population. With significant defections of military men from the crown and the formation of militias devoted to the popular cause, the opposition acquired force of its own. The popular bloc, connected and often led by members of the bourgeoisie, started to gain control over parts of the state apparatus.

The lawyers, officials, and other bourgeois who seized the state apparatus in 1789–1790 rapidly displaced the old intermediaries: landords, seigneurial officials, venal officeholders, clergy, and sometimes municipal oligarchies as well. "[I]t was not a rural class of English-style gentlemen," declares Lynn Hunt, "who gained political prominence on either the national or the regional level, but rather thousands of city professionals who seized the opportunity to develop political careers."[13] At a local level, the so-called Municipal Revolution widely transferred power to enemies of the old rulers; patriot coalitions based in militias, clubs, and revolutionary committees and linked to

Parisian activists ousted the old municipalities.[14] Even where the old power-holders managed to survive the Revolution's early turmoil, relations between each locality and the national capital altered abruptly. Village "republics" of the Alps, for example, found their ancient liberties—including ostensibly free consent to taxes—crumbling as outsiders clamped them into the new administrative machine.[15] Then Parisian revolutionaries faced the problem of governing without intermediaries; they experimented with the committees and militias that had appeared in the mobilization of 1789 but found them hard to control from the center. More or less simultaneously they recast the French map into a nested system of departments, districts, cantons, and communes, while sending out *représentants en mission* to forward revolutionary reorganization. They installed direct rule.

Given the unequal spatial distribution of cities, merchants, and capital, furthermore, the imposition of a uniform geographic grid altered the relations between cities' economic and political power, placing insignificant Mende and Niort at the same administrative level as mighty Lyon and Bordeaux.[16] As a result, the balance of forces in regional capitals shifted significantly: In the great commercial centers, where merchants, lawyers, and professionals already clustered, departmental officials (who frequently came, in any case, from the same milieus) had no choice but to bargain with the locals. Where the National Assembly carved departments out of relatively uncommercialized rural regions, the Revolution's administrators overshadowed other residents of the new capitals and could plausibly threaten to use force if they were recalcitrant. But in those regions they lacked the bourgeois allies who helped their confreres do the Revolution's work elsewhere and confronted old intermediaries who still commanded significant followings. In great mercantile centers such as Marseille and Lyon, the political situation was very different. By and large, the federalist movement, with its protests against Jacobin centralism and its demands for regional autonomy, took root in cities whose commercial positions greatly outpaced their administrative rank. In dealing with these alternative obstacles to direct rule, Parisian revolutionaries improvised three parallel, and sometimes conflicting, systems of rule: (1) the committees and militias; (2) a geographically defined hierarchy of elected officials and representatives; (3) roving commissioners from the central government. To collect information and gain support, all three relied extensively on the existing personal networks of lawyers, professionals, and merchants.

As the system began to work, revolutionary leaders strove to routinize their control and contain independent action by local enthusiasts, who often resisted. Using both cooptation and repression, they gradually squeezed out the committees and militias. Mobilization for war put great pressure on the system, incited new resistance, and increased the national leaders' incentives for a tight system of control. Starting in 1792, the central administration (which until then had continued in a form greatly resembling that of the Old Regime) underwent its own Revolution: the staff expanded enormously, and a genuine hierarchical bureaucracy took shape.[17] In the process, revolutionaries installed one of the first systems of direct rule ever to take shape in a large state.

That shift entailed changes in systems of taxation, justice, public works, and much more. Consider policing. Outside of the Paris region, France's Old Regime state had almost no specialized police of its own; it dispatched the Maréchaussée to pursue tax evaders, vagabonds, and other violators of royal will and occasionally authorized the army to quell rebellious subjects, but otherwise relied on local and regional authorities to deploy armed force against civilians. The Revolutionaries changed things. With respect to ordinary people, they moved from reactive to proactive policing and information-gathering: instead of simply waiting until a rebellion or collective violation of the law occurred, and then retaliating ferociously but selectively, they began to station agents whose job was to anticipate and prevent threatening popular collective action. During the Revolution's early years, Old Regime police forces generally dissolved as popular committees, National Guards, and revolutionary tribunals took over their day-to-day activities. But with the Directory the state concentrated surveillance and apprehension in a single centralized organization. Fouché of Nantes became minister of police in the Year VII/1799, and henceforth ran a ministry whose powers extended throughout France and its conquered territories.[18] By the time of Fouché, France had become one of the world's most closely policed countries.

Going to war accelerated the move from indirect to direct rule. Almost any state that makes war finds that it cannot pay for the effort from its accumulated reserves and current revenues. Almost all warmaking states borrow extensively, raise taxes, and seize the means of combat—including men—from reluctant citizens who have other uses for their resources. Pre-revolutionary France followed these rules faithfully, to the point of accumulating debts that eventually forced the calling of the Estates-General. Nor did the Revolution repeal the rules.

The French used their own new system as a template for the reconstruction of other states. As revolutionary and imperial armies conquered, they attempted to build replicas of that system of direct rule elsewhere in Europe. Napoleon's government consolidated the system and turned it into a reliable instrument of rule.[19] The system survived the Revolution and Empire in France and, to some degree, elsewhere; Europe as a whole shifted massively toward centralized direct rule with at least a modicum of representation for the ruled.

Resistance and counterrevolutionary action followed directly from the process by which the new state established direct rule. Remember how much change revolutionaries introduced in a very short time. They eliminated all previous territorial jurisdictions, consolidated many old parishes into larger communes, abolished the tithe and feudal dues, dissolved corporations and their privileges, constructed a top-to-bottom administrative and electoral system, imposed expanded and standardized taxes through that system, seized the properties of emigrant nobles and of the church, disbanded monastic orders, subjected clergy to the state and imposed on them an oath to defend the new state church, conscripted young men at an unprecedented rate, and displaced both nobles and priests from the automatic exercise of local leadership. All this occurred between 1789 and 1793.

Subsequent regimes added more ephemeral changes such as the revolutionary calendar and the cult of the Supreme Being, but the early Revolution's overhaul of the state endured into the nineteenth century and set the pattern for many other European states. The greatest reversals concerned the throttling of local militias and revolutionary committees, the restoration of or compensation for some confiscated properties, and Napoleon's Concordat with the Catholic church. All in all, these changes constituted a dramatic, rapid substitution of uniform, centralized, direct rule for a system of government mediated by local and regional notables. What is more, the new state hierarchy consisted largely of lawyers, physicians, notaries, merchants, and other bourgeois.

Like their prerevolutionay counterparts, these fundamental changes attacked many existing interests and opened opportunities to groups that had previously had little access to state-sanctioned power—especially the village and small-town bourgeoisie. As a result, they precipitated both resistance and struggles for power. Jean-Pierre Jessenne's study of Artois (the department of Pas-de-Calais) uncovers a moderate version of the transition.[20] It reveals a region where before the Revolution nobles and churchmen held a little over half of all land as against a third for peasants, where 60 to 80 percent of all farms had fewer than 5 hectares (which implies that a similar large majority of farm operators worked part-time for others), where a quarter of household heads worked primarily as agricultural wage-laborers, where taxes, tithes, rents, and feudal dues took a relatively low 30 percent of the income from leased land, and where a fifth of rural land went on sale with the revolutionary seizure of church and noble properties—in short, where agricultural capitalism was well advanced by 1770.

In such a region, large leaseholders (fermiers) dominated local politics, but only within limits set by their noble and ecclesiastical landlords. The Revolution, by sweeping away the privileges of those patrons, threatened the leaseholders' power. They survived the challenge, however, as a class, if not as a particular set of individuals: many officeholders lost their posts during the struggles of the early Revolution, especially when the community was already at odds with its lord. Yet their replacements came disproportionately from the same class of comfortable leaseholders. The struggle of wage-laborers and smallholders against the *coqs de village* that Georges Lefebvre discovered in the adjacent Nord was less intense, or less effective, in the Pas-de-Chalais. Although the larger farmers, viewed with suspicion by national authorities, lost some of their grip on public office during the Terror and again under the Directory, they regained it later and continued to rule their roosts through the middle of the nineteenth century. By that time, nobles and ecclesiastics had lost much of their capacity to contain local powerholders, but manufacturers, merchants, and other capitalists had taken their places. The displacement of the old intermediaries opened the way to a new alliance between large farmers and bourgeoisie.

Jessenne tells us nothing about the political process by which direct rule descended on revolutionary France. For that, we must turn to such studies as Colin Lucas's vivid portrayal of Terrorist Claude Javogues, agent of the Revolution in his native department of the Loire.[21] Javogues was one of those ordinary people, cast into extraordinary circumstances by the Revolution, whose careful portrayal Richard Cobb has long urged on historians. Javogues stood higher on the ladder of wealth and power than Cobb's tailors and housemaids—he was a member of the Convention—but without the Revolution he would surely have ended his life in comfortable provincial obscurity. His close kin were lawyers, notaries, and merchants in Forez, a region not far to the west of Lyon. The family was on the ascendant in the eighteenth century, and Claude himself was a well-connected thirty-year-old *avocat* at Montbrison in 1789.

Four years later, Javogues was a hard-drinking, irascible, vociferous *représentant en mission* sent home to help organize the defeat of rebel Lyon and to reestablish the supremacy of the Republic in the newly created department of the Loire, whose capital was St. Etienne. The anonymous reviewer for the *Times Literary Supplement* (unmistakably, and inimitably, Richard Cobb himself) summed up Lucas's portrait of Javogues as agent of the Terror:

> Here was this blustering *bellâtre*, foaming and roaring up and down his native Department, even biting people, the veins sticking out of his enormous, bull-like forehead, shaggy eyebrows, a revolutionary giant, nearly always with food in his mouth, frightening women out of their wits, pinching their bottoms and making coarse references to the size and spaciousness of part of the female anatomy, apparently living in an almost permanent state of rage.[22]

The Convention dispatched this raging bourgeois bull to the Loire in July 1793 and recalled him in February 1794. During those six months, Javogues relied heavily on his existing connections, concentrated on repression of the Revolution's enemies, acted to a large degree on the theory that priests, nobles, and rich landlords were the enemies, neglected and bungled administrative matters such as the organization of food supply, and left behind him a reputation for arbitrariness and cruelty.

Yet Javogues and his co-workers did, in fact, reorganize local life. In Lucas's account, we learn about clubs, surveillance committees, revolutionary armed forces, commissars, courts, and *représentants en mission*. We see an almost unbelievable attempt to extend the direct administrative purview of the central government to everyday individual life. We recognize the importance of popular mobilization against the Revolution's enemies—real or imagined—as a force that displaced the old intermediaries. We therefore gain insight into the conflict between two objectives of the Terror: extirpation of the Revolutions' opponents and forging of instruments to do the work of the Revolution. We discover again the great importance of control over food as an administrative challenge, as a point of political contention, and as an incentive to popular action.

Contrary to the old image of a unitary people welcoming the arrival of long-awaited reform, local histories of the Revolution make clear that France's revolutionaries established their power through struggle, and frequently over stubborn popular resistance. Most of the resistance, it is true, took the form of evasion, cheating, and sabotage rather than outright rebellion; it employed what James Scott calls "weapons of the weak."[23] Where the fault lines ran deep, however, resistance consolidated into counterrevolution: the formation of effective alternative authorities to those put in place by the Revolution. Counterrevolution occurred not where everyone opposed the Revolution, but where irreconcilable differences divided well-defined blocs of supporters and opponents.

France's South and West, through similar processes, produced the largest zones of sustained counterrevolution.[24] The geography of executions under the Terror provides a reasonable picture of counterrevolutionary activity. The departments having more than 200 executions included: Loire Inférieure (3,548), Seine (2,639), Maine-et-Loire (1,886), Rhône (1,880), Vendée (1,616), Ille-et-Vilaine (509), Mayenne (495), Vaucluse (442), Bouches-du-Rhône (409), Pas-de-Calais (392), Var (309), Gironde (299), and Sarthe (225). These departments accounted for 89 percent of all executions under the Terror.[25] Except for the Seine and the Pas-de-Calais, they concentrated in the South, the Southwest and, especially, the West. In the South and Southwest, Languedoc, Provence, Gascony, and the Lyonnais hosted military insurrections against the Revolution, insurrections whose geography corresponded closely to support for federalism.[26] Federalist movements began in the spring of 1793, when the Jacobin expansion of the foreign war—including the declaration of war on Spain—incited resistance to taxation and conscription, which in turn led to a tightening of revolutionary surveillance and discipline. The autonomist movement peaked in commercial cities that had enjoyed extensive liberties under the Old Regime, notably Marseille, Bordeaux, Lyon, and Caen. In those cities and their hinterlands, France fell into bloody civil war.

In the West, guerrilla raids against republican strongholds and personnel unsettled Brittany, Maine, and Normandy from 1791 to 1799, while open armed rebellion flared south of the Loire in parts of Brittany, Anjou, and Poitou beginning in the fall of 1792 and likewise continuing intermittently until Napoleon pacified the region in 1799.[27] The Western counterrevolution reached its high point in the spring of 1793, when the Republic's call for troops precipitated armed resistance through much of the West. That phase saw massacres of "patriots" and "aristocrats" (as the proponents and opponents of the Revolution came to be called), invasion and temporary occupation of such major cities as Angers, and pitched battles between armies of Blues and Whites (as the armed elements of the two parties were known).

Historians have not disputed what happened in the West—especially south of the Loire—for fifty years or more. Even the militantly anticlerical Alphonse Aulard, writing eight decades ago, had the main sequence right:

> The Vendean, Breton, and Angevin peasantry did not at first rise in support of royalty, but in support of their clergy and against military service. Strongly attached to their priests, they were opposed on general grounds to the application of the civil constitution of the clergy, and had attended the Masses of non-juring priests at farm-houses, in chapels, or in the forest. . . . Between March 10th and 15th a rising took place, to cries of *Pas de milice!* No enlistment! and almost immediately there was a cry for their former priests. It was these priests who stirred the peasantry to anger, and presided over the first acts of civil warfare, and the first massacres of republicans.[28]

Aulard's imputation of motives now seems naive, and no recent historian has so baldly stated the idea of the priests as agitators, but students of the Vendée still see that they must explain first the popular response to the Civil Constitution and then the reaction to the levée en masse of March 1793. Since the 1960s, furthermore, we have had a relatively clear idea of who participated on both sides, and when. The real controversies have concerned three issues: (1) whether similar class alignments set off revolutionaries and counterrevolutionaries in the regions of sustained insurrection south of the Loire and in those of scattered but persistent Chouannerie (guerrilla warfare) to the north, (2) fundamental causes of the counterrevolution, and (3) intentions of the principal actors. On those important scores, alas, little is settled: If the old ideas of a gigantic counterrevolutionary plot led by nobles and of a peasantry blindly loyal to king and country have almost disappeared from serious accounts, historians still disagree vigorously over sufficient causes and deep intentions.

As it happens, the bicentennial-bound French have recently been debating the counterrevolution in a new light. A remarkable book by Reynald Secher, ominously titled *Le génocide franco-français* [Genocide Among the French], has thus labeled the repression of the successive counterrevolutions that broke out in the regions south of Nantes and Angers between 1793 and 1795.[29] "Genocide" means that the French state deliberately undertook to extirpate an entire people. Laurent Ladouce summarizes the terms in which Secher's book has entered public discussion:

> Many "progressive" thinkers and historians still approve or justify the anti-religious fervor of the revolutionaries. They are thus challenged by a recent discovery made by a 32-year-old historian, Reynald Secher. Secher presented a remarkable doctoral thesis at the Sorbonne, subtitled "The Franco-French Genocide." His thesis demonstrates that the inhabitants of the Vendée region, after they surrendered to the Republic armies in 1793, were systematically exterminated in 1794 by order of the convention led by Robespierre. About 117,000 civilians—including women and children—were massacred, in order that the "race" of Vendeans be obliterated as a hindrance to the progress of the Revolution.[30]

Ladouce further remarks that when Secher appeared on the literary television show *Apostrophes,* his critics "did not deny what was contained in his book. They argued that the terrifying facts he exposed in his book were the logical and almost inevitable result of The Reign of Terror."[31]

If Secher had in fact established the massacre of 117,000 civilians, he would indeed have forced all historians of the counterrevolution to amend their analyses. As one of the author–critics who appeared on that fateful television broadcast with Reynald Secher, however, I deny both that we conceded his facts and that he has established them by means of precise reasoning and solid documentation. Michel Vovelle comments bitterly on the controversy:

> A whole literature is forming on "Franco-French genocide," starting from risky estimates of the number of fatalities in the Vendean wars: 128,000, 400,000 . . . and why not 6000,000? Despite not being specialists in the subject, historians such as Pierre Chaunu have put all the weight of their great moral authority behind the development of an anathematizing discourse, and have dismissed any effort to look at the subject reasonably.[32]

Clearly Secher's claims deserve close attention.

What did Secher do? First he completed a thoughtful, modest Third Cycle thesis (rough equivalent of an American Ph.D.) about the revolutionary experience of his own village, La Chapelle-Basse-Mer, not far northeast of Nantes.[33] In the published version of the thesis, he adopted arguments I had proposed twenty-five years before, and others had confirmed since then: that conflicts within communities generalized into a region-wide confrontation of an antirevolutionary majority based in the countryside with a prorevolutionary minority having particular strength in the cities; that the split began to form with the application of the Civil Constitution of the Clergy, and the oath to support it, in 1790–1791; that from then on local conflicts grew ever graver and alignments more sharply defined, with the choice between priests who rejected and those who accepted the ecclesiastical oath providing the most salient issue; that the conscription of March 1793, with the attendant question of military exemptions for Republican officials and National Guard members, broadened the antirevolutionary coalition and brought the young men into action.[34]

Secher illustrated these widely accepted points with copious quotations from the archives, interpreted them as establishing the incomprehension and ideologically driven zeal of revolutionary authorities, and ended with a decisively negative balance sheet for the Revolution. He described the bloody repression of counterrevolutionary La Chapelle-Basse-Mer but did not pronounce the fateful word "genocide." Aside from taking a distinctly antirevolutionary tone and stressing the defense of threatened religion somewhat more than other recent historians, Secher cast his village study in conventional terms.

With *Le génocide franco-français*, Reynald Secher took a more daring line. *Le génocide*, his thesis for the Doctorat d'Etat, began with a generalization of the standard arguments to the whole region of counterrevolution south of the Loire, the departments of Vendée, Deux-Sèvres, Loire-Inférieure, and Maine-et-Loire. Although La Chapelle-Basse-Mer served him repeatedly as a reference point, Secher illustrated the arguments with wide citations of national and regional archives. (My confidence in Secher's scholarship faltered, however, when I noticed that, with minor changes of wording and without citation of my work, he had copied at least two passages, including the references to archival sources, from my earlier book. Clearly someone should check Secher's other claims to have consulted the archives.)[35] Even his graphic account of repression, with Republican armies burning, smashing, and killing as they marched from village to village, however, drew on sources that were widely known to historians of the Vendée a half-century ago. Maniacal Carrier, who drowned boatloads of suspected counterrevolutionaries in the Loire, and ruthless Turreau, whose "infernal columns" of Republican troops undertook to level the whole region, have long burdened narratives of the counterrevolution.

Secher broke with conventional historiography, nevertheless, in assessing the damage done by revolutionary repression. On the basis of almost no evidence, Secher portrayed the prerevolutionary Vendée as more prosperous than the rest of France—the better to emphasize the devastation wrought by war and repression. He then used dubious methods to estimate the losses of population and housing attributable to the counterrevolution and its repression. In *La Chapelle-Basse-Mer*, he had established the minimum number of fatalities by using a parish register in which the local priest listed 421 residents (of a population of about 3,230 in 1792) killed by Republican forces between 1793 and 1797, and had argued from the trend in registered births between 1789 and 1800 that the total loss of population was actually on the order of 700 to 770.[36] For housing losses, Secher used a procedure that inflated the value, if not the number, of missing houses.

Le génocide generalized those procedures. For housing, Secher used claims residents filed in 1810–1811 to receive compensation from the government for dwellings destroyed during the counterrevolution. An applicant stated the dwelling's value before its razing, reported whether it had been rebuilt, and gave its present value if rebuilt. In an unstated number of communes spread across the counterrevolutionary region, Secher implausibly took the claimed predestruction value as his measure of financial losses and used the total number of houses existing at the time of the claims (fifteen to eighteen years after the counterrevolution's height)as a base for calculating the proportion of all housing destroyed. By these doubtful means he estimated that the counterrevolutionary region lost 18 percent of its dwellings and 19 percent of its housing value.[37]

For population loss throughout the region, Secher counted the total number of births recorded in the parish registers of an unstated number of communities distributed across four departments in 1780–1790 and 1801, computed an annual average, multiplied it by twenty-seven, then subtracted the later figure from the earlier. The procedure relies on three unjustifiable assumptions: (1) a constant birth rate of about thirty-seven per thousand population, (2) no net migration, (3) a net population loss entirely due to excess deaths in the counterrevolution and its repression. In France as a whole, fertility began a sharp decline around 1790.[38] Best estimates of crude birth rates in the four departments actually run:[39]

	France	*Deux-Sèvres*	*Loire-Inférieure*	*Maine-et-Loire*	*Vendée*
1801–1805	31.8	28.7	30.8	29.4	32.5
1860–1810	31.2	27.3	28.9	26.8	34.0

Thus the region as a whole had fertility levels that were declining, and lower than those of France as a whole, during the later years of the Revolution. Most likely they were already declining during the 1790s.

In a region where fertility was beginning to decline significantly, where thousands fled the turmoil, and where marriage frequencies almost certainly dwindled, all three of Secher's assumptions cast doubt on his results' validity. They attribute the region's entire population loss to massacre and then inflate that loss by underestimating the population at the period's end. They fail, finally, to make any allowance for deaths inflicted by counterrevolutionaries. By means of these faulty procedures, Secher estimated that "117,257 people disappeared between 1792 and 1802—14.38 percent of the population."[40] Pierre Chaunu then glossed the estimate as "120,000 dead in a fiftieth of the [French] territory during about eighteen months" and concluded that "A desperate rebellion provoked by the attempt to force these people to serve a profane cause . . . led to the premeditated genocide of a people."[41] He thus froze a series of analytic errors into an ostensible historical fact. According to a recent review of the Revolution's cost:

> Estimates of the number of vicitims vary sixfold: At least 100,000, at most 600,000. The 117,000 dead mentioned by Reynald Secher included only the departments of the *Vendée militaire*. The highest number comes from Pierre Chaunu, speaking as a master demographer . . . and including Blues and Whites, those dead by sword, hunting rifle or military gun, victims of illness and of famine in that burned-out country, people summarily executed, and those who died from wounds when no one could treat them: civil wars are inexorable.[42]

The author, René Sédillot, then opts for a "median" estimate of 400,000. A mistaken interpretation has entered history—at least as argued by critics of the Revolution.

Let me be clear: At times, both "patriots" and "aristocrats" deliberately massacred defenseless civilians in the Vendée. The Terror claimed more lives in Loire-Inférieure than in any other department.[43] The Convention's agent Carrier did, in fact, write from Nantes that "90 of the people we call refractory priests were locked up in a boat on the Loire. I have just learned, and the news is quite certain, that they all died in the river."[44] From January to May 1794 the "infernal columns" of General Turreau did, indeed, march through the counterrevolutionary zone burning, looting, smashing, and shooting. Thousands died in the Vendée. No one disputes those facts. The questions concern whether destruction occurred on the scale that Secher argues, whether the facts justify the term *genocide*, whether the very logic of the Revolution required the degree of destruction that actually occurred, and whether France would have been better off without the Revolution. My own answer to each of these questions is no. But any answer rests on a set of moral and political judgments that are inherently contestable.

Without attempting to arrive at definitive answers to the probing questions, we can see that the West's counterrevolution grew directly from the efforts of revolutionary officials to install a particular kind of direct rule in the region: a rule that practically eliminated nobles and priests from their positions as partly autonomous intermediaries, that brought the state's demands for taxes, manpower, and deference to the level of individual communities, neighborhoods, and households, that gave the region's bourgeois political power they had never before wielded. In seeking to extend the state's rule to every locality, and to dislodge all enemies of that rule, French revolutionaries started a process that did not cease for twenty-five years. In some ways, it has not yet ceased today.

In these regards, for all its counterrevolutionary ferocity, the West conformed to France's general experience. Everywhere in France, bourgeois—not owners of large industrial establishments, for the most part, but merchants, lawyers, notaries, and others who made their livings from the possession and manipulation of capital—were gaining strength during the eighteenth century. Throughout France, the mobilization of 1789 brought disproportionate numbers of bourgeois into political action. As the revolutionaries of Paris and their provincial allies displaced nobles and priests from their critical positions as agents of indirect rule, the existing networks of bourgeois served as alternate connections between the state and thousands of communities across the land. For a while, those connections rested on a vast popular mobilization through clubs, militias, and committees. Gradually, however, revolutionary leaders contained or even suppressed their turbulent partners. With trial, error, and struggle, the ruling bourgeoisie worked out a system of rule that reached directly into local communities and passed chiefly through administrators who served under the scrutiny and budgetary control of their superiors.

This process of state expansion encountered three huge obstacles. First, many people saw opportunities to forward their own interests and settle old scores open up in the crisis of 1789. They either managed to capitalize on the opportunity or found their hopes blocked by competition from other actors; both categories lacked incentives to support further revolutionary changes. Second, the immense effort of warring with most other European powers strained the state's capacity at least as gravely as had the wars of Old Regime kings. Third, in some regions the political bases of the newly empowered bourgeois were too fragile to support the work of cajoling, containing, inspiring, extracting, and mobilizing that revolutionary agents carried on everywhere; resistance to demands for taxes, conscripts, and compliance with moralizing legislation occurred widely in France, but where preexisting rivalries placed a well-connected bloc in opposition to the revolutionary bourgeoisie, civil war frequently developed. In these senses, the revolutionary transition from indirect to direct rule embodied a bourgeois revolution and engendered a series of antibourgeois counterrevolutions.

NOTES

1. Alexis de Tocqueville, *The Old Régime and the French Revolution* (Garden City, N.J.: Doubleday, 1955), p. 60.

2. Michel Antoine, *Le Conseil du Roi sous le règne de Louis XV* (Geneva: Droz, 1970); Douglas Clark Baxter, *Servants of the Sword: Intendants of the Army, 1630–70* (Urbana: University of Illinois Press, 1976); William H. Beik, *Absolutism and Society in Seventeenth-Century France* (Cambridge: Cambridge University Press, 1985); Julian Dent, *Crisis in Finance: Crown, Financiers, and Society in Seventeenth-Century France* (Newton Abbot: David and Charles, 1973); Daniel Dessert, *Argent, pouvoir, et société au Grand Siècle*

(Paris: Fayard, 1984); Robert R. Harding, *Anatomy of a Power Elite: The Provincial Governors of Early Modern France* (New Haven: Yale University Press, 1978); A. Lloyd Moote, *The Revolt of the Judges: The Parlement of Paris and the Fronde* (Princeton: Princeton University Press, 1971); Sharon Kettering, *Patrons, Brokers, and Clients in Seventeenth-Century France* (New York: Oxford University Press, 1986).

3. For the uneven geographical distribution of royal institutions of control, see Bernard Lepetit, "Fonction administrative et armature urbaine: Remarques sur la distribution des chefs-lieux de subdélégation en France à la fin de l'Ancien Régime," *Institut d'Histoire Economique et Sociale de l'Université de Paris I, Recherches et Travaux,* 11 (1982): 19–34. For the crucial place of corporate institutions in royal relations with localities, and their transformation during the Revolution, see Gail Bossenga, "City and State: An Urban Perspective on the Origins of the French Revolution," in Keith Michael Baker, ed., *The French Revolution and the Creation of Modern Political Culture.* 1: *The Political Culture of the Old Regime* (Oxford: Pergamon, 1988); and Bossenga, "La Révolution française et les corporations: Trois exemples lillois," *Annales; Economies, Sociétés, Civilisations* 43 (1988): 405–426.

4. Bossenga, "La Révolution française," 405–426; Bossenga, "City and State," pp. 115–140.

5. Gunnar Artéus, *Till Militärstatens Förhistoria. Krig, professionalisering och social förändring under Vasasönernas regering* (Stockholm: Probus, 1986); Peter Burke, "City-States," in John A. Hall, ed., *States in History* (Oxford: Blackwell, 1986); Eric J. Evans, *The Forging of the Modern State: Early Industrial Britain, 1783–1870* (London: Longman, 1983); Marjolein 't Hart, "Taxation and the Formation of the Dutch State, 17th Century," paper presented to the Vlaams-Nederlandse Sociologendagen, Amsterdam, 1986; Jonathan I. Israel, *The Dutch Republic and the Hispanic World* (Oxford: Clarendon Press, 1982); Leon Jespersen, "The *Machtstaat* in Seventeenth-Century Denmark," *Scandinavian Journal of History* 10 (1985): 271–304; Sven A. Nilsson, "Imperial Sweden: Nation-Building, War and Social Change," in Sven A. Nilsson, ed., *The Age of New Sweden* (Stockholm: Livrustkammaren, 1988); Ervin Pamlényi, ed., *A History of Hungary* (London: Collet's, 1975); Traian Stoianovich, "Model and Mirror of the Premodern Balkan City," *Studia Balcanica.* III: *La Ville Balkanique XVe–XIXe siècle* (1970): 83–110; Ernst Werner, *Die Geburt einer Grossmacht—die Osmanen (1300–1481)* (Vienna: Böhlhaus, 1985); Andrzej Wyczanski, "La frontière de l'unité européenne au XVIème siècle: Liens—cadres—contenu," in *Actes du Colloque Franco-Polonais d'Histoire* (Nice: Laboratoire d'Histoire Quantitative, Université de Nice, 1981).

6. Raymond Grew, "The Nineteenth-Century European State," in Charles Bright and Susan Harding, eds., *Statemaking and Social Movements* (Ann Arbor: University of Michigan Press, 1984); Arno Mayer, *The Persistence of the Old Regime* (New York: Pantheon, 1981).

7. M. S. Anderson, *War and Society in Europe of the Old Regime 1619–1789* (London: Fontana, 1988); Gunnar Artéus, *Krigsmakt och Samhälle i Frihetstidens Sverige* (Stockholm: Militärhistoriska Förlaget, 1982); Richard Bean, "War and the Birth of the Nation State," *Journal of Economic History* 33 (1973): 203–221; Geoffrey Best, *War and Society in Revolutionary Europe, 1770–1870* (London: Fontana, 1982); Klaus-Richard Böhme, "Schwedische Finanzbürokratie und Kriegführung 1611 bis 1721," in Goran

Rystad, ed., *Europe and Scandinvia: Aspects of the Process of Integration in the 17th Century* (Lund: Esselte Studium, 1983); Otto Busch, *Militarsystem und Sozialleben im alten Preussen 1713–1807: Die Anfänge der sozialen Militarisierung der preussisch-deutschen Gesellschaft* (Berlin: de Gruyter, 1962); Sir George Clark, "The Social Foundations of States," in F. L. Carsten, ed., *The New Cambridge Modern History*. 5: *The Ascendancy of France, 1648–88* (Cambridge: Cambridge University Press, 1969); James B. Collins, *Fiscal Limits of Absolutism: Direction Taxation in Early Seventeenth-Century France* (Berkeley, Los Angeles, London: University of California Press, 1988); Brian M. Downing, "Constitutionalism, Warfare, and Political Change in Early Modern Europe," *Theory and Society* 17 (1988): 7–56; Michael Duffy, ed., *The Military Revolution and the State, 1500–1800* (Exeter: University of Exeter, 1980; Exeter Studies in History, 1); Samuel E. Finer, "State- and Nation-Building in Europe: The Role of the Military," in Charles Tilly, ed., *The Formation of National States in Western Europe* (Princeton: Princeton University Press, 1975); Jean-Philippe Genet and Michel Le Mené, eds., *Genèse de l'Etat moderne. Prélèvement et Redistribution* (Paris: Editions du Centre National de la Recherche Scientifique, 1987); Alain Guillerm, *La pierre et le vent. Fortifications et marine en Occident* (Paris: Arthaud, 1985); J. R. Hale, *War and Society in Renaissance Europe, 1450–1620* (New York: St. Martin's, 1985); Jan Lindegren, "The Swedish 'Military State,' 1560–1720," *Scandinavian Journal of History* 10 (1985): 305–336; William H. McNeill, *The Pursuit of Power: Technology, Armed Force and Society since A.D. 1000* (Chicago: University of Chicago Press, 1982); Geoffrey Parker, *The Military Revolution: Military Innovation and the Rise of the West, 1500–1800* (Cambridge: Cambridge University Press, 1988); Josef V. Polisensky, *War and Society in Europe, 1618–1648* (Cambridge: Cambridge University Press, 1978); Simon Schama, "The Exigencies of War and the Politics of Taxation in the Netherlands 1795–1810," in J. M. Winter, ed., *War and Economic Development: Essays in Memory of David Joslin* (Cambridge: Cambridge University Press, 1975).

8. J. E. D. Binney, *British Public Finance and Administration 1774–92* (Oxford: Clarendon Press, 1958); Norman Chester, *The British Administrative System, 1780–1870* (Oxford: Clarendon Press, 1981); Emmeline W. Cohen, *The Growth of the British Civil Service 1780–1939* (Cambridge: Cambridge University Press, 1965); Eric J. Evans, *The Forging of the Modern State: Early Industrial Britain, 1783–1870* (London: Longman, 1983); William Kennedy, *English Taxation 1640–1799* (New York: Augustus Kelley, 1964; first published in 1913); Peter Mathias and Patrick O'Brien, "Taxation in Britain and France, 1715–1810: A Comparison of the Social and Economic Incidence of Taxes Collected for the Central Governments," *Journal of European Economic History* 5 (1976): 601–650.

9. George C. Comninel, *Rethinking the French Revolution: Marxism and the Revisionist Challenge* (London: Verso, 1987); William Doyle, *The Ancien Régime* (Atlantic Highlands, N.J.: Humanities Press International, 1986); Jean Egret, *La pré-Révolution française* (Paris: Presses Universitaires de France, 1962); Georges Frêche, *Toulouse et la région Midi-Pyrénées au siècle des Lumières (vers 1670–1789)* (Paris: Cujas, 1974); Bailey Stone, *The Parlement of Paris, 1774–1789* (Chapel Hill: University of North Carolina Press, 1981).

10. For surveys of popular collective action during the early Revolution, see Richard Cobb, *The Police and the People* (Oxford: Oxford University Press, 1970); Colin Lucas, "The Crowd and Politics between *Ancien Régime* and Revolution in France,"

Journal of Modern History 60 (1988): 421–457; John Markoff, "Contexts and Forms of Rural Revolt: France in 1789," *Journal of Conflict Resolution* 30 (1986): 253–289; Charles Tilly, *The Contentious French* (Cambridge: Harvard University Press, 1986).

11. John Markoff, "The Social Geography of Rural Revolt at the Beginning of the French Revolution," *American Sociological Review* 50 (1985): 761–781; Markoff, "Contexts and Forms of Rural Revolt," 253–289.

12. For the telling contrast between members of parlements, who came overwhelmingly from noble families and who generally lined up against the Revolution, and provincial magistrates, largely bourgeois and at least passive supporters of the Revolution, see Philip Dawson, *Provincial Magistrates and Revolutionary Politics in France, 1789–1795* (Cambridge: Harvard University Press, 1972), esp. chap. 8.

13. Lynn Hunt, *Politics, Culture, and Class in the French Revolution* (Berkeley, Los Angeles, London: University of California Press, 1984), p. 155; for detailed studies of provincial bourgeois in the Revolution, see Michel Vovelle, ed., *Bourgeoisies de province et Révolution* (Grenoble: Presses Universitaires de Grenoble, 1987).

14. Lynn Hunt, *Revolution and Urban Politics in Provincial France: Troyes and Reims, 1786–1790* (Stanford: Stanford University Press, 1978).

15. Harriet G. Rosenberg, *A Negotiated World: Three Centuries of Change in a French Alpine Community* (Toronto: University of Toronto Press, 1988), 72–89.

16. Ted Margadant, "Towns, Taxes, and State-Formation in the French Revolution," paper presented to the Irvine Seminar on Social History and Theory, April 1988; Ted Margadant, "Politics, Class, and Community in the French Revolution: An Urban Perspective," paper presented to Conference on Revolutions in Comparison, University of California, Los Angeles, 1988; Marie-Vic Ozouf-Marignier, "De l'universalisme constituant aux intérêts locaux: Le débat sur la formation des départements en France (1789–1790), *Annales: Economies, Sociétés, Civilisations* 41 (1986): 1193–1214; Patrick Schultz, *La décentralisation administrative dans le département du Nord (1790–1793)* (Lille: Presses Universitaires de Lille, 1982).

17. Clive H. Church, *Revolution and Red Tape: The French Ministerial Bureaucracy 1770–1850* (Oxford: Clarendon Press, 1981), chap. 3. In response to the financial crisis, Minister Loménie de Brienne had already established a national treasury in 1788; the revolutionaries then consolidated the organization, expanded its scope, and nationalized the debt: J. F. Bosher, *French Finances, 1770–1795: From Business to Bureaucracy* (Cambridge: Cambridge University Press, 1970), chaps. 11 to 15.

18. Jacques Aubert and Raphaël Petit, *La police en France: Service public* (Paris: Berger-Levrault, 1981), p. 84; Jacques Aubert et al., *L'Etat et sa police en France (1789–1914)* (Geneva: Droz, 1979); Iain A. Cameron, "The Police of Eighteenth-Century France," *European Studies Review* 7 (1977): 47–75; Robert M. Schwartz, *Policing the Poor in Eighteenth-Century France* (Chapel Hill: University of North Carolina Press, 1988).

19. Owen Connelly, *Napoleon's Satellite Kingdoms* (New York: Free Pess, 1965).

20. Jean-Pierre Jessenne, *Pouvoir au village et Révolution: Artois 1760–1848* (Lille: Presses Universitaires de Lille, 1987).

21. Colin Lucas, *The Structure of the Terror: The Example of Claude Javogues and the Loire* (Oxford: Oxford University Press, 1973).

22. "The Bull Who Bearded the Terrible Twelve," *Times Literary Supplement*, 26 October 1973, p. 1320.

23. James C. Scott, *Weapons of the Weak: Everyday Forms of Peasant Resistance* (New Haven: Yale University Press, 1985).

24. Quick reviews of resistance to the Revolution and its conquests both inside and outside of France appear in François Lebrun and Roger Dupuy, eds., *Les résistances à la Révolution* (Paris: Imago, 1987). In Jean Nicolas, ed., *Mouvements populaires et conscience sociale, XVIe–XIXe siècles* (Paris: Maloine, 1985), see especially Alan Forrest, "Les soulèvements populaires contre le service militaire, 1793–1814"; and Colin Lucas, "Résistances populaires à la Révolution dans le sud-est," in Gwynne Lewis and Colin Lucas, eds., *Beyond the Terror: Essays in French Regional and Social History, 1794–1815* (Cambridge: Cambridge University Press, 1983)—see especially Colin Lucas, "Themes in Southern Violence after 9 Thermidor," and Gwynne Lewis, "Political Brigandage and Popular Disaffection in the South-East of France 1795–1804."

25. Donald Greer, *The Incidence of the Terror during the French Revolution* (Cambridge: Harvard University Press, 1935), p. 147.

26. Alan Forest, *Society and Politics in Revolutionary Bordeaux* (Oxford: Oxford University Press, 1975), chap. 5; James N. Hood, "Protestant–Catholic Relations and the Roots of the First Popular Counterrevolutionary Movement in France," *Journal of Modern History* 43 (1971): 245–275; James N. Hood, "Revival and Mutation of Old Rivalries in Revolutionary France," *Past and Present* 82 (1979): 82–115; Gwynne Lewis, *The Second Vendée: The Continuity of Counter-Revolution in the Department of the Gard, 1789–1815* (Oxford: Clarendon Press, 1978); Martyn Lyons, *Révolution et Terreur à Toulouse* (Toulouse: Privat, 1980); William Scott, *Terror and Repression in Revolutionary Marseilles* (New York: Barnes and Noble, 1973); Michel Vovelle, "Massacreurs et massacrés. Aspects sociaux de la Contre-Révolution en Provence, après Thermidor," in Lebrun and Dupuy, eds., *Les résistances à la Révolution*.

27. Paul Bois, "Aperçu sur les causes des insurrections de l'Ouest à l'époque révolutionnaire," in J.-C. Martin, ed., *Vendée-Chouannerie* (Nantes: Reflets du Passé, 1981); T. J. A. Le Goff and D. M. G. Sutherland, "Religion and Rural Revolt in the French Revolution: An Overview," in János M. Bak and Gerhard Benecke, eds., *Religion and Rural Revolt* (Manchester: Manchester University Press, 1984); Jean-Clément Martin, *La Vendée et la France* (Paris: Le Seuil, 1987).

28. Alphonse Aulard, *The French Revolution* (London: Unwin, 1910), 2: 306–307.

29. Reynald Secher, *Le génocide franco-français. La Vendée-Vengé* (Paris: Presses Universitaires de France, 1986).

30. Laurent Ladouce, "Was France the Fatherland of Genocide?" *The World and I,* January 1988, p. 686.

31. Ibid., p. 687.

32. Michel Vovelle, "L'Historiographie de la Révolution française à la veille du Bicentenaire," *Annales Historiques de la Révolution française* 272 (1988): 119.

33. The truncated published version appeared as *La Chapelle-Basse-Mer, village vendéen. Révolution et contre-révolution* (Paris: Perrin, 1986).

34. Charles Tilly, "Civil Constitution and Counter-Revolution in Southern Anjou," *French Historical Studies* 1 (1959): 172–199; "Local Conflicts in the Vendée Before the Rebellion of 1793," *French Historical Studies* 2 (1961): 209–231; "Some Problems in the History of the Vendée," *American Historical Review* 67 (1961): 19–33; "Rivalités de bourgs et conflits de partis dans les Mauges," *Revue du Bas-Poitou et des Provinces de*

l'Ouest no. 4 (July–August 1962): 3–15. *La Vendée. Révolution et contre-révolution* (Paris: Arthème Fayard, 1970); Claude Petitfrère, *Blancs et bleus d'Anjou (1789–1793,* 2 vols. (Paris: Champion, 1979). For reservations as to the generality of the rural–urban split in all the West's counterrevolutionary regions, see T. J. A. Le Goff and D. M. G. Sutherland, "The Revolution and the Rural Community in Eighteenth-Century Brittany," *Past and Present* 62 (1974): 96–119; T. J. A. Le Goff and D. M. G. Sutherland, "The Social Origins of Counter-Revolution in Western France," *Past and Present* 99 (1983): 65–87; Donald Sutherland, *The Chouans: The Social Origins of Popular Counter-Revolution in Upper Brittany, 1770–1796* (Oxford: Clarendon Press, 1982); and Roger Dupuy, *De la Révolution à la Chouannerie. Paysans en Bretagne 1788–1794* (Paris: Flammarion, 1988).

35. Compare the descriptions of events in La Séguinière, Saint-Lambert-du-Lattay, and Saint-Aubin-de-Luigné in Secher, *Génocide,* pp. 88–89, with accounts of the same events in Tilly, *Vendée,* pp. 254–255.

36. Secher, *Chapelle-Basse-Mer,* pp. 154–155. Actually the series begins with 115, 139, 102, and 127 births in 1789–1792 and ends with 74, 120, 105, and 77 births in 1797–1800, whose variability provides little evidence—logical or statistical—of any trend whatsoever. For cautions concerning any computations of revolutionary population losses in the Vendée, see François Lebrun, "Les conséquences démographiques de la Guerre de Vendée: L'exemple des Mauges," in Lebrun and Dupuy, eds., *Les résistances à la Révolution.*

37. Secher, *Génocide,* p. 265.

38. Yves Blayo, "Mouvement naturel de la population française de 1740 à 1829," *Population* 30 (Special Number, 1975): 15–64; David R. Weir, "Life Under Pressure: France and England, 1670–1870," *Journal of Economic History* 44 (1984): 27–47.

39. Etienne van de Walle, *The Female Population of France: A Reconstruction of 82 Départements* (Princeton: Princeton University Press, 1974), pp. 125, 349, 364, 435, 453. The figures are female crude birth rates, which provide a good approximation of total crude birth rates and an excellent indication of trends and differences. According to these figures, the proper multiplier for Loire-Inférieure around 1803 was 34; by 1808 it was 37.

40. Secher, *Génocide,* p. 253.

41. Pierre Chaunu, "Avant-propos," in Secher, *Génocide,* pp. 23, 24.

42. René Sédillot, *Le coût de la Révolution française* (Paris: Perrin, 1987), p. 28.

43. Donald Greer, *The Incidence of the Terror during the French Revolution* (Cambridge: Harvard University Press, 1935), p. 38.

44. Alphonse Aulard, ed., *Recueil des actes du Comité de Salut Public* (Paris: Imprimerie Nationale, 1895) 8: 505.

FOUR

Cultural Upheaval and Class Formation During the French Revolution

Patrice Higonnet

Was the French Revolution a social revolution? The answer obviously depends on what the word *social* means. But in one way or another, generally received common sense will surely answer, yes. Isn't history "a seamless web?" Doesn't the French Revolution, from its very complexity, have to be defined as a social, or perhaps even a "socioeconomic," dysfunction? Our answer, informed by a driving sense of the uniqueness of the French Revolution, will be categorical. The French Revolution was not a social revolution. Its first cause was neither economic nor social, in the classical sense of either word. Its motor was instead the complicated cultural transformation of the country's possessing, administrative, and educated elites in the preceding century. The politics of 1789–1799 had as their origin the prerevolutionary restructuring of ancient assumptions on the nature of the public and the private. Restated, this is to say that the first cause of the Revolution lay in the elites' renewed definitions of both the empowered self and the empowered nation. Particularly important also was the nature of the politicized relationship that the elites assumed would soon regulate their regenerated universe.

This "problématique" can be considered under various headings, the nature of the Republican idea in France, its origins before 1789, its decay during the decade of Revolution, and its effect on French politics from Bonaparte to Pétain.

I

For nearly a thousand years, French society had revolved—in theory certainly and in growing reality as well—around the notion of ordered and intermediary bodies (privileged guilds, estates, corps, parishes, regions, clients, families). As Delamare wrote in his *Traité de Police* of 1705:

> l'homme est tellement né pour la société, qu'il en fait son objet favori & sa principale satisfaction. De-là vient que dans l'ordre de la nature, non content de ce premier lien qui ne fit de tout le genre humain qu'une grande société, il a recherché avec empressement des unions plus étroites, d'où se sont formés dans la suite les familles, les Villes, & les plus grands Etats; & dans chacun de ces Etats, des societez encore plus intimes, par les emplois & les professions particulières.[1]

In the middle decades of the seventeenth century, however, the social and administrative elites of the French nation began to rethink the shape of their collective life. By the 1780s, for reasons that are still opaque but which we will try to address, two poles had come to focus their energies on this score: first, meritocratic individualism, about whose nature and merits they were seemingly quite clear; and, second, what might be called, for want of a better term, "public life," a realm whose scope had widened steadily since the creation of the "Old Régime" in the mid-seventeenth century, a great transformation that holds our particular attention since that same trajectory from the corps to the nation has been widely reversed in our own times.

Nature, reason, humanity, *civisme*, sacrifice, people, and nation were varyingly used at various times to approximate this communitarian social nebula.

The terms *private* and *public*, which had had relatively little relevance only decades before, gradually acquired overwhelming cultural centrality. Montesquieu's popularity in France during the 1780s derived from his individualistic denunciation of arbitrary rule and not, as it did in America, from his defense of intermediary bodies or from his concern for the benefits of mixed government. The venality of offices, which had been allowed in the minds of Frenchmen by the collapse of the public and the private, was universally decried, even by the *parlementaires* whose social existence depended on it. Meritocratic academies gained at the expense of painters' guilds. Intellectualized, Parisian, and "ungendered" salons—where divisions of status were, if not ignored, at least suspended—waxed as the model of court life as Versailles waned. Privilege, heretofore a kind of private law, now became synonymous with abuse. The state itself, under the indirect aegis of the physiocrats, gave the (fitful) signal for an attack on feudalism and corporatism, especially in Paris. Of similar relevance to the rise of the new and "a-religious" ethic of the private and the public were many newly introduced institutions: masonic lodges, for example, with their coded, neoparliamentarian rules of order; "lycées"; and "sociétés de pensées," where nobles and nonnobles found common cultural ground. Reference should also be made, though this is less clear, to the educational institutions of the times, some of whose programs and personnel were renewed in the third quarter of the century.

These new foci of social life, then, were the staging areas for transformed definition of the public and the private, and for new patterns of sociability and thought. Their effect was felt in the near and distant corners of social life, in the explicit redefinition and secularization of public fêtes, for example; or in the increasing reluctance to consider Protestants and Jews as members of subprivileged groups rather than as individuals entitled by nature and reason to freedom of opinion.

A less important but perhaps more symbolic consequence of this reordering of priorities was the enlightened interest in pornography, which can be defined as the intimate and illicit made outrageously and illicitly public, as the interface between unrestrained individual desire and undefined natural circumstance. Sade's fantasies have suggestive relevance to the structure if not the content of Jacobin thinking on the relationship of nature to man and "others."[2]

A similar if inverted effect of this same reordering found expression in the conceptual opposite of pornography, that is to say, in a new and highly gendered literary genre, the epistolary novel. In *La Nouvelle Héloïse* and *Les Amants de Lyon*, the private and exemplary letters of a blameless woman were made public for the edification of the public, but only after the heroine's more or less suicidal and wholly apolitical death. Here, womanly self-sacrifice allowed the licitly private to be made licitly public as well.

The effect in eighteenth-century France of the invention or development of secularized privacy (an ancient English locution that to this day has no strict equivalent in the French language) can best be traced in the recently rewritten history of women in eighteenth-century France. The traditional political and public role of females (as queens, royal mistresses, or, more humbly, as vicarious voters in elections to the second estate in 1788–1789) was recoded, devalued, or even eliminated. Women (and children, whom they were held to resemble psychologically and physiologically, in the pitch of their voices, for example) were removed from the public eye and placed at the center of private life. Quite typically, Diderot, in the *Encyclopédie*, considered citizenship as an exclusively masculine concern:

> on n'accorde ce titre (de citoyen) aux femmes, aux jeunes enfants, aux serviteurs que comme à des membres de la famille d'un citoyen proprement dit; mais ils ne sont pas vraiment citoyens.[3]

This redefinition of feminized, private life had very wide effect. It spilled over into matters as varied and numerous as how and where men and women should work; children's literature and birthday celebrations; a concern for domestic comfort; for better heat and better smells; for women's bodies and the joys of sex; and for the virginal white muslins with which women were ordinarily enrobed, both in the paintings of the counterrevolutionary painter Vigée-Lebrun and in David's elaborate settings of revolutionary fêtes. The sustained antifeminism of nearly all revolutionary leaders, from Chaumette to Robespierre and Amar (with some conspicuous exceptions, especially of Condorcet, a child of Reason more than of Nature, and the heir of Poulain de la Barre's Cartesian reasonings) finds its first and most obvious origin in the widely shared belief that the private sphere of woman could not be fused directly with the public life of men. It is curiously expressive that revolutionary anticlericalism should have had as one of its rhetorical motifs the forced marriage of heretofore culturally androgynous Catholic priests, a ceremony that might involve his entering a closed confessional in priestly (and womanly) robes in order to emerge from it reborn, régénéré, since attired in the manly—and public—uniform of the national guard.

The puzzling extent of the revolutionaries' antifeminist (and anticlerical) aggressiveness allows us also to apprehend the deep insecurities created in the minds of men by this Great Transition in the reshaping of sexual roles.[4] Public men and public women were set at the two extremes of a new ethic whose requirements had only been uncertainly interiorized by both men and women.[5] Marginal groups would pay the price of that insecurity in the years to come.

In similar if converse fashion, the rise of a new conception of the secularized public good (and of the "nation" as its prized institutional locus) found expression in the desire to depersonalize power and in the attendant desacralization of the monarchy, after 1750 especially. Architecturally, the newly discovered majesty of the public sphere was given physical expression not in palaces, as before, but in impressive, geometrically shaped and balanced squares (the first of them being in Paris, the Place des Vosges conceived in the reign of Henry IV; the last, the Place de la Concorde in 1754) and in the spacious, ordered cours and allées of Paris and many provincial cities like Nancy, Bordeaux, and Rheims, a spatial model so successful that it was soon copied all over Europe by would-be-modernizers from Lisbon to Copenhagen.

Though nationalism as a term was not coined until the revolutionary and imperial armies of the Grande Nation had made their aggressive effect painfully obvious from Madrid to Moscow, the reality of French nationalism and of militarized patriotism was everywhere visible long before 1789. The War of American Independence was very well received in Paris: "They tell me," wrote a delighted John Adams, "it is the first Time the French Nation ever saw a Prospect of War, with Pleasure."[6] It was popular in part as the first major conflict that the crown financed nearly exclusively from loans and not from taxes. But nationalism was yet more relevant to the zeal aroused by the struggle against perfidious Albion. Paradoxically, Britain was at once an accepted social and economic model and the national enemy, so that masculine suicide—at times defined either as an individuated gesture, as "l'acte le plus libre," as a Catonian gesture of empowered and national self-sacrifice— was also (and contradictorily) held to be an "English disease." The nation became a standard unit of social measurement with the development of statistics and of social analysis.

Many, and perhaps even most, nobles were unable to resist this cultural shift: unable to persist in the view that theirs was an immanent unit in an integrated society of traditional Orders. Some aristocrats did stumble backward onto the wholly factitious theory of the distinct, Frankish racial origin of the noble-born. But the more representative response of nobles was, optimistically, to reconsider the role of the French nobility as a nationally useful and mercantile group, or as a remilitarized fraternity of trained and skilled officers whose self-appointed task would be to defend the fatherland more efficaciously and more professionally as well.

The nation became a standard point of cultural reference: a new feeling for national and public life found expression in the growing and archival interest for the historial origins of the French state, of French chivalry, and of the French or Frankish races. Latin now seemed less important than the national French language to these "moderns" who nurtured a thriving and corresponding disdain of local dialects. Many schemes of national education were floated here and there, one of them by an otherwise highly reactionary parlementaire, La Chalotais. By the time of the Revolution, the French had even developed a national musical canon, a repertoire of often-performed works which emphasized patriotic continuity rather than mere esthetic novelty.

It is critical to understand that this new and enlightened, private/public polarization of "a-religious," elitist sensibility was not perceived by its votaries as being conflictual. Sensibility, it may be useful to add, is more appropriate to describe the situation of prerevolutionary France than is the term *ideology*. Like social classes whose yearnings they express, ideologies ordinarily presuppose conscious and antagonistic allegiances. But to the contrary, the sensibility of the French prerevolutionary elite actively assumed the effortless social and political reconciliation of universally acknowledged principles.

Commentators who reflected on the gradual, meliorist emergence of the (feminized) private and the (masculine) public easily assumed that this newly discovered ecumenism was embedded in the books of Nature and/or Reason which previous generations had only falteringly and partially deciphered. Heuristically, many schools of thought might be harnessed to justify these new categories of social thought: Cartesian innovations as well as the more traditional principles of natural law were easily adapted to current needs. The new cultural arrangements, it was thought, needed only to be conceptualized in order to realize themselves in practice. Revealingly, many thinkers were indifferent to the political context that would best realize their schemes. Before the 1780s, there was not much to choose, it seemed to many, between the rule of parliaments or of enlightened despots.

The social costs of the new ethic were drastically underestimated by meliorist "philosophers" who perceived the past as a record of failures never to be repeated. Nearly to a man (few of them were women), the philosophes assumed that the new social model would make existing social distinctions irrelevant or, at least, *transparent*, to use a term that has been appropriately used to describe Rousseau's seminal interpretation of man's ideal social condition. Indeed, during the 1780s it was widely held (in Paris) that the inhabitants of the newly emancipated, thirteen colonies, regenerated by independence and—as Brissot was to explain in 1792—by virilizing war, had already succeeded in reaching this Republican and fraternal goal. Americans, they concluded, had brought forth in their wilderness near-perfect replicas of the ancient republics.

A suggestive parallel can also be drawn between the expectation of civic harmony-to-come, which they assumed would soon characterize French public life, and the harmony that many French couples expected to find immediately, in their current, private, and maried life. Significantly, the political involvement of wives and husbands during the Revolution was often intertwined. On the side of the Revolution, the Rolands, Desmoulins, Roberts, and Condorcets, come to mind, as do also Pauline Léon and the enragé, Leclerc; the analogs on the right are Charette's Vendéan "amazons" like Mme. de Bulkeley and Thérèse de Moëllien, or, for that matter, the king and queen. In the apt words of Dominique Godineau, "l'existence de couples de militants est une donnée du mouvement populaire parisien."[7]

It is in this central assumption of social and cultural, private and public harmony (and in its failure) wherein lie the origins and the failure also of "l'esprit révolutionnaire." Jacobinism, which was to be the ideologized and politicized essence of that sensibility, pointedly harked back to lost ideals of classical antiquity. It was, in Benjaminian terms, a political phantasmagoria, a utopia that dreamed the future as the reincarnation of an imagined, classless, and harmonious past.

In the mind of the revolutionary elites, liberty (or the modern freedom of the individual) and equality (a common and classic access to the all-encompassing politics of the commonwealth) were to be conciliated by Republican fraternity, in our own times a risible public slogan, but a critical concept for Frenchmen and women at the time: "la République," Roland was to explain in September 1792 to the newly arrived *Conventionnels*, "est une seule et même chose que la fraternité."

To use the terms but not the argument of Albert Hirschman's excellent book, public interest was not displaced by private greed or passion. To the contrary, the two were aggressively perceived as separate halves of a complementary dynamic. For Montesquieu, the apparent inequality of meritocratic reward was actually a proof of equality, provided that all men were equally free to develop their varying abilities. Likewise, the giving of alms plain and simple was a poor idea since it discouraged individual endeavor. But the final effect of that wiser kind of charity that required the poor to become productive individuals would be to raise the disadvantaged to a suitable standard of civic equality.

In a more noble register, Lafont de Saint-Yenne, the first modern art critic, urged French artists to imitate Roman models, because in that ancient Republic, "every private person having his part in governance [of the state], the good constitution of the State became his private and personal interest."[8] Many philosophes were quite conscious of the wide gap that was implied by the simultaneous defense of property and of civic humanism; but they generally assumed that this difference could be transcended by the creation, in Rousseau's words, of an "égalité morale et politique." The voluntarist politicization of difference was to be a path not to conflict but to be unprecedented cultural integration.

Rousseau, the universally famous and solitary "Armenian" hermit of the Ile Saint-Pierre, the most representative figure of his age, a man whose life and works were to be a model for revolutionaries great and small, male or female, conceptualized this universalist ethic as the General Will, a masculinist moral universe within which an empowered and sovereign citizen might commune with his neighbors through the civil religion of a revived polis.

The *Social Contract*, it is true, was not widely read; but thousands of men— and women, especially—wept over the analogous message of *La Nouvelle Héloïse*. They communed with Saint-Preux, the suicidally prone, narcissist, self-obsessed and sensual hero of this epistolary novel who had managed to find a place in the patriarchal, fraternal family that revolved around his beloved Julie. In Rousseau's world view, man's nature, though not invariably communitarian and good, was nonetheless distinctly pliable. Man, if touched by social rather than divine grace, could—with the help of his fellow men— make himself good. Saint Vincent de Salles had explained, in the previous century, that the purpose of a Christian education was to break the sinful nature of the individual child. Rousseau proposed instead to nurture the child's desire to love and to be loved by others: "the vices and misfortunes of children," he reminded the subjects of the French king, "are chiefly the effect of the unnatural despotism of the father."

Public and private were everywhere held by the prerevolutionary elites to be in potentially consensual, antiauthoritarian, neo-Republican accord. So was it, for example, that the first and appointed task of contented women in the home was voluntarily to begin to shape through principle and affection the sensibility of future civic-minded or even Republican, fraternal, and public figures. The sudden popularity of the *rosières*, or "queen of virtue," much praised by Target, the first lawyer of his day,[9] was expressive of this new and integrated private/public perception. Personal integrity and the upholding of public morality were enmeshed as the integrated, cardinal principles of the day. And in a higher (and later) register, the mutuality of the private and the public were to be reproduced in the (universalist) Declaration of the (private) Rights of Man of August 1789, which emphasized less the specific and inherent, imprescriptible rights of the citizen, than his total empowerment in the context of the nation-state. It was indeed this simultaneously naturalized and nationalized quality that in the eyes of its makers essentially differentiated the French statement from its inferior and more positivistic, Virginian antecedents.

In a lower but more immediate key, the craving of the reading public for a collapse of public and private values was inversely evinced in its horrified fascination for tales of courtly and monarchic corruption. The Diamond Necklace affair was the cause célèbre of the 1780s. Countless revolutionary politicians would also learn, in time, to fear politically crippling accusations of corruption, of having placed their private gain before the public weal. In this context, Danton and his foil Robespierre immediately come to mind. Only a genuinely base man, replied Robespierre to the Girondin Louvet in November 1792, could refuse to see that his entire sense of self must have the national good as its purpose. Ortega y Gasset aristocratically derided Joseph Chénier's denigration of Mirabeau: "Je considère qu'il n'y a pas de grands hommes sans vertu."[10] But this was to miss the point of Chénier's unspoken and wholly representative argument.

Before 1789, the detailed contours of the constitutive private and public elements of the new French collective identity were carefully annotated. On one side, rigidly moralizing distinctions were developed between positive and negative definitions of private life, that is to say, between those shapings of privacy that did dovetail with the public good and those which failed that acid test.

The physicality of breastfeeding was pleasing. Female sexuality in marriage was likewise much praised: the Desmoulinse's double-bed was for them and others the symbol of an emotionally and politically collaborative marriage. For Choderlos de Laclos, the author of the celebrated (and ironically epistolary) *Liaisons Dangereuses*, the sexuality of women could not be denied (as was made obvious in countless statements ranging from novels to "sexuated" representations of male and female skeletons); but within happy, mutually satisfying marriages this potent force of nature might well be tamed. (Choderlos was a prerevolutionary partisan of divorce, which was to be legislated in September 1792.)

Simultaneously, however, perverted female sexuality (i.e., a private yearning that sought fulfillment irrespective of the public good) was much feared. Lesbianism now suddenly seemed far more threatening than male homosexuality, which in the recent traditionalist past had still been punished by burning at the stake. Dr. Tissot's criticism of female onanism, or *tribadisme* as it was then known, was warmly stated.

Republicanism for men, by contrast, often verged on homosexual, masculine friendship. In David's *Oath of the Horatii*, it united masculinized citizens in militarized and fraternal amity, just as it relegated women to the bosom of familial love, ordinarily inscribed in the devalued, bottom-righthand corner of vast canvasses. In the Year II, Romme, the self-sacrificing and fraternal "martyr de prairial," insisted on marrying any widow of a fallen and revolutionary soldier who might be assigned to him by his Parisian Section: this highly subjectivized but self-sacrificing Jacobin aimed to commune with both the Nation and an unknown, fallen, comrade through a female body, now become like other material and social forms, a "transparent" and almost irrelevant object.

In this same context of sexualized politics, Marie Antoinette, her pre-revolutionary reputation, and the obscenities of her trial readily come to mind also, as does, on the other shore, the relatively unimpeded progression of Cambacérès and Fiévée from Republic to Empire and the more checkered career of Chaumette during the Revolution.[11]

Similar distinctions, positive and negative, were applied to the public side of the reconceptualized vision of sociability as well. Aged, country nobles who had grown poor in the unrewarded service of the state were much praised. Court nobles were by contrast despised, and this same distinction of "corrupt court and worthy country" was widely held, even in 1789–1790—even by Brissot, a man who lived from the crumbs he snatched from the tables of the titled great, and even when the more worldly and younger nobles of Paris and Versailles had repeatedly shown themselves to be the manifestly more liberal at the Estates-General than their troglodytic country cousins. In that same mode, it is worth noting that in 1793–1794, the most victimized of all nobles—both male and female—were parliamentary aristocrats, that is to say the most enlightened and wordly patrons of arts and letters. It did not matter that many of these often-enlightened jurists were as private persons (like Hérault de Séchelles and Le Peletier de Saint-Fargeau) personally liberal. In the lottery of execution, their established reputation of indifference to the public good was an insurmountable handicap.

In short, by 1789, in many noble and nonnoble minds alike, the newer categories of private and of public (like those that defined the male or female) took precedence over the older distinctions of estates and corps as the structuring elements of *l'imaginaire social*. Rousseau, Thomas, Diderot, Mme. d'Epinay, and countless others pondered the question of woman's nature. And implicit in the background of the frequently raised question, "What is woman?" was, as has been said, the more dreaded if silent theme, "What is man?"[12] Where did his self begin and end? Could it fully express itself in privatized social life? The emphatic declaration of man's rights and responsibilities in August 1789 can be read as an answer to hidden, unstated questions of gender as well as to the more explicit dilemmas of public politics.

II

The question inevitably arises of the social and economic origins of this new and soon to be politicized cultural world view. Was 1789 the more or less efficient *machine de guerre* of the nascent and irresistible French bourgeoisie, a frustrated, increasingly prosperous and antinoble group with a narrow if distinct cultural and economic configuration? Or was it instead a broader cultural upheaval, staged by a wide and educated public with divergent interests and materially unreformed origins?

To go one step further, can the Revolution be conceived as the well-nigh doomed effort of a socially heterogenous elite to institutionalize (in the face of historical legacy and popular resistance) a radically new and complementary, highly volatile and even self-destructive view of the private self and the social self? Generations of Marxist historians assumed that revolutionary politics were the necessary effect of antecedent social and economic change. Many historians would now wish to turn that assumption on its head: revolutionary politics failed precisely because the culture of the elites did not supply a solid material foundation.

The supposed material origins of Enlightenment thought are well known. Who would choose to ignore the strains caused by population growth or minimize increases in the volume of trade with the development of a comprador economy, on the Atlantic coast especially? Of relevance also are the rise of the national debt and the increased circulation of money. Many other factors of this type have been closely investigated: that is, the stabilization of the currency after 1724; improved communications under the aegis of the state and its trained employees; the gradual displacement of sharecropping by leaseholding (in Babeuf's Picardy, at least); incipient regional specialization and industrialization; the standardization of prices within an incipiently national market; introduction of new crops; and so forth. A century of excellent and relentless research allows an impressive extension of this point of view. Much is to be learned also from the material evolution of the French nation's constituent groups: pressed for funds, many nobles, parlementaires especially, did their best to revive lapsed and antique feudal dues. French peasants suffered especially: more numerous, unwilling or unable to go abroad or to leave the land for cities where the demand for labor was low, many of them were caught in a cruel bind between rising prices and an essentially unchanging productivity. Beggary was widespread, and much feared, in prerevolutionary urban and rural France.

But few historians of the Revolution would choose today to make of these transformations the determining base of some epiphenomenal cultural or political superstructure. The older arguments will not hold. The rhythm of cultural change far outstripped that of its material analog: in the main, France in 1789 was still as it had always been, a collection of "immobile villages." Unlike London, Paris was primarily an administrative center that grew relatively little in the eighteenth century, and which remained more focused on the production of luxury goods than on modern industry or international commerce. The creation of the Bank of England in 1694 antedates that of the Bank of France by more than a century. The relative immaturity in the eighteenth century of French private and state finance (and the attendant importance of foreign Protestant and Swiss bankers like those honest brokers, Necker and Clavière) needs no emphasis. Their presence speaks loudly to the relative financial backwardness of the French economy.

It is of great consequence that the French bourgeoisie, much of it marked by Jansenism, was, like the great majority also of French working people, visibly uninterested in the capitalist applications of the laws of supply and demand. Unlike the American and English political elites of the times, the French revolutionary political class had its roots in the professions, in law above all else, and not in business. The mercantile interest was socially marginal in France before 1789, and politically marginal after that as well in the nation's Assemblies, after 1791 especially.

Economic travails were often the catalyst of political radicalization after 1789, and especially for the urban poor; but they were never its first cause. The execution of the king was, for example, more relevant to the surge of the enragés in the spring of 1793 than was the competition of the army and the urban poor for scarce and more expensive food.

It is for reasons of this kind ultimately futile and even misleading to find the origins of cultural change in the material transformations of French society. Material change coincided with the cracking of the cake of custom, but it was more a sign than a cause of that event. The cardinal principles of the French Enlightenment have to be understood as a terminus ad quem, as the "vectors of new perceptions of reality,"[13] rather than as the mere consequence of some deeper cause. In the postrevolutionary words of Roederer, the institutions of the Ancien Régime were more injurious than they were onerous. A century of materialist explanation needs to be reinterpreted and transcended.

Unfortunately, historians who agree that the origins of the Revolution were more cultural than material have also found it extremely difficult to discuss these origins in a convincing way. The counting of books is a disappointing lode. Ideologically undiscriminating tabulations—which are of necessity sterile intellectually—ordinarily reveal the surprising (and of course deceptive) conservatism of the reading public.

An emphasis on the seamier side of the Enlighterment (that is to say, the reification rather than the interpretation of pornography) is likewise problematic, especially when a historiographical choice of this kind is, as it were, "institutionalized": it is highly conjectural to hypostasize the existence of a French Grub Street, of a supposed self-conscious milieu of scribblers and pamphleteers, many of whom in actual fact were either courtiers or the isolated hired pens of high-flying polemicists. Developed networks of information certainly existed even before the Revolution: on September 19, 1783, over a hundred thousand Parisians, forming perhaps the largest crowd that had ever been seen in France, knew that they should go to Versailles in order to witness the ascent of Montgolfier's hot-air balloon. To ignore the journalistic mediatization of information during the French Revolution would be very unwise: Hébert, Roux, Marat, Brissot, Desmoulins, Robespierre, and Mirabeau were all journalists of a kind. The creation of a typographical school run by women and for women is surely one of the most indicative *faits-divers* of the Revolution. But the torrent of the French Revolution cannot be plausibly presented as the subcategory of frustrated prerevolutionary journalistic ambition. Marat's Plan de Législation Criminelle of 1779 was certainly incendiary, but as his doctrinaire and Marxist biographer, Massin, interestingly points out, Marat was then at the height of his social success, and the radicalization of his polemical ideas owed more to the recent successes of America's revolutionaries than to his private concerns.

Far more critical in the background of cultural change than these pamphleteers was the emergence in enlightened France of "public opinion" as an accepted point of reference. The Republic of letters, it has often been suggested, was an antecedent of republicanism sans phrases. But public opinion was understood by all (including the hired hacks who tried to influence it through scurrilous text and image) to be the expression of the nation's renewed elite, and not of its marginal members at all. Symbolically, the first apologist of this "reine du monde" was Necker, minister to the king, a religious man who remained, in the end, more a partisan of enlightened despotism than of parliamentary monarchy sans phrases.

Institutional and political antecedents also appear promising as a possible cause of deep-seated cultural transformations. High on that list are the modernizing effects of the Ancien Régime itself, its leveling effect on "feudalism," a development whose consequences are well known to the readers of Tocqueville. The names of Lebrun, a client of Maupeou in the early 1770s who became second consul in 1799, and that of the future Baron Louis (in the 1780s a friend of Calonne and, many years later, himself a minister of finance) are eloquent symbols of the modernizing and official continuity that links the so-called Old Regime to the admittedly streamlined Napoleonic and post-Napoleonic state. The Bourbon monarchy did not succeed in modernizing French social institutions, but it did a great deal to make older arrangements obsolete.

More critical yet as possible causes for the rise of a new private and public vision of the common good are explanations that center less on the external forces (be they material, cultural, or political) that attacked traditional corporatism in France, than on the internal decay of that ancient system.

For a variety of reasons, many of them related to the French state's incessant need for money, the prestige of judicial and administrative traditionalism vanished as its scope increased. In some sense, traditionalist institutions in monarchic France simply collapsed under their own weight. (In Spain, a "backward" country, professional corporatism was by 1789 much more lightly felt than in France: women there had been given the right to enter any profession of their choice already in 1784; the venality of offices was unkown south of the Pyrénées; and outside of Catalonia, the institutions of provincial particularism were as a rule politically inconsequential.)

Behind the decay in France of corporatism and monarchic traditionalism was also to be found the self-destructing bent of its constituent institutions. Feudalism, as Tocqueville emphasized, no longer fullfilled any useful purpose. Its judicial and financial vestiges were bitterly criticized by many noble and official publicists. Guilds likewise neared collapse under the strains of internal rivalries. The momentary unpopularity of a church that rejected both tolerance and millenarian zeal has often been described but needs to be emphasized: the French in the 1780s were a religious people whose religiosity was dangerously incapable of finding expression in a church that had simultaneously rejected popular millenarianism and the enlightened individuation of religious forms. The humiliation of Jansenism, for example, was still deeply felt in 1789, as was to be attested by the careers of Grégoire and Lanjuinais. The Catholic church on the eve of the Revolution was a troubled institution, more torn by doubts than at any time since the Reformation: perhaps as many as twenty thousand clerics abjured their priesthood in 1793–1794, and three thousand of them chose to marry.

The weakness of the monarchy and the decline of its patriarchal myth in an age of incipient nationalism were also critically relevant to the rise of a countervailing political ethic. Though France in 1685 brought the idea of absolute monarchy to its European zenith, the prestige of enlightened despotism as a method of government was weaker in late eighteenth-century France than in any other continental country. By the 1780s, and perhaps long before, literate Frenchmen had given up on the idea of "reform from above." The servants of the French king were no more efficacious than their master: unlike its Prussian analog, the French bureaucracy was incapable of sustained and independent political action. Important also were diplomatic difficulties and the inability of the French state to maintain armed forces commensurate with its international goals.

Nationalist passions can likewise be seen as both a cause and effect of change. The growing prestige (and masculinization) of public life heightened the sense of nationhood. Nationalism in turn reinforced the new categories of the private and the public. The elite of the French nation, with its eye on Britain's domestic economic achievement and her mortifying, worldwide military successes, resented the inability of the Bourbon state to marshal the energies of the French people. As has been remarked, the subjects of Louis XV and of his grandson had a lively—and grating—sense of French economic backwardness and of Britain's military, industrial, commercial, financial, and imperialist superiority. Bonaparte spoke knowingly when he said that the victory of Fontenoy had given the French monarchy an extra forty-five years of life, but it did no more than that.

The fit between domestic and international concerns was tight: the failure of the crown's bureaucracy to enact institutional modernization at home dovetailed in the public mind with its failure to impose its will on foreigners, as was seen in Holland especially in 1787. The waning prestige of this "visible hand," the decay of the mercantilist/absolutist state, crystallized the rising appeal in the minds of French men and women of new sensibilities, soon to become demanding systems of ideology. Some of these, like physiocracy, emphasized individualistic economic effort. Others, in the works of Mably for example, emphasized communitarian values. But all of them were ecumenical visions that assumed the possible creation of a transparent state, of an "invisible hand," that might effortlessly express the will of a united people.

III

Revolutionary politics can also be explained in this same cultural and institutional framework, as an unprecedented and unrepeatable drama, a unique if ominous performance whose backdrop was the unstable reshaping of the nation's collective identity before 1789.

The political trajectory after 1789 of the nation's possessing notables and of their intellectualized clients—some rich, some poor—all of them moving in uneasy and shrinking accord with the plebs of Paris, cannot be explained as a "superstructural" event. Revolutionary politics were not some impoverished effect that corresponded mechanically to some neatly labeled layering of capitalist society. (The sequence, we might add, ordinarily runs,

1. organicist, landowning nobles;
2. high, "grand-bourgeois" Feuillant constitutionalist;
3. upper-middle-class Voltairean Girondins;
4. middle-class Rousseauist Jacobins; and
5. the anticlerial plebs, itself split between (5b) the Hébertist petite-bourgeoisie and (5c) the more populist and democratic enragés.)

Pedagogically useful as this nomenclature may at first appear, it is however more sensible to envisage the events of the 1790s without reference to some supposed prerevolutionary structure of class. Politics were the signs of the decomposition of an initial cultural and political consensus that was centered on an unstable vision of the self and society. It may well be that without accidents of routine politics (war, shortages, betrayals) the claims of revolutionary unanimism would not have unfolded as characteristically as they did. But in revolutionary times, difficulties of some kind are bound to emerge. Some revolutions succumb to unforeseen events, and others not. What matters in the end is more the inner logic of political assumptions than the nature of the serendipitous happenings that catalyze its emergence.

L'esprit révolutionnaire matters more than the events that brought it forward, and this spirit eventually proved to be unstable, violent, and tyrannical. Although the right of all (male) citizens to pluralist self-expression was theoretically recognized in the Constitution of 1791 (just as the more dramatic right to insurrection was likewise to be enshrined in the unapplied Constitution of 1793), the more fundamental vision shared by all the revolutionaries was that of a united, romanized cité in which regenerated individuals might find self-fulfillment as citizen–warriors struggling to maintain a unanimous and wholly politicized nation–state.

In the words of Le Chapelier, who was to be in rapid succession a founder and a bitter enemy of Jacobinism, "Il n'y a plus de corporations dans l'Etat; il n'y a plus que l'intérêt particulier de chaque individu, et l' intérêt général."

Regenerated by liberty, French men and women, though in fact hardly prepared to give up the day-to-day benefits and security of a corporatist world order, thought themselves on the verge of a new epoch: "L'idée du bonheur," Saint-Just was to explain in 1794, "est neuve en Europe." Emancipated from the theoretical constraints of corporate life but unafraid of class tensions whose full impact they could not yet apprehend, the French gave unbridled scope to their social imagination, and to their lyric enthusiasm. At the stroke of a pen, law codes were abolished and new territorial arrangements drawn up. Language, religion, education, marriage were all to be reformed. Everything seemed possible for the better in 1789, and, as it happened, for the worse in 1794.

In the minds of its framers, the new revolutionary and universalist state was ultimately to guarantee the natural rights of all men (as against the American system of 1787 whose purpose was to defend the positive rights of enfranchised men). At the same time, the French obsession on the unity of the state's political purpose gradually but inexorably eroded a concern for the civic rights of individual citizens.

At first, in 1789–1791, civil society seemed more important than the state but, by 1793–1794, the revolutionary definition of sovereignty placed civil society at the mercy of the state, very much as Bodin had advised should be so and as Hobbesian or Ludovician, monarchic absolutism had also assumed to be true.[14] By placing the nation between the citizen and the exercise of his natural rights, the French possessing class in August 1789 set the stage for that very decomposition of individual liberties that it most feared.

In the first months of the Revolution, the new individualist and universalist ethic (l'esprit révolutionnaire) with its mix of the private (symbolized by women) and of the public (the realm of the warrior–citizen) found an almost universal audience among the members of the French educated and possessing class, some of them nobles, and others not. Politically, after the initial difficulties of June and July 1789, "right" and "left," that is to say, at this point, both monarchists and constitutionalists, whether nobles or non-nobles, whether owners of feudal dues or enlightened reformers (many people in fact cumulated these two roles), were in basic accord on the practicalities of reform. The defeated and "unmasked" parlements had lost all credibility. The liberality of the nobles' *cahiers de doléances* is well known. It seems highly likely that most of the noble-born were in August and September of 1789 resigned or, in thousands of cases, even enthusiastic about the new order of politics.

In the early fall of 1789, right and left (somewhat misnamed in this early context since these terms arose only in 1792 when the earlier equilibrium of 1789 had broken down) differed only in the emphasis they gave to the constituent part of the newly politicized cultural synthesis: some of the actors in 1789–1790 were more eager to ignore the past in order to develop both the new individuated rights of private persons and of the universalist, Grande Nation. Others thought it prudent to meld their novel sense of what the public/private should be with the rhetorical legacy of the Ancien Régime. But nearly everyone looked for some compromise between the old and the new systems, between the legacy of the past, of king, church, and nobles (when taken as private persons), and the integrated values of liberty, equality, and fraternity. Preferences were not everywhere the same, but the numbers of genuinely reactionary, organicist emigrés could in 1789 be nearly counted on the fingers of one hand. In 1789–1790, conservatives—like Cazalès and Royou—were Enlightenment figures of a kind who accepted the need for institutional reform and popular consultation.

And on the side of change, during these same early years, even ardent Jacobins were convinced monarchists, *amis de la Constitution*, respectful of religion and tepid in their application of the new legislation on the abolition of feudal dues. "Revolutionizing" Republicans in 1790 were as scarce as were the organicist conservatives. Louis XVI was probably more popular in 1789–1790 than any French monarch had ever been. In short, the cleavage of politics in 1789–1790 was set first within the new and ecumenical definition of private/public culture, of individualism effortlessly entwined with communitarian forms; and second within the monarchic legacy of French history.

Only later did dissenting actors set themselves outside that double context. It was only with the breakdown of consitutional monarchy in 1791–1792, and only then, that the initial arrangements broke down on two fronts. The right—prompted as it was by the civil constitution of the clergy, the abolition of nobility, and the humiliation of the monarch—did indeed regress to religious integrism on a trajectory that would soon lead it to political organicism. And the popular left simultaneously advanced from a rejection of individualism in economic life toward an embryonic and organicist consciousness of class that was best expressed by Babeuf in 1796.

But in early 1790, no one even remotely suspected that either one of these upheavals was in the making. In Sieyès's initial and highly representative world view, the nation–state (wholly sovereign to be sure, but—for the moment and practically speaking—nearly invisible) and its empowered citizens were not to be separated by any kind of institution of any kind. Jews (from Bordeaux) were given complete equality as private individuals and resolutely denied a collective existence as "a nation within the nation." The situation of nobles and of the nobility was similarly envisaged. The French state was to be at once universal and invisible: it might monopolize the realm of collective representation but, practically speaking, it was to remain a cipher. Sieyès even argued against the suppression by the state of tithes.

Existing material arrangements, including even many feudal dues, were not immediately affected by the assertion of the new individualist–universalist state. As Sieyès, again, explained in September 1789, France was not and could not yet be a democracy. The material ordering of civil society was, in the main, left untouched, even though the subjects of the French king were now declared to be the citizens of a fraternal state. With the Le Chapelier law, as shall be seen, the revolutionary state agreed merely to enforce contracts whose individuated terms it had no right to shape. It would likewise eventually passively agree to dissolve the marriages of childless and consenting adults on their request. Significantly, the Jacobin clubs, which claimed to embody a hegemonic Public Opinion, simultaneously presented their associations as groups of atomized individuals whose natural, self-evident task was merely to be the mouthpiece of a preexisting, single, public, and national will.

By the summer and fall of 1791, however, Jacobins moved away from the first part of their initial stance. Their desire to find a compromise between the old and the new atrophied and died. They had wished at first to nationalize church and king, just as they had been eager to compensate the owners of abolished feudal dues. But after the king's flight to Varennes in June 1791 which was after the fact condoned by many Constituent deputies, the Jacobins realized that they alone truly expressed the sovereignty of the people. The clubs would have to supplant the Assembly politically in order to transform society, institutionally and culturally, through censorship and, if need be, Terror.

But the second facet of their world view remained unchanged. To the bitter end, Jacobins were to be resolute in their determination to uphold their vision of the empowered, politicized male citizen within an empowered and wholly sovereign nation. Jacobinism was first and foremost the ideologized and Janus-faced quintessence of l'esprit révolutionnaire, at once bourgeois and universalist.

The Jacobins never wavered in their opposition to "factions" and to selfish and sectarian, feminized aristocracies (not to be confused with nobles). Jacobins were unbending in their defense of civic equality whose claims were still lightly felt in 1789–1791. Political parties were wholly foreign to their way of thinking, and the clubs persistently presented themselves not as a particularist association at all, but as the united hierophants of mankind. In the subsequent words of Saint-Just, Jacobins were later to become a *conscience publique*, the apostles of a national will that had proved to be less self-conscious than they had at first assumed.

Uncompromisingly national and unbendingly individualistic, Jacobins were also, and of necessity, rigidly antipluralist. The original, federal and Madisonian American solution of 1787, which also sought to blend private interest and public good, did not and could not have many echoes in the Grande Nation. Surprisingly, the *Federalist Papers* were translated into French by a friend of the painter David in 1792. (Madison, Hamilton, and Gay were even awarded honorary French citizenship in 1793!) But Louis Sébastien Mercier, a polymath linguist, a member of the Cercle Social, and a former *Conventionnel*, wrote of these essays that they had been hopelessly misunderstood by the Montagnards. They had failed to see, he explained, that this American text

> est précisément un ouvrage contre le fédéralisme, en ce qu'il tend à ramener toutes les parties d'un état à l'unité de gouvernement, cette unité que Brissot vouloit, ainsi que nous tous, qui avons signé la proclamation aux départements pour la sûreté extérieure de la France et pour son union interne.[15]

But however statist and antipluralist they might be, the Jacobins nonetheless remained equally adamant in their defense of private property. Their universalism was at once boundless and dramatically circumscribed. Property, like women, was for them a private concern that could not be politicized. These embattled citizens were the mortal foes of the redistributive *loi agraire*. As private persons, the Jacobins were avid purchasers of *biens nationaux* but, revealingly, this desire to profit privately from the Revolution did not affect the Jacobins' conviction of being in good faith. These defenders not just of private property but of the local entrepreneur's right to rule in his own factory, these resident and ensconced officers of localized national guards, were also dedicated patriots, eager to equip—and at their own expense—those poorer citizens who had sacrificially volunteered to join the nation's warring armies. Jacobinism was fueled not only by the militant defense of private property and the strident denuciation of an impossible equality of wealth, it was ennobled also by the eulogistic glow of civic virtue. A good citizen might very well be a patriarchal and propertied father.

The critical theme of regeneration bridged for them the gap between selfishness and responsibility, both within the family and within the state.

Only regenerated and politicized citizens, they now fully understood, might uniformly realize their purified self in the state, regardless of their varying private situations as owners (or nonowners) of property. Empowered by an *amour de soi* that was purged of *amour propre*, regenerated Frenchmen would eventually form a regenerated France: "J'ai osé concevoir," wrote Lepelletier (a noble-born Jacobin) of a school designed to train the revolutionary male elites, "une plus vaste pensée [than that of mere instruction]."

> [Et] considérant à quel point l'espèce humaine est dégradée par le vice de notre ancien système social, je me suis convaincu de la nécessité d'opérer une entière régénération et, si je peux m'exprimer ainsi, de créer un nouveau peuple.[16]

And should regeneration not suffice to create that sense of the private self that could realize itself fully in the public sphere, the Jacobins, unable and unwilling to reshape property relations, vigorously worked to establish equality in other realms, in education, in the ability to speak a national and equalizing language, and in the reshaping also of space and time. As Romme wrote:

> Le temps ouvre un nouveau livre à l'histoire; et dans sa marche nouvelle, majestueuse et simple comme l'égalité, il doit graver d'un burin neuf les annales de la France régénérée. . . . L'ère vulgaire fut l'ère de la cruauté, du mensonge, de la perfidie, de l'esclavage; elle a fini avec la royauté, source de tous nos maux.[17]

The widely accepted revolutionary call to define as complementarily heroic both individualism and the public good (a mix that I have elsewhere described as "bourgeois universalism") found many applications in revolutionary France. It took on rhetorical substance in the prosodies and orchestrations of revolutionary fêtes, where extremely complicated scores involved the contrapuntal performances of choristers and highly trained soloists, all of them echoes of the nation's united will. The thirst for unanimity appeared also in the civic and Pantheonic cult of great and immortal individuals: bodies might turn to dust, but the people's remembrance of Barra and Viala, of Lepelletier, Chalier, and Marat could never be erased.

The collective apotheosis of the politicized and masculine self likewise explains in large part the public display of wounded bodies, the worship of fallen heroes, and the widespread fascination for the communitarian suicide of would-be legislators. Voluntary death, described by the Montagnard Conventionnel Lequinio as "l'acte le plus libre," was everywhere perceived, from royalist right to the populist, Babouvian left, by all actors of the revolutionary drama, as both the supreme assertion of the Faustian self and as a triumphant act of civic education. Even Pâris, the royalist assassin of Le Peletier who had voted the death of Louis XVI, mimetically killed himself. Republican schoolchildren were given as their models the voluntary deaths of Barra and Viala, the exemplary and fallen child heroes of revolutionary war and civil war. (A festival to commemmorate the death of Barra had been scheduled for 10 Thermidor.) Staged and exemplary suicide was a model of death and becoming that appealed to Girondins like Condorcet or Mme. Roland (who did not actually kill themselves) and to Buzot, Roland, Clavière, and Pétion who did; to Montagnards like Saint-Just and Robespierre, who waited for execution, and to Lebas or the "martyrs de prairial" who chose to take their own lives; to Babeuf who stabbed himself in the dock at Vendôme, and to Doctor Bach who chose to end his days mutely at the foot of Liberty's statue on the Place de la Révolution, shortly after Bonaparte's successful and liberticide, military coup.

So was it also that Charlotte Corday's suicidal and deeply irrational murder of Marat (a figure whose private life was itself consumed by revolutionary struggle and who had threatened to fire a bullet in his brain on the very floor of the Convention) should have been particularly troubling for the dedicated, male revolutionaries of the day: Corday's Plutarchian and politicized determination inverted their deepest public expectations, just as Marat's vulnerable, exposed, naked and bathing body inverted centuries of iconographic clichés. (The Républicaines Révolutionnaires, who more than any others orchestrated Marat's burial, insistently carried his tub in their processions.)

Corday's was a sacrificial and heroic gesture: this, the Jacobins could easily understand. But the death and transfiguration of this young woman also formed and, to their intense dismay, became an archetypally masculine statement. Corday's desire to save republican France from Marat was doubly defiant, politically and sexually. It is hardly coincidental that after her execution, Corday's body was anatomically examined, in David's presence, in the hope that she might not have been a virgin: the idea of a doubly public woman would have been more easily encompassed.

The Jacobin's expected fusion of the private and of the public explains also the deeper nature of the d'Allarde and Le Chapelier laws in the late spring of 1791, laws that abolished all associations and therefore served, as Marx correctly explained, to clear the decks of French society for the elaboration in the next century of individualistic capitalism and industrialization.

In some obvious sense, of course, the motivation of this legislation lay in the plain defense of the manufacturer's immediate interest: banal strike-breaking is a meaningful aspect of the story. But the deeper point of these laws related instead to the expectation that the invisible hand that governed social relations would effortlessly reconcile the private and the public good in business and in industry as it had already done in high politics and in the family. Symbolically, Desmoulins opined in 1791 that this abolition of the guilds would thrill the poor: "Il y aura des illuminations dans les mansardes."[18]

An analogy can be drawn here between the expected complementarity of monetized life, which Le Chapelier assumed would soon take shape, and the meritocratic fraternity of military life. Heroic authority was in its original intent exemplarily democratic. The careers of Napoleon's future marshals after 1800 started from the belief in 1793 that the unquestioned lead of elected officers would reinforce the fraternal democracy of military life.

That industrialism, Bonapartism, and a sexist Code Civil emerged as the unforeseen consequences of revolutionary individualist/universalist action is not to deny the thoughtfulness of the Jacobins' original impulses.

The year 1789 was a unique (and thrilling) moment of cultural and political optimism, a *bonne nouvelle*, coming as it did at the unfettered and libertarian, liberating intersection between the old and new structurings of French social life; that is to say, at a unique moment never to be repeated, when the constraints of "traditionalism" had lapsed, and when those of bourgeois modernity were not yet felt: Jacobinism was an *ilusión*, in the two senses of that Spanish word.

But these new constraints did surface, of course, and with a frightful vengeance made worse for initial misunderstandings. The ferocity of 1794 gives us the measure of the headiness of 1789, when "to be young was very heaven."

Inexorably, as events revealed the heretofore unsuspected extent of egoism and *aristocratie*, the sphere of the public began to devour the realm of what was to have been private. With the Club des Citoyennes Républicaines Révolutionnaires, women struggled to emerge into the public sphere. With the maximum, the sanctity of private property was questioned by the sansculottes. The Jacobins had brought into being that which they most feared.

Revolutionary praxis shook Jacobinism to its foundations. In their initial conceptions, especially as regarded the rights of private property, the Constituents had assumed, in their practice at least, that civil society was to be an immanent form. The purpose of politics was to make possible the transcendence but not the transformation of social forms, once feudalism had been abolished.

Nonetheless, the logic of the Jacobins' argument on the nature of the public good and of its relationship to private virtue, gradually led the Constituents or their Jacobin successors dictatorially to place a still unvirtuous (and rebellious) society at the disposal of the state that they now controlled.

The Jacobins soon found themselves to be the unwitting instruments of social and economic changes with which they could not cope; but even before these appeared, the first of the structural problems that sapped the dictatorialized, individualist/universalist synthesis of the propertied revolutionaries was, very simply, the hopeless irrelevance of their vision of state and society to the lives and sufferings of most French men and women.

Jacobin cultural construct might please educated, enlightened, and propertied individuals—most of them, obviously, bourgeois, but many of them nobles (like Lafayette, the Lameths, Talleyrand, Condorcet, the Le Pelletiers [one a murdered Montagnard, the other a Babouvist], Antonelle, Hérault, Barras, Soubrany, and countless others). But in spite of this, Jacobinism bore little relevance to the daily life of ordinary people, if only because the constitutionalists quickly excluded millions of "passive" citizens from their universalist pact. Indeed, it is a measure of the unpopularity of traditional corporatism and the Old Regime (as it is also of the Patriotic party's control of word and image) that, in May and June 1789, the deputies of the Third Estate who represented the interest of a fraction of the nation's population should have effortlessly succeeded in presenting themselves as the spokesmen of a united and embattled people.

The appeal of the new ethic was very narrow. Most French peasants (and according to William Reddy, much of the French bourgeoisie as well!) were deeply suspicious of the laws of the market. Their rationality was focused on the private survival of their family as a group, rather than on their public prosperity as producers. Bourgeois individualism and republican universalism, defined as they were in relationship to property, held an especially small promise for women and especially for peasant women (surely a third of the nation's inhabitants) who proved to be the least prorevolutionary of all French social groups, as well they might be since now doubly disenfranchised as both females and nonowners of property. Even propertied and enlightened women were very ambiguously situated to the calls of republican public life—as Mme. Roland would discover—since their role was to support it from afar: "Restez à vos places," explained Amar to the Citoyennes Républicaines, "ne sortez point de vos demeures. . . . Il ne faut pas qu'un ménage reste un seul instant désert."[19]

More troubling yet were the many politically unforeseen and problematic implications of republican universalism. Conceived as negation, and for that reason practically defined less in its own right than as the antithesis of the principles of the Ancien Régime, revolutionary universalism created unexpected difficulties for itself at every step. The inclusion of Jews and of Protestants especially had certainly been one of its stated goals before 1789; but very few universalist public figures before that date had given sustained thought to its implications for the freed *gens de couleurs* in the colonies, not to speak of black slaves. Indeed, the universalist message, as Jacques Revel has pointed out, created political problems where none had existed before, with speakers of dialects for example, or with Jews, again, who had been a fragmented and unimportant corps before 1789 but now became a more homogeneous "nation within the nation." Freemasonry was an eccentricity that a sated and avuncular Ancien Régime could easily tolerate. Catholicism was a universalist system that revolutionary Jacobinism was bound to deny.

But the acid test of the Jacobins' universalist zeal was of course in the answer they gave to the wholly unexpected claims of the urban poor, and more particularly of the politicized Parisian poor, male and female, who were given unprecedented prominence by their ability to coerce a recentralized French state, by the factional instability of revolutionary politics, by the eroding effect of depreciating paper currency in 1793, and by the ensuing competition for bread between Paris and the army in that same year.

Hic Rhodus, hic salta! Here was the cleavage that was to define the French bourgeoisie after 1794, and which in 1792 already—after the September massacres especially—began to separate the formerly united and revolutionary party. In late 1792–1793, the patriots of 1789 split in two. On the losing side were the warmongering Girondins, ensconced in power, who had seen the handwriting of class on the wall and who were now desperate to stop the Revolution in order to preserve it. Many of them were lawyers and, in order to justify their stand, these jurists easily rediscovered the words of freedom and choice (and free enterprise) which they had so recently forgotten. Principle was to be sure at the heart of their politics but only in the sense that the Girondins genuinely wished eventually to save a Revolution that they identified with their place within it. In order to reach that greater and more distant goal, the short-run opportunism of the Girondins was boundless. Their transparent calculations gave great offense.

Arraigned against them were their former brethren, the opposing and more principled Montagnards who, despite the reality of sans-culotte demands, persisted in their still-powerful if increasingly irrelevant universalist vision of a harmonious public good. Here was an idealistic goal whose pursuit after the September massacres now implied the endorsement of horrendous popular violence. In the spring of 1793, the uncertain but republican deputies of the Plaine settled the issue between the two groups by choosing for the more determined Mountagnards.

Contrary to what most Marxist and even anti-Marxist historians have supposed, the Jacobin "patriots"—Girondins and Montagnards—had originally been all of one mind, and in the main of one social origin as well. Many of them had been close friends (Marat and Brissot, Robespierre and Desmoulins). In 1793, what distinguished Robespierre from Brissot was less a difference in the origins or nature of their political and universalist/individualist culture, than the timing of their ultimately similar responses to the threat from below. Robespierre's hostility in the fall of 1793 to the dechristianization that was urged by the sans-culottes clearly echoed the Girondins dismay after the September massacres of 1792. And looking forward, the Incorruptible's denunciation of Chaumette and Fouché likewise prefigured the Thermidorean reaction of 1795.

The gap in 1793 between former and current Jacobins (i.e., Girondins and Montagnards) basically occurred because the Revolution failed in ways that none had expected could occur since their first and united animosity had been overwhelmingly focused on the destruction of the Old Regime. In principle, all Jacobins from Barnave to Saint-Just were in rough agreement: all of them had started in 1789 from the assumption that in their great crusade, private and public goals could easily be fused. Nearly all of them were hostile to the involvement of women in politics. None of them were particularly sympathetic to money or modern industry: Sieyès did admire Adam Smith's exposition of the advantages that might accrue from the division of labor, but went on to apply that principle not to social life but to politics (Rousseau had been wrong; deputies like himself, he thought, fully represented the nation at large; the task of voters was to vote, and that of representatives was to represent).

The inability of the propertied revolutionaries of all hues to resolve the gap between their universalist vision of transparent social forms and the reality of Parisian popular life strikes us with hindsight as having been little less than inexorable. We see the inevitability of the debate between Montagne and Gironde on what should be done with the Parisian sans-culottes. But to the participants, that same gap came as a complete surprise. That the Revolution would only be able to go forward with the help of the self-assertive Parisian plebs was something that few observers had foreseen, even in the summer of 1792.

In May and June 1793, with the help of the sans-culottes and of their enragés spokesmen and women (on whom he turned at once), Robespierre made good his universalist claims against the Girondins. In October 1793, women's societies were shut down. Vendean counterrevolution was destroyed. The nation in arms repulsed its foreign enemies. But Robespierre's system was deeply at odds with itself. The problem of Jacobinism was less in its ability to crush its opponents than in resolving its own contradictions. It was possible to institutionalize momentarily both the death penalty for partisans of the Loi Agraire and the decrees of Ventôse, which, in the version of Saint-Just, held out the possibility of land redistribution. But it was impossible to reconcile durably the conflicting goals that Jacobinism desperately sought to unite.

In 1789–1791, the various conflicting pieces of the Jacobin world view were easily fitted into a seamless whole. In 1793–1794, these arrangements decomposed. Jacobins as private persons continued to purchase biens nationaux while eulogizing the poor whom they simultaneously terrorized; but their professions of faith that had met at first with nearly universal approval gradually came to elicit nearly universal detestation. In late March 1794, Robespierre managed to execute the Hébertists who wished to use the sans-culottes to push the Terror forward. In early April, he executed the Dantonistes who wished for the Terror to stop. But by this time, Robespierre had few friends left. In the words of Saint-Just, the Revolution was "frozen."

In 1789–1791, even prudent social conservatives like Barnave, Lameth, and Mirabeau had been Jacobins, but in the hour of their trimuph, in 1794, Jacobins were very thin on the ground. Even before the fall of Robespierre in July, attendance in the clubs fell off. Jacobinism had been an irresistible political movement in 1791–1794, but it nearly vanished, and without much struggle, in late 1794–1795. Robespierre's system was less overthrown than it was unable to stand the weight of its contradictions: in the unstable Jacobin ideology of 1793–1794, the vision of the public good could no longer encompass both the defense of individualist property on the right, and the sansculottes' growing material and communitarian claims on the left.

Though by no means impossible in theory, this mix had become practically impossible in the spring of Year II. The differences that the philosophes had indolently thought republican politics might sublimate had in actual fact become wholly impossible to manage. Recourse to violence and Terror now came instinctively to frustrated statesmen who as private persons may well have been shocked by the physicality of violence and physical punishment, but whose first political concern had become the destruction of their myriad and ever more numerous enemies.

Inexorably, tragically, and to the dismay and even disbelief of its votaries, the Jacobin phantasmagoria had become an oppressive and murderous nightmare. In Vergniaud's words, the Revolution, like Saturn, devoured its own firstborn.

Taine conceptualized Jacobinism as the collective aspiration of revolutionary psychopaths, but it is more fruitful to see the *clubistes*, or many of them at least, in Derridian terms as the "sites" of conflicting forces whose deeper structures they could not grasp. True, many Jacobins, like Brissot, were consciously and outrageously manipulative; but contemporary accounts of conscious motivation are of curiously limited use in the understanding of French revolutionary politics. They do convey powerfully the amazement of admiring or horrified spectators; but it often happens that their frequently personalized accounts (Marat's cruelty, Robespierre's intransigence, Danton's audacity) are conceptually impoverished.

In any instance, by 1795, most Jacobins had come to regret their past. Men can learn from their mistakes. After 1794 (with the exception of the more obdurate, and much to be admired, communitarian "Martyrs de prairial," who were executed in 1795) all of the bourgeois patriots gradually realized that their private/public phantasmagoria had failed. As François Furet has aptly written, on 9 Thermidor, society recaptured politics. Going one step further, one might see in the drama of Robespierre's fall the birth pang of French civil society in modern times. Social fact, now conceptualized as an entity in its own right, triumphed over utopian hope. The revolutionary definition of legitimacy (i.e., the simultaneous pursuit of the rights of man in a universalist and even terroristic state) lost all significance, and the Thermidoreans were left with their threadbare claims as wielders of established and Republican legality,[20] a much-eroded concept that they themselves continued to violate in a tragicomic series of militarized coups from 1797 to 1799.

After having fallen away, bit by bit, from Jacobin orthodoxy in 1792–1794, the revolutionaries gradually reentered, bit by bit, in 1795–1797, a new and decidedly conservative Thermidorean consensus that merely parroted the heroic republicanism of Year II.

In 1791, on Robespierre's motion, the deputies of the Constituent Assembly had selflessly (and uniquely) declared themselves ineligible for reelection; in 1795, the Conventionnels selfishly ruled that two-thirds of their number would have to be included by the voters in the new assembly. Inevitably, the enemies of Robespierre, himself much hated, also lost whatever popular audience Jacobinism may have had—and beyond the limits of southeastern France that audience had never been too large. A politicized fear of the demanding poor now became the generalized catalyst of middle-class, nationalistic, and persecutory, anti-clerical republican politics, a system that desperately tried to stake an ever-shrinking, propagandistic middle ground, between royalist aristocrats on the right and impenitent *buveurs de sang* or *anarchistes* on the left. As a title, *De la Force du gouvernement et de la nécessité de s'y rallier* of 1795 is Benjamin Constant's unwitting and comic masterstroke.

The Thermidoreans' reassertion of social structures as the matrix of political action, or, restated, the claims of bourgeois civil society to construe the nature of private contracts as it saw fit, had many lamentable effects for all socially marginal groups, especially after the seizure of power by that modern and unprincipled condottierre, Napleone de Buonaparte: slavery was reimposed; husbands whose wives committed adultery in their legal domiciles acquired the legal right to murder delinquent couples should they be found in flagrante delicto. In any dispute, the word of the employer was always to matter more than that of his employee. Property became the focus of the Code Civil: employers managed it; workers did not have it; wives entrusted it to their husbands.

Overall, the historical loss was great, but the diminution of the public sphere did have one positive effect, namely the tentative expulsion of Terror and of murderous violence from routine politics.

The institutionalization of social transparency in May–June 1789 (that is to say, the breakup of a society of Estates) marked the instantaneous escalation of both popular and middle-class violence: a great gap distinguishes the classic, church–king popular violence of the Réveillon riots in April 1789 from the ghastly decapitations and eviscerations that occurred in July 1789 after the fall of the Bastille. Barnave's celebrated "ce sang était-il si pur?" of this same epoch also comes to mind. It is hardly fortuitous that the most egregious instance of popular violence—the September massacres—and of the middle-class violence—the Terror—should have coincided with the sudden and renewed, desperate assertion of republican classlessness, with its attendant collapse of traditionalist restraints.

So was it also, if from the other shore, that the reassertion of punitive social forms in 1795—now become those not of ancient Estates and order, but of modernizing social class—marked both the abrupt end of popular violence and the simultaneous, militarization and legalistic codification of republican violence.

The same collapse of accepted social categories that had made possible the lyricism of 1789, also transformed mild and ordinary individuals into persecutory tribunes, whose ability to punish was deployed by their detestation of anticivic "factions" and conspiracies. Good and evil were mixed without precedent in the minds of the Jacobins.

The destruction of restraints made ennobling heroism and self-sacrifice possible, but so did it simultaneously engender debasing cruelty. Marat's personality speaks to this bizarre mix of motives: kind in his personal relations, Marat protected some of his political enemies (like Lanthenas and Théroigne de Méricourt), and, as has been said, the man was deeply admired by the Républicaines Révolutionnaires of Claire Lacombe. But Marat was also the pathological apologist of blind execution, the apologist of the September massacres, a man who could and did arouse murderous and irresistible hatred.

The lifting in the summer of 1789 of man's mind-forged manacles was not without its costs. The revolutionaries had fully intended to banish not just violence but madness and "un-reason" from their regenerated universe, as Barère explained in Messidor of the Year II. During the Terror, however, the guillotine became a worshiped fetish, and recourse to it, a magical solution: "quand il y avait la guillotine, il y avait du pain. Et maintenant, il n'y a plus de pain."

From 1789 to 1794, ambiguities of motivation—and of morality—(like those of Marat) were common coin: in a now-celebrated pamphlet entitled *Français, encore un effort!*, the Marquis de Sade puckishly urged liberated Frenchmen to legalize rape and murder. After 1795, however, androgynous statements of this type became exceptions to a renewed rule of prosaic government. The decline of the Revolution's romantic imagination was also a signal for a return to law and order, however inadequate it may have been.

To paraphrase the words at once witty and profound of Marc Richir, the bourgeoisie did not (in 1789) make the Revolution. It was the failed universalist Revolution of 1793–1794 that brought into being a particularist, law-abiding, and unimaginative middle class that even privileged writers (Constant, Stendhal, Balzac, Flaubert, Baudelaire) instinctively knew to hate.

It was the varyingly perceived understanding of conceptual contradiction that sequentially forced the Jacobins of 1789 to give up, one by one, their shared and earlier vision of unshackled private interests effortlessly reconciled to unrestrained public good.

IV

Finally, the politics of the French Revolution also mark the beginnings of the history of modern France. We read forward to the Revolution from the shape of republicanism broadly defined under the Old Regime. We read forward from the revolution to the French civil wars of the nineteenth and twentieth centuries.

The most distinctive effect for France of the Revolution was to disjoin its political and social trajectories for a century and a half. The iconographically varied and ubiquitous political discourse of the Jacobin Revolution, with its fascinating and, by now, much-studied representational wealth and extravagance, became a self-referential and hegemonic universe of discourse. What it did not include (that is to say, the particularisms of region, class, and gender) could not be spoken.

The most important if invisible effect of this success was to make impossible in France the political representation of the corporate values that continued to underpin much of French daily life. A great deal is implied by Napoleon's basic inability to withdraw ordinary rights of citizenship from even his weakest subjects, namely, Jews, whose outmoded, particularist, and even privatist customs he so disliked. And the Restoration was no more able to achieve on behalf of the landowning nobility as a whole what Napoleon had tried to impose on the Jews, a distinct social existence recognized by law.

To the dismay of the ultramontanes like the young Lamennais, the church under Charles X, though privileged within the postrevolutionary state, was hardly favored as a freestanding entity. The grandmaster of the post-Napoleonic university might well be a cleric, but control of education was never handed over to the church, pure and simple. And the officialized inability of the restored, neotraditional monarchy of "Charles the Simple" to recreate a corporatized France was echoed in the internalized assumptions of even those Frenchmen who ought to have been most sympathetic to its organicist world view: surprisingly, most noble-born electors in 1830 voted against the *ultracisme* of Charles X. Louis-Philippe, like the royalist dukes of 1871 who founded the Third Republic, could only function politically by stealing other people's leftist clothes, which they often tried to do, but with no durable success.

Though the defense of "leftist" or communitarian values in French republican doctrine was after 1795 feeble to a degree (the near travesty of Renouvier's *solidarisme* comes to mind), the revolutionary interdict of 1789–1791 on the political representation of "rightist" or corporate values, of church, monarchy, and nobility, remained by contrast durable and strong. The year 1789 did not durably transform the material face of the French nation, but it most certainly set its political agenda by making impossible the expression of traditional corporatism in France and to a degree that has no analog in any other European nation of the time.

The spectacular variety and richness of life within the borders of an entity called France found its principal and impoverished public image in the flattened and distorting mirror of a centralized, distant, and bureaucratic state. An esthetic analog would.have been to make of official and historicizing, *lêché* painting the only tolerated mode of expression for the French pictorial imagination, to make of Delaroche or Gérôme, rather than Manet or Degas, the first painters of "Paris, Capital of the Nineteenth Century." The bureaucracy of the Ancien Régime had been concerned to raise the power of the king, but the revived centralism of the French state in the nineteenth century had as its effect to reduce particularisms and culturally to assimilate a socially atomized population.

Commodity fetishism, wrote Walter Benjamin, couples the living body to the inorganic world. The stultifying memory of Jacobinism fastened the richness of French life to a *passéiste* and sterile understanding of the French Revolution, an understanding that resurfaced historiographically as "the Social Interpretation of the Revolution."

Equality before the law was obviously a critical conquest (and one that would elude American blacks until our own time). The French and Republican definition of civil rights was conditional in its dependence on the nation, but it was in other respects genuinely universalist. At the same time, of course, the costs of transforming "peasants into Frenchmen" was very high, as was also the "domestication" of women.[21] From 1870 to 1918, France was (with Switzerland and San Marino) Europe's only durable Republic. But this unusual triumph was not without its many shadows. The republican left did triumph over royalist right in France, but late-nineteenth-century French republicanism, regardless of its good intentions, found it strangely difficult to make room for the "neocorporatist," particularist interests of the working class: men make their history, wrote Marx, but they do not make it as they please: "the traditions of all the dead generations," he concluded, "weigh like a nightmare on the brains of the living."

Without doubt, the numerous institutional achievements of the Third Republic were of lasting and liberating substance: the recognition of syndicalism in 1884, the encouragement of the peasant cooperative movement, the general extension of primary and secondary education to women (all of which were bitterly opposed by the right) were significant landmarks of popular empowerment. A juxtaposition of republican France and Wilhelminian Germany speaks mountains. Nonetheless, the fact remains that in the end, the Republic's voice was not one of those it chose, for its own reasons, to protect. The function if not the ostensible purpose of the republican scholarship system (of whom Daladier was a typical product) was more to coopt popular talent into the bourgeoisie than to provide a voice for the nation's popular majority.

The evolution of industrial capitalism in France was, by Anglo-American standards, unusually slow. The history of department stores is more relevant to the history of French capitalism than was the creation of mines and factories. But in spite of this muted and facilitating tempo in the realm of things, in spite of its emphasis on capitalism as a system of consumption rather than of production, the progression in France from liberalism-to-welfare-state in the realm of politics was unusually painful and disputed and, revealingly, when it finally occurred, Catholics on the right played a greater role in its inception than did the Socialists on the left.

In a parallel (non)development, the political emancipation of women was more quickly achieved in Britain than in France.

The Republic's premier Radical Socialist party certainly managed to ensconce itself after 1870 in the loyalties of a republicanized French peasantry that was close in spirit to the "petite-bourgeoisie" of urban France, but the existence of this popular audience in the countryside did not affect the social and procedural conservatism of its chosen representatives. Ominously, the obsessive assertion by French liberals of the nation as the only legitimate political and social entity, implied that the doctrines of the moderate left could never hope to secure in France the durable allegiance of the urban working class.

On the one hand, race, as a working political concept, was excluded from postrevolutionary discourse in France: though French more than German civil society seemed to be in 1895 a promising seedbed for anti-Semitic horrors, national French racialist complicity in the Holocaust was not as horrendous as might have been imagined: foreign Jews were disgracefully abandoned to their fate by the Vichy regime, but Jews of French nationality were fitfully protected. The French Revolution and its concept of citizenship, though socially limited, was not a cipher. In that protective and important sense, the French Revolution was an undoubtedly progressive event.

On the other hand, sex and class, like race, were also excluded by the ruling republicans as matrixes of political action. The strikingly mixed legacy of the French Revolution was to make of class and gender the cornerstones of a repressive social life (i.e., to engrave the feared memory of 1792–1795 when male and female sans-culottes had dared to raise their voices) and to deny the relevance of these concepts to public political life (i.e., to reinscribe in the nineteenth century the universalist, classless memory of 1789, but in the eviscerated and readjusted form that had served the socially conservative goals of the Directory in 1795–1799).

The failure of the fraternal Revolution split French society into social fragments that its anticorporatism was designed precisely not to heal, and this fragmentation ran deep. The ecumenical feelings of 1789 did not last. But the reverse most certainly could be said of the bitter class memories of 1792–1795 and of the attendant near-panic of the possessing class. The failed political application in 1793–1794 of an antecedent cultural and universalist upheaval engendered a divisive social earthquake that drastically altered French and even European social life for nearly two centuries to come.

Struck by the violent resolution in 1793–1794 of its innermost cultural contradictions, deeply alarmed by the anti-individualist drift of Jacobin communitarianism, the French possessing class that had accepted republicanism in 1792 developed, after 1800, a new and countervailing detestation of any politicized communitarian statement, however feebly generous it might be. The Rousseauistic and literary urge to privatize the experience of women now found explicit institutionalization in law and politics. (French women were not granted the vote until 1945.) The day-to-day fear of the urban poor that the French elite had begun to experience in the practice of daily life before 1789 but which could not be fully articulated at that time, was, with the failure of the French Revolution, violently stated in 1795 as the bourgeois detestation of the buveurs de sang, soon to become in the 1840s the celebrated "classes laborieuses, classes dangereuses."

In some material sense, by retarding French economic growth and by strengthening the hold of two precapitalistic groups—the landed, professional middle class and the peasantry—the great Revolution of 1789 did momentarily arrest the drift toward a modern society of classes. The inability of peasants (those celebrated potatoes in a sack) to think in class terms is well known, as is Robespierre's detestation of banks and money. But in the larger scheme of things, the French Revolution dramatically sharpened class and gender lines. The terroristic breakdown of the Revolution deployed class consciousness in France as would never have occurred in a more placid context. If one of its short-run effects was to reduce the condition of women to a level that in many significant ways was inferior to the one they had enjoyed in the last decades of the Old Regime, so was one of its long-run effects to set the stage for the republican massacres of the weak in 1848 and 1871. "La République is very fortunate," mused Louis-Philippe in exile. "It can afford to shoot the people."

The French Revolution created the bourgeoisie and, countervailingly, so did it help to create a doctrinally intransigent working class. From the seed of sans-culottism, and largely by reaction, working-class consciousness emerged as well. After the dramatic precedent of 1789, the theater of politics spontaneously produced the fruitless revolutions of the left in June 1848 and March of 1871. Proudhonism yielded to Marxist theories of class war and revolutionary violence. History, wrote Jean-Paul Richter, is the "Place La Morgue where everyone seeks the dead kinsmen of his heart."

V

Was the failed, terrorist, and class-bound denouement of the Revolution a fated event? Was Jacobinism doomed to failure? Ought we to speak of causes rather than of mere origins? The temptation to conclude affirmatively on this issue is quite strong. To be sure, in the newly created United States, some compromise was reached in much the same years between the Radical Whigs' communitarian ideology of virtue and the fearsomely individualist and capitalist nature of American social life. But the newly independent Americans were a profoundly religious people with a sharply defined communitarian, Golden Past that they yearned to recreate in a secularized republic. They were, after their war of Independence, convinced antimonarchists, with no historical reason to fear the variegated and unpredictable implications of pluralistic liberalism. Almost miraculously, the shape of American history during the last decades of the eighteenth century made possible in that new country the very synthesis of private gain and public good that proved to be so illusive in France.[22]

The ingredients of political catastrophe in the Grande Nation were by contrast very numerous, ranging as they did from a fabled and Tocquevillean incapacity for self-government to an atavistic neoreligious yearning for ideological, social, and political unity. These were great liabilities, compounded as they were by the incomplete nature of French economic change in the eighteenth century: the foundations of economic individualism in France were too weak to check after 1791 the drift toward holistic and terroristic virtue. Had the French Revolution been a social revolution, whose political discourse corresponded to some social bedrock, the ideological *dérapage* of revolutionary politics could hardly have occurred as it did. But it was, as it were, an antisocial revolution whose trajectory hinged on the inner logic of Jacobin ideology, and on the unavoidable if gradual realization of its inner contradictions.

Thermidor, as has been said, was aptly described by François Furet as the revenge of social forces over politics. We can extend this insight to prerevolutionary France as well. Jacobinism failed because its connection to the fabric of French social life was too weak. The origins of Jacobinism, of l'esprit révolutionnaire, were in a prerevolutionary cultural upheaval whose connection to new commercial and economic forms had been peripheral or even negative. More relevant to its genesis were ultimately ephemeral institutional mutations. The origins of Jacobinism were not in the development of capitalism within the framework of the Old Regime but in the categorical (and unstable) cultural rejection of traditionalist institutions by the propertied elite.

Simultaneously meritocratic and nationalist, the enlightened reader could no longer make his peace with the historicist particularism of the Old Regime, but he was not, for all that, prepared to construct a pluralist polity. The breakdown of revolutionary Jacobinism is implied by the divided, schizophrenic nature of antecedent French and enlightened thought, which was unable to sort out the rights of the individual from the responsibilities of the citizen. Its failure was embedded also by the setting of this mixed political culture in the tolerant but deceptive social void of a decaying Ancien Régime, when the older constraints of corporatism no longer seemed necessary but where the newer tensions of a society of class had not yet appeared.

Carlyle was right, then, if for the wrong reasons. In the late 1780s, the French Ancien Régime was, just as he wrote, doomed to bloody death. But the Revolution was to be no more able to avoid bloodshed and self-destruction than the Ancien Régime had been able to adapt itself to the needs of modern life.

NOTES

1. Delamare, *Traité de Police*, vol. 1., chap. 12, "Des Confrairies" (Amsterdam, 1729).

> Man is so obviously born for social life, that he makes of it his favored concern and his principal satisfaction. Hence his search for narrower associations in the natural order of things: not content with the first link which make of humankind one vast and single society, he has avidly sought other and more narrow unions, from which emerged in time families, Cities, and even greater States; and, in each one of those States, even more intimate societies, through particular professions and employments.

2. See my *Class, Ideology, and the Rights of Nobles During the French Revolution* (Oxford: Oxford University Press, 1981).

3. Cited by Dominique Godineau, *Citoyennes tricoteuses* (Alinéa, 1988), p. 15.

4. On this score, see the illuminating introduction by Elizabeth Badinter in *Paroles d'hommes (1790–1793)* (Paris: P.O.L., 1989), p. 34.

5. Thus, in the royalist newspaper *Journal de la ville et de la cour*, 16 May 1792: "Puisqu'il est impossible de trouver des hommes capables d'occuper longtemps la place de ministre, pourquoi ne pas recourir à Mmes Condorcet et Théroigne? Elles ont assez de talent pour être femmes publiques."

6. Butterfield, Lyman Henry, ed., *The Adams Family Correspondence*, letter to R. H. Lee (Cambridge: Harvard University Press, 1963), 4:172.

7. Dominique Godineau, *Citoyennes Tricoteuses*, p. 213.

8. *Sentiments sur quelques ouvrages de peinture, sculpture et gravure, écrits à un particulier en province* (Paris, 1754), pp. 91–92.

9. See "The Rose-Girl of Salency: Representations of Virtue in Prerevolutionary France," in *Eighteenth-Century Studies* (Spring 1989): 395–412.

10. José Ortega y Gasset, "Mirabeau el Politico" (1927) in *Obras Completas* (Madrid: Alianza Editorial, 1987), 3: 608.

11. Rumors of Chaumette's homosexual past were widely known.

12. See Anthoine Léonard Thomas, Diderot, Madame d'Epinay, *Qu'est-ce qu'une femme?* with a preface by Elizabeth Badinter (Paris: P.O.L., 1989).

13. See Lynn Hunt's review of the *Handbuch politisch-sozialer Grundbegriffe in Frankreich 1680–1720* in *Journal of Modern History* 60, 2 (June 1980): 387.

14. See Lucien Jeaume, *Le Discours Jacobin et la démocratie* (Paris: Fayard, 1988), and my review of this important book in *Commentaire* (Fall 1989).

15. Louis Sébastien Mercier, *Le Nouveau Paris*, ed. Fuchs, Pougens, et Crémer (Paris, 1798), 2: 100–101.

. . . is precisely an anti-federalist work, in that it strives to bring back all the parts of a state to a unicity of government, to that very unicity which Brissot wanted, as we all did, we who signed a proclamation to the departments on behalf of the exterior safety of France and of her internal union.

16. "I dared to conceive," wrote Lepelletier de Saint-Fargeau (a noble-born Jacobin) of a school designed to train revolutionary male elites, "of an inspiration more vast than that of mere instruction. Having considered the extent to which the human species has been corrupted by the vice of our former social system, I became convinced of the need to operate a complete regeneration and, if I dare to speak in this manner, of the need to create a new people."

17. As Romme wrote, "time opens up a new book in the history of man; and in its new and majestic march, as simple as equality, time needs to engrave anew the annals of regenerated France. The former era was a time of cruelty and mendacity, of perfidy and slavery. It ended with the monarchy, source of all our misery."

18. Cited in P. Barret and Jean Noël Gurgand, *Ils Voyagaient la France: Vie et traditions des compagnons du tour de France au 19e siècle* (1980), p. 93.

19. Cited in Elizabeth Badinter, *Paroles d'hommes (1790–1793)* (Paris: P.O.L., 1989), p. 33.

20. François Furet, *Interpreting the French Revolution*, trans. Elborg Forster (Cambridge: Cambridge University Press, 1981), p. 74.

21. Bonnie Smith's *Ladies of the Leisure Class* (Princeton: Princeton University Press, 1981) gives an unrivaled description of that process, but her interpretation of women's reaction to this change seems to us highly problematic.

22. This comparison is developed in Patrice Higonnet's *Sister Republics: The Origins of French and American Republicanism* (Cambridge: Harvard University Press, 1988).

FIVE

Jews into Frenchmen: Nationality and Representation in Revolutionary France

Gary Kates

On 2 January 1792 in the center of the northeastern French town of Nancy, recently elected political leaders gathered to officiate at a new kind of patriotic ceremony. Standing before the town council were fourteen of Nancy's most notable Jews, including the Grand Rabbi, ready to swear an oath of allegiance to the young regime. "The oath that we are about to take," announced Berr Isaac Berr, the lay leader of the local Jewish community, "makes us, thanks to the Supreme Being, and to the sovereignty of the nation, not only men, but French citizens." Never again, they believed, would French Jews be the victims of persecution because of their "religious opinions." Berr, however, made it perfectly clear that he did not believe emancipation meant assimilation. "Each of us will naturally follow the religion of his father," he remarked to his gentile countrymen. "Thus, we can be loyally attached to the Jewish religion and be at the same time good French citizens. Yes, Messieurs, that's what we will become. We swear it to you."[1]

In his response to this avowal, the mayor of Nancy happily welcomed Berr's remarks and declared what he thought to be the fundamental rationale behind Jewish emancipation: "Society must never investigate the beliefs of a citizen. Whatever the form he uses to honor the divinity does not matter so long as he obeys the Laws and serves his country." Then the mayor read the oath, which proclaimed the Jews' loyalty to the nation, to the laws, to the king, and to the Constitution. Each of the Jews responded: "I do swear."

Meanwhile, at Bischheim-au-Saum, a village near Strasbourg, Jews had a more difficult time convincing municipal leaders that they were worthy of emancipation. The town council kept putting off at least five eminent Jews who wanted to take the oath by declaring that every oathtaker must cross himself. That was the only way, the council insisted, that they could be sure that the person was telling the truth. The Jews refused to cross themselves, arguing that it was a violation of their newly won religious freedom. In March 1792, negotiations broke down over this point until both sides appealed to the departmental Directory, a regional authority that spoke on behalf of the central government. The Directory agreed with the Jews, stating that the law required "simply the obligation of taking the civic oath, without prescribing either the form nor the manner in which it will be made." The Directory ordered the town to go ahead with its ceremony.

Because of the controversy, thirty local national guard troops were assigned to the ceremony, which was finally set for 18 April. As the ceremony was beginning, however, there were cries from the crowd, particularly from the national guardsmen, for the Jews to remove their hats. The Jewish leaders refused to do so, claiming that one should never make an oath in God's presence without covering the head. The crowd, of course, argued the reverse, and the municipality was forced to cancel the event, lest it turn into a riot. Once again both sides appealed to the Directory, and once again the Directory sided with the Jews, accusing the town council of obstructing the law. Finally, on 30 April, at the insistence of the Directory, the five most prominent Jews of Bischheim succeeded in swearing allegiance to their country, thereby winning their full political rights.

These ceremonies, the result of the law passed by the Constituent Assembly on 27 September 1791 which granted full political rights to Ashkenazic Jews, allow us to examine the ways in which Jewish emancipation was received at the local level. We find leading Jews stubbornly determined to acquire full political rights and equally determined to maintain their religious identity. At the same time, we see French revolutionary leaders insisting on the principles of equality before the law and religious freedom, even at the risk of offending local constituencies. Consequently, ever since these early days of the French Revolution, Jewish emancipation has been seen as something of a watershed in both French and Jewish history. For the French, the law meant that their country was the first modern European nation–state to offer Jews political equality. For the Jews, emancipation meant the beginning of their "Haskalah," the end to the ghetto and centuries of forced separation from gentiles. For both French and Jews, then, Jewish emancipation signaled an entirely new kind of epoch: secular, free, and tolerant.

Yet now, in the midst of the bicentennial celebration of the French Revolution, it has become increasingly difficult to see the emancipation movement in such a sanguine light. The tragic events of our own century have made emancipation at best problematic, and perhaps even irrelevant. From the Dreyfus Affair to the Holocaust, the overriding theme of European Jewry has been its destruction, not its liberation. Berr Isaac Berr pledged that his people would survive as Jews, because it is natural for people to follow "the religion of their fathers." But except for a few very rare families, few French—indeed, few European—Jewish families today can trace their genealogy back to the eighteenth century. Those Jews who did not assimilate were murdered or, if they were lucky, were forced to flee Europe. For many in the generation who lived through the Holocaust, the destruction of European Jewry in this century has made eighteenth-century Jewish emancipation seem like a tragic farce.

Among the most eminent of this generation who share that perspective is Rabbi Arthur Hertzberg. Holder of a Distinguished Chair at Dartmouth, former head of the World Zionist Congress, regular contributor to the "Op-Ed" page of the *New York Times*, as well as to the *New York Review of Books*, Rabbi Hertzberg has established himself as one of the most prominent intellectuals in the American Jewish community, and his book, *The French Enlightenment and the Jews: The Origins of Modern Anti-Semitism*,[2] quickly became the definitive discussion of the subject. Its argument is original and disturbing. Until Hertzberg, most writers held the view that modern anti-Semitism was a right-wing phenomenon that surfaced during the late nineteenth century in opposition to the liberal ideas usually associated with the French Revolution. But Hertzberg turned that contention upside down: twentieth-century anti-Semitism, he claimed, is not in conflict with French revolutionary ideology but in fact stems from it. "Modern, secular, anti-Semitism," he wrote, "was fashioned not as a reaction to the Enlightenment and the Revolution, but within the Enlightenment and Revolution themselves."[3] For Hertzberg, Jewish emancipation was the first step in the long march to Auschwitz.

Hertzberg did not simply claim that those who opposed emancipation were anti-Semitic but argued further that even the proemancipation legislators contributed to modern anti-Semitism: they saw emancipation as the only way to assimilate the Jew and rid France of its "Jewish problem." Once Jews lost their communal autonomy and faced the centralized state as individual Frenchmen, Hertzberg claimed, their days were numbered. The hostility of the Jacobins to all religious expression during the Terror offered Hertzberg the proof that he needed.

Hertzberg's argument managed to combine the ideas of three influential Jewish intellectuals: Hannah Arendt, Jacob Talmon, and Asher Ginzberg (better known as Ahad Ha'am). From Arendt's *Origins of Totalitarianism*, Hertzberg gleaned two fundamental concepts: first, that in the modern age the revolutionary left and the radical right are equally repressive. Since revolutionary change most often depends on the coercive power of the centralized state, its impact on the individual is bound to be tyrannical. Second, Arendt claimed that anti-Semitism had played a crucial role in recent European history. "Political developments have driven the Jewish people into the storm center of events," she wrote. The way that Europe treated its Jews could be taken as a bellwether of the quality of European political culture.[4]

Arendt had specifically noted that these features were true only for the contemporary world. She pushed back her analysis to the last decades of the nineteenth century, but no further. Although elsewhere Arendt was later highly critical of the French Revolution, nowhere did she accuse the Jacobins of establishing a totalitarian or anti-Semitic state.[5] For her, modern racial anti-Semitism was novel and distinct from older attitudes, preventing any explanation of the Holocaust from reaching back as far as the eighteenth century.

Jacob Talmon's *Origins of Totalitarian Democracy* provided that continuity for Hertzberg. In Jacobinism, Talmon discovered "a vision of society of equal men re-educated by the State in accordance with an exclusive and universal pattern."[6] Like Arendt, Talmon considered the radical left to be as repressive as the right. The Jacobins had acted fanatically, he believed, systematically violating individual liberties on behalf of a messianic ideal. But while Talmon attacked the liberal ideals of the revolutionary left, he ignored Jewish emancipation altogether.

Both Arendt and Talmon, then, sought to discredit the revolutionary left and provide a historical model that justified a more moderate approach to political change. Moreover, like Hertzberg, Arendt and Talmon were both dedicated Zionists, committed in their personal lives to developing an authentic Jewish political culture. Arendt had worked for Youth Aliyah (Jewish immigration to Palestine) programs before World War II and had published articles during the 1940s on Zionist strategy. Talmon moved to Israel after an education in Britain and taught for years at the Hebrew University in Jerusalem. Both, in short, were highly suspicious of the emancipation process as well as the promises of the revolutionary left. But neither of them blamed modern anti-Semitism on the French revolutionary emancipators.[7]

For the notion that the emancipation process *itself* lay at the root of modern anti-Semitism, Hertzberg drew on the writings of Ahad Ha'am (1856–1927), the Zionist "secular rabbi" who first began to write in his native Russia during the 1880s and finally moved to Palestine in 1921. Ahad Ha'am had directly attacked France and French Jews for their faith in political emancipation, charging that the Jews' so-called freedom was little more than a mirage. "Their condition may be justly defined as *spiritual slavery under the veil of outward freedom*," he wrote in 1891 (emphasis added). "In reality they accepted this slavery a hundred years ago, together with their 'rights'; but it is only in these evil days that it stands revealed in all its glory." Ahad Ha'am condemned Jews for giving up their separate national identity not so much because he distrusted France, but rather because he did not believe that Jews could maintain a religious identity of any significant value in an epoch in which the broader culture had become almost completely secular. Accepting even the best of circumstances for the emancipated Jew, Ahad Ha'am insisted on asking a nagging question: Why would French Jews choose to remain Jewish "for the sake of certain theoretical beliefs which they no longer hold, or which, if they do really and sincerely maintain them, they might equally hold without this special name, as every non-Jewish Deist has done?"[8]

It is a tribute to Hertzberg's rhetorical skills that he was able to combine distinct arguments from these three thinkers into a powerful interpretation that blamed the tragic events of the twentieth century on the French revolutionary emancipation process itself. "It is strange that he did not even mention the Jewish question during the Revolution," Hertzberg wrote of Talmon.[9]

> Here there can be no doubt whatsoever that the Revolution was "totalitarian." Almost all of those who helped to emancipate the Jews, from Grégoire through Robespierre, had in mind some vision of what they ought to be made to become. Talmon's critics may be correct in maintaining that the main body of the revolutionaries, the political center, were willing to leave men to be themselves within the new political order. It was these very people, however, who made demands not only on the public behavior but also on the inner spirit and religion of the Jews. Here the Revolution appeared at its most doctrinaire.

Hertzberg put the blame for modern anti-Semitism on the proemancipators themselves, especially on left-wing deputies who hoped to push France in a more democratic direction. Behind such logic is a clear Zionist agenda. Since the Haskalah, when Jews emerged from their communal autonomy, Western nation–states have faced essentially three choices with regard to their Jewish communities: integration, expulsion, or destruction, or encouraging the establishment of a separate Jewish state. Clearly the French revolutionaries chose the first alternative and, in fact, never seriously contemplated any of the others. The novelty of Hertzberg's argument is that he discredits integration by associating it with expulsion or destruction. Insofar as the French expected Jews to assimilate into French society and culture, they had no respect for Judaism or the Jewish people, he charges. Emancipation was just another way for the French to get rid of their Jews. In this view Zionism was and remains the only response to modernity that is good for Jews.

The problem with Hertzberg's argument is not with his ideology; the notion that Jews are a nation entitled to their own state is certainly legitimate. Rather, it is Hertzberg's understanding of history that is problematic. His interpretation of the French Revolution is highly reductionist. He conflates different phases of the Revolution together, assuming that the achievements of the liberal Constituent Assembly were merely a prelude to the Terror; Hertzberg ignores the differences between the democratic movement of 1790–1792 and the sans-culottes movement of 1793–1794.[10] Worse, by pulling the debates over emancipation out of their proper political context, he distorts the views of the proemancipators as well as the antiemancipators, who were, obviously, more concerned about the fate of France and her revolution than with Jewish national destiny. Finally, Hertzberg's analysis does an injustice to the Jews themselves. Berr Isaac Berr and hundreds of others who took the loyalty oaths required for full emancipation were not simply fools deceived by their countrymen but patriots who were exploiting a historic opportunity.

Despite these flaws in his analysis, Hertzberg has focused on some genuine historical problems concerning Jewish emancipation which still require attention: given that the Declaration of the Rights of Man and Citizen was passed in August 1789, why did French Jews have to wait two years before being offered full political rights? Why did the proemancipators equate emancipation with assimilation? Why did they have so little respect for the integrity of an autonomous Jewish identity that they expected Jews to dissolve their official communal institutions?

Perhaps the most amazing aspect of Jewish emancipation is that it happened at all. French Jews, in fact, constituted only a tiny fraction of French society. Moreover, they were concentrated into relatively few towns. Some 3,500 Sephardic Jews lived in and around Bordeaux, 30,000 Ashkenazic Jews lived in Alsace and Lorraine, and perhaps 500 others lived in Paris. Nor was their participation in the Revolution particularly noteworthy. There were no Jews, to my knowledge, elected to any of the national assemblies during the Revolution. And outside of the debate over their own fate, it is difficult to think of one Jewish writer, journalist, or political activist who played more than the most minor role. It is likely that the vast majority of Frenchmen, including those deputies sitting in the Constituent Assembly, had never met even a handful of Jews, if that many.

These facts have led Eugen Weber to argue that "the Jewish question was a *Jewish* question," that is, of interest only to Jews. "Most normal French," he asserted to a rather dismayed audience at a 1985 conference on the history of Jews in France, have not cared about Jews and don't care to think much about them now. Outside of Alsace, "the French thought about Jews hardly at all. They had other fish to fry."[11] But surely Weber was exaggerating. Otherwise, how do we explain the inordinate amount of attention given to the Jewish issue by the French revolutionaries? No agenda has ever been more full than was the Consitutent Assembly's. It had to deal with such crucial issues as the constitution, taxation, the reorganization of the church, and an increasingly recalcitrant king, not to mention their own internal disputes and factions. Many other pressing issues, such as women's rights, were ignored. Certainly it was not imperative that the Constituent Assembly deal with the Jewish question; and at least some deputies did not think it was worth it. "We have even more important matters to deal with," exclaimed the moderate leader Guy Target during one of the debates:

What we say in regard to the Jews affects only a part of society; but to establish a judiciary, to determine the size and manner of the French army, to establish a financial system, here are three issues that interest the entire kingdom, and which require immediate action.[12]

But the Jewish question did not go away. Leaders of the National Assembly kept returning it to the agenda. Even the Paris municipal legislature considered Jewish emancipation very important, though there were only five hundred Jews living in the capital. At one point during the early weeks of 1790, nearly every one of Paris's sixty district assembiles debated the issue and, by an overwhelming majority, urged the National Assembly to fully emancipate all Jews.[13]

Thus Target was off target on one major point: few people treated the debate on the Jews as concerning only "a part of society." Non-Jews chose to address this issue because the emancipation debate was not really about the Jews at all. Since there were so few Jews in France, and since they played little role in the Revolution, they were easily turned into symbols of something else. Various groups and writers, including the Paris Communal Assembly and the national Constituent Assembly, used the issue to test what was then perhaps the most fundamental political question: Would the promises inherent in the Declaration of the Rights of Man and Citizen translate into equal political power for all Frenchmen, regardless of status, or would those leading the Revolution stop short of democracy by limiting the political power of certain kinds of people? The debate over Jewish emancipation was thus a debate over what it meant to be a French citizen.

In fact, it has been argued that French Jews did not need emancipation, at least no more so than any other group in France. Although we think of the era before the French Revolution as a bleak period in Jewish history, the status of the Jew was much better in France during the last decades of the Old Regime than in most other European countries. Old Regime society was corporate and particularistic. The law recognized individuals only insofar as they held membership in a legal group. A tailor needed the protection of his guild, a priest his religious order, a merchant his town corporation, and so on. In this respect, Jews were considered legitimate subjects of the king if they were attached to a legally recognized Jewish community. Political life usually consisted of each separate group gaining its own privileges from the royal government at the expense of every other group. As Salo Baron noted sixty years ago, throughout the eighteenth century French Jews were particularly adept at securing special laws for their communities. "Even then they belonged to the privileged minority which included nobles, clergy and urban citizenry."[14] This is perhaps an exaggeration but, at least in terms of legal advantages, the political status of most Jews was greater than that of most peasants. Jewish communities prospered at the pleasure of the royal government and often against the muffled shouts of the peasants who, especially in Alsace and Lorraine, were hostile to Jews. Despite local bigotry, by the eve of the Revolution royal reformers such as Malesherbes were calling for further reform. So long as the central government continued its policy of protecting Jewish interests, French Jews could reasonably expect to be optimistic about the future.

But the French Revolution threw the status of the Jews into confusion. Without their privileged and autonomous communities, Jews were vulnerable to the passions of the local peasants and small shopkeepers. If the new French government became decentralized, Jews might even stand to lose much more than they might gain by the new changes. The Constituent Assembly first discussed the Jewish question on 28 September 1789 because northeastern French Jewish communities had asked for protection from popular violence that had broken out during the summer. The moderate leader Stanislas Clermont-Tonnerre and the radical priest Henri Grégoire urged the Assembly to adopt the following decree:

> The Assembly decrees M. the President to write to the public officials of Alsace that the Jews are under the safeguard of the law and require of the king the protection that they need.[15]

This bill passed with no opposition, and its importance should not be minimized. On the one hand it continued the policies of the old central government of protecting Jews against local persecution and, in that sense, represented no great change for Jews. But insofar as it brought Jews under the same laws as everyone else, it gave them a high degree of civic equality. This was very close to de facto emancipation. Why, then, did it take the Assembly another two years (and hours of tumultuous debate) to go any further?

At about the same time, the Assembly was working out the electoral laws that would operate under the new constitution. Although the Assembly pledged that the constitution and its laws would apply equally to all citizens, they nonetheless made a fundamental distinction between two kinds of citizens: Active and Passive. Both kinds of citizens were treated equally under the law and held the rights guaranteed in the Declaration of the Rights of Man and Citizen. The difference between them was that only active citizens could vote and hold public office. The most important qualification for active citizenship was wealth: one had to pay a direct tax that amounted to three days' wages for an average worker. In addition, there were gradations of active citizenship. For example, only those who paid an annual tax of about fifty-one livres—a sum well out of reach of most Frenchmen—were eligible for seats in the National Assembly.

Hertzberg and others have ignored the fact that the 28 September 1789 decree effectively transformed Jews into passive citizens. From that day on, no one in the Constituent Assembly denied Jews the basic rights guaranteed in the Declaration of the Rights of Man and Citizen; all agreed, for example, that Jews ought to be free to observe their own religious opinions and should not be forcibly converted. The issue, then, became not one of religious freedom, but rather of the extent to which Jews were qualified to be active citizens. In other words, Hertzberg's claim that "the battle for the Emancipation very nearly failed" needs to be radically qualified: what nearly failed was the attempt to secure the rights of active citizenship for Jews.[16]

Thus when we turn to the debates concerning Jewish rights that took place at the Constituent Assembly on 23–24 December 1789 and 28 January 1790, we find that the bill in question focuses on aspects of active citizenship:[17]

> That non-Catholics, who will have otherwise fulfilled all the conditions prescribed in previous decrees for becoming an elector and eligible [for public office] could be elected to all ranks of administration, without exception.

In December this bill passed only when Jews were specifically excluded from it. One month later, a similar bill gave the rights of active citizenship to the Sephardic Jews of Bordeaux and Avignon. But a majority of the Assembly refused to "emancipate" the Ashkenazic Jews of eastern France. Why?

Opposition to offering Jews the rights of active citizenship came from three overlapping groups. First were a small core of deputies from Alsace, most notably Jean-Francois Reubell. They clearly echoed the popular anti-Semitism of their region, reflecting a fear of Jewish financial power and, above all else, of usury. Because Jews were concentrated primarily in this part of France, these attitudes were isolated, and this group alone could not have persuaded a majority of their colleagues to vote against Jewish active citizenship.

A second and larger group consisted of clergymen and friends of the church who saw French nationality in religious terms. What concerned the Abbé Maury, for example, was the notion that emancipated Jews could be elected to positions of leadership in what he assumed should be a Christian nation. He thought the prospect of a Jewish judge pronouncing justice on a Christian defendant absurd; for him, the law derived from the sovereign will of a people, 99 percent of whom were Christians. But this did not mean that Maury wished to expel the Jews:

> They must not be persecuted. They are men; they are brothers; and it is an anathema to even consider talking about intolerance. You have already recognized that nothing should be done about their religious opinions, and since then you have assured Jews the broadest protection.[18]

In short, even Maury, among the Constituent Assembly's most conservative and "theocratic" deputies, recognized the importance of the September 1789 decree and was not offended by the idea of Jews living in France as passive citizens; rather, what disturbed him was the possibility of being ruled by them.

Finally, a coalition of conservative deputies wanted to exclude Jews from political life because their goal was to restrict active citizenship to as small a group as possible. These deputies, such as Prince de Broglie, hoped to transform active citizenship into a new kind of aristocracy. Jews, Protestants, actors, urban workers, sans-culottes—anyone who was not of the highest class, they felt, should be denied the right to vote and hold office.

These three groups also had in common the belief that French Jews, especially the Ashkenazim in eastern France, constituted a separate nation within France. The differences in language, dress, marriage, and obviously religious rituals made the Jew as different from the Frenchman as an Englishman or Dane. "The Jews collectively are a *corps de nation* separate from the French," charged Reubell. "They have a distinct role. Thus they can never acquire the status of an Active Citizen."[19] When all was said and done, this was the most effective argument of the antiemancipators, successful enough to retard full emancipation until the final days of the Constituent Assembly.

The concept of nationality was extremely important in French revolutionary ideology precisely because it replaced the idea of subjects kept apart by privilege with the notion of citizens brought together through their common national identity. For its leaders, the French Revolution was precisely the act of the French nation repossessing the sovereign state from king and aristocracy. The "people" and the "nation" were often, but not always, considered the same thing. When the people acted according to their self-interest, they were merely a collection of individuals. But when the people shared a common interest, their actions were perceived as expressing the national will.

This definition of nationality, so important for the development of political ideas during the Revolution, is most clearly seen in Sieyès's popular pamphlet, *What Is the Third Estate?* In it, Sieyès described three stages of national development. At first there are a great number of isolated individuals who wish to unite, but they do not yet recognize a common interest. "The second period is characterized by the action of the *common* will. . . . Power exists only in the aggregate. The community needs a common will; without singleness of will it could not succeed in being a willing and acting body." This was the point at which the Revolution occurred. Finally, Sieyès distinguished a future "third period from the second in that it is no longer the *real* common will which is in operation, but a *representative* common will."[20]

Drawing heavily upon Rousseau, Sieyès's ideas were radical because they negated the political legitimacy of all corporate bodies. The Revolution dissolved them all, leaving in their place individuals whose rights were protected by their membership in a nation–state. In this sense "the Jewish question" boiled down to the following problem: Did Jews constitute a nation distinct from the French (and thus were not part of the new sovereign body)? Or were Jewish communities essentially autonomous corporations, like any other in the Old Regime? This was the essential issue that divided proemancipators from their opponents. The antiemancipators believed that during the Old Regime, Jewish communities constituted both corporations and a separate nation. Therefore although the Revolution had dissolved corporations, it still left the nationality problem unresolved. Antiemancipators, such as the Abbé Maury, therefore proposed something of a compromise: in return for the elimination of Jewish corporate autonomy, Jews ought to be given the basic rights of passive citizens. But insofar as their nationality makes them distinct from the sovereign, they should be refused the rights of active citizenship.

The proemancipators constructed their argument around the notion that the Jews of France did not constitute a separate nation but merely a corporation, which, like other corporations, was in dire need of "regeneration." Clermont-Tonnerre offered the best-known version of this position: "One must refuse everything to the Jews as a nation, and give everything to the Jews as individuals. . . . It would be repugnant to have a society of noncitizens in a state, and a nation within a nation."[21] Commenting on the debate, future Girondin chief Jacques-Pierre Brissot predicted that those Jews who were given the rights of active citizens would "lose their particular characteristics." Their "admission to eligibility will regenerate them."[22]

Arthur Hertzberg is correct to see in the proemancipation position the call for an end to Jewish distinctiveness. But he is mistaken in his assertion that this position was the seedbed for anti-Semitism or totalitarianism. The necessity for some kind of "regeneration" stems from the French revolutionary conception of representation. In some representative systems, the deputy is supposed to represent the interests of the majority of voters who elected him. But during the French Revolution, to quote Sieyès again, "every deputy is representing the entire nation."[23] In contrast to the United States, in which legislators represent different interests and constituencies, the French expected their leaders to search only for the one true will of the nation. Any group of deputies who openly represented a particular interest or constituency separate from the national will was considered a dangerous faction. Thus no significant differences could be allowed to arise between a deputy and his constituency, much less between the deputies themselves.

This concept of representation had important implications for the Jews of France. Since granting rights of active citizenship to Jews would make them eligible for various offices, the possibility arose that a Jew could represent a nation that was overwhelmingly Christian, when most of those Christians were ineligible to hold political office. How could a Jewish elector, for example, participate in an election for a bishop (such elections began in late 1790)? Proemancipators such as Sieyès and Grégoire resolved this dilemma by arguing that the Jewish politician should think only about the welfare of the entire nation, relegating his Jewish life strictly to the private sphere. In order for him to adequately represent the true interests of his nation, his own Jewishness, while remaining personally important to him, must have no political significance.

The Ashkenazic Jews did not win their full political rights until the final days of the Constituent Assembly in September 1791. By then the political mood of the country had changed drastically. Many aristocratic deputies had become disgusted by the pace of revolutionary change, and they were fleeing the country. The moderate leaders were less convinced that the king would abide by the new constitution, and they feared that power would fall into the hands of radical republicans. In this new political context, granting Jews the rights to active citizenship no longer seemed so dangerous. Thus when the popular leader Adrien Duport urged his colleagues to "declare relative to the Jews that they can become French Active Citizen," they decreed that all Jews must have the same rights to "becoming Active Citizens" as any other citizen. Thus "emancipation" was equated with active citizenship, while passive citizenship had long ago been assumed by everyone.[24]

These debates over Jewish emancipation do not reveal an anti-Semitic or even a mean-spirited Constituent Assembly. The hypothesis that emancipation itself provided the seedbed for later tragedies turns out to have been based on a distorted view of French revolutionary politics. Insofar as the Jews were concerned, the early French revolutionaries basically carried on the liberal policies of the preceding government. Anti-Semitism was a local affair, confined to northeastern France. The political status of French Jews changed between 1789–1791 because Frenchmen themselves were transformed from subjects of a kingdom to citizens of a nation. If the Constituent Assembly spent many noisy hours over the fate of the Jews, it was because "the Jewish question" raised issues fundamental to their own identity: it helped to define the secular character of the state, the meaning of active and passive citizenship, the nature of representation, and the place of corporate bodies within the new regime. It also gave radical and moderate politicians an issue they could use to fight the power of the church and the aristocracy.

More fundamentally, the debates over Jewish emancipation reveal not a Jewish problem but a problem the *French* had defining nationality and representation. Unlike the newly created United States, the French did not conceive of representation in terms of separate interests; only a unitary national will could be the ultimate political expression of French sovereignty. This approach impeded the development of a "loyal opposition," as well as of party politics, and it led France away from political stability. Hertzberg may be correct that this kind of democracy is not good for Jews; indeed, it may not be good for anyone. But this is a political problem and has little to do with anti-Semitism.

Zionist critics distrust the emancipation process because they correctly believe that it represented a renunciation of an autonomous Jewish national destiny. But it is wrong to blame emancipators like Clermont-Tonnerre and Grégoire for what would happen to Jews 150 years later. Worse, it makes fools of those Jews who, since Berr Isaac Berr, have believed in the integrity of the diaspora. In fact, the French Revolution offered French Jews a historic opportunity. Emancipation gave every Jew the *choice* of being Jewish. Participation in the Jewish community was no longer a legal obligation but became instead a moral duty. Only in this context could Jewish identity become a matter of intense personal concern.

NOTES

Funds for researching and writing the essay on which this chapter is based were generously provided by the Faculty Development Committee of Trinity University. I would like to thank John Martin, Judi Lipsett, and Char Miller for their valuable suggestions.

1. David Feuerwerker, *L'Emancipation des juifs en France de l'Ancien Régime à la fin du Second Empire* (Paris, 1976), pp. 429–441. The account from Bischheim-au-Saum also comes from this source.

2. Rabbi Arthur Hertzberg, *The French Enlightenment and the Jews: The Origins of Modern Anti-Semitism* (New York: Columbia University Press, 1968).

3. Ibid., p. 7.

4. Hannah Arendt, *The Origins of Totalitarianism* (New York, 1973 [1951]), p. 7. Hertzberg comments on Arendt in *The French Enlightenment*, pp. 6–7.

5. See Hannah Arendt, *On Revolution* (New York, 1963).

6. J. L. Talmon, *The Origins of Totalitarian Democracy* (New York, 1970 [1952]), p. 250.

7. For Arendt see Elizabeth Young-Bruehl, *For the Love of the World: A Biography of Hannah Arendt* (New Haven, 1982). Given Talmon's commitment to Zionism and his interest in Jewish history, it is curious that he was silent about Jewish Emancipation. This omission has caused some confusion among his colleagues. On the one hand, Yehoshua Arieli insists that Talmon "perceived the 'Jewish problem' of modern Europe and the modern world as the touchstone, the main indicator and precipitate, of the major trends and problems of modern times, indicating the degree of virulence of the collective neuroses as well as accelerating them." But British political theorist John Dunn is probably closer to the truth when he claims that Talmon's most basic problem was not the Jewish question but rather: "Why exactly is the political character of Communist regimes such an unremitting disaster?" See the articles by Arieli and Dunn in *Totalitarian Democracy and After: International Colloquium in Memory of Jacob L. Talmon* (Jerusalem, 1984), pp. 25, 42. For Talmon's interest in Jewish history and politics see his *The Unique and the Universal* (New York, 1965), and *Israel Among the Nations* (New York, 1970).

8. *Selected Essays of Ahad Ha'Am*, trans. Leon Simon (New York, 1970 [1912]), pp. 177, 184. For Hertzberg on Ahad Ha'am see *The Zionist Idea*, ed. Arthur Hertz-

berg (New York, 1981 [1959]), pp. 248–277; and Arthur Hertzberg, *Being Jewish in America: The Modern Experience* (New York, 1979), p. xiii.

9. Hertzberg, *The French Enlightenment*, p. 363.

10. On the tendency to reduce the French Revolution to the Terror alone, see Ferenc Fehér, *The Frozen Revolution: An Essay on Jacobinism* (Cambridge, 1987), pp. 1–30.

11. Eugen Weber, "Reflections on the Jews in France," in Frances Malino and Bernard Wasserstein eds., *The Jews in Modern France* (Hanover and London, 1985), p. 17.

12. *Archives parlementaires de 1787 à 1860. Recueil complet des débats législatifs et politiques des chambres françaises. Première série (1787 à 1799)*, 88 vols. to date (Paris, 1867–) (hereafter cited as *AP*), 11: 710.

13. On Paris see S. Lacroix, "Ce qu'on pensait des juifs à Paris en 1790," *Revolution française* 30 (1898): 91–112.

14. Salo W. Baron, "Ghetto and Emancipation: Shall We Revise the Traditional View?" *The Menorah Journal* 14 (June 1928): 517; Salo W. Baron, "Newer Approaches to Jewish Emancipation," *Diogenes* 29 (Spring 1960): 56–81. For a more general survey see also Feuerwerker, *L'émancipation des juifs*, pp. 3–48.

15. *AP*, 9: 201.

16. Hertzberg, *The French Enlightenment*, p. 339.

17. *AP*, 10: 782.

18. *AP*, 10: 757.

19. *AP*, 11: 364.

20. Emmanuel Joseph Sieyès, *What Is the Third Estate?*, trans. M. Blondel (London, 1963), pp. 121–122.

21. *AP*, 10: 754.

22. *Patriote français*, 24 December 1789, p. 2.

23. Quoted in Keith Michael Baker, "Representation," in Baker, ed., *The French Revolution and the Creation of Modern Political Culture. 1: The Political Culture of the Old Regime* (Oxford, 1987), p. 488.

24. *AP*, 31: 372.

SIX

The French Revolution as a World-Historical Event

Immanuel Wallerstein

The significance or importance of the French Revolution has usually been analyzed in one of two ways: as an "event" in French history which has its course and consequences; or as a phenomenon that had a specific influence on the history of other countries. I wish in this chapter however to view the French Revolution as a world-historical event in the very specific sense of its significance and importance in the history of the modern world system as a world system.

As we know, the literature on the French Revolution of the last thirty years has reflected a gigantic intellectual battle between two principal schools of thought. On the one side, there has been the so-called social interpretation, of which Georges Soboul has been the central figure and which traces its lineage to Lefebvre, Mathiez, and Jaurès. This viewpoint has built its analysis around the theme that the French Revolution was essentially a political revolution of the bourgeoisie who were overthrowing a feudal Ancien Régime.

A second camp has emerged in "revisionist" criticism of the social interpretation of the French Revolution. This second camp has no accepted collective name. The two leading exponents of this view have been first Alfred Cobban and then François Furet. This camp rejects the concept of the French Revolution as a bourgeois revolution on the grounds that eighteenth-century France can no longer be meaningfully described as "feudal." Rather, they suggest that it can better be described as "despotic" and the French Revolution seen as a political explosion of antidespotic libertarian demands.*

---

*The so-called Atlantic thesis is an amalgam of these two perspectives, although it was presented initially prior to the revisionist work. The Atlantic thesis is that the French Revolution was both bourgeois and antidespotic. It is furthermore world-systemic in that its origins and that of the other more or less simultaneous "Atlantic" revolutions were in the common fount of Enlightenment thought. One can see this as marrying either the best or the worst of the other two theses.

The key difference this makes in the analysis of the actual events revolves around the interpretation of the political meaning of the insurrection of 10 August 1792. For Soboul, this insurrection was a "second revolution" ushering in a democratic and popular republic. For Furet, it was exactly the opposite. It was the closure of the path leading to the liberal society. It was no doubt a second revolution, but one that represented not the fulfillment of the first but its *dérapage*. Thus, for Soboul, Robespierre and the Mountain represented the most radical segment of the French bourgeoisie and therefore a force for liberation; for Furet, Robespierre and the Mountain represented a new (and worse) despotism.

In this debate the lines are clearly drawn and are certainly familiar ones in terms of twentieth-century European politics. Indeed, as has often been said, this debate is as much an argument about the Russian Revolution as it is about the French Revolution. It is important nonetheless to see what premises are *shared* by the two camps in rhetorical battle. They both share a model of history that is developmental and which assumes that the units that develop are states. (The Atlantic thesis also shares this model.) For the social-interpretation school, all states go through successive historical stages, the most relevant transition in this case being that from feudalism to capitalism, from a state dominated by an aristocracy to one dominated by a bourgeoisie. Ergo, the French Revolution is simply the moment of dramatic or of definitive transition, a moment that was however both necessary and inevitable. For the "liberal" school, the process of modernization involves the renunciation of a despotic state and its replacement by a state founded on liberal principles. The French Revolution was an attempt to make this (not inevitable) transition, but one that was abortive. The drive to freedom remained latent in the French polity and would be resumed later. For Soboul, since the Revolution was bourgeois, it was the point of departure for liberal democracy in France. For Furet, after the dérapage, the Revolution became itself an obstacle to liberal democracy.

It is interesting to see, therefore, how each side treats the long war with Great Britain that began in 1792 and continued (with interruptions) until 1815, that is, long past the Jacobin period. For Soboul, the war was essentially launched from abroad by the French aristocracy who, losing the civil war, were hoping to recoup their position by internationalizing the conflict. For Furet, the war was desired by the revolutionary forces (or at least by most of them) as a way of pursuing the revolution and strengthening it.

No doubt one can make a plausible case for each of these explanations of the immediate origins of the war. What is striking is that there seems to be, in these analyses, no consideration of whether or not a Franco-British war might have occurred at this time in the absence of anything resembling an internal French revolution. After all, there had been three successive major wars between Britain (or England) and France over a period of a century, and from the perspective of today we might think of the 1792–1815 wars as simply the fourth and last of these major wars in the long struggle for hegemony in the capitalist world-economy.

I shall briefly summarize here an analysis expounded at length in the first two chapters of volume 3 of *The Modern World-System* (1989) without the supporting data found in the book.[1] I do this merely as background for the argument I wish to make about the ways in which the French Revolution as a world-historical event transformed the world-system as a world system. I start with the assumption that the capitalist world-economy existed as an historical system since the "long" sixteenth century with boundaries that from the beginning included England and France, and that therefore both countries had been functioning for all this time within the constraints of a capitalist mode of production and had been members of the interstate system that emerged as the political framework of the capitalist world-economy.

Such a "world-systems perspective" leaves little room for the most fundamental assumptions of the two main scholarly schools concerning the French Revolution. The French Revolution could not have been a "bourgeois revolution" since the capitalist world-economy within which France was located was already one in which the dominant class strata were "capitalist" in their economic behavior. The "capitalists" in that sense had no need of a political revolution in particular states in order to gain *droit de cité* or to pursue their fundamental interests. This of course does not exclude the fact that particular groups of capitalists might have been more or less happy with the public policies of their states and might have been willing, under certain conditions, to consider political actions that ended up by being in some sense "insurrectionary," thereby changing the structures of given state institutions.

In contrast, the world-systems perspective gives equally little place to the underlying assumption of the revisionist school (or schools), who take as central a putative macro-struggle between the advocates of political despotism and the advocates of political liberalism within each state, and see a sort of vector of modernity in the drive for liberalism. "Liberalism" in a world-systems perspective is seen rather as a particular strategy of the dominant classes utilizable primarily in core zones of the world-economy and reflecting among other things a lopsided intrastate class structure in which the working classes are a much lower percentage of the total population than in peripheral zones. At the end of the eighteenth century, neither England nor France yet had effective "liberal" institutional structures, and neither would have them for another century or so. The dérapage of 1792, if that is what one wants to call it, had no greater long-run significance than what might be thought of as the parallel dérapage of 1649 in England. Seen from the perspective of the twentieth century, Great Britain and France are not significantly different in the degree to which "liberal" political institutions prevail in the two centuries. Nor are they significantly different from say Sweden, which had no dramatic set of events comparable to the English or French Revolutions.

What can be noted about England and France is that, once Dutch hegemony in the capitalist world-economy began to decline in the mid-seventeenth century, these two states were the competitors for the hegemonic succession. The competition could be seen in two principal arenas: in their relative "efficiencies" of operation in the markets of the world-economy, and in their relative military–political strengths in the interstate system.

In this long competition, 1763 marked the beginning of the "last act." The Peace of Paris marked Great Britain's definitive victory over France on the seas, in the Americas, and in India. But, of course, it simultaneously laid the bases for the acute difficulties that Great Britain (and Spain and Portugal as well) were to have with their settler populations in the Americas, and which led to the process of settler decolonization that originated in British North America and spread everywhere.

We know that the American War of Independence attracted eventually a French involvement on the side of the settlers which, in the 1780s, greatly aggravated the fiscal crisis of the French state. To be sure, the British state also faced great budgetary dilemmas. But the 1763 victory made it easier for the British to resolve these difficulties in the short run than for the French state. Witness, for example, the role of "Plassey plunder" in relieving British state indebtedness to the Dutch.

The French state found it politically impossible to solve their fiscal problem through new modes of taxation and had no access to the equivalent of Plassey plunder. This explains their willingness to enter into the Anglo-French Commercial (Eden) Treaty of 1786 to which the French king agreed in good part on the grounds that it would create new sources of state revenue. Its immediate impact was in fact economically disastrous and politically unnerving. The *cahiers de doléance* were full of complaints about the treaty.

If one looks at the comparative efficiencies of French and British agricultural and industrial production in the eighteenth century, it is hard to make a case for any significant British lead. As of 1763, the French were if anything "ahead." But despite the fact that the economic realities were very similar, at least up to the 1780s when Britain was perhaps doing a little better, it is true that there was an (incorrect) perception in France after 1763 of France "falling behind." This was probably an illusion whose elaboration became a rationalization for the military defeat of 1763. There seems to have been a similar illusion prior to 1763 among the English that they were "behind" France, an illusion apparently effaced after 1763. In any case, this sense on the part of the French-educated strata helped also to create the justification for the Eden Treaty.

When the king convened the Estates-General, the general atmosphere (the defeat of 1763, the fiscal crisis of the state, the error of agreeing to the Eden Treaty, all compounded by two successive bad harvest years) created the political space for the "runaway" situation we call the French Revolution, a "runaway" situation that basically did not end until 1815.

One could say that the period 1763–1789 in France was marked by an unwillingness of French elites to accept defeat in the struggle for hegemony with Great Britain, exacerbated by a growing feeling that the monarchy was unwilling or unable to do anything about the situation. The wars of 1792–1815 were therefore part of the fundamental logic of the French revolutionaries, seeking to restructure the state so that it would be capable of finally overcoming the British foe.

From the strictly relational perspective of the Franco-British struggle in the interstate system, the French Revolution turned out to be a disaster. Far from permitting the final recouping of the defeat of 1763, France was beaten militarily more definitively in 1815 than it ever had been, because this time the defeat was on land, where French military strength lay. And far from allowing France to overcome the previously largely fictive economic gap with Great Britain, the wars created this gap for the first time. In 1815 it was true to say, as it had not been in 1789, that Great Britain had a significant "efficiency" lead over France in the production of goods for the world markets.

But were there not at least significant internal economic transformations in France as a result of the Revolution? When the dust settled, it turned out that the transformations were less startling than is often asserted. The larger agricultural entities for the most part remained intact, although no doubt there was some change in the names of the property owners. Despite the presumed "abolition of feudalism," such constraints on "agricultural individualism" (to use Marc Bloch's phrase) as *vaine pâture* and *droit de parcours* survived until late in the nineteenth century. The yeoman class (such as the *laboureurs*) emerged stronger than before, but largely at the expense of the smallest producers (such as the *manoeuvriers*). The agricultural reforms were at times noisy, but they fit into a slow steady curve of parallel change in much of western Europe over several centuries.

As for industry, guilds were abolished to be sure. And internal tariffs disappeared, thereby creating a larger unfettered internal market. But let us not forget that before 1789 there already existed a zone without internal tariff barriers, the Five Great Farms, that included Paris and was approximately the size of England. The Revolution did of course revoke the Eden Treaty and France once again, quite sensibly, returned to protectionism. The state did acquire a new administrative efficiency (the linguistic unification, the new civil code, the creation of the *grandes écoles*), which no doubt was very helpful to France's economic performance in the nineteenth century.

But from a strictly French point of view, the balance sheet of the French Revolution is relatively meager. If it was the "exemplary" bourgeois revolution, this doesn't say much for the value or the force of such revolutions. As a struggle against despotism, we have the word of the theorists of this position that it did not turn in a stellar performance. Of course, we could celebrate it on Tocquevillian grounds: the French Revolution was France's fulfillment of its state-creation, the achievement of bureaucratic centralization that Richelieu and Colbert sought but never quite completed. If so, one might understand French celebration of this event as the incarnation of French nationalism, but what should the rest of us celebrate?

I believe there is something for the rest of us to note, and perhaps to celebrate, if somewhat ambiguously. I believe the French Revolution and its Napoleonic continuation catalyzed the ideological transformation of the capitalist world-economy *as a world-system*, and thereby created three wholly new arenas or sets of cultural institutions that have formed a central part of the world-system ever since.

We must begin with the perceived meaning of the French Revolution to contemporaries. It was of course a dramatic, passionate, violent upheaval. In what might be called its primary expression, from 1789 (the fall of the Bastille) to 1794 (Thermidor), the Great Fear occurred, "feudalism" was abolished, church lands were nationalized, a king was executed, and a Declaration of the Rights of Man was proclaimed. This series of events culminated in a Reign of Terror, which finally ended with the so-called Thermidorian Reaction. Of course, dramatic events did not cease then. Napoleon came to power and French armies expanded throughout continental Europe. They were greeted originally in many areas as carriers of a revolutionary message, and then came to be rejected later in many areas as bearers of a French imperialist drive.

The reaction everywhere in Europe among the established authorities was one of horror at the undermining of order (real and potential) represented by the French revolutionary virus. Efforts to counter the spread of these ideas and values were implemented everywhere, and most notably in Great Britain where a very exaggerated view of the strength of possible sympathizers led to an effective repression.

We should note in particular the impact of the French Revolution (including Napoleon) on three key zones of the "periphery" of the world-system: Haiti, Ireland, and Egypt. The French Revolution's impact on St.-Domingue was immediate and cataclysmic. The initial attempt of White settlers to capitalize on the Revolution to gain increased autonomy led rapidly to the first

Black revolution in the world-system, a Black revolution which, over the succeeding decades, all other players (Napoleon, the British, the White settler revolutionaries in the United States and in Latin America) sought in one way or another to destroy or at least contain.

The French Revolution's impact on Ireland was to transform what had been an attempt by Protestant settlers to gain autonomy (as had the analogous group in British North America) into a social revolution that for a time drew together both Catholics and Presbyterian Dissenters into a common anticolonial movement. This attempt, hitting at the very heart of the British state, was turned aside, undermined, and repressed, and Ireland was all the more closely integrated with Great Britain by the Act of Union of 1800. The result however was to create an endemic internal political issue for Great Britain throughout the nineteenth century, its equivalent *mutatis mutandis* of the U.S. political issue of Black rights.

In Egypt, the Napoleonic invasion resulted in the emergence of Egypt's first great "modernizer," Mohamed Ali, whose program of industrialization and military expansion seriously undermined the Ottoman Empire and almost established a powerful state in the Middle East capable eventually of playing a major role in the interstate system. Almost, but not quite— Mohamed Ali's efforts were eventually successfully checked, as were all similar efforts in the periphery for a century.

To all of this must of course be added the settler decolonization of the Americas. No doubt, this was not the doing (alone) of the French Revolution. The American War of Independence predated the Revolution. But its sources lay in the same post-1763 restructuring of the geopolitics of the world system, and it made appeals to the same Enlightenment doctrines to legitimate itself as did the French Revolution. The Latin American independences of course then came in the wake of the same geopolitical restructuring, reinforced by the successful models of both the American and French Revolutions, plus the devastating political consequences of Napoleon's invasion of Spain in 1808 and the abdication of the Spanish monarch.

All in all, it added up to a political whirlwind of a kind that had never been known before in the modern world. Of course there had been previous periods of turmoil, but their impact had been different. The English Revolution no doubt shared many features with the French Revolution—in England. But its effect outside of England was quite limited, in large part because there was no "Napoleonic" conquest associated with it. And no doubt the Reformation–Counterreformation turmoil was every bit as wrenching as the French revolutionary turmoil. But it was not focused around issues of political order, and the ultimate outcome, although involving real political restructuring, seemed not to raise questions about the political legitimacy of rulers and governmental structures per se.

I think the bourgeoisie, or if you prefer the capitalist strata, or if you prefer the ruling classes, drew two conclusions from the "French revolutionary tur-moil." One was a sense of great threat, not from what might be done by the Robespierres of the world, but from what might be done by the unwashed masses who seemed for the first time to be contemplating seriously the ac-quisition of state power. The French Revolution proper had several times almost "gotten out of hand" not because some "bourgeois" were seeking political changes but because some "peasants" or some "sans-culottes" or some "women" began to arm themselves and to march or to demonstrate. The Black slaves of St.-Domingue did more than demonstrate; they actually seized state power, a political development that turned out to be even more difficult to contain and turn back than the rebellions in France.

These "uprisings" might of course be assimilated analytically to the re-curring food riots and peasant uprisings of prior centuries. I believe the world bourgeoisie perceived something different was occurring, that these "uprisings" might better be conceived of as the first truly antisystemic (that is, anti-capitalist-system) uprisings of the modern world. It is not that these antisystemic uprisings were terribly successful. It was simply that they had occurred at all, and that therefore they were the harbinger of a major qualita-tive change in the structure of the capitalist world-system, a turning point in its politics.

The world bourgeoisie thereupon drew, I believe, a second and very logi-cal inference. Constant, short-run political change was inevitable, and it was hopeless to maintain the historical myth used by previous world-systems and indeed even by the capitalist world-economy up to that point, that political change was exceptional, often short-lived, normally undesirable. It was only by accepting the normality of change that the world bourgeoisie had a chance of containing it and slowing it down.

This widespread acceptance of the normality of change represented a fun-damental cultural transformation of the capitalist world-economy. It meant that one was recognizing publicly, that is expressively, the structural realities that had in fact prevailed for several centuries already: that the world-system was a capitalist system, that the world-economy's division of labor was bounded and framed by an interstate system composed of hypothetically sovereign states. Once this recognition became widespread, which seems to me to have occurred more or less in the period 1789–1815, once this discourse prevailed, three new institutions emerged as expressions of and responses to this "normality of change." These three "institutions" were the ideologies, the social sciences, and the movements. These three institutions comprise the great intellectual/cultural synthesis of the "long" nineteenth century, the in-stitutional underpinnings of what is sometimes inaptly called "modernity."

We do not usually think of ideologies as institutions. But this is in fact an error. An ideology is more than a *Weltanschauung*. Obviously, at all times and places, there have existed one or several Weltanschauungen that have determined how people interpreted their world. Obviously, people always constructed reality through common eyeglasses that have been historically manufactured. An ideology is such a Weltanschauung, but it is one of a very special kind. It is one that has been consciously and collectively formulated with conscious political objectives. Using this definition of ideology, it follows that this particular brand of Weltanschauung could only be constructed in a situation in which public discourse accepted the normality of change. One needs to formulate an ideology consciously only if one believes that change is normal and that therefore it is useful to formulate conscious middle-run political objectives.

Three such ideologies were developed in the nineteenth century—conservatism, liberalism, and Marxism. They were all world-systemic ideologies. It is no accident that conservatism was the first to emerge institutionally. It is clear that the new recognition of the normality of change posed urgent dilemmas to those of a conservative bent. Edmund Burke and Joseph de Maistre saw this clearly and quickly. They saw they needed to make an intellectual case for the slowest possible pace of change. But more importantly, they realized that some kinds of change were more serious than others. They gave priority therefore to preserving the structures that in turn could serve as brakes on any and all precipitate reformers and revolutionaries. These were of course the structures whose merits conservatives lauded: the family, the "community," the church, and of course the monarchy. The central motif of conservative ideology has always been "tradition." Traditions are presumed to be there, and to have been there for an indefinitely long time. It is argued that it is "natural" to preserve traditional values because they incarnate wisdom. Conservative ideology maintains that any tampering with traditions needs a strong justification. Otherwise, disintegration and decadence follow. Hence conservative ideology is the incarnation of a sort of Cassandra-like cultural pessimism, inherently defensive in nature. Conservatives warn against the dangers of the change that now has become considered normal. The short-run political implications may vary enormously, but in the middle run conservatism's political agenda is clear.

Liberalism is the natural ideology of normal change. But it needed to become an ideology only after conservatism had emerged. It was English Tories who first called their opponents "liberals" in the early nineteenth century. To be sure, the idea of the individual's right to be free from the constraints of the state has a long history that predates this moment. The rise of the absolutist state brought in its train the advocates of constitutional government. John Locke is often considered the symbolic incarnation of this line of thought. But what emerged in the nineteenth century was liberalism as an ideology of consciously enacted reform, and this did not really exist in the seventeenth or eighteenth centuries. This is also why I believe the oft-cited difference between early nineteenth-century "minimal state" liberalism and late-nineteenth-century "social state" liberalism misses the point. The exponents of both had the same conscious political agenda: legislative reform that would abet, channel, and facilitate "normal change."

Marxism then came along quite late as the third ideology of the nineteenth-century world. Perhaps some would prefer to think of socialism as the third ideology. But over time the only variety of socialist thought that became truly distinguishable from liberalism as an ideology was in fact Marxism. What Marxism did, as an ideology, was to accept the basic premise of liberal ideology (the theory of progress) and add to it two crucial specifications. Progress was seen as something realized not continuously but discontinuously, that is by revolution. And in the upward ascent to the good or perfect society the world had reached not its ultimate but its penultimate stage. These two amendments were sufficient to produce an entirely different political agenda.

It should be noted that I have not discussed the social bases of these different ideologies. The usual explanations seem to me too simple. Nor is it at all clear that the emergence of these three ideologies depended on specific social bases, which is not to say that there has been no historic correlation between social position and ideological preference. What is important is that the three ideologies were all statements about how to deal politically with "normal change." And they probably exhausted the range of possibilites for plausible ideologies to be institutionalized in the nineteenth-century capitalist world-economy.

Political agendas are only one part of what one needs to deal with "normal change." Since these agendas represented concrete proposals, they required concrete knowledge of current realities. What they needed in short was social science. For if one didn't know how the world worked, it was difficult to recommend what one might do to make it work better. This knowledge was more important to the liberals and Marxists since they were in favor of "progress," and thus they were more prone than the conservatives to encourage and frequent social science. But even conservatives were aware that it might be useful to understand reality if only in order to conserve (and restore) the status quo (ante).

Ideologies are more than mere Weltanschauungen; social science is more than mere social thought or social philosophy. Previous world systems had had social thinkers, and we still today benefit by reading them, at least some of them. The modern world-system was of course the heir of a so-called Renaissance of (especially) Greek thought and built on this edifice in many ways. The rise of the state structures, and in particular of the absolutist state, led to a special flourishing of political philosophy, from Machiavelli to Bodin to Spinoza, from More to Hobbes and Locke, from Montesquieu to Rousseau. Indeed this was a stellar period in the production of such thought, and nothing quite matches it in the post-1789 era. Furthermore, the middle and late eighteenth century saw the emergence of work in economic philosophy almost as rich as the political philosophy: Hume, Adam Smith, the Physiocrats, Malthus. One is tempted to add: Ricardo, John Stuart Mill, Karl Marx.

But none of this represented the institutionalization of social science. Social science, as it came to be defined in the nineteenth century, was the empirical study of the social world with the intention of understanding "normal change" and thereby being able to affect it. Social science was not the product of solitary social thinkers but the creation of a collective body of persons within specific structures to achieve specific ends. It involved a major social investment that was never previously the case with social thought.

The principal mode of institutionalizing social science was by differentiation within Europe's traditional university structure which, by 1789, was virtually moribund. The universities, which at that point in time were scarcely vital intellectual centers, were still largely organized in the traditional four faculties of theology, philosophy, law, and medicine. There were furthermore relatively few universities. In the course of the nineteenth century, there occurred a significant creation of new chairs, largely within the Faculty of Philosophy, to a lesser extent within the Faculty of Law. These chairs had new names and some of them became the forerunners of what today we call "departments."

At first it was not clear which "names" of putative "disciplines" would prevail. We know the outcome, however. By the end of the nineteenth century, six main "names" had survived and more or less become stabilized into "disciplines"—anthropology, economics, geography, history, political science, and sociology. They had become institutionalized not only within the university system, now renewed and beginning again to expand, but also as national scholarly associations, and in the twentieth century as international scholarly associations.

The "naming" of the disciplines—that is, the structure of the presumed division of intellectual labor—reflected very much the triumph of liberal ideology that was (and is) the reigning ideology of the capitalist world-economy. This also explains why Marxists were suspicious of the new social science, and why conservatives have been even more suspicious and recalcitrant.

Liberal ideology involved the argument that the centerpiece of social process was the careful delimitation of three spheres of activity: those related to the market, those related to the state, and those that were "personal." The last category was primarily residual, meaning all activities not immediately related to the state or the market. Insofar as it was defined positively, it had to do with activities of "everyday life"—the family, the "community," the "underworld" of "deviant" activities, and so forth. The study of these separate spheres came to be named political science, economics, and sociology. If political science was the last name to be accepted, it was primarily the result of an archaic jurisdictional dispute between the Faculties of Philosophy and of Law, and not because the operations of the state were deemed less worthy of study. All three of these "disciplines" developed as universalizing sciences based on empirical research, with a strong component of "applied science" attached to them.

Parallel to this, the "name," history, was manifestly redefined. This is the great transformation represented by the work of Ranke. Ranke's great critique of what had been previously produced under the "name" of history is that it was too "philosophical," insufficiently "historical." This is the import of writing history *wie es eigentlich gewesen ist*. History had really occurred. What had happened could be known, by turning to the "sources" and reading them critically. The history that now became institutionalized was rigorously idiographic.

Three things are to be noted in the emerging institutionalization of these four so-called disciplines, as they developed in the nineteenth cnetury. First, they were concerned primarily, almost exclusively, with a few core countries of the capitalist world-economy. Second, almost all scholars worked on materials concerning their own country. Finally, the dominant mode of work was empirical and concrete, even though for the three so-called nomothetic disciplines (economics, sociology, political science) the object was said to be the discovery of the "laws" that explained human behavior. The nationally based, empiricist thrust of the new "disciplines" became a way of circumscribing the study of social change that would make it most useful for and supportive of state policies, least subversive of the new verities. But it was nonetheless a study of the "real" world based on the assumption that one could not derive such knowledge deductively from metaphysical understandings of an unchanging world.

The nineteenth-century acceptance of the normality of change included the idea that change was only normal for the civilized nations, and that it therefore was incumbent on these nations to impose this change on the recalcitrant other world. Social science could play a role here, as a mode of describing unchanging customs, thereby opening the way to understanding how this other world could be brought into "civilization." The study of the "primitive" peoples without writing became the domain of anthropology. The study of the "petrified" peoples with writing (China, India, the Arab world) became the domain of Orientalism. For each field the academic study emphasized the elements that were unchanging but was accompanied by an applied, largely extra-university domain of societal engineering.

If the social sciences became increasingly an instrument of intelligent governance of a world in which change was normal, and hence of limiting the scope of such change, those who sought to go beyond the limits structured by the world bourgeoisie turned to a third institution, the movements. Once again, rebellions and oppositions were not new. They had long been part of the historical scene, as had been both Weltanschauungen and social thought. But just as Weltanschauungen now became ideologies and social thought became social science, so did rebellions and oppositions become antisystemic movements. These movements were the third and last of the institutional innovations of the post-1789 world-system, an innovation that really emerges only after the world revolution of 1848.

The essential difference between the multiple prior rebellions and oppositions and the new antisystemic movements was that the former were spontaneous, short-lived, and largely uncoordinated beyond the local level. The new movements were organizations, eventually organizations with bureaucracies, which planned the politics of social transformation. They worked in a timeframe that went beyond the short run.

There were to be sure two great forms of such antisystemic movements, one each for each main theme of the "French revolutionary turmoil" as it was experienced throughout the world-system. There were the movements organized around the "people" as working class or classes, that is, around class conflict, what in the nineteenth century came to be called first the social movement, then the socialist movement. And there were the movements organized around the "people" as *Volk*, as nation, as speakers of a common language, what came to be known as the nationalist movements.

This is not the place to recount the arduous but effective institutionalization of socialist and nationalist movements as state-level organizations seeking state power within the states in which they were located or which they intended to establish. It is the place to note that, despite their appeal to "universal" values, the movements as they were constructed were all in effect state-level structures, just as the social sciences, despite their appeal to "universal" laws, studied de facto phenomena at the state level. Indeed, it was only the ideologies, of the three new "institutions," that managed to institionalize themselves somewhat at the world level.

What then can we say has been the true legacy of the French revolutionary turmoil? It clearly transformed the "cultural apparatus" of the world-system. But it did so in an extremely ambiguous way. For, on the one hand, one can say that it permitted the efflorescence of all that we have come to associate with the modern world: a passion for change, development, "progress." It is as though the French revolutionary turmoil allowed the world-system to break through a cultural sound barrier and permit the acceleration of the forces of "change" throughout the world that we know occurred.

But, on the other hand, the French revolutionary turmoil, by creating the three great new institutions—the ideologies, the social sciences, the movements—has created the containment and distortion of this process of change and simultaneously has created the blockages of which the world has become acutely conscious in the last twenty years. The post-1789 consensus on the normality of change and the institutions it bred has now at last ended perhaps. Not in 1917, however, but rather in 1968.

If we are to clarify our options and our utopias in the post-1968 world-system, perhaps it would be useful to reread the trinitarian slogan of the French Revolution: liberty, equality, fraternity. It has been too easy to pose liberty against equality, as in some sense the two great interpretations of the French Revolution have done, each interpretation championing if you will one half of the antinomy. Perhaps the reason that the French Revolution did not produce either liberty or equality is that the major powerholders and their heirs have successfully maintained that they were separate objectives. This was not, I believe, the view of the unwashed masses.

Fraternity meanwhile has always been a pious addition, taken seriously by no one in the whole long post-1789 cultural arena, until in fact 1968. What the "normality of change" has been interpreted, by all and sundry, to mean has been the increased homogenization of the world, in which harmony would come out of the disappearance of real difference. We have of course discovered the brutal fact that the development of the capitalist world-economy has significantly increased the economic and social disparities and therefore the consciousness of differences. Fraternity, or to rename it in the post-1968 manner "comradeship," is a construction to be pieced together with enormous difficulty, and yet this fragile prospect is in fact the under-pinning of the achievement of liberty/equality.

The French Revolution did not change France very much. It did change the world-system very much. The world-scale institutional legacy of the French Revolution was ambiguous in its effects. The post-1968 questioning of this legacy requires a new reading of the meaning of the popular thrusts that crystallized as the French revolutionary turmoil.

NOTE

1. Wallerstein, Immanuel, *The Modern World-System*, III: *The Second Era of Great Expansion of the Capitalist World-Economy, 1730–1840s*. (San Diego: Academic Press, 1989).

PART TWO

The Terror

SEVEN

Saint-Just and the Problem of Heroism in the French Revolution

Miguel Abensour

Translated by Frank Philip

DE LA NATURE . . . : LATE 1791–1792

In 1947, Professor Carnot, a descendant of the great Carnot, presented to the Bibliothèque Nationale a collection of Saint-Just's unknown manuscripts, *De la nature de l'état civil, de la cité ou les règles de l'indépéndance du gouvernement* ("On the Nature of Civil Society, the City, or the Rules of the Independence of Government"). Albert Soboul first published them as "Un manuscrit inédit de Saint-Just" in *Annales historiques de la Révolution française* (vol. 23, 1951); a second edition followed in a bilingual collection of Saint-Just's writings published in Italy under the title *Frammenti sulli Istituzioni repubblicane seguito da testi inediti* (Einaudi 1952).[1] *De la nature*... is fundamental in the strictest sense of the term: it is Saint-Just's first, incomplete expression of the principles of his political philosophy, one in search of a foundation. These writings throw new light on the enigma of Saint-Just, who shines through his myth. His intentness of mind, his dawning philosophical development, and his will to base revolutionary action on truth, demand that we consider an often overlooked aspect of Saint-Just as theorist. This is important even though certain figures like Brissot, Marat, and Dezamy, who compared him to Billaud-Varenne, and Edgar Quinet, who compared him to Fichte, as well as Lucien Febvre, recognized him as a thinker. Can we still cling to the classic interpretation of Saint-Just as embodying the contradiction between the theory of *Social Contract* and revolutionary practice? Thanks to this discovery of one of the most coherent theoretical formulations of Jacobinism in the making, should we not rather perceive the *continuity* between Saint-Just's theory of nature and his action, or better yet, by taking "the force of circumstances" into account, inquire about the actual political effects of what seems to be a dogmatic conception of nature and the state of nature? Up to what point may we see the failure of the Jacobins (admitted by Saint-Just in the formula, "The Revolution is frozen") as reflecting the inadequacies, the blind spots of their theory? Rather than taking to task the divorce of theory from practice, viewed as an irremediable fate, would it not be better to discern what is at fault in the theory?

First we need to date the manuscript. Albert Soboul, the first publisher, proposed three possible dates of composition: first around 1790–1791; then the first few months of the Convention, between September 1792 and April 1793; finally between April 1792 and 9 Thermidor. Based on an internal critique of the manuscript, we have proposed another dating that seems to have gained current acceptance.[2] Taking as our point of reference the issues of slavery and divorce, we maintain that the manuscript must have been written between 24 September 1791 and 20 September 1792, the date slavery was abolished in France and divorce introduced. *De la nature*. . . would thus date from midway between *L'esprit de la Révolution et de la Constitution de France* (1791) and *Fragments sur les institutions républicaines*, probably written in Year II. This is an important point, for as we note the repetition of certain themes characteristic of *De la nature*. . . in the *Discours sur la Constitution de la France* (24 April 1793) and in the second *Fragment des institutions républicaines*, we can better appreciate the distinctiveness of Saint-Just's political style. Unless we take *De la nature*. . . as a philosophical starting point from which the young revolutionary leader's thoughts and actions flowed, we shall inevitably be dumbfounded by the continual interaction between his political theory and his practice, and between his actions and his principles, where his concern focused on not letting action distort principles. For the inner rhythm of this movement depends on the periodic recurrence of a philosophy of nature, which serves as a kind of springboard for each new plunge. Hence the central role that *De la nature*. . . occupies in Saint-Just's development, and thus, regarding this kernel of his doctrine and vital representation, we need to grasp the modulations of meaning that punctuate Saint-Just's story.

RECONSTITUTION OF THE *DE LA NATURE*. . . MANUSCRIPT

For Saint-Just the state of nature meant, in the usage of the political theory of the time, "the state of man before civil governments were instituted." He describes this state as social, for society, a natural given and a fundamental and historically prior phenomenon, precedes the individual and not vice versa. The individual only appeared when the social body began to disintegrate. This natural human society accounts for a universal phenomenon manifested on every level on the scale of creatures, with certain differences of intensity varying from species to species, depending on the intelligence and sensitivity of those subjected to the society. Man, the most sensitive and intelligent creature, is born for an enduring society, for he is born to possess an ensemble of natural relations originating in human needs and affections. There are two kinds of possession, personal possession, which originates in man's affections—including the relations arising from the ties between person and person—and real possession, which originates in needs and includes relations arising from the self's occupation, the exchange of goods, and business in general.

Apart from this, from man to man, everything is identity. Identity, the affective and psychological underpinning of social life, has a fundamental place in Saint-Just's political thought, and an analysis of this concept helps us define the societal state and provide a diversified picture of it. Saint-Just's first proposition describes the societal state as a harmonious alliance between independence and life in society. The basis of this complementarity is membership in a species: "Everything that breathes is independent of its species, and lives in society in its species."³ Identity of origin, the precondition for this state, and its corollary, equality, make it possible to rid social life of every instance of domination caused by some difference in power. Unflagging vigilance is needed to preserve identity and equality, and thus to maintain the harmony of the societal state. Inequality of any kind destroys the original identity and introduces into the species or society a heterogeneity that is necessarily a catalyst of dissolution and which fractures the unanimous society into so many distinct and hostile groups. As a result, otherness is the source of an antisocial state, namely, the "savage" or "political" state. In fact, the social state disappears when we are thinking not of the relations between creatures of the same species but the relations between species, for the emergence of difference breeds rivalries and the will to dominate. Every social body thus presents two aspects, depending on whether it is viewed from the inside or the outside. Within a homogeneous society, independence is allied with sociability. But when this society confronts a different society, the societal state vanishes, giving way to the law of politics or preservation, along with its characteristic phenomena of resistance and force. Saint-Just expresses this in a second proposition: "Everything that breathes has a law of politics or preservation against what is not its society or species."⁴

Thus, the two different states coexist. The localization of each of the states depends on which group one envisages. According to Saint-Just, up to the level of the group "people" (peuple), all groups, family, the tribe, are recognized as more identical than different. Thus they live in the societal state. We find the point of transition from identity to otherness at the level of the people, and that is where the solution of continuity intervenes to create the political state. Saint-Just makes the following terminological distinction: "The societal state is the relation between men and men. The political state is the relation between one people and another."⁵

This contrast gives rise to a fundamental idea: force or constraint is to be proscribed, for it destroys social unity. When we replace a relation of identity

and equality with a relation of constraint or domination, the prior unity
breaks up, giving way to a conflict between those using force and those they
oppress; the binary category of master and slave appears. This is why the
definitions of the societal state and the political state are transformed. In
ridding themselves of any precise content, they lose their original meaning
and become general and theoretical concepts, with the aid of which Saint-
Just defined relations other than those between men and the state of nature,
or between peoples. The societal state becomes a normative or regulative
concept, and the political state a descriptive category. Saint-Just clearly
affirms the autonomy and specificity of the social by contrasting a *society*, an
immanent and internally experienced unity, with an *aggregate*, which is an
apparent society and a purely formal unity, an externally imposed and not
internally experienced cohesion. The political state designates every relation
based on force, inequality, and constraint. And Saint-Just unhesitatingly
equates so-called civilized life with savage life. He describes history as the
disappearance of the social under the impact of the generalization of the
political, which, not restricted to the relations between peoples, has also
ruled those between cities, and eventually destroys the relations between men.

This evolution involves two orders of causes: the theoretical causes, and
the more specifically historical causes. Humanity has reached the savage
state because of two fundamental errors. In the first place—and this is the
main cause—men have ignored the distinction between the internal and
the external relations of a society, the former being destined to unanimity, the
latter to division and war. Men have confused social right and political right.
As a result, the city (civitas) has been based on principles that are foreign to
its kind, and its internal structure has approached that of the general society
of people, separated by a quantitative difference instead of, as in the beginning, a qualitative difference. Ever since, men have lived among themselves
in the relation of a people to another people. The primordial phenomenon of
participation has faded away; we only see an order of juxtaposition. The
principal manifestation of this confusion between the social and the political
is the creation of the complex forces of government. The second and more
moral cause of this development has to do with man's increasing estrange-
ment from nature, first through ignorance, then through the systematic will
to denaturalize man. The leading role in this disfigurement of man's image is
played by religious law, which lent its support to all the encroachments of
domination and bondage.

The historical description is much more concise. In the earliest societies—
Saint-Just is thinking of the Franks and the Teutons—the people had no
magistrates; acting as both their own princes and their own sovereigns, the
peoples had only chiefs to ensure external preservation. The political state
emerged with the divorce of the roles of prince and sovereign from the people,
and with the creation of the magistrate, who never ceased to oppress the

people. This separation came about when the people lost their penchant for assemblies and turned away from the life of the city to dedicate themselves to commerce, agriculture, or conquest. It was then that the political contract, which Saint-Just conceived as a twofold convention, intervened in history, including a pact of union by the citizens among themselves and a pact by the citizens to submit to power.

Saint-Just envisaged the reconstruction of the legitimate city (civitas) from a theoretical viewpoint and a political viewpoint. From a theoretical point of view, we need to reverse the course of history and recover for the social the domain that rightly belongs to it, and thus limit the political to the relations between peoples. Social right must inform the reconstruction of the "city," basing it on nature, that is, on integration and participation in an organic totality, as contrasted with coordination and, *a fortiori*, subordination. That is why Saint-Just denounces the idea of a social contract at the origin of society. By its very structure, the contract is just a means for achieving a compromise between various antagonistic forces. Furthermore, to enact a contract is bad in itself, for it is an attempt to constrain nature and ignore the natural harmony that rests on the reciprocity between, on the one hand, sociability—the basis of possession and ownership of the national territory— and, on the other hand, property and possession, the most certain guarantees of society's preservation. This natural harmony is, however, the fruit of hierarchical laws according to the relations engendered by the society. At the top of the hierarchy Saint-Just places social relations—the direct relations of men in the simple quality of being human—and their more complex relations as citizens. The laws of these relations are independence and ownership, which means that each man is the owner of his body, his will, and himself. These two most abstract laws constitute the fundamental norms with which all legal rules must be consistent. Thus, the civil laws governing possession must follow the rule of equality that translates on the civil plane as the norm of social right. Because of certain matters of fact, Saint-Just grants the lawmaker a latitude in the practical arrangement of the conformity between the social state and the civil state in a somewhat more concrete manner. When this harmony is respected, society regenerates and perpetuates itself, and there seems to be no need for external and authoritarian intervention. And Saint-Just emphasizes the possession that progressively becomes the surest catalyst of social spontaneity as it reveals how decisive civil relations are in strengthening or crushing the social body if they are not based on independence and equality. The anthropological and legal notion of possession issues in a nonantagonistic and harmonious solidarity whose primary source is affinity, and which finds itself confirmed in the set of natural and necessary mediations deriving from the needs and affections of men. From a political viewpoint, the very title of the manuscript, whatever the grammar suggests, indicates how the rule of independence from the government should be based on "nature," which is understood in the narrow Rousseauistic sense.[6] Saint-Just's mistrust gives rise to a solution as direct as it is negative: the "city" must have no separation between the magistrate and the sovereign; it is enough to exclude the magistrate from the "city" forever. This, however, is more a matter of logical and ideal conclusions than of real political solutions. Saint-Just formulated other negative imperatives like the creation of a public force that is not an organ of oppression or division. The government must be limited to the exercise of one function only: external preservation. Thus, it involves an ad hoc military leader more than a genuine government.

From a strictly political point of view, *De la nature . . .* is decidedly unsatisfying. Positive solutions are lacking, and here Sain-Just's ideas reflect the incompleteness of the manuscript. This incompleteness, however, is not alone responsible for the lacunae. We need to reckon with the deeper proclivities of the young and doctrinaire Jacobin. Torn between the demands of the social law that "does not tolerate either the elevation or the abasement of anyone" and the necessity for self-preservation, Saint-Just affirmed his resolute opposition to the domination to which, in his view, politics was in the main reduced. Several times over, in lapidary phrases, he condemns the phenomenon of power. Social right imposes a ban on the distinction between the governing and the governed, which damages the original cohesion and builds the city on the disastrous opposition between the weak and the strong. This radical critique, revealing that Saint-Just belonged to a minority in the tradition that knew how to separate the being of the social from the division into masters and subjects, is not aimed at any particular political form. Nevertheless, he absolutely rejects politics as such, including the rule of force. Ignorant of the creative spontaneity of the social state, politics institutes violent ties instead of natural ties. Political law is to be proscribed, for within the city it separates, while social law unites. Surprisingly, the reader senses a genuine hatred of politics in someone who aspires to appear on the world's political stage, as though he were judging politics only on the basis of the monarchical experience. Saint-Just writes, "I'll speak of political law no more, I have struck it from the state."[7]

NATURALISM, PRIMITIVISM, AND THE THEORY OF SOCIAL RIGHT

Now that we have reconstructed his thinking, what is its overall significance? Saint-Just uses a collective tool: he thinks in terms of the idea of nature. What is his conceptual field? What are its harmonic elements?

Saint-Just is clearly aware of the topicality of the theme and its ambiguity. Rather than calling the very concept of nature into question, however, he asserts its primacy and atemporal character. "Sovereign nature is the chief right, it is for all time!"[8] Determined to establish the unequivocal and ahistorical truth of this concept, Saint-Just meant by nature "the point of exactness, justice, and truth in the relations between things or their morality," which exists outside of any human intervention, in contrast to the artificial. An objective moral order is implied here into which convention does not enter. Society should be based on nature, for it is not the product of artificial creation, the work of man, but a natural given that exists prior to man and exists independently of him. Saint-Just considers that this social order or "natural morality," which exists parallel to the physical order, is ruled by laws producing not necessary relations but intelligent relations that provide some purchase for human action, even though this nonautonomous objective order is not foreign to a divine order. Nothing, then, is more foreign to this idea than legal voluntarism, and it is more akin to classical natural right than to individual or revolutionary natural right. The human mind should content itself with "reading" the laws of the natural order that are imposed on it from the outside; however, the faculty is granted to it to arrange its different elements and to project the arrangements between the social law and the practical exigencies of the civil state.

Saint-Just pushed his social naturalism quite far; society finds not only its basis in nature, but also a solution to the complex relations it begets and the guarantee of its robustness, no matter what its stage of historical development. The spontaneous harmony of nature is the opposite of force, the real basis of contemporary societies. On the note of a studied idyllic optimism, and an even more rigorous and coherent naturalism, Saint-Just excluded reason, an artificial faculty, from the conceptual field. At the end of *De la nature. . .*, we observe a clear drop in tension; after pitting himself against common conceptions and aggressively reversing their usual meanings almost entirely, "savage state" meaning for him "civil" or "political state," and "social state" meaning "state of nature," Saint-Just returns to the standard terminology of his time: "In nature men love each other. In social life they take care of each other. . . . I have called social life the life of men united by a written contract, not to be misunderstood."[9] Saint-Just denied that reason was a natural faculty, maintaining that in the state of nature it virtually did not exist and emerged in history only as a substitute for and as a degenerate form of the earliest intelligence. Thus reason, a mere a posteriori to the accident by which humanity proceeded from the social to the savage state, is the only tool left to man for working out the political contract and organizing society on relations of force. This conception of reason as generator of political or savage life, a tool for constraining nature, shows how far Saint-Just distances himself from rationalism, even if his writings seem not to altogether exclude some good use for reason. The precedence given to the original intelligence over reason betrays a tendency toward a quite radical primitivism.

Indeed, in Saint-Just's thought, novelty is synonymous with error. He chose the attitude of regret; his mind, his awareness, are irresistibly turned toward what is no longer. His is an essentially chronological primitivism: the perfect state of humanity existed at the origin of the human race; history is merely a long decline. This is why Saint-Just rejects history, for history is evil and *alteration* is a key word in his philosophy of history. Every society turns corrupt as it gets away from its earliest state. Though he professess a theory of decline, Saint-Just is convinced of man's natural goodness. What is actualized in the change from the social to the savage state is not a defect in human nature; there was no fall owing to some innate corrupting passion of human nature, but merely an accident, for which the sole factor responsible was theologico-political subterfuge. There is therefore an antinomy between the deterioration of the human soul and its original innocence. This contradiction can be resolved only by the discovery of a socially created unreason at the base of contemporary societies. Thus a kind of temporal breach opens between the social and the savage states; we necessarily rediscover the latter if we move in the opposite direction. The result is the prescription of static imperatives, without any search for a dynamic means that would point a way to the social state. No vision of the future appears in *De la nature.* . . . Both the word and the idea of progress seem unknown to Saint-Just; historical time seems to be unfamiliar.

Historical indeterminism at least does not preclude hope; nature is associated with the earliest society, which does not prevent nature from ordering and ruling the current society. Nature was not created just for the wilderness. Cognizant of a certain growing economic complexity in the society of his time, Saint-Just still asserts that it must not be concluded from "some relations that business, agriculture, and industry have established among men, that they cannot be governed naturally."[10] Men are thus free to return to a natural social form and, if present society is based on nature, "relations will arise from each other, and business and industry will again find laws in nature."[11] A clear cultural primitivism—the rejection of a form of civilization—takes on and enriches itself with Saint-Just's social values. In the face of nascent capitalism, which he opposes, Saint-Just exalts the earliest society where men did not suffer from greed but achieved happiness by rest and the meeting of primary needs.

In the face of this radical repudiation of every form of power and authority within the city, are we warranted in thinking Saint-Just is arguing for anarchy? This interpretation ignores the still rough idea of rights that permeates *De la nature* . . . and culminates in the idea of a necessary harmony between social right and civil right. Saint-Just himself explicitly denies the charge that he is a theoretician of anarchy: "Where there will be no powers, there will be no anarchy."[12] At first blush this answer seems specious, but it puts us on the right track; we must dissociate right and power, and we can conceive of a legal order free of constraint and authority. Saint-Just's political ideas belong to the stream of social right that George Gurvitch defined as follows: "The autonomous right of communion in which each active, concrete, and real totality embodying some positive value is integrated objectively."[13] The analogy is not merely terminological but involves the form of sociability and the essence of right that Saint-Just advocated as the basis of the city. This is confirmed by the critical aspect of Saint-Just's thought. The form of sociability Saint-Just is arguing against as the rule of political law clearly contains the obverse of the one for which he was striving. The political tie results in a sociability via interdependence where essentially distinct individuals are reciprocally delimited and have merely an external connection. When political law enters the civil state, most natural relations are experienced as conflict, and relations of union are replaced by those of dependence. Because in this society others are seen as impediments and one's relations to them as antagonistic, the city becomes a mere assemblage of hostile and divided citizens, caring for one another in terms of the balance of forces and connected only through the state, which superimposes itself on them from the outside.

It follows that the legal expression taken by this form of sociability must be an order of coordination, namely, the contract, the necessary tool of mediation between separate individuals. Conversely, the desirable form of sociability is spontaneous. Its distinguishing sign is the network of union, all the more intimate because the whole precedes the parts, and each person lives for all. Interpersonal relations are experienced as friendship or love— because it is a form of sociability by interpenetration in which, despite differences, identity prevails and generates a resolutely anticontractual right of integration: social right.

It thus seems that Saint-Just's contrast between social right and political right exactly matches the contrast between social right (right of integration) and individual right (right of coordination) and, in terms of specific legal expression, between statutory right and contractual right. By placing Saint-Just in the stream of social right, we get a clearer view of the main features of his thought: doctrinaire naturalism, anti-individualism, and opposition to any theory of the contract.

Let us pursue this analysis a bit further and get a clearer view of the theory of social right. After questioning the city's need of civil laws and concluding in the affirmative, Saint-Just writes: "The city will thus have its laws, so that each, following the rule of all, is connected to all, and for the citizens to have no connection to the state, but only between themselves, they form the state, and the source of the laws will be possession, not the prince or the convention."[14]

This sentence expresses principles essential to the overall interpretation of Saint-Just's thinking: first, the principle of the distinction between society and state, and the assertion that the state is based on society and not vice versa. The state, the contractual mediation of wills, does not create society; society, the relations of affections and needs that are concretized in possession, creates the state. Society is conceived as an organism, an organic total-ity: "The social body resembles the human body, all its mechanisms con-tribute to harmony."[15] The social body spontaneously secretes a common social right, the end result of the relations of human needs and affections, of Hegel's "civil society." "In all engagements the civil rule should be copied from the social rule. Because they are confounded, the social nexus is tight-ened and, as I have said, all parts of the *society that subsists of itself by a natural principle* is connected by the civil rule."[16] The social order thus exists as autonomous, independent of the statist order that merely disturbs the initial spontaneous order.

Finally, and above all, the main function of social right is integration. The totality, the "social body," is immanent; it does not externally transcend the members of the city but emanates from the experienced reciprocity of needs and affections, from possession, which begets union—a concrete, dynamic, endlessly renewed participation from the whole to the parts and from the parts to the whole. "The right of man to nature or independence, the right of citizen to citizen, is possession, the right of a people to people is force. *In these relations and in the correspondence of these things we find the unity of the social body. The social body preserves itself because in these relations it is united.*"[17] Any individualism is thus clearly excluded: the man who is bound in a network of natural and nonviolent bonds lives spontaneously for all, and with all the greater ease when the community to which he belongs has a task to perform, that of its own preservation and defense from outsiders.

Hence Saint-Just's radical opposition to a contractual and artificialist conception of society and to any theory of individual right. In this respect the theory of law in *De la nature . . .* is symptomatic. Any voluntarist basis for right is to be forsworn; thus the law expresses not the general will but nature. And the role of expressing nature falls to the lawmaker, sage, or philosopher, but not the prophet.

Finally, Saint-Just conceived of possession as a defective right (the *jus abutendi* is missing), checked, harmonized, relative, functional—in short, a social property. It is the prototype of the theory of social right according to which the needs of the community guide the regulation of possession, quite unlike the property born of Roman right. Saint-Just's conception of man's owning himself does not come under the category of possessive individual-ism, for the individual is conceived as part of a larger whole whose organic unity he must strengthen by his economic or affective projection.

We cannot fail to be struck by an almost systematic anti-Rousseauism at the three successive levels of the philosophy of history, the theory of society, and the basis of rights. And above all, like Billaud-Varenne in his *Éléments de républicanisme* (Year I), Saint-Just criticizes Rousseau for rejecting the thesis of natural sociality.

THE PARADOXES OF SAINT-JUST:
FROM THE REVOLUTION AS RESTORATION TO THE
REVOLUTION AS ABYSS

How does *De la nature* . . . shed light on Saint-Just's action, his revolutionary development? His conversion to the Terror and his anguish in the face of the glaciation of the Revolution?

Charles Nodier, the enthusiastic publisher of *Institutions républicaines* (1831), perhaps best described the paradox of Saint-Just: "The unfortunate Saint-Just . . . was not a heartless man . . . he had tenderness and even convictions from which our improved civilization recoiled in contempt . . . he believed, which is much stronger, in respect for one's forebears and in the cult of emotion. . . . *He was an extremely backward philosopher compared to the age we live in.*"[18] The Archangel of the Terror made a fetish of ancestors: "Age is what our country worships," he wrote in *Institutions républicaines*. Let us try to unravel this paradox.

The first element is that this young man, the very embodiment of the Revolution, based his action, strange as it may seem, on classical natural right. Though invoking nature may be in a critical relation to tradition, the idea of limitation peculiar to classical natural right, teleological thought, and an idea of right not based on subjective foundation makes this idea incompatible with the modern idea of revolution. With the logic of a philosophy of freedom and not of virtue, the modern idea of revolution involves a subjective conception of right while also aiming at an emancipation seen as infinite movement.

Now the assertion of natural sociality, positing an objective ahistorical order in the name of nature, the declared mistrust of the individual or general will, the repeated rejection of the contract as a model, the theory of the lawmaker—all these features put Saint-Just, a crafter of the modern world, in the ranks of the ancients. So his appeal to virtue takes on a certain sense. Though Saint-Just associated the revolution with the people, he uncoupled the founding of the Republic from the popular will and assigned the job and the monopoly to the lawmaker, the elected interpreter of nature. This is an odd doctrine in that Saint-Just professed an idea of natural right that tended toward egalitarianism and hence was more Christian than classical in inspiration. This paradox resulted from Saint-Just's anti-Rousseauism; claiming, unlike Rousseau, that "the Golden Age is behind us," and thus making himself vulnerable to Fichte's critique, Saint-Just could not have access to the dialectical view of history in Rousseau's second *Discourse*; furthermore, he altered the idea of nature that in Rousseau had served as a critical hypothesis in the affirmation of a past reality that asserted itself as the truth of the earliest society. Dogmatizing Rousseau in this way, Saint-Just took away the conflictual tension because, for him, the return to the "city" and the return to nature had to be merged.

The revolution is thought of more on the model of astronomy—which implies the idea of a return to an earlier position—than within the strictly political field, from the classical concept of stasis or of modern thinking about the upheavals leading to an idea of conflict and social division.[19]

But is this idea of revolution a modern idea? Doesn't Saint-Just fatally lack the muse of perfectibility? Divorced from the idea of freedom and married to nature, revolution is directed less at liberation or the invention of a new social order than at "renaturalization," the restoration of a natural order effaced by centuries of monarchical decay that is denounced in the judgment of the king as "a crime against nature." The aim of the revolution is to redirect society into the orbit of nature, returning to an order seen as natural, away from the new, and to set limits that are all the more constraining for they are seen as objective. "I do not sever the bonds of society, but society has severed all those of nature. I do not seek to institute novelties, but to destroy novelties."[20] This orientation to the past, this hatred of novelty, this "misoneism," helps explain the fundamentalist climate of this idea, which goes along with the Jacobin puritanism oscillating between the images of the hero and the saint. This does not appreciably change the image of the revolutionary; he appears less possessed by a passion for freedom than irresistibly attracted to the founding of an order that, although proclaimed in the name of the revolution, still displays all the features of a generalized codification of the forms of existence.[21]

There appears an even more striking paradox: not content to associate the revolution with a plan to restore nature, Saint-Just calls for the revolution to be accomplished without politics, even to be *opposed* to politics. "We should not be afraid of changes, the peril is merely in how they are affected, all the world's revolutions are part of politics. That is why they have been steeped in crimes and calamities. Revolutions that are born of good laws and that are conducted by skilled hands would change the face of the earth without shattering it."[22] Good laws? He means laws resting on nature.

Must we see in this surprising declaration of the young and doctrinaire Jacobin a resurgence of the Augustinian doctrine that identifies politics with evil? This would imply that Christianity's hold on Jacobinism—the distinctively Christian ways of thinking about politics—is more crucial than has usually been thought. Referring the cohabitation of men to a spontaneity of the social with, moreover, a placing of the *polis* beneath the *societas*, leads to the disparagement of politics. This lowering of the political sphere shows how much Saint-Just, despite his reference to classical natural right, fails both to acknowledge the dignity of politics and to recognize an uncircumventable constitutive dimension in the plural existence of men.

As demonstrated, the contradictions are numerous, but the essential contradiction involves making the modern practice of revolution serve a pre-modern idea of rights and society.

Can we see here one of the roots of the Terror? The evils ascribed to politics must entail a downgrading of political mediation, even if Saint-Just declared, in his *Sur la Constitution*, that "natural polity" was not his aim. What else if not a *twofold rejection of politics* (the rejection of mediation or confusion with the logic of another order) was Saint-Just asserting when he wrote: "The principle of a republican government is virtue; the alternative is terror. What do people want who want neither virtue, nor terror?"[23] He called for a return to nature, and not humanity, as the destination of the city, and his conception of the revolution as the way to bring about this return fosters the illusion in which politics is confused with morality. It is important not to expose politics to an "overload" or to derail it by giving it a mission beyond its capacities—in this case, the reform of conscience or the diminution of selfishness. This was Kant's warning in 1793, when he distinguished between the political community and the ethical city, explicitly describing the dangers of a politics of virtue:

> We may call a union among men with simple laws of virtue following these prescriptions, an ethical society; and, to the extent that these laws are public, we may call it order, that is, an ethical civil society (in contrast to a legal civil society) or an ethical community. . . . Every political state doubtless desires to exercise domination over minds according to the laws of virtue, for in cases where its means of coercion are insufficient, because the human judge cannot see into the minds of men, virtuous intentions could secure what is wished. But woe unto the lawmaker who wants to use force to secure a constitution for ethical ends, for not only would he thus create the opposite of this constitution, but he would also weaken his political constitution and remove all its solidity."[24]

Thus when Saint-Just initiated what seemed to us to be "a new march" with the plan of *Institutions républicaines*, an outbreak of Terror, and, one might say, a critique of Jacobinism from within, he does not elude the movement of a return to a prepolitical state of nature.[25] The idea of institution, in relation to a critique of the law—"obeying laws, that is not clear," wrote Saint-Just—again points to nature, to the will to reestablish a natural order with access to objectivity. But we cannot fail to observe a hardening in this Jacobin lawmaker determined to shape republican institutions so that an orientation to nature would be combined with an enduring mistrust. Hence, along with the enthusiasm for creating institutions goes the appeal to heroism, to "the soul of the republic": "The day when I am convinced that it is impossible to give the French people manners that are gentle, energetic, sensitive, and implacable against tyranny and injustice, I shall plunge a dagger into my heart."[26] The suicide of the hero opposes the death of nature.

A new and paradoxical movement is formed: starting from a fundamentalist plan to reestablish the city on natural foundations, Saint-Just couldn't deny himself an act of foundation or, more precisely, of self-foundation. The issue of the French Revolution becomes the issue of heroism. Viewed from political philosophy and not from romanticism, heroism is a constitutive dimension of the Revolution. Heroism is the Revolution's magnetic field. For want of recognizing the existence of the "central sun" (G. Büchner), of measuring its energetic effects, the magnetization of consciences, according to Chateaubriand a "redoubling of life," the interpreter may fail to understand or even to think of the revolutionary. A modern Brutus, a regicide with the halo of his youth and his name, appearing suddenly on the public stage at the king's trial, Saint-Just exhibited the heroic experience par excellence, that of a rebirth.

Jules Michelet, who had read his Plutarch as well as Vico, had a political understanding of the Revolution. Furthermore, he did not separate this way of understanding from a consideration of heroism. Thus he knew better than anyone how to uncover the logic of heroism as an active, autonomous force in the Revolution. That is why he insisted on emphasizing the incessant commotion that Saint-Just's intervention provoked at the time of the king's sentencing. "This speech had an enormous effect on the trial. . . . Immature or not, exaggerated or not, it was powerful enough to set the tone for the whole trial. It determined the pitch; one continued to sing to the tune of Saint-Just."[27] It was the experience of a beginning, the start of the Republic, an appeal to the unknown, but also a beginning for Saint-Just, torn from the obscurity of a private citizen and suddenly propelled into the light of public space. "Who was to wield the sword. . . . A new man was needed, unshackled by any philanthropical precedent," wrote Michelet.[28]

Reading Saint-Just's speech, we see how this event indissolubly mingled the experiences of birth and founding, both necessarily connected with the death of the king. "The same men who will judge Louis have a republic to found: those who attach some importance to the just punishment of a king will never found a republic. . . . For me, I see no middle way: this man must reign or die . . . the mind that judges the king will be the mind that founds the republic. The theory of your judgment will be the theory of your magistratures."[29] Or again, "the revolution begins when the tyrant ends."[30]

But a question immediately arises concerning what Michael Walzer, drawing on the work of E. Kantorowicz, has rightly described as "public regicide," which he sees has the special feature of an attack on the inviolability of the monarchy, a transgression of the "sacred terror" of theologico-political origin which attaches to the twofold body of the king, both mortal and immortal.[31] Can we change the face of the earth without shattering it? Doesn't revolutionary action involve uncontrollable effects, all the more so as, in Saint-Just's case, it was not a matter of judging the king but of fighting him and bringing him down like an enemy? Can one still cherish the illusion of returning to good laws, dependent on nature? Is not the revolutionary experience as a beginning, at the same time an exposure to unpredictability? Saint-Just himself did not fail to compare the revolution to birth: "We have opposed sword to sword, and freedom is founded; it has emerged from chaos and with man who cries at birth. . . . Everything begins thus under the sun."[32]

Did not the public regicide, an unprecedented rupture owing to the radicalness it required, ruin the very idea of nature? The revolution would leave the comforting shores of a return to the natural order and brave the tempests of freedom to take on the unknown of a new experience of freedom, as freedom to do good *and* evil. This is the change from a revolution of restoration to a revolution of the abyss. At the same time Saint-Just was seeking the point where the revolution must *stop*, "at the perfection of happiness and of public freedom by law." He voices his anxiety about the identity of the Revolution which from now on is problematic, that is, disguised, and about the vertiginous movement of freedom, for it is a movement toward the infinite. "We speak of the height of the revolution, who will fix it? It is movable."[33] Testing the impossible?

In the face of this gap, heroism in turn becomes a paradoxical experience. Though Saint-Just gazes with melancholy at "the beauty that is no longer" (Rome, Sparta), he still confesses to a metamorphosis of heroism, and very consciously draws on what P. Lacoue-Labarthe described concerning Hölderlin as a general crisis of *imitatio*, following the collapse of a tradition. "The disappearance of every rule and every model, of every codification in art."[34] And the poet, no stranger to revolutionary disorder, consumes himself "in the practically *ex nihilo* creation of a pure work or of a new art." On 25 April 1794, Saint-Just announced, "Have no doubt of it, everything around us must change and end, for everything around us is unjust; victory and freedom will cover the world. Scorn nothing, but imitate nothing of what has gone before us. *Heroism has no models.* It is thus, I repeat, that you will found a powerful empire with the boldness of genius and the power of justice and truth."[35]

In exactly the same speech, "Sur la police générale, sur la justice, le commerce, la législation et les crimes des factions," Saint-Just limns the portrait, the model of the revolutionary man, "the hero of good sense and honesty," meaning the privileged interpreter, perhaps even the guardian of the Revolution. "As his goal is to see the Revolution triumph, he will never find fault with it, but he condemns his enemies without involving himself with them, he does not violate the Revolution but illuminates it, and jealous of its purity, he is circumspect in speaking of it, out of respect."[36] With furious speed the cutting edge of the word *regicide* is followed by an homage to revolutionary exemplariness. This change of tempo displays the paradoxical trajectory of heroism; the energy of the beginning, propelled by the *initium*, reverses itself and becomes testimony and force for stopping, becomes a limit imposed on revolutionary élan. A new image is drawn of the custodian of the criteria for good and evil, the judge of moderation and exaggeration. Heroism has no models; when the ground of nature is revealed, exposed to this vacuity, the hero immediately transforms himself into a model, into a force of impossible "modeling."

At this nodal point, the logic of heroism encounters the logic of democratic invention so well elucidated by Claude Lefort.[37] Deprived of the canon of nature, how can we then determine the line between liberty and license? After the unprecedented dismemberment of the social in and by the king's death—a proof of the vertigo vis-à-vis the unknown of a society that no longer turned to nature but was confronted by the new—after the loss of reference points, how to recodify, remake the criteria of the reference, redraw the identifying frames of reference, remake the body (Claude Lefort), if not by offering the body of the revolutionary hero as the incarnation of a new sacred thing, as the support for an identification, if not by connecting the power to an exemplary body?

The more Athenian than Spartan Camille Desmoulins, who loved to chortle at the gods and idols, said of Saint-Just that he "carried his head like the Blessed Sacrament." The echo comes back to us of Lucile Desmoulins's cry in *Danton's Death*, "Vive le roi!" hailed as the word of freedom by Paul Celan, who grew up with the writings of Pierre Kropotkin and Gustave Landauer.[38] Though Saint-Just, by creating his own myth, took part in the invention of what Stendhal called the "beautiful modern," and at this distance still exerts fascination, we should keep in mind the final lines of Michelet's 1869 preface to *Le Tyran*: "Happily, time passes. We are a bit less dim-witted. The rage for incarnation, carefully inculcated through Christian education, messianism, passes. At length we understand the counsel Anacharsis Clootz left when he died: 'France, be cured of individuals.'"

NOTES

1. All the references in this article refer to this edition: Antoine de Saint-Just, *De la nature. . .*, in *Frammenti sulli Istituzioni repubblicane seguito da testi inediti* (Torino: Einaudi, 1952).

2. J.-P. Gross, "Essai de bibliographie critique," in *Actes du Colloque Saint-Just* (Paris: PUF, 1968), pp. 343–463.

3. *De la nature. . .*, p. 135.

4. Ibid.

5. Ibid.

6. The same passive meaning is found on p. 142, where Saint-Just writes: "The natural pact excludes any particular force that is independent of the sovereign." This should read, "with regard to the sovereign."

7. *De la nature.* . . , p. 156.

8. Ibid., p. 157.

9. Ibid., p. 175.

10. Ibid., p. 143.

11. Ibid.

12. Ibid., p. 148.

13. George Gurvitch, *L'Idée du droit social* (Paris: PUF, 1932), p. 15.

14. *De la nature.* . . , p. 158.

15. Ibid., p. 152.

16. Ibid.

17. Ibid., p. 146.

18. Jean Richer, "Charles Nodier de la Révolution française," in *Philosophies de la Révolution* (Paris: Vrin, 1984).

19. M. J. Lasky, *Utopia and Revolution* (Chicago, 1976), pp. 239–259.

20. *De la nature.* . . , p. 161.

21. Michael Walzer, *The Revolution of the Saints* (New York, 1976).

22. *De la nature.* . . , p. 155.

23. *Frammenti*, p. 49.

24. Kant, *Religion Within the Limits of Reason Alone*, 1793.

25. Miguel Abensour, "La théorie des institutions et les relations du législateur et du peuple selon Saint-Just," in *Actes du Colloque Saint-Just* (Paris: PUF, 1968), pp. 239–290.

26. *Frammenti*, p. 47.

27. Jules Michelet, *Histoire de la Révolution française*, vol. 2 (Paris: La Pleiade, 1952), p. 79.

28. Ibid., p. 73.

29. Saint-Just, *Discours et Rapports* (Paris: Editions Sociales, 1957), pp. 63, 65, 67.

30. Saint-Just, *Oeuvres* (Paris: Vellay, 1908), 1 : 398.

31. Michael Walzer, *Regicide and Revolution* (Cambridge: Cambridge University Press), 1974.

32. *Discours*, pp. 186–187.

33. *Frammenti*, p. 52.

34. Hölderlin, *Hymns, Elegies and Other Poems* (Paris: Gallimard, 1983), Introduction, p. 8.

35. *Discours*, p. 196.

36. Ibid., p. 183.

37. Claude Lefort, *L'invention démocratique* (Paris: Fayard, 1981).

38. Paul Celan, *Le méridien* (Mercure de France, 1971).

EIGHT

Violence in the French Revolution: Forms of Ingestion/Forms of Expulsion

Brian Singer

Like all writings, this chapter has a varied provenance. But the one "gesta-tive line" that I should like to pursue by way of introduction concerns the difficulties in thinking about violence. Acts of violence immediately raise a number of moral issues, which tend to determine the direction of enquiry. To speak of violence, it is feared, is to justify violence—unless such speech is explicitly directed at its condemnation. But to condemn violence is to place it under a subtle (but no less strict) form of censure. And in order to break the censure, and thereby open up violence as a topic of discussion, violence must be tamed theoretically, as well as restricted practically. Generally, this is done by binding violence to the modes of instrumental rationality, even as violence by itself appears as what is most threatening to rationality in all its forms.

No less a thinker than Hannah Arendt has claimed that the essence of violence, its very substance, lies with its instrumentality.[1] Violence is a means to an end. Thus violence will receive the right of entry into a utilitar-ian calculus. Too little violence, and the end may not be achieved; but too much violence is morally wasteful, when not simply counterproductive. Vio-lence may be one of several means to the realization of an end, in which case its costs must be measured against those entailed by the use of the alternate means. Or it may be only means to the realization of that end, given the character of the resistance of those opposed to that end. Here the investiga-tion of violence is limited to its uses, its effectiveness, its necessity. It is a matter of the establishment of a calculus to establish the judicious (if not the just) use of violence. An instrumental rationality brackets—though only partially—the question of ends in order to produce a morality of the means. When "good" violence can be separated from "bad" violence, violence can be rendered, at least to some extent, acceptable.

Of course, the investigation does not stop here. The discussion of the "rational" employment of violence soon moves to consider the "rationality" of the actors and their motives. The "rationality" of the actors: their social background, their institutional affiliations, their relation to the law—in short, their "respectability." The "rationality" of the motivations: Are the actors consciously striving for concrete goals worth attaining?—here the question of ends returns, but in the more manageable form of (material) interests. And again, in both cases violence can be justified, if not necessarily legitimated, in the name of pragmatics.

In truth, the attempt to establish rules for the rational use of violence has a long history, dating back at least as far as Machiavelli. After all, such an enquiry does have eminently practical implications for the practice of politics. And it enters, almost necessarily, into our most casual judgments when confronting violent events. Yet the instrumentalist calculus of violence is fraught with all kinds of problems—even should the delicate balance between means and ends not be upset (when either the means—the violence—are judged unacceptable independent of the ends, or the realization of the ends is considered so imperative that all means employed on their behalf are condoned).

Suppose, however, that the balance is maintained. There remains the problem that violence can enter a utilitarian calculus only in a stable, narrowly circumscribed situation. Numerous suppositions follow: at the very least, the ends must be limited, the consequences foreseen, and the contingencies held at bay. And one will want to argue that such suppositions can never be met in toto, that the "virtues" of violence can never be entirely ensured in the face of *fortuna*. And what applies in general, applies with far greater force to the type of situations that we shall be examining: a revolutionary situation. For in the latter, as we shall see, the violence is not always directed at a well-defined enemy who poses some clear and immediate threat. Nor is the violence, ultimately, directed at some limited, short-term end, but to the creation of a new regime, a new humanity. And above all, revolutionary situations entail a state of continuous and extreme flux: it is not just that circumstances are always changing, or that the rules of the game are constantly being rewritten; the fact is the very definitions of what is real and unreal, possible and impossible, true and false, are all being shifted from their moorings.

But beyond the question of whether the instrumentalist perspective can deliver an adequate portrayal of the reality of violence (and without considering whether the actors understand their violent acts in purely instrumental terms), there are the moral questions raised by this perspective. In truth, the latter does not really seek to provide a pure description of reality and will admit as much in rare moments of self-reflection; on the contrary it attempts to describe violence not as it is but as it ought to be when "rationally" applied. And yet at the same time, in the name of a certain "realism," it would denude that realm of the "ought" of its utopian dimension. The result is that an ideal violence is substituted for the ideals that violence sometimes claims to serve.[2] In the attempt to be at once "realist" and "idealist," the perspective proves neither realistic nor, to be sure, idealistic: at worst, the artificially perfected image of an imperfect world with which to construct a morality for the amoral.

This is not to mention those discussions of the uses of violence which shift the terms, slipping from an analysis of the instrumentality of violence to an analysis of its "functionality." Here, where one speaks of the symbolic uses of violence in terms of cathartic release, social solidarity, or boundary definition and maintenance, or in terms of its regenerative powers, violence becomes an end in itself, opening up a possible whirlpool of apologetics.

To consider violence as, essentially, an instrument is not, as is so often hoped, to render it morally neutral. It does, however, tend to make violence theoretically transparent. Instrumentalized, violence appears without any interest in itself outside of the means/end context in which it is inserted. It is reduced to purely quantitative terms, a medium of action whose only content is the degree of force it embodies. As a tool, violence lacks any expressive capacity; as the result of a rational choice, violence, even if employed by institutions, cannot itself take on an institutional character. Within such a perspective, violence is denied any relation to culture. There can be no concern with the forms of violence, with the possibility that certain forms of violence are characteristic of certain kinds of society. In a word, to treat violence instrumentally is to choke off the possible elaboration of what might be termed a *sociology* of violence.

Now the elaboration of such a sociology is no easy matter. It will, relative to the commonsense understanding of violence regarding "the logic of the social," appear to engage in a number of paradoxes. For just as violence first appears opposed to rationality, violence also appears contrary to society, or more precisely, to its existence in terms of institutions, forms, and expressions. Let me explain. First, violence as the negation of form: generally speaking, violence is seen as either the primordial chaos out of which form develops, or as the final chaos in which form is to be engulfed. Second, although violence may not necessarily be opposed to expression, it does appear as opposed to communication: either it appears as prior to language, expression without articulation, the utterance of a brute subjectivity, or as posterior to language, where communication, exhausted of its resources, breaks down. Finally, violence as contrary to institution: where the latter supposes not just form but the continuity of form, violence appears as the disruption of routine, a rupture in the temporal continuum, the introduction of an unstable, unpredictable, and uncontrollable element threatening the social order.

To elaborate a "sociology" of violence, then, is to restore to violence, or at least to some violence, its character as institution. It is to understand violence as form, as a "cultural" form if one will, as a social "ritual" as well as a collective instrumentality. And it is to examine the different forms of violence as instituted in different societies as, in each case, telling us something about that society, as expressive of that society, and of its "self-understanding." One might wish to see such a sociology as providing a hermeneutics of violence through which the larger "social text" can be interpreted. Alternately, the remainder of this chapter may be read as an introduction to a possible history of violence.

The discussion begins with a brief examination of George Rudé's well-known work on popular violence, *The Crowd in the French Revolution*. This book may be considered as representative, though not in any rigorous sense, of the instrumentalist approach. My own, more "sociological" approach will emerge out of a critique of this work. Because I am following here on the heels of Rudé, and because of limitations of time, space, and research, my analysis will be based almost exclusively on Parisian events. However paradigmatic the Parisian case, I recognize this as a limitation, and all conclusions should, therefore, be treated tentatively.

RUDÉ'S POPULIST HISTORY

George Rudé begins his book by proposing that the revolutionary crowds cannot be treated as abstractions. Though the abstractions of the left are criticized, that is, the image of the popular movements as embodying the "People," it is soon obvious that it is the abstractions of the "right" which are his real target.[3] Here he is speaking of the image of the revolutionary crowds as "inchoate mobs," anarchic and blindly destructive, "drawn from criminal elements or the dregs of the city population." Or to quote the rhetoric of one Edmund Burke, "bands or cruel ruffians and assassins, reeking with . . . blood" and embodying "all the unutterable abominations of the furies of hell."[4] George Rudé seeks to undermine these "abstractions" ("stereotypes" seems the more appropriate word) by pursuing, at least implicitly, three lines of enquiry: the first is concerned with who commits the violence, their quality as social actors; the second with their motivations and intentions, the reasons for the violence; and the third with the uses of violence, its instrumentality as a means for the realization of the ends posited by the intentions and motivations. These "lines of enquiry" then can be considered as forming the book's underlying "theoretical" framework. Though in truth, this is not a theoretical work, and the underlying framework hardly constitutes its originality, let alone its importance. If we must be eternally grateful to Professor Rudé and his travails, it is for having brought empirical data to the discussion of popular revolutionary violence, and thus proof positive to his counterdemonstration.

Consider then the more concrete lines of investigation that, roughly speaking, correspond to the above lines of enquiry. Again we can speak of three lines. In the first place, throughout the book, while relating the history of the crowd's actions, George Rudé provides a body count, showing that the revolutionary crowds did not engage in large-scale, uncontrolled bloodletting. Generally speaking, the number of victims during the *journées révolutionnaires*—and by victims, one understands the unarmed and defenseless, and not the Swiss Guards killed in pitched battle—were few, rarely more than a handful, hardly the stuff to fuel the fires of counterrevolutionary nightmares.

In the second place—and this in many ways is the core of the book's research—he demonstrates that the revolutionary crowds were not composed of the unemployed, the underemployed, the petty criminal, the marginal, the vagabond, those who were called, in a language still resonating with the feudal past, *les gens sans aveu* (literally, those who had not taken an oath, and thus had no clear place within the social order, however lowly, those therefore who were the very embodiments of a social dis-order). This "underclass," it seems, were hardly major participants on the stage of the Revolution in any real sense. The revolutionary crowds were largely composed, to be sure, of sans-culottes (literally, those without breaches, that is, those who wore trousers—the wearing of stockings up to the knee being a major mark of the social divide of the time). But what George Rudé demonstrates is that it was the most stable, most law-abiding elements of the sans-culottes who participated in the revolutionary events, those whose remnants some fifty years later would be considered petty-bourgeoisie or, if one will, lower middle class. Though participants from higher classes—that is, bourgeois, *rentiers*, merchants, civil servants, and professionals (breaches and all)—as well as participants from the lowest classes, were not entirely absent, it was the workshop masters, craftsmen, shopkeepers, petty traders, journeymen and, more rarely, wage earners who predominated.[5]

Lastly, the author considers the motives for participation in the revolutionary crowds. It comes as no surprise that he finds that "bribery and corruption," or "the quest for loot," were not "major factors stimulating revolutionary activity."[6] Nor does he consider the revolutionary crowds to be acting from the irrational instincts posited by the crowd psychology inaugurated by Gustave Lebon.[7] Such right-wing shibboleths are quickly dismissed. He does admit that the revolutionary crowds acted, in part, out of political motives, having "enthusiastically supported and assimilated the objects, ideas, and slogans of the political groups in the National Assembly, Cordeliers, and Jacobin Clubs whose leadership they acknowledged and in whose interest they demonstrated, petitioned, or took up arms."[8] But it is not simply a matter of the sans-culottes passively following the initiatives of the republican bourgeoisie. The sans-culottes had their own reasons for engaging in street action, reasons that were foreign to the interests and experience of their erstwhile bourgeois allies, and which account for the force and continuity of the social ferment of the revolutionary period. The sans-culottes' primary concerns, Professor Rudé asserts, were with more basic issues: those dealing with the provisioning of cheap and plentiful food in the face of shortages and high prices. And he goes on to note that the reasons for their actions were continuous with a long history of popular disturbances, dating back at least several centuries. These were not new struggles, seeking the establishment of a new, hitherto unknown order. "[T]he *sans culottes* intervened" he states, ". . . to reclaim traditional rights and to uphold standards which they believed to be imperilled by the innovations of ministers, capitalists, speculators, agricultural 'improvers,' or city authorities."[9] These were defensive reactions, or in the words of Charles Tilly, "reactive struggles"; they sought to defend tradition and community against the threats posed by the newly emergent state and economy. They were the type of popular struggle that prevailed during the period prior to the consolidation of the nation–state and capitalist economy, after which new struggles of "proactive" character would arise.[10]

Without delving into this last point, which, despite its considerable interest, is not germane to my discussion—and which, in fact, is not central to George Rudé's discussion, being the horizon to which the latter points toward its end—let us very briefly summarize his argument. The revolutionary crowds, he seems to be saying, were largely composed of the lower classes to be sure, but of their more respectable elements. These crowds engaged in revolutionary actions for reasons that were reasonable, if somewhat archaic. Lastly, respectable and reasonable, these actions, as measured by the level of violence, were relatively moderate. This is a sympathetic portrait. The three lines of investigation lead, both implicitly and explicitly, to a defense of the sans-culottes' revolutionary actions. The book is meant to be a history from below; and indeed the bulk of the book is composed of a chronicle of the Revolution's history as presented by a history of the journées révolutionnaires. The villains of the piece are those located above. Notably, the first two estates, that is, the aristocracy, the clergy, and other counterrevolutionaries. But also, if to a slightly lesser degree, the republican bourgeoisie and their state. George Rudé follows here the historiography of Albert Soboul wherein the sans-culottes and the revolutionary bourgeoisie are posed as, depending on the period, the best of allies and the worst of friends. The Jacobin state, in particular, is condemned for completely eliminating the sans-culottes' capacity for autonomous action, thus cutting itself off from its popular base of support, and mounting a Terror that was excessive and arbitrary. In short, this is a history of popular movements that would also be a populist history.[11]

Now, my problem with the book lies not with its populism, nor with the morality tale hidden therein. What I find difficult to accept is that the "popular" actors must, in order to be rended historically acceptable, be made into rational actors. With the exception of their context, they would be like us, or like we would like to believe ourselves to be. One would hardly think that they came from another time, let alone another culture. For them violence would be a mere resource, something to be mobilized, in itself neutral, transparent.

This is to say that it is not my intention to criticize Professor Rudé's characterization of the social composition of the revolutionary crowds. Nor will I dispute his characterization of their motives, at least directly. My intention is not to attack Professor Rudé on his chosen terrain but to shift the terrain and open up new areas for discussion.

THE SEPTEMBER MASSACRES

Let me begin with a brief comment concerning the images of popular violence against which George Rudé directs his argument. This imagery was not invented by right-wing historians after the revolutionary events; the perception of the revolutionary mob as composed of the lowest, least-stable elements of the population was common to the time. And it was not just the wealthy and counterrevolutionary who feared the vast underworld of the desperately poor and criminal. As George Rudé is not unaware, almost all sectors of society, including the revolutionary, and the revolutionary sansculotte, shared the same fears relative to les gens sans aveu; and almost all sectors were equally willing, when confronted with social disturbances contrary to their perceived interests, to blame the same people. In other words, the stereotyped images of the revolutionary mob constitute less a historical argument, or even a political argument, than a widely shared social prejudice, both then and now and in times intervening. As such, this prejudice must be considered part of the reality it purports to describe; for it is part of the motivations and intentions of the Revolution's actors; indeed it seems to have a social dynamic of its own, almost independent of the multiple uses to which it was put. On more than one occasion, it was rumors, almost always false, concerning the least favored part of the population, that set the popular movements in motion. What historians refer to as the Great Fear, the peasant insurrections of the summer of 1789 which swept away the old rural order, was precipitated by rumors that Paris was expelling its surplus population, casting into the countryside a confused and hungry mass that would pillage farmer and farm alike. And again it was "lesser fears" that were the catalyst of several of the journées révolutionnaires in Paris, the sans-culottes rising in self-defense against imaginary threats posed by the same desperate elements, presumed in the pay of some counterrevolutionary conspiracy. In truth, as we shall see, this most unfortunate sector of the population was more likely to be the victims of popular violence than its perpetrators. As a target, the object of George Rudé's critique is simultaneously weak and resilient: weak in the sense that no great imagination is required to see that the stereotypes are largely false, the result of what is generally known as scapegoating; and resilient in the sense that for this very reason they will always be with us.

There is another point that must be brought out here. How can Professor Rudé speak of the revolutionary actors as reasonable when those he would defend hold the very prejudices that he would attack? Or better, how can one speak, whether implicitly or explicitly, of rational actors, when the grounds of their actions lie within a social imaginary composed, at least in part, of rumors and hearsay?[12]

Beyond all questions concerning the actors, their social composition, their "rationality," what can be said about their violence? George Rudé as suggested, leaves an impression of moderation, but only by neglecting, if not entirely ignoring, what are known as the September Massacres of 1792. The ostensible reason for his neglect has to do with the paucity of evidence relative to those who participated in the massacres. No one wanted to admit their participation after the event for, unlike the other journées revolutionnaires, there was little to gain and much to lose in any such admission.[13] The only real data comes three years after the massacres, and one year after the fall of Robespierre and the Jacobin party, when judicial proceedings were brought against thirty-nine persons for alleged participation in the massacres—and then all but three were acquitted for lack of evidence.[14] However, despite the lack of hard data relative to social composition, the character of the event remains clear. And the character of the September Massacres was so exceptional, that it must be considered in some detail.

What immediately strikes the observer about the September Massacres is the extent of their violence. The number of victims—again among the unarmed and defenseless—exceeded by far anything that had occurred previously. George Rudé provides a maximum estimate of 1,400 executed, and this figure has not been exceeded by more recent estimates.[15] Admittedly, the September Massacres occurred under exceptional circumstances. Paris, it then seemed, was threatened with foreign invasion, the leaders of the invading forces had threatened widespread reprisals against the revolutionaries, and the Parisian populace was, understandably, affected by a nervous ferment. And yet the massacres appear not to have been a panic reaction. They appear to have been, at least in part, premeditated, and they unfolded in relative calm. The ostensible reason for the massacres was the presence in the prisons of numerous counterrevolutionaries, many of them rounded up during the last journée révolutionnaire, August 10, when the monarchy had fallen. There were rumors of a *complot des prisons*, a conspiracy amongst the prisoners against the Revolution,[16] and on the second of September the prisons were invaded by the revolutionary crowds. However, it must be said that the massacres were not limited to the prisons, or by what one usually understands as prisons, and the largest number of the victims was not counterrevolutionaries. At least 70 percent of those executed were common-law prisoners: common thieves, prostitutes, forgers, vagrants, and the like—that is, precisely, the gens sans aveu, the eternal scapegoats discussed above.[17]

In this regard, it is perhaps surprising that George Rudé seeks to serve the September Massacres with reasons—reasons, one might add, not far removed from those given by the *septembriseurs* themselves. For he writes that "[u]nsavoury as the episode must appear in itself, the massacres. . . completed the destruction of the internal enemy some weeks before" the defeat of the external enemy at Valmy.[18] One wonders in what sense most of the victims were enemies of the Revolution, and in what sense those who were enemies of the Revolution, being in prison, were threats to the Revolution. Even if there was a complot des prisons—for which there is no evidence—it should hardly have to be said that it would have been highly unlikely that these prisoners could have (1) escaped the prisons, (2) armed themselves, and (3) successfully confronted an armed and vigilant, revolutionary populace. Born in fear, fueled by rumor, and directed at a wide, imprecise array of victims, this journée révolutionnaire, perhaps more than any other, cannot be reduced to the terms of a means–end rationality, let alone justified in such terms. The violence was, in a sense, "too total."

Now George Rudé is not a "rational-choice" theorist in any rigorous sense. He does not seek to demonstrate that the massacres resulted from the rational pursuit of the self-interests of the *massacreurs*, nor that the means chosen in the pursuit of these interests were perfectly adequate to the designated ends. He does, however, implicitly believe that the revolutionary actors were reasonable and that their actions are to be understood as such. And this belief results in some rather blatant revolutionary apologetics.[19] In claiming the "utility" of the massacres, George Rudé is perhaps justifying less the rationality of the events than the "rationality" of the Revolution itself, or at least of the "popular Revolution," understood as a whole that must be rescued from the taint of ambiguity and defended in all its peripeties. Here, most definitely, I must part company with Professor Rudé and let him continue to fight, some two hundred years later, the Revolution's battles, and with almost the very same arguments.[20]

The importance of the September Massacres does not simply lie with the number of its victims. Many historians see the massacres as marking the beginning of the end of popular violence. Already several weeks prior to September, Danton, then the minister of justice, had declared: *Que la justice des tribunaux commence, et la justice du peuple cessera.*[21] And after the massacres, almost all parties with influence on the government agreed that a special apparatus had to be established to carry out revolutionary justice and monopolize the violence carried out in its name. Accordingly, the events of September are seen as marking the last important outbreak of what is sometimes called the Popular Terror, which was to be replaced by the official Terror of the Revolutionary Government. As such, a line is drawn after the September Massacres, distinguishing popular violence from state violence, the latter being explicitly presented as a means to stop the "popular executions," while satisfying the sans-culottes' desire for "prompt justice."

My account is going to be somewhat different. I will not situate the rupture after the September Massacres with the construction of a governmental apparatus specializing in "revolutionary justice."[22] Without denying the value of the more common account, I shall place the September Massacres themselves at the point of rupture. For my rupture concerns not those who carried out the violence, but the forms of that violence.

FORMS OF VIOLENCE

I shall try to give some idea of what I mean by "forms" by briefly describing the crowd violence that accompanied the previous journées révolutionnaires, as compared with the violence of the September Massacres.[23]

Popular violence prior to the September Massacres made a spectacle of the victim and his mutilation. Examine the typical course of events: the sans-culottes are in a state of insurrection. Crowds form on the street. Someone who, by position or reputation, excites popular hatred, usually a priest or aristocrat, is seized and threatened with being *lanterné*, that is, hung from the nearest lamppost. At this point someone tries to intervene, usually an agent of the government, displaying the symbols of his office and of the government's revolutionary legitimacy. This person (or persons) attempts to reason with the crowd and remove the potential victim from the clutches of his or her tormentors. While admitting the possible culpability of the object of the crowd's wrath, he speaks the language of the Law, claiming that the forms of due process must be followed and a proper trial held. This discourse is often shouted down, in any case ignored, and the person who gave it is forced to withdraw. If it was an agent of the government, a report will be written up, relating the efforts of the authorities and the failure of these same efforts—a report that can then be presented in the case of a judicial enquiry. Once the law, and those who speak in its name, have been explicitly rejected, the crowd makes good its threat. The poor wretch is indeed strung up from the nearest lamppost and, once dead, the head is separated from the body and placed at the end of a pike. An evisceration then takes place, with various organs also finding themselves at the end of pikes. These will then form the front of a somewhat macabre procession. A rope will be tied to the foot of the body, which will be dragged behind. This procession will tour the major streets of the city, visiting key public places, as well as, on occasion, places of particular significance to the victim. The procession will be accompanied with much rejoicing, gallows humor, and threats to do similar things to similar people. Witnesses to the procession will join in, shout words of encouragement, turn away, vomit in doorways, and some women will faint. Once the procession is over, the various pieces of the corpse will go on semipermanent display, usually near the gates to the city or section, or some other public place.

At this point, one might remember that George Rudé had spoken, relative to the violence of the revolutionary crowds, of their moderation. And he is right, if one speaks of the violence in purely quantitative terms. However, what little violence there was, was maximized as spectacle. Indeed, one suspects that it was because the choreography was so violent, that its quantity was, relatively speaking, restrained.

Consider now the character of the September Massacres. Again, one speaks of the "typical" case. The massacres did not occur in the street, they were not public, in the above sense. The objects of the crowds' wrath were the inmates of the prisons and other "total institutions" of the period; and the violence was restricted to the confines of these institutions, their courtyards, and immediate vicinities. It was not simply a general slaughter, conducted in complete anarchy, or at least not as the slaughter proceeded. Again the authorities, municipal and national, sent deputations to calm the crowds and to either stop or moderate the butchery.[24] And again they failed and were forced to retreat, sometimes under the threat of physical violence. At about the same time, however, persons who are described as strangers to the sans-culotte milieu,[25] but who were not agents of governmental authority, and without any mandate, stopped the executions, installed themselves behind a table, and organized "popular tribunals." In effect, justice was improvised. Juries were formed, judges named, a prosecutor established, the prison records obtained. The prisoners were then brought before this tribunal one by one, their identities and the reasons for their institutional confinement verified. A short interrogation followed, after which the prisoner would be declared either innocent or guilty. If declared guilty, there was but one penalty: the prisoner would be pushed beyond the threshold of a doorway, whereupon he or she would be bludgeoned or hacked to death with whatever instruments were available. The bodies of the victims were left to accumulate in a pile. A short while after the butchery had ended, the authorities carted the bodies to the outskirts of Paris, where they were buried in pits covered with chalk.

The contrast between the September Massacres and the outbreaks of popular violence that preceded it are striking. Two points stand out: the absence or presence of the mutilation and display of the corpses, and the role of the law. Let us consider the second of these points first.

We saw that during the acts of popular violence someone, usually someone official, would seek to have the crowd respect the due process of law, and that his demands would, inevitably, be rejected. Indeed, so often does the discourse of those who speak of the law get repeated and with always so few results, that one suspects that its real purpose lay elsewhere. Rather than being an attempt to save the victim, or to have justice served (in its forms at least), one suspects that this discourse served as a ritual of exclusion whereby the authorities separated themselves from the crowd and washed themselves of all responsibility for its actions.[26] Such a course of action, or more precisely, nonaction, is not without its uses, but the result is an explicit demonstration of the law's impotence and an implicit admission of the government's unofficial tolerance for the ensuing events. And neither could be tolerated by many of the revolutionary leaders, particularly those of a more radical persuasion. They sought—and indeed, they believed one of the Revolution's central aims to be—to reduce the distance between the law and the people; and this meant not only making the law an expression of the sovereign will of the people, but bringing the people under the sovereign authority of the law. And not the least of the implications of this conjoining of law and people was the placing of all violence committed by the people in the name of the Revolution under the authority of the Law. An imperative made all the more necessary in their minds by the increasing demands on the part of sansculotte spokesmen for the execution of the Revolution's enemies, and by the increasing likelihood of more and more extensive outbreaks of popular violence.[27] Now, as noted, during the September Massacres the "people" would deny the law as represented by the duly constituted authority of both the National Assembly and the Commune. And yet, they would not reject the authority of the law per se, as witnessed by the establishment of improvised tribunals with their makeshift justice. One might say that they rejected the official representatives of the law but not the law itself. In effect, what one is witnessing with the September Massacres is the transformation of popular violence into "popular justice."[28] And as an act of justice, the massacres would not differ all that much, as regards their form, from the acts of an official justice, which would also have its tribunals, juries, prosecutors, and its examination of written documents, and so on. It is in this sense that the September Massacres, rather than marking the culmination of popular violence, introduced a rupture that anticipated the official Terror to come. And as the anticipation (and reflection) of a new, more regularized form of violence, the September Massacres can be said to mark the end of popular violence. Not the least of the Jacobins' claims to legitimacy was their promise to end the outbreaks of crowd violence. And in fact, the Jacobin insurrection of 31 May 1793 was the first journée révolutionnaire not accompanied by popular executions.[29] The cadavers would mount under Jacobin rule, but what were called the *scènes de horreur*, "the scenes of horror," had ended.[30]

This brings us to the second point of comparison: the mutilation and display of corpses. During the September Massacres, although the dismemberment of corpses was not entirely absent, nor was it the rule. Nor was there the parade of dismembered and mutilated bodies which had accompanied the earlier journées révolutionnaires. In short, the spectacle of violence was absent.[31] In fact, the Parisian populace only became fully aware of the extent of the executions once the carts, carrying the bodies of the victims to the city's outskirts, threaded their way through the city streets—and it was at that point that popular opinion began turning against the massacres.[32] In truth, one suspects that had the violence of September taken the earlier form, there might have been fewer victims. Violence as spectacle is public, and the public, it seems, while not adverse to a certain *frisson*, would have balked at too many corpses. Besides, the execution of large numbers of people requires a more efficient use of time than allowed for by the dismemberment and display of body parts. In this regard too, the official Terror follows the pattern set by the September Massacres, where spectacle was abandoned for efficiency.[33]

Now this, admittedly, might appear contrary to general impressions. One often thinks of the public executions of the Terror as a spectacle. Books like *The Scarlet Pimpernel* or *The Tale of Two Cities* have filled our minds with images like those of the *tricoteuses*, those old hags who knitted beside the guillotine, cackling with glee as the heads rolled. But although the manifestly gruesome aspects of these executions are not to be denied, this is to miss something of their historical significance. The guillotine was invented by the good doctor Guillotin as an efficient and painless method of execution and, compared to the earlier practices of the Ancien Régime, it was.[34] Moreover, though the guillotine first operated in the central square of Paris, as the state Terror proceeded, it was moved to the outer suburbs, and finally, during the last days of what has come to be known as the "Grand Terror," most of the executions took place, like those of the September Massacres, within the prisons or their courtyards.

There is more to this change in forms, however, than merely the introduction of a more efficient, instrumentally rational mode of public execution. These two forms involve not just a relation to collective violence but a relation of "society" to that violence—a relation that reflects back on that society and can tell us something about it. For such violence is of a given society, and is thus expressive of that society, of its order, and of the modalities by which that order is affirmed. In order, then, to express something of this relation, and of the difference in this relation between the two forms, I am going to resort to two contrasting metaphors: a metaphor of ingestion and a metaphor of expulsion. In the one case, the anterior form, it is as though the social body seeks to devour its victims; whereas in the other, it is as if the victims are to be expelled from the social body.

In the first case, the violence is visible to all and thus engages the entire social body, at least vicariously. Again, the victims are cut up and cut open, the pieces mounted on the ends of metal implements and made to circulate through the major arteries of the city, with the entire populace being made to partake, if not necessarily savor, the repast. Moreover, whenever such violence is described, whether by the Revolution's sympathizers or detractors (though almost always by the literate and respectable classes, who were appalled at the "savagery" of the popular classes), the descriptions are couched in the terms of a vocabulary of digestion: those participating in such acts are inevitably called "cannibals," "anthropophagi," or *buveurs du sang* (blood-drinkers); and they are described as threatening to "bite off the head of an aristocrat" (or sometimes of a "bourgeois"), or to "eat their liver," "open up their stomach and eat the intestines," and so on; and, to be sure, particularly nasty sans-culottes are rumored to have actually carried out these threats (though such rumors are probably all apocryphal).[35]

The second form of violence, by contrast, employs a vocabulary of expulsion (but note: not of excretion, the polar opposite of ingestion). Here one finds a language of exclusion, with reference to either the ancient practices of ostracism or the newer language of the contract: one is pushed "outside the city," or "outside the protection of the law," or one is "returned to the state of nature"). Or alternatively, one hears the language of the purge, often supplemented by a whole panoply of medical metaphors that speak of the need to cut off gangrenous members or surgically remove diseased tissue.

Now, this second, more sanitized vocabulary has to be related to the language of Enlightenment, by which I understand something different from but not entirely unrelated to the Enlightenment as philosophical movement. Although there is still much argument about the Revolution's relation to the philosophical Enlightenment, there can be no doubt about the Revolution's constant, and constantly reiterated, use of the language of Enlightenment.[36] In a million and one speeches, texts, and theatrical representations the same message is repeated: society is to be enlightened; light is to shine on all society, and thereby eliminate all the areas of darkness; the entire topography of caves and crags, mountains and valleys, where shadows are cast, dark deeds committed, and diabolical plots hatched, is to be leveled. Accordingly society will form a single, smooth surface, where everyone will be visible to everyone else and where conformity to the law will result from continuous, mutual surveillance.[37]

And beyond the language of Enlightenment, there lies the horizon of an institutional project. For this was the period, broadly speaking, of what, since the work of Michel Foucault, has been termed the "Great Enclosure," when what had come to be perceived as "deviances" were removed from society and placed within an increasingly differentiated series of enclosed institutional spaces. A point not without relevance to the September Massacres and their tendency to confuse political with social deviancy. For not only, as noted earlier, were the victims common-law prisoners, as well as political prisoners, but with the invasion of the Bicêtre and the Saltpetrière (which were hospices as well as prisons), unemployed beggars and vagabonds, abandoned and delinquent young adolescents, as well as the insane, also found themselves before the bar of the revolutionary tribunals. In effect, the massacres tended to encompass almost all the newly emergent institutions of individual sequestration. It is as though a mechanism was being constructed which pushed the logic of social exclusion ever deeper. As though ever-widening circles of those who had been excluded from the visible realms of social intercourse were to be expelled from even the invisible realms of social separation; while the violence that purged those who had been excluded was itself to be expelled from the realms of general social visibility. As if the snake could swallow its own tail.[38]

LAW AND SOCIETY

It is at this point that I wish to conclude, though in another sense I have only just begun. There remains the question of the larger significance of the changes that I have sought to articulate. The violence of which I have spoken was neither a mere tool, whose only significance lies in its effectiveness relative to the purposes it was meant to serve; nor was it some sort of preinstitutional chaos out of which a regularized social life would be shaped, and which, as such, escapes interpretation, because without shape itself. To speak of the forms of violence is to speak of violence as part of society, and as expressive of the society of which it is a part. Indeed, to speak of the forms of violence may be to provide a unique perspective on society, here on both a society in eclipse and a society emergent. In what follows, I will restrict myself to some brief and very general comments, which, it is hoped, point in the direction of further enquiry.

1. One is tempted to claim that popular violence, as regards the mutilation and display of corpses, merely reflected the practices of the crown under the Ancien Régime. For the latter also made a spectacle of the dismemberment of those it had condemned to die—and in manners that could be quite extravagant. (In this regard popular violence was relatively "humane," the victim not being made to die a "thousand deaths" under torture.) Where popular violence most clearly differed from the violence of the crown, was in its relation to the law. Yet here too, one might argue, the crown's violence conformed to the principles of the Ancien Régime. According to the latter, since the law proceeded from above, only those closest to its source, that is, only those in the upper reaches of the hierarchy, could be the law's representatives; the general populace, being mired in a profane reality, was by definition incapable of participating in the formulation, pronouncement, or

execution of the law. As such, popular violence could not but be a rejection of the law. Only with the September Massacres, with what I called the transformation of "popular violence" into "popular justice," did the general populace begin to assimilate something of the modern conception of the law and its "egalitarianism."[39] Only in a Republic, Montesquieu had said, can the people be imbued with the "spirit of the laws." In this sense, it is perhaps not entirely coincidental that the massacres occurred only weeks after the fall of the monarchy.[40]

2. One does not want, however, to assimilate completely the violence of the revolutionary crowds to the principles and practices of monarchic justice (which, one should add, underwent major changes during absolutist rule). Popular violence did not simply reject the law, it inverted the law, turning the hierarchical order upside down in a carnival-like atmosphere. And as a carnivalesque inversion, one is tempted to see in such violence the signs of a separate popular culture. (The existence of the latter being suggested, not least of all, by the mixture of incomprehension and disgust with which such violence was greeted by its "bourgeois" critics—critics who, it must be remembered, often condoned the equally sanguinary movements of the "national razor.")[41] Here a brief reference can be made to the book on popular culture by the Russian literary critic Mikhail Bakhtin, entitled *Rabelais and His World*. In this work the carnival is perceived as a truly popular festival, for unlike, say, the "ceremonies of the Law," it is not offered by, or with reference to, any external, transcendent source of power or truth. And in a hierarchical society, where all order is perceived to proceed from above, the carnival, by virtue of its "immanence," can only proceed in accordance with a certain, albeit welcome, disorder. For the duration of the festivities, the sanctity of the existing forms of the coercive sociopolitical organization are mocked, its rules and injunctions suspended and, in an atmosphere of terrible gaiety, carnival "rights and freedoms" reign supreme.[42] Furthermore, in this atmosphere of carnival violence, as Mikhail Bakhtin writes, "the kitchen and the battle meet and cross each other in the image of the rent body."[43] Images of culinary anatomization and dismemberment are common, and the dismemberment of individual bodies is clearly related to the dismemberment of the social body, the latter being literally turned inside out, with what Bakhtin calls the "material bodily lower stratum" acquiring ascendancy over the more heady realms of the upper strata. Finally, the individual body of carnivalesque imagery is portrayed as "grotesque," composed of exaggerated protuberances reaching out to the world, and equally exaggerated orifices through which all bodily transactions with the world pass. Mikhail Bakhtin contrasts this grotesque body to the classical image of the body which was revived in the high culture of the early modern era. With the latter, the body was presented as formed of smooth, impenetrable surfaces that "contained" it, closing it off as a separate completed phenomenon:

All signs of its unfinished character, of its growth and proliferation, were eliminated; its protruberances and offshoots were removed, its convexities . . .
smoothed out, its apertures closed. The ever unfinished nature of the body
was hidden. . . . The accent was placed on the completed, self-sufficient individ-
duality of the given body. . . . The inner processes of absorbing and ejecting
were not revealed.[44]

One is tempted to transpose here the image of the individual body to that of
the social body held by the revolutionaries who were, in this as in all else,
very much classicists.

3. This brings me to a third point, one that concerns what might be called
the delineation of the social body or, more precisely, of society.[45] I am not
speaking here of a geographical or territorial delineation, though a few words
about the latter may serve to illuminate what I am speaking of. In the Ancien
Régime, the geographic extent of the kingdom stretched as far as the
monarch's authority; the latter, however, tended to become weaker the
further removed it was from the monarch's original domain, till it faded into
a sort of no-man's-land at its farthest reaches. In a similar manner, it was
held that the force of the law weakened the further removed its point of
application from its point of origin.[46] Which is to say that as the law moved
from its source in divine principle, through its terrestial representatives in the
first two Estates, and down to the lower reaches of the social hierarchy, it was
supposed that its hold became ever more tenuous, men's actions being im-
pelled by appetites increasingly removed from the ideals embodied in the
legal order. What this suggests is that, even as the legal order defined the
societal order, the order thus defined was necessarily much narrower than
"society" or collective existence, particularly in its more profane aspects.
With the Revolution all this changed. The law no longer moved vertically,
down a hierarchy, but "horizontally," where it was to apply to all, with
equal force and in an equal manner. One consequence of this "horizontal"
positioning, which should be noted, was that the law, and the societal order
that it was to establish, could no longer be inverted, only overthrown. The extension of the law in this sense, with its egalitarianism, its universalism and seri-
ousness, was opposed to carnival forms and "their whole psychology of two
worlds."[47] In this sense, the law was the perfect instrument of revolution.

Another consequence, a more significant consequence for our present purposes, was that the legal order was held to define not just a societal order but
"society" itself. In the utopian longings of the revolutionaries, law and society were to be coequivalent: the law was to constitute society, the pure
product of a legislative project; while the society thus constituted was to be
so designed as to uphold the "sovereignty of the law" and its rigors. To be
sure, this revolutionary apotheosis of the law could not last. For the law retained a trace of its transcendence: by its very rationality and visibility, by the
very fact that it *demanded* obedience, it could never be identical to society.[48] And

as it became all too obvious that the hold of the law was (necessarily) weak, the imperative was to discover the "real" society, the society beneath the laws, constituted of a deeper order barely visible to the social actors, an order located, at least in part, outside the self-conscious workings of their rational faculties.[49] But even as the legal order was, relative to the definition of social reality, to be replaced by either a "natural order" (variously defined) or a nonrational, normative order, the law still served, without remaining identical to society, to trace the limits of behavior in society. An exoskeleton of the permissible, failure to conform to the law placed one outside society, depriving one of the rights the latter guarantees and the protection it affords. And it is only when the boundaries of society are thus demarcated, that the logic of exclusion discussed above can begin to operate.

4. The last point: by drawing a line separating social from antisocial behavior, the law establishes what, ideally, lies outside society as well as within. And not the least of the things is to be pushed beyond the societal frontiers is all violence that originates outside the law and its application. We are faced here with what Max Weber considered one of the defining characteristics of the modern state: its monopolization of the legal use of violence (along with its corollary, the pacification of society). But what of this legal, or better, legalized, violence that establishes the boundaries and banishes the criminal and his crime outside the "gates of the city"? Is it to be part of the order it enforces, with full rights of visibility? Or do the means of enforcement belie the order to be enforced, and not just because of the resemblance of legalized violence to its illegal counterpart? Within the Ancien Régime things were clear. The violence of power was presumed necessary, the very reflection of its strength. As power moved ever deeper into the lower regions of the hierarchy, the recourse to violence was deemed increasingly necessary to enforce what could only be a minimal, grudging obedience. Moreover, power made itself visible through its violence; it had to appear spectacular and arbitrary (capable of terrible deeds, but also of acts of grace) if it was to mark its distance from common mortals. It was only when the nation was sovereign and power was said to emerge from society at large, that its violence, at least when directed internally, would appear as weakness, the sign of a division internal to its source. It was only when the law was the supposed expression of a general will that the (frequent) recourse to legalized violence would suggest that the law was not general and the people were far from infused with its spirit. At worst, the violence of the law might indicate the existence of an undeclared civil war, itself the possible sign of governmental tyranny.[50]

Now it would be difficult to assert that the modern state had been more, or for that matter, less violent than that of the Ancien Régime. But where modern states have been violent, they have almost invariably sought to cover the extension of their violence with the simultaneous removal of that violence from the sight of, and more generally, intercourse with, society. Indeed, one might read the history of state violence since the French Revolution as continuously attempting to improve on this logic.[51] In this regard, the twentieth century, with its concentration camps and gulags, has been particularly fertile, with perhaps the most recent refinements coming from Argentina, that piece of Europe in Latin America. With the *desaparecidos* of the 1970s, not only was there an attempt to render the violence invisible (it was officially denied; those slated for execution being picked up by police and soldiers in civilian uniform). Not only was there an attempt to render the identities of the victims invisible (their identities were removed from official records, their bodies buried in unmarked graves or dropped over the ocean), as well as those of their persecutors (they gave themselves false names, sometimes false identities; the law under whose authority they operated was, when not ignored, made into an official state secret). But there were, as well, attempts to make even the sites of violence "disappear." For not only were the sites where victims were held, interrogated, and executed closed to public view, there were, apparently, attempts to render these sites mobile, lest, by virtue of the evidence of geography, they be susceptible to public exposure. This must all count as a significant improvement in the logic of exclusion; beyond the acts of incarceration, and of death by incarceration, it is the traces of such acts that are systematically eliminated.[52]

We are here, to be sure, far removed from the events of September 1792. But something began in that month, another history, different connections, with unexpected and unrecognized lines of descent. It would, of course, be absurd, during the bicentennial of the French Revolution, to establish a separate anniversary for the September Massacres. What perhaps began with the latter is too deeply buried in our modernity, too far removed from questions of political partisanship, and too dark in its character and implications to admit of the prestige of an inaugural event. In something as epochal, total, and complex as the French Revolution, it is its deepest, most obscure aspects to which we remain the most tightly bound.

NOTES

1. Hannah Arendt, "On Violence," in *Crisis of the Republic* (New York: Harcourt Brace Jovanovich, 1970), p. 106.

2. As a morality of the means it would bracket the question of ends, or at least of ultimate ends, whether stemming from universal values, or the more particular values of the analyst. And yet, almost inevitably, the latter return, unannounced and unquestioned. For the question of the actor's "rationality" tends to be subject to the analyst's social prejudices; whereas that of the "rationality" of the actor's motives tends to be prey to the author's moral prejudices.

3. "Michelet's use of le peuple corresponds, of course, far more closely to the facts . . ." George Rudé, *The Crowd and the French Revolution* (London: Oxford, 1967), p. 232.

4. From *Reflections on the Revolution in France*, cited in ibid., p. 2.

5. Indeed Professor Rudé is able, by virtue of his archival searches, to pinpoint for each of the *journées révolutionnaires*, which categories of sans-culottes were present, and from which sectors of Paris they came, thus shedding considerable light on the individual character of each of the events.

6. Rudé, *The Crowd and the French Revolution*, pp. 191–196.

7. Ibid., pp. 219–221.

8. Ibid., p. 199.

9. Ibid., p. 225.

10. Charles Tilly, *From Mobilization to Revolution* (Reading, Mass.: Addison-Wesley, 1978), pp. 145–149.

11. In truth, the book is not entirely consistent in this regard. The "rationality" of a "defensive reaction" cannot but be "bounded" by its failure to adapt to history and its "innovations." In a later book, *Ideology and Popular Protest* (New York: Pantheon, 1980), even the rationality of "proactive struggles" (those of unions, for example) will be considered limited, and limiting. Rationality here—and it is truly a revolutionary "rationality"—would consist not in adapting to history but in mastering it. However, notes George Rudé, echoing Lenin if not Lukács, those subject to history (i.e., the popular classes) are of themselves in no position to become subjects of history.

12. Richard Cobb's work in particular is invaluable for charting the social and geographical topography of these rumors and fears.

13. The term *septembriseur* was not the least of the epithets used to discredit one's opponents in the factional infighting that was to consume the revolutionary camp. An excellent essay on the "difficulties" in using the archival evidence to study the *journées révolutionnaires* is the first piece in Richard Cobb's *The Police and the People. French Popular Protest 1789–1820* (London: Oxford University Press, 1970), pp. 3–48.

14. Rudé, *The Crowd in the French Revolution*, p. 111.

15. Ibid., p. 110. On these events one should consult the classic work of Pierre Caron, *Les Massacres de septembre* (Paris: Maison du Livre Français, 1935); and the more recent piece by Frédéric Bluche, *Septembre 1792. Logiques d'un massacre* (Paris: Robert Laffont, 1986).

16. There is some evidence, however, that the rumor only developed after the massacres had begun. See Bluche, *September 1792*, pp. 29–30.

17. "*Surprisingly*, only one quarter of the prisoners were priests, nobles, or 'politicals'. . . ." Rudé, *The Crowd in the French Revolution*, p. 110 (my emphasis).

18. Ibid., p. 112.

19. Though in truth, he does speak much later in the book of the massacres as a consequence of "mass hysteria." Ibid., p. 225.

20. Others have sought to place the "rationality" of the *septembriseurs'* actions within the internal struggles of the revolutionary camp, their real purpose being, it is claimed, to terrorize the more moderate elements. Now although there is some evidence that certain elements were willing to use the massacres to advance their interests in the factional struggles, such maneuvers appear as a sideshow to the main event. Nor did any moderate die in the violence. Nor, generally speaking, were the moderates (i.e., the Girondins), as judged by their press, any more or less critical of the events, as they were taking place, than their more radical counterparts. It was only later, after public opinion had turned against the massacres, that the Girondins

sought to distance themselves from the events, while portraying their more radical enemies as morally compromised. See Bluche, *Septembre 1792*, pp. 73–76, 201–205.

21. Ibid., pp. 22–23.

22. One might wish to date the beginnings of the construction of this apparatus with the formation of the Committees of Public Safety and General Security in February of 1793, though one could also date these same beginnings in August of 1792—that is, just prior to the September Massacres—when the first hesitant steps were taken in the establishment of the *guillotine permanente*, the revolutionary tribunals, and the committees of surveillance.

23. What follows is indebted to Bernard Conein,"Le tribunal et la terreur du 14 juillet 1789 aux 'massacres de septembre.'" *Les révoltes logiques*, no. 11 (Winter 1979–1980): 2–24.

24. Though the attitude of the municipal authorities, in particular was rather ambiguous and has become the object of some controversy. See Bluche, *Septembre 1792*, pp. 151–183.

25. Conein, "Le tribunal et la terreur," pp. 18–19.

26. Ibid., pp. 10–11.

27. Already in the month prior to the September Massacres, the Commune of Paris was petitioning the National Assembly for the authority to establish a special tribunal that would be responsible for judging and punishing political crimes. This tribunal was to be composed of citizen–judges elected by the sectional assemblies, the idea being to place all public executions under the authority of the Commune, while simultaneously associating the sans-culottes, or at least their politicized elements, with the new reorganization of the judicial apparatus. And in fact, on August 17, the National Assembly did agree to the formation of a new tribunal, though one composed of judges elected not by the sectional assemblies, but by special electoral bodies and on the basis of professional criteria. Ibid., pp. 16–17.

28. Indeed those radicals who sought to justify, or at least excuse, the events of September argued that because the people had organized themselves into tribunals (though the evidence suggests that the "people" did not organize the tribunals, but simply recognized tribunals organized "from without") these events were not to be represented as "massacres," but as an act of justice, of people's justice, the just punishment of the Revolution's opponents.

29. Conein, "Le tribunal et la terreur," p. 23.

30. In truth, there was one last outbreak of popular violence—after the fall of the Jacobins. On the first of Prairial (May 20, 1795), during the last desperate "revolt" of the sans-culottes, the deputy Féraud was killed and his head paraded on a pike.

31. These claims apply only to Paris. In the provinces, the "echoes" (and they were rather faint) of the September Massacres still involved the mutilation and display of corpses. See Bluche, *September 1792*, pp. 103–121.

32. Ibid., pp. 75–76.

33. Here a certain caution has to be added to Natalie Zemon Davis's claim that the "rites of violence," particularly in their more carnivalesque forms, serve to produce the "conditions for guilt-free massacre." Although they may help the killers to "forget that their victims are human beings," in the French Revolution at least, the real massacres occurred outside the framework of such rites. "The Rites of Violence,"

Society and Culture in Early Modern France (Stanford: Stanford University Press, 1965), p. 181.

34. Although the observation of movements of the face and body after decapitation led to a lively debate as to whether the guillotine actually delivered its promise of instant death. See "Notice historique et philosophique sur la vie, les travaux et les doctrines de Cabanis," which introduces P.-J.-G. Cabanis, *Rapports du physique et du moral de l'homme* (Geneva: Slatkine Reprints, 1980), pp. XXI–XXII.

35. Cobb, *The Police and the People*, pp. 87–88. Cannibalistic imagery in popular revolts has a longer history. See for example Emmanuel Le Roy Ladurie, *Les paysans de Languedoc* (Paris: S.E.V.P.E.N., 1966), pp. 398–399; and *Carnival in Romans* (New York: George Braziller, 1979), pp. 179–180.

36. See Brian Singer, *Society, Theory and the French Revolution* (New York: St. Martin's, 1986), pp. 46–47; Jean Starobinski, *1789: Les emblêmes de la raison* (Paris: Flammarion, 1979), pp. 31–37; and Mona Ozouf, *La fête révolutionnaire* (Paris: Gallimard, 1976), p. 119.

37. Singer, *Society, Theory and the French Revolution*, pp. 47 and 193; Michel Foucault, "The Eye of Power," reprinted in *Power/Knowledge: Selected Interviews and Other Writing 1972–77* (New York: Pantheon, 1980), p. 153.

38. Since writing this essay, I have been asked to say something about violence from the "right." In this regard, an exceptional article by Colin Lucas on the "White Terror" ("Themes in Southern Violence After 9 Thermidor," in Gwynne Lewis and Colin Lucas, eds., *Beyond the Terror: Essays in French Regional and Social History* [Cambridge: Cambridge University Press, 1983]) can provide a few comparisons. The popular culture of the southeast was not that of Paris, and the violence in the former was rooted in (the decomposition of?) youth organizations and charivaris which had long disappeared in Paris. Moreover the counterrevolutionary communal violence had an intensely local character (it being, apparently, a tacit rule that the victims and their tormentors had to know each other) that did not obtain in Parisian conditions. However, the violence was public: if the crowds did not participate in the killings, as in Paris, they were always there as witnesses; and bodies were mutilated, though curiously not by the killers but by the crowds after the event (though mutilation did not have the obligatory character it did in Paris—indeed, the victims were not always killed, but subjected to traditional forms of humiliation or restitution). What about the relation to the law? Obviously, such violence took place outside the framework of the law and its forms. Colin Lucas does not tell us if the representatives of the law remonstrated before the crowds, only to be explicitly rejected. But in another sense, he does suggest that it was the (former) representatives of the law, those who had upheld it the most rigorously, who were the "privileged" targets of the violence. For those murdered during the White Terror were not simply Jacobins, but those Jacobins who had applied the revolutionary laws the most inflexibly, who had thus, in the name of a larger collective entity and more general norms, ignored the community and its more traditional, tractable ways of settling conflicts and easing tensions. These were truly the "reactive struggles" mentioned earlier, pitting the community against the external, encroaching, and innovative powers of the nation, with its legal universalism, and the state, with its military, fiscal, and legal centralization.

39. One usually understands this egalitarianism as "equality before the law"; but

it also encompasses an "equality behind the law," whereby everyone participates, in principle equally, in the formulation and carrying out of the law. It is the very meaning of popular sovereignty.

40. Admittedly, during the religious strife of the sixteenth century, the crowds often claimed for themselves the role of the magistrate (and cleric). But beyond the fact that the religious and political authorities often participated in the crowd's actions, and were almost always willing to justify them, the crowds were, by acting in the name of the sacred, presumably approaching the transcendence of the law. Perhaps in a hierarchical society, the explicit rejection of the law and its forms only occurs when it is the hierarchy itself that is being attacked. See Davis, "The Rites of Violence," pp. 164–169.

41. Incomprehension, if not always disgust, almost always suggests the copresence of two incommensurable cultures. Too often historians have searched for the existence of a separate popular culture in what turns out to be the fragments of an earlier elite culture, reworked for consumption by the lower strata. Such seems to have been the fate of the research into the *bibliothèque bleue*—a fate that was not entirely unpredictable, given that, by definition, a *bibliothèque* of whatever color will be tied, however tenuously, to the world and culture of the literate. See Robert Mandrou, *De la Culture populaire aux XVII et XVIIIe siècles* (Paris: Stock, 1964); and Geneviève Bollème, *La Bibliothèque bleue* (Paris: Julliard, 1971).

42. Mikhail Bakhtin, *Rabelais and His World* (Cambridge, Mass.: MIT Press, 1968), pp. 9–11.

43. Ibid., p. 197. See also pp. 192–194 and 207.

44. Ibid., p. 29.

45. In a sense, the Revolution will mark the displacement of the social body by society. For once the former is no longer tied to the image of the individual body of the monarch, collective existence can no longer be represented quite so easily in corporeal (if not necessarily, organic) terms.

46. For purposes of clarity I am exaggerating here: the absolutist regime sought a certain, partial consolidation of its territory, and of the law enacted therein.

47. The expression is taken from Natalie Davis, "The Reasons of Misrule," in *Society and Culture in Early Modern France*, p. 120.

48. At least not without being internalized, and thus losing its character as "law." Singer, *Society, Theory and the French Revolution*, pp. 110–123.

49. In truth, one should add that this search is complicated by the existence of another, parallel search. For the society, born of the continuous reversibility of is and ought, is held to exist not just as an object to be investigated in its deep structures, but as a subject to be constantly interrogated as regards the surface movements of will formation, public opinion, and fashion.

50. Singer, *Society, Theory and the French Revolution*, pp. 86–87.

51. And what about antistate violence? Terrorism is spectacle or it is nothing, without, however, being popular. Generalizations are dangerous, but an extraordinary example of truly popular violence has recently been provided by the overthrow of the Duvalier regime in Haiti. Here the populace took to the streets in a festival atmosphere to search out ex-members of the paralegal police force of the ancien régime, the *tonton macoutes*. *Macoutes* who were found were executed, and, as in the French

Revolution, their dismembered bodies were borne in triumph by the crowds. More-over, the events were filmed, presumably by participants, and video cassettes were distributed underground throughout Haiti and the Haitian diaspora. However, un-like the French Revolution, the crowd violence was not limited to a few "symbolic" victims. But then a "revolution" had not really occurred; and once, under the pres-sure of "liberal" allies, the killings stopped, momentum was lost and forces of the old regime were able to reassert themselves. I owe this information to a personal com-munication by Nina Schiller.

52. Paul Virilio/Sylvere Lotringer, *Pure War* [New York: Semiotext(e), 1983], pp. 88–89.

NINE

The Cult of the Supreme Being and the Limits of the Secularization of the Political

Ferenc Fehér

REPRESENTATIVE INTERPRETATIONS

In two centuries of history writing, perhaps the most contentious aspect of the history of the French Revolution is the domain of explanations concerning the conflict of the Revolution with the church and religion. Not only are the explanations sharply divergent as far as conclusions and interpretive terms are concerned, but, more importantly, the explanatory schemata are not even coextensive. Some of the pertinent theses regard the relationship of the consecutively dominant revolutionary groups to the church and to the "religious issue" as an interconnected and continuous process, a relationship that gradually developed or degenerated from mutually tension-laden but earnest attempts at cooperation into terror and civil war. For others, there is absolutely no connection between the fiasco of the efforts to reform the church by the new nation–state on the one hand, and the new revolutionary cult of the Supreme Being on the other.

Given the primarily political character of the issue, conspiracy theories quickly surfaced on both the right and the left. In the very period of the revolutionary storm, the famous Abbé Barruel set the dominant tone[1] for the two-centuries-long debate by flatly denouncing the gloomy drama as the end result of the plot of the philosophes, the freemasons, the men of the Enlightenment. Although over the next century, research methods matured from mere puerile accusations to academically respectable techniques, ultramontanism even in de la Gorce's magisterial work[2] remained fundamentally committed to the thesis of a premeditated and orchestrated leftist conspiracy. In the nineteenth-century republican narratives written in the style of Hugo, the similarly dubious story of a "counterconspiracy" of priest and nobleman in alliance with the barbarously ignorant and bigoted peasant of the *bocage*, inevitably emerged.[3]

An incomparably more serious approach, one which constitutes a venerable tradition of interpretations from Madame de Staël to Jean Jaurès[4] and which is still present on the academic scene,[5] detects dilemmas where others only discover sheer manipulation, ill will, and factional spirit. These mention mistakes, sometimes of tragic magnitude, instead of deviously hatched plots. However, the different versions of this type of theory have one problematic feature in common: they are atomistic readings of the religious drama of the Revolution, a drama that has a thoroughly interconnected plot, a tightly interwoven texture, and a continuous structure.

Edgar Quinet,[6] the representative theorist of a third schema, refers to the "missed historical opportunity" of the alliance between religious and secular democracy. With certain modifications, his theory is an organic continuation, as well as a revision, of the aspirations and illusions of *Le cercle social* of Fauchet, Grégoire, and Bonneville. This debating club of the most democratic stream of the future *Église constitutionnelle* tried to create a new and plebeian Catholicism, and, so at least its founders believed, it was destined to become the religious center of the Revolution.[7] Quinet expands the confused overtures of Le cercle social into a world history of radical Christianity.

Aulard misreads Quinet's position as one recommending Protestantism for a panacea to the French Revolution.[8] In fact, Quinet interprets the story of Christianity (both Protestant and Catholic) as humanity's great "novel of education" to political democracy. According to Quinet, the genuine spirit of Christianity had resided not in the papacy but in the councils, the "hermeneutical conventions" of equals who had, beyond the work of the free interpretation of the text, created the first system of a representative spiritual government.[9] The devastating inroads of the barbarians were needed to erode Christian democracy and to usher in, with the pope as an adequate *primus inter pares*, centuries of a degenerate aristocratic rule over the Church of Christ which were also long periods of a total religious decay.[10] But the "eighteenth of Brumaire" of Gregory VII, this revolutionary absolute monarch, overthrew the rule of a dissolute oligarchy and, in putting "morals on the order of the day" and demanding that popes should become saints, guided Christianity into a "social pact" with the world.[11]

The results of Gregory's revolutionary coup were in turn dissipated by both Catholic and Protestant church bureaucracies. It could have been one more powerful reason for the French Revolution, the this-worldly heir of Christian democracy, to assist the slender but surviving forces of democratic Christianity instead of tinkering with the bureaucratic rebuilding of the old edifice. The tragedy in the event was due to the historical circumstance that France was the only major country that lived its political revolution prior to its religious revolution.[12] Therefore the spirit of the Revolution, despite the secular language, remained deeply Jesuitic and inquisitional in its vituperative rhetoric and coercive measures against both the old and new Gallican church. The great historical opportunity of an alliance between secular and religious democracy was thus missed.

Without doubt, Quinet's story is one of the representative grand narratives of the conflict between the (official and oppositional) church and the Revolution, and it is one recounted with great persuasive force and verve. However, the premise, the reconcilability of church democracy and the democratic nation–state as equal political partners, is, in my view, a premodern conception, and one that has been correctly criticized by H. Maier.[13]

The most celebrated debate in French historiography on the conflict between the old and new church and the Revolution, on the character and appraisal of both the dechristianizing movement and the Cult of the Supreme Being, is the Aulard–Mathiez controversy.[14] Despite the clamor of the mêlée, the factual disagreements between these doyens of revolutionary historiography are minimal, although their evaluations of the story are sharply divergent. In addition, neither side draws the philosophical consequences of their own respective positions. In his early, major book on the issue, Aulard indeed believed that dechristianization as a popular movement had started only with the Jacobin dictatorship, that it had had hardly any antecedents, and that it had taken but very slender roots. Mathiez, in contrast, spotted the beginnings of the movement already in the 1790 Feast of the Federation. He also marshaled considerable supporting evidence of a ceremonial and ritual culture that grew out of the Revolution and outside of the church, one that became a competition to both refractory and constitutional Catholicism. This new ritual served as the basis and the raw material for the popular movement of dechristianization and the Cult of Reason or (and this was in Mathiez's opinion a mere change of name) the Cult of the Supreme Being. However, Aulard frankly admits in his later book on the same issue that he had initially underestimated the deep religious indifference of the French (above all the peasant) masses. Thus their factual statements, if not their assessments, drew considerably nearer. At the same time, Mathiez ought to have made a philosophical argument to prove his major point, namely, the identical character of the Cult of Reason and the Cult of the Supreme Being, since this is a theoretical and not an archival issue. And what is the most painful feature of this famous, tumultuous, but in the last analysis not particularly rewarding controversy, is the fact that neither Aulard's comprehensive books, which cover the whole story, nor Mathiez's writings on the issue provide an integral theory of the conflict between the church and the Revolution.

The postwar research on this classic topic has been characterized by a revealing ambivalence. On the one hand, the impetus given to historiography by social and cultural anthropology and by the *Annales* movement has yielded significant results in exploring the subterranean world of popular religious imagination and habits and the survival of pre-Christian rites and their transformation in the revolutionary storm. Beyond providing a wealth of data, this has enriched us with new insights.[15] On the other hand, we face a telling lacuna whenever we try to address the revolutionary policies on the church and religion on the basis of more recent narratives.[16] This time, the cause of the silence is not embarrassment in the teeth of a "delicate" problem, but rather universal ennui. The postwar world of technological and social rationalization seems to be convinced that both fanatical and quasi-religious anticlericalism as well as a redemptive politics with its revolutionary substitutes for transcendental beliefs belong irretrievably in a vanished world.

This chapter is based on a diametrically opposed conviction. The writer believes that the fiasco of the revolutionary reform of the Gallican church and the story of the subsequent reaction, of the attempts to create a revolutionary religion in an all-out critique of political reason, together write a drama in two acts, the second act of which cannot be understood without the first. They together recount a paradigmatic fable about the dogmatic fury of rationalization and secularization in the early days of what seemed to be the ultimate victory of the Enlightenment, about its necessary fiasco, about the backlashes of an overzealous rationalization, and about the limits of political secularization.

THE FURY OF RATIONALIZATION AND THE REVOLUTIONARY FIASCO

One of the very few consensually shared opinions by historians of the French Revolution is that the Gallican church was ripe for reform on the eve of the Revolution and that this was a widely held goal at the end of the Old Regime both within and outside the church.[17] The historians' general perception of the near-universal recognition of the need for rationalization in the age may create the illusion that it was an easy task. In fact, as the Revolution had to learn very soon, and at a heavy price, *rationalization* is not a homogeneous term but an umbrella word. In the mouth of the advocates of the internal reform of the church, the term meant streamlining, modernization. In the interpretation of the philosophes and their political successors, it simply implied the application of the uniform principles of reason to society as a whole and therefore, by implication, also to the affairs of the church. The homogeneity and uniformity of the catchword "rationalization" was a common but dangerous illusion of the prerevolutionary Enlightenment. The stumbling blocks involved in the issue can be identified in very simple questions: What kind of rationalization, uniform or sphere-specific? Rationalization by whom? And, finally, Rationalization on behalf of whom?

Once these questions are posed, the almost inextricable complexity of the situation that had developed already before the Revolution[18] becomes apparent. For almost two centuries a trend had been emanating from the court "to rationalize" the inherent contradictions of Gallicanism on its own behalf. After eliminating the authority of Rome, the monarchs also intended to destroy the representative system of the church as a competitive political authority within the absolutist rule.[19] Absolute princes could not be satisfied even with the decaying representative system that was reigning supreme within the church, in part because it was a bastion against royal inroads and in part because it could have served as a dangerous example. Nor could they ever accept the claim of the church to maintain an independent legal system parallel to their jurisdiction. The much discussed issue of *appel comme d'abus*, a common device of the court and parlements against the church, is telling proof of this incessant and irreconcilable conflict of parallel legal systems.[20] The "royal rationalization" of the church was therefore a strong option. At the same time, however, it was never implemented, nor even seriously attempted, and for good reason. Without the sanction of an independent, authoritative, and wholly spiritual power, the absolute monarchy would have been reduced in the eyes of an ever more influential public opinion into common tyranny or oriental despotism.[21]

The attempts on the part of the parlements to rationalize the church were even more self-contradictory. Their famous and much discussed "egoism" was not a moral but a sociological category. The parlements constituted a professional corporation within the system of Estates. And a corporation cannot reform another corporation under the sign of universalistic claims notwithstanding the high degree of formal rationality of the parlements' demand for a unified legal system. The victory of the parlements would have resulted either in the total monopoly of a legal aristocracy over the legislature and the administration of justice or in the further strengthening of the absolute rule of the prince.

"Society," or "the public opinion," an entity that until the Revolution had no sociologically perceivable body, regularly proposed its own versions of rationalization for the whole social world, including the clergy. Philosophical theses (of "tolerance," of an education based on "reason" and not "prejudice," of civil or natural religions) were widely advertised. Bereft of public forums of deliberation, however, the future liberal and radical actors of the revolutionary assemblies, who were to have a prominent role in shaping the church policies of the Constituent Assembly, had no opportunity to conduct discussions on the future political options of the sweeping reform of the church. The frequent statements of historians concerning the total unpreparedness of the revolutionary politicians for dealing with this enormous task merely describe the result of precisely this political lacuna.

Future reformers and revolutionaries frequently boasted about the "supreme rationality" of their ideas. But in fact, they were of the worst schools of rationality. They were imbued with the dominant spirit of *étatisme*. As a considerable contingent of them (Treilhard, Durand de Maillane, Martineau) had served as legal experts in the parlements, they brought a badly needed expertise on the issue of the clergy into the revolutionary legislation. This expertise, however, was at the same time inextricably interwoven with factionalism and the spirit of tit-for-tat. Some others, for example Camus and Lanjuinais were either surviving vestiges of a long-suppressed Jansenism, Protestants like Barnave, or professed libertines like Mirabeau. Their masterplans of rationalization could, at least, be suspected by friend and foe alike of being less than an expression of impartial justice and coolly inquisitive reason.[22] Beyond this far-from-negligible moral consideration, the future experts on church issues for the Revolution never even explored the following fundamental issues, without which no blueprint could be termed rational. First, what status were they going to grant to the church: that of a reformed corporation, a separate and independent association, or a state agency? Second, it was a foregone conclusion of some, and the increasingly prevailing option of others, not to declare even a reformed Catholicism as the national religion. But were they not thus undermining Gallicanism and opening the door to the influence of Rome from which no radical social transformation could expect beneficial results? Third, if they were to reduce the church to the role of a state agency without integrating its dogma into the founding principles of the state, could the result of this decision be anything but the creation of a rebellious servant rather than a useful spiritual arm of the state?

Paradoxically, the drive for reform within the church was motivated by the very fact that the church was the best-organized and the most streamlined of all three Estates. The need for reform grew out of the needs of an already existing but defective internal rationalization, not from the total absence of systemic rationality. The church had a representative "political" system of its own, one that could be termed an aristocratic parliamentary republic within an absolute monarchy. It had its own judiciary system, which, though constantly threatened by the court and the parlements, was powerful enough within its own walls. While enjoying exemption from taxation and making only "voluntary contributions" to the royal budget, it had its own enormous wealth and system of taxation. The church employed huge and separate bodies of (political, fiscal, theological, and educational) bureaucracies and, although submitting to the political hegemony of the court, it enjoyed a virtual independence from Rome and had a political representation in the court as well as a wide influence over secular affairs.

At the same time, the whole elaborate and highly rationalized system suffered from maladies that were surprisingly similar to those of the Ancien Régime as a whole. As a result of exactly the same principles of selection and appointment, the caste of the prelates became an aristocratic network to the same degree as did the clique of commanding officers in the royal army. The church went through the same process of unstoppable and irreversible fiscal crisis as the court, and basically for the same reasons (the luxury of the upper layers combined with the structural impossibility of financial modernization). The church also had its own rebellious Third Estate, the curés, the priestly democracy with their strong "Richerist" ideology, Christian egalitarianism, gestures of defection, and explicit political demands for the democratization of the "parliamentarianism" of the church.[23]

The modernizers of the church, who lent moderate support to rationalization both internally and to "society at large," were suffering from the same delusions as their secular counterparts when they assumed harmony between the various options of rationalization. From a sweeping rationalization of France as a whole, they could only expect to lose, not gain. For at least one consequence of a general rationalization must have been predictable: the demise of the Gallican church as an independent and impenetrable corporation. Furthermore, there were different and conflicting strategies of rationalization–modernization even within the church. What seemed rational for the *haute clergé* meant the betrayal of the interests of the Richerist curés and vice versa; the Richerist dreams of a renewal of the church on the bases of a primordial, poor but moral Christianity, was for the episcopal aristocracy tantamount to a total abandonment of the institutional past and present of the church, and thus not only treason but also total irrationality. Clearly, each and every scenario of rationalization was on a collision course with each and every other.

It is common knowledge that within a year after the elections to the Constituent Assembly, the rationalizing program of the Third Estate transpired as victorious and irrevocable, literally wiping out all other alternative approaches to rationalization. The confiscation of the wealth of the church and the introduction of the Civil Constitution of the Gallican church comprised everything the political elite of the Third Estate was to say and legislate on the issue. And once the Constituent Assembly confiscated the wealth of the clergy, it practically excluded both options of an intrachurch rationalization. Only two alternatives remained: the separation of the church, no longer an Estate, from the state, that is, "laicization" or the merger of the church and the state; that is, the reduction of the new church to the rank of a state agency.

When the Civil Constitution decided in favor of the second option, this fundamental document transformed priests into state agents, the Gallican church into a *clergé salariée*. It brought greater social equality into the church by considerably raising the income of the curés and allocating to the episcopate salaries that, though high, no longer provided for a lifestyle comparable to the aristocratic luxury of prelates under the old regime. The Civil Constitution imposed a kind of work discipline on the clergy which was in harmony with their new identity as *fonctionnaries*. It demanded "job training" and the introduction of meritocratic principles in ecclesiastic appointments. It solved the internal fiscal problems of the church in the most radical fashion: the once enormously rich corporation ceased to be an independent economic unit.

A great rationalizer of the territorial organization of France, the Constituent Assembly also drastically reorganized the dioceses, transforming them into units basically coextensive with the new *départements*. Thousands of church positions were either abolished outright or slated for extinction once the incumbents died or retired. An overwhelming majority of religious corps and orders of century-long standing were dismantled overnight as ones not fulfilling a "socially useful" function. The ultimate act was the formal destruction of the internal parliamentarism of the church together with its separate corporative legislation. Once all internal political mechanisms of the church, including the councils or church assemblies, had been abolished, it seemed perfectly "logical" to the *Comité Ecclésiastique*, as well as to the majority of the Constituent Assembly, that the priests of the Catholic church should be elected by the *citoyens actifs* irrespective of their religious beliefs or lack thereof, as well as of their denominational affiliation. Finally, the Civil Constitution completed the work of centuries of Gallicanism in a form absolute monarchs had never expected and church leaders had never wanted. It severed all relations between the Church of France and Rome apart from the empty gesture of recognizing the pope as the "visible head" of Catholic Christianity.[24]

Despite the deserved ill-reputation of the church policies of the Revolution, it would be unfair to describe the Civil Constitution as merely a document of doctrinaires. On several points, the drafters were backed sometimes by the majority, sometimes by a considerable minority of the *cahiers*,[25] and, above all, they were propelled by their own firm principles of a general and uniform social rationalization. Their first principle was that the emancipation of "society," which was for them tantamount to making the Third Estate general, be dependent on the political homogenization of the "national body." They were equally convinced, and on this point posterity has never questioned them, that the abolition of the prerogatives of the church (its position as a corporate feudal landlord, its exemption from taxation, its special system of jurisdiction and administering justice) was a precondition of transforming the confused network of privileges into the homogeneous system of universal rights. Finally, it was also self-evident to them that rationalization equaled modernization and that the latter was tantamount to *functionalism*. Defining a function as socially useful was naturally a public issue pertaining to the competence of the sole authority in which the national will was invested: the Constituent Assembly. Generally jealous of associations, it never occurred to these radical rationalizers that an association may have either the authority or the competence to define its functional utility within its own borders.

From this dogmatic belief in the necessary homogeneity of *ratio*, a tyrannical spirit in the church policies of the Revolution immediately transpired. Together with the estate or corporation, they also abolished the association, a framework in which "society" could freely organize itself in various (not necessarily political) forms. By combining the system of election of church functionaries with the general political system of elections, they not only showed unmasked contempt for a millennial tradition, they also demonstrated that, for them, the new agency could only serve political purposes. As a result of this gesture alone, the church, reformed or unreformed, lost its raison d'être. It was therefore more than a passionate polemical invective, but indeed the truth of the matter that Camus, a Jansenist, threw down as a gauntlet in front of the reluctant or oppositional members of church representatives in the Constituent Assembly: a sovereign (i.e., the nation) not only can give orders to a religious agency, it can also change the religion of a nation by decree.[26]

"Rationalist fanaticism" crowned its work with the famous issue of imposing the obligation of an oath on the clergy. There is no point in rehashing here this well-known episode that made the breach between the church and the Revolution final. The important aspect is its overtly tyrannical and inherently absurd character. The oath, in itself a quasi-religious gesture that attested to the slowly emerging political fundamentalism of the new nation–state even before the Jacobin takeover, was imposed on Catholic priests in the name of a new sovereign, the nation. This sovereign was not Christian (it regarded itself as secular); it had refused earlier to declare Catholicism the national religion, for tactical reasons certainly, but also for reasons of principle.[27] And yet, at the same time, it felt it had a prerogative to legislate on all issues of religious doctrine.

Was the breach, at least in the early period of the conflict, reparable? In other words, was the conflict merely tactical in character, a matter of the revolutionaries' lack of prudence? The alliance of church and Revolution was undoubtedly a fact for a very short period, and sustaining this alliance seemed on the surface to be one of the feasible options. I am convinced, however, that the idea of a long-term alliance between church and Revolution was illusory right from the start, and the clash concluding in violence and terror was necessary, at least by the then-existing premises of the revolutionaries. The rift had firm roots in the very structure of the revolutionary ideology, most particularly in the idea of *popular sovereignty* as it then transpired.

Popular sovereignty started to emerge as a theroetical problem at the very moment it ceased to be a polemical concept used against a monarch whose existence as a sovereign could never be in doubt.[28] Arendt called it an outright tautological concept (over whom can the people be sovereign? she asked). She suspected that the term had only been preserved in order to activate occasionally the inherent totalitarian features of democracy: the oppression of a dissenting minority in the habitual fashion of sovereigns.[29] The undeniable tension in the very structure of the term stems from the fact that it had indeed retained the duality that was so brilliantly analyzed by Kantorowicz concerning the "King's two bodies." One of these bodies is natural; the other is transcendental–supernatural. The first can be the vessel of a criminal, tyrannical, or sick soul. Yet the other body is sacred in a dual sense: it is inviolable, barred from sacrilegious hands because it is annointed by God, and it is the repository of the Christian ideas inherent in sovereignty.

In the new concept of sovereignty, borrowed from the monarch by the victorious *peuple*, a similarly dual body of the new ruler was incarnate. The "natural part" was embodied in the empirically existing citizens and their elected agencies which together constitute the "body politic." This body had both the advantage and the disadvantage of being a body only in a metaphorical sense. It had the great pragmatic advantage of being imperishable; for example, it could not be decapitated like the king in his natural person. On the negative side, in the merely metaphoric body of the collective sovereign, its will was never unequivocal. It invariably transpired as the awkward aggregate of individual volitions and opinions which could only be summarized by a clumsy political arithmetic. In addition, the collective body politic had at least as many sources of "erroneous functioning" as the single body politic of the monarch. Le peuple could just as easily have a poor judgment in the selection of its agents and could thereby alienate its own inalienable rights just as the prince had. It could get entangled in internecine strife that made the body politic ungovernable. It could be possessed of various kinds of political furies that made it its own worst enemy, driving the citizens into the collective political hysteria of *nous ne voulons pas être libres*. It might easily become a menace to other collective body politics as well as the tyrant of its own dissenting minority.

For this reason, another supranatural–metaphysical body politic is needed as a principle of correction. In addition to the actual–empirical rule of the people, the idea of the popular sovereignty is necessary. It is no exaggeration to call it supranatural. It is meant to be immortal in the sense that it was not supposed to vanish even if every single member of the empirical body politic rejected it in a moment of political hysteria or if the people's representatives ruled as tyrants and banned the use of the term. Furthermore, in this metaphysical domain, the dispersion of pragmatic wills no longer presented a problem; here general will ruled and legislated.

It is small wonder, then, that the newly conceived idea of sovereignty was irreconcilable with the old Christian idea of the sovereign's supranatural body as a copy of the hierarchical character of the Christian universe. Nor is it surprising that in moments of political exaltation and "enthusiasm" (the latter was to become a key concept of Robespierrism), the new sovereign was regularly blown out of all proportion, even sacralized in the new political metaphysics. For the sacralizing of the political or the project of "redemptive politics" is inherently present in the dualistic structure of popular sovereignty, as is, of course, the idea of the constitution, an entirely rational answer to all enigmas of the "empirical body" of the collective sovereign.

The rationalizing fury of the first revolutionary wave intended to homogenize the whole social and political body under the sign of the metaphysics of *la nation.* It recognized no deviations (or to use the Weberian term, spheric rationalities) not only because it perceived them as so much stubborn and resistant irrationality in disguise, but also because it suspiciously sensed in them the hydra of corporatism and the relapse into the presocietal condition of estates. The rationalizers had to sanctify, and thus mystify, the new sovereign to such an extent that, by their tyrannical overrationalization, they also prepared the ground for the most irrational type of politics: the redemptive one. The end result of doctrinaire rationalization and tyrannical functionalization was the complete fiasco of the church policy of the Revolution.

The term *fiasco* has to be qualified in several aspects. True enough, the outcome of the clash between church and Revolution was a major disappointment on *both* sides; not just for the revolutionaries, but also for the counterrevolutionaries. A nationwide civil war with one side under the banner of a humiliated Catholic church never broke out. Instead, the civil war was restricted to the Vendée. In the heat of the clash, however, an irreconcilable schism between left and right was created in France which lasted for almost two centuries. Experts unanimously agree that almost until the late 1970s–early 1980s (when the pattern began to change), a Catholic vote was a rightist vote and vice versa.[30] Furthermore, the revolutionaries very soon came to realize that they had paid a heavy price in creating a state agency that was useless for them on all counts. This applied even to the "plebeian" or democratic wing of the reformed and nationalized church. The constitutional church never succeeded in embracing the majority of the believers and, instead of defusing the religious opposition, its very existence brought back the atmosphere of the religious wars in France together with the category (and the concomitant passion) of heresy. The religious schism undermined Gallicanism, the work of a long line of monarchs (which the Revolution had actually planned to bring to fruition) and brought back an unexpected protagonist absent from the French political scene for two centuries: the pope. Finally, and perhaps most importantly, the fury of rationalizing dogmatism activated that aspect of the new order which has been termed by Talmon "totalitarianism in democracy" or "totalitarian democracy."[31] When Treilhard silenced the opposition during the debate on the Civil Constitution by saying that, when the sovereign deems a reform necessary, no one can oppose it,[32] it was the language of Louis XIV and of future totalitarian dictators. It reduced the citizens to the status of mere subjects.

The result of this fiasco transpired, both in the political elite and at the social bottom, in the form of a deep disillusionment with rationalization and political secularization. Tyrannical rationalization and functionalism, acting on the belief that it was crowning the venerable tradition of the Enlightenment, had created a political and spiritual vacuum that came to be filled by violent dechristianization, an anarchist scenario, and a new political religion that was an explicit critique, as well as a partial rejection, of political reason. This is why, in my view, the story of the Cult of the Supreme Being has to be understood as not merely related to the fiasco of the revolutionary church policy but also as a direct response to it.

THE CULT OF THE SUPREME BEING AND THE CRITIQUE OF POLITICAL REASON

Was the "religious revolution" a popular movement to which Robespierre, the Jacobin Club, and the Convention added nothing apart from some terminological polish and a legally binding form, or was it a manipulative campaign of the political elite? As is well known, the first is Mathiez's position (which also inherently condones the whole movement). The second, the Aulard thesis, establishes a diametrically opposed explanation. In terms of the latter, it was the ominous *représentants en mission* (symbolically: Fouché) who initiated the turmoil.

Both of these one-sided interpretations face several unresolvable difficulties. In the Mathiez version, the radical novelty of the Cult of the Supreme Being has disappeared. Had the whole work already been done by the anonymous activists, his own hero's philosophical efforts to introduce a "moral world revolution" would be, by implication, reduced to empty rhetoric. Nor can the vehemence of Robespierre's political campaign against at least certain contingents of the movement be accounted for on these premises. In the Aulard scenario, the popular movement, of which he was the great historian, either remains an irrelevant symptom of the general upheaval or, at the very best, is reduced to an easy excuse for the introduction of Robespierre's new state religion, the function of which remains, for Aulard, on the whole mysterious.

I propose a third approach to the issue, the methodological bases of which I have set forth in *The Frozen Revolution*. It is modeled on the Jacobin elite's attitude toward the policy of the *maximum général*. The idea of a terroristic economic policy was equally promoted by (sometimes the same) popular activists; it was similarly expropriated and, in a modified form, declared the official policy of the dictatorship by the political elite.[33] The maximum général was a nihilist scenario precisely in the sense that it displayed an enormous destructive power without the capacity of creating anything durable. At the same time, it was a popular initiative of great strength, especially in the very power bases of the dictatorship, the Parisian districts, which suffered most from the collapse of the economic policy of the Revolution.

The power center, the Montagne, the Club of the Jacobins, and Robespierre himself, were watching the new movement with utmost suspicion and jealousy. They were convinced, in a manner similar to the famous dictum of Saint-Just, that no positive legislation on economy, on this almost natural domain within society, is possible. Even the most resolute radicals, Robespierre above all, hated anarchism. In certain aspects, they always remained statesmen of the Enlightenment who wanted to usher in the era of the rule of reason. At the same time, they shared at least one feeling with the suspicious demagogues of social turbulence: an increasing disillusionment with the supposedly self-regulatory rationality of the market. But they were not prepared to relinquish even a part of their authority. When it turned out to be impossible to control the popular thrust for maximum général with fine speeches, they expropriated the main demand of the movement, made it state policy, thoroughly transformed it, and used the modified result as a powerful weapon for, among other uses, crushing dangerous agitators. Something frighteningly similar happened in the case of the Cult of the Supreme Being.

Right from the beginning, there had indeed emerged several, and widely heterogeneous, trends and motifs on the lower echelons of the revolutionary process which prepared the ground for the final showdown. A number of eminent scholars, old and new, have proved how a system of symbols and ceremonies had been accumulating during the revolutionary events, anniversaries, and festivities from the Feast of the Federation in 1790 onward. These symbols and ceremonies were initially only instinctively profane and political, instead of religious, but they gradually paved the way for a new cult.[34] Perhaps the philosophically deepest observation concerning the sociopolitical vacuum that needed to be filled with this new cult, a crucial testimony about the strong need for a new political religion, reaches us through centuries from the most unexpected quarters: from Madame de Staël. Her premise is that "Representative monarchies cannot succeed absolute monarchies but through the change of dynasty, republics cannot succeed monarchies but through the change of religion."[35] And although her final considerations were dictated by the experience of "the socail question" after Thermidor, at least certain sections of her thought would have found unhesitant support from the man whose head fell in Thermidor and who had always been a suspicious observer of the antipatriotism of the rich. Here is the conclusion drawn from the premise:

The unique interest of people in France is to acquire a sum of available money. They act with such agitation as those on a shipwrecked vessel would grab any plank that would bring them to the shore regardless of what happens to the crew. One defies the other, and no one offers assistance. . . . There is no longer even a hypocrisy of language in personal relationships. Personal interest is so highly exalted by all sorts of fears of which it is composed that mentioning virtue, sacrifice, devotion would, in a manner of speaking, produce the effect pedantry did in other times. . . . Under the reign of the Terror a sort of passion inhered in the barbarism that was exercised. Those people were ferocious animals who satisfied their instinct rather than greedy men who offered sacrifice to their interest. Whoever commits cruel acts these days in France is solely inspired by calculating what the gamble of this or that agent of the power can be. It is better to bail out your life than defend it. . . . No one listens to reason of any kind for the issue is invariably one of selfish motives . . . am I wrong therefore to believe that we have to look for aid in the religious ideas?[36]

It is not *civil religion* (whose best-known champion in the French Revolution was, typically, an American, Thomas Paine) that is at issue here, but the *religious underpinning* of the Revolution in the face of the destructive atomization by an unrestrained free market, which erodes all republican virtues and leaves only sheer, and in bad times ferocious, egoism in the arena. The common feature in Robespierre and Madame de Staël is that they both drew a surprisingly similar conclusion from the rationalizing fiasco of political reason as well as from the new problems unleashed by the very process of the Revolution. Both gradually came to realize that tinkering with new editions of the old religion is futile. Both believed therefore that, in contrast to the mere change of the forms of monarchy, what they called the "Republic" needed a change of religion. However, both knew that the free state is in reality linked with the free market, that the citizen is also an egoistic man. Will the Republic be anything else but the constant battlefield of egoistic interests if reason, whose other name is calculation, is the sole guide? Are egoists, ordinarily full of contempt for "spiritual powers" and "higher principles," capable of sacrifice, devotion, justice? Both asked the question, and they answered it in the negative. In addition, neither believed, for different reasons, that egoistic man can be altogether eliminated from the social arena. At this point, because Robespierre added the power of the terroristic state as a restrictive–protective measure against the uncontrollable fury of unrestrained egoism, whereas de Staël remained for her entire life a passionate enemy of the Terror, their ways parted. But their dilemma remained valid for the whole lifetime of the French Revolution as well as for other revolutions and for "republics" functioning in "normal" times. Their fundamental and irreconcilable difference on "the socially useful function of the salutary terror" had the further consequence that while de Staël made efforts to devise a new religion for the Republic, but one which operates in the private sphere, Robespierre decided that the terroristic state is the adequate locus for a "religious revolution from above."

Robespierre faced an enormously complex problem during the months the idea of a religious revolution must have gradually been taking shape in his thoughts. As a young deputy of the Constituent Assembly, he had been in the forefront of the drive for the Civil Constitution. Although, as he was to admit later, he was always a bad Catholic and influenced by a philosophy whose Protestant dimensions were not particularly hidden, he still believed that the old religion, once sufficiently broken and humiliated, could be streamlined and used by the Revolution in a subaltern position. However, his illusions totally evaporated under the impact of Vendée and the evident uselessness of the constitutional church in channeling the counterrevolutionary sentiments. When the dechristianizing movement, both in spontaneous and organized forms, emerged in late 1793–early 1794, he immediately smelled anarchism and his term of accusation was *atheism*.

Robespierre emphasized several times, most emphatically in his crucial speech in Floréal on the Supreme Being, that he was not a metaphysician but a statesman with philosophical intent.[37] For him, every social trend that tended to destroy the old belief without creating a new one transpired as *anarchist* atheism, because it created a dangerous political–spiritual vacuum that, Robespierre firmly believed, would be filled with the spirit of Vendée. This is why the genuinely atheist Cloots and the anti-Christian but religiously mystical-minded Chaumette were uniformly accused of atheism, a charge which, if erroneous on philosophical grounds, was completely consistent in terms of a terroristic logic.

Although perhaps Rousseau's thunderous invectives against the idle disbelievers, the enemies of humanity, reverberated in Robespierre's charges of atheism with counterrevolutionary intent when he committed his list of accusation to paper, the atheist–anarchist (whose epitome was the despised Fouché) appeared to him as a modern type, one not identical with the aristocratic libertine.[38] Robespierre, who hated Diderot but who was to a degree familiar with his writings, could have encountered such a specimen in *Rameau's Nephew*. This new type of atheist was a gambler with ideas and commitments. His republican virtue was pure affectation or hypocritical theater behind which lurked either corruption (as in the case of Fabre d'Églantine) or a criminal lust for power. At any rate, the haughty atheist's superhuman challenge to God and the immortality of the soul was more than the attitude of a virtuous citizen and, as such, it was suspect.

The venture of expropriating the results, channeling the destructive energies, and reshaping the options of the popular movement in the positive form of the Cult of the Supreme Being could find very few constructive elements to build on among the debris left behind by the dechristianizers. It shows Robespierre's mettle, indeed his tyrannical genius, that he extracted from this meager material, as well as from his own amateurish philosophical erudition, the project of a religious revolution. Mathiez believes otherwise. His thesis is that Robespierre added nothing but a new name to what had already been created by anonymous militants, namely, the Cult of Reason.[39] I will try to prove, first, that names do count and that the "Cult of Reason" was inadequate for Robespierre's own purposes; and second, that the "Supreme Being" was the only overarching term that could serve the Robespierrist "republic of virtue."

As we now see from the end result, the following principles were leading Robespierre in the masterplan of the new cult. First and foremost was that the Enlightenment, with its spirit of unshakeable trust in the omnipotence of reason, had proven inadequate in the storms of revolution. There had been just too many areas where reason's promises were self-confident but its actual performance catastrophic. Although reason remained one of our guides in Robespierre's view, it has an in-built penchant to be perverted into mere calculation; therefore it must be closely supervised. Furthermore, reason is lame without enthusiasm, which cannot be generated from rationality alone. The explicit ban on the mainstream of the Enlightenment in the speech of Floréal, the outburst against Diderot's more rational-than-enthusiastic patriotism, bears out the truth of this interpretation.[40]

Robespierre's second guiding principle was that the new religion must be political, not just civil (an idea he had inherited from Rousseau), and therefore that it must be a cult enforced by the Republic of Virtue. Political religion and "Republic" reciprocally presuppose each other. Without the republican power, the new cult could not maintain itself against the wave of anarchy. This is why in a special decree that was pushed through in the Convention, "the French people recognized the existence of the Supreme Being and the immortality of the soul" in the same manner as parliaments recognize the existence of a new state.[41] On the other side, the Republic of Virtue would be lacking in moral foundations without the legally decreed idea of the Supreme Being. Robespierre provided a laconic maxim of moral politics or politicized morals: "Immorality is the basis of despotism, as virtue is the essence of the Republic. . . ."[42]

The third ground rule of the new cult was that it was not allowed to infract the organizational monolithism of *démocratie dirigée*. As far as we can ascertain from the interpretation given to it by Payan (who in the last period of the dictatorship following the fall of both *ultras* and *citras* emerged as the major translator of Robespierre's implicit intentions), it was a categorical decision of the center that the new political religion should have neither priests nor a separate institutional existence.[43]

Finally, the new cult was not meant to be the continuation of any traditional belief, dogma, or religion; it was arbitrarily created. This fact alone (of which the new prophet was proudly aware) attested to the growing self-confidence of the new revolutionary in handling the social world as an artifact, instead of a natural, and therefore unalterable, order.[44] The "artificially" created Cult of the Supreme Being had a single, explicitly political, task: to solve all the unresolved problems of the Revolution, the Republic of Virtue. Its functions can be derived from this assigment alone.

The first and overarching function has already been mentioned: to provide a moral grounding for the "Republic," which was never a technical term in Robespierre's vocabulary. Although for him both constitutional monarchy and aristocratic (Girondist) republic were variations on the same old theme, Republic writ large represented a completely new phenomenon in the moral and political history of humankind. This novel creation could not possibly rest on tradition (because the latter was one of servitude), nor could it be based on the self-interest of those who find the Republic more profitable than the rule of the prince. In fact, Robespierre's almost general suspiciousness toward his own former comrades-in-arms in the last months of the dictatorship, his growing obsession with the hydra of an internal counterrevolution, was rooted precisely in his experience (or perception) that the majority of them served the Republic for their own selfish interests. Mathiez, who endorsed his paranoid vision without reservation, provides a good summary of Robespierre's attitude:

> Robespierre . . . showed that all the crises of the Revolution had been caused by more or less avowed *agents of despotism—that is to say, of crime*: by Lafayette, "who invoked the Constitution in order to restore the royal power"; by Dumouriez, "who invoked the Constitution in order to protect the Girondin faction against the National Convention"; by Brissot, who desired to turn the Constitution into "a shield to parry the blow which menaced the throne"; by "Hébert and his accomplices, who demanded the sovereignty of the people in order to slaughter the National Convention and annihilate the republican government"; by Danton, "indulgent to every crime, involved in every plot, promising protection to villains and fidelity to patriots; adroitly explaining away his treachery by the pretext of the public weal." . . . Robespierre examined into the means of putting an end to these crises, and *defined the principles which ought to guide the Convention, and with which it ought to imbue the souls of Frenchmen, so that they might at last become insensible to the snares of despotism.*[45]

"To imbue the souls of Frenchmen" and to make them "insensible to the snares of despotism" are terms of indoctrination the functions of which are manifold. But all of these functions can be grounded and fulfilled by the *sacralizing of the political authority* from which indoctrination emanates and which, in turn, draws its legitimacy from the end result of this indoctrination process.

For Robespierre, "the happiness of the people" was the major item on the political agenda. And without having ever heard the name of Immanuel

Kant, he was on this point, as on so many others, in a surprising harmony with Kant (of course, only within an overarching disagreement), who contended that while freedom unites, the quest for happiness divides.[46] Robespierre discovered the roots of this divisive impact of the quest for happiness in "egoism," and he was prepared to apply the sword of the Terror to the egoism of the rich, and even to restrain the poor with coercive measures. But he was too great a statesman to miss the point that force cannot survive on its own premises nor can it bring cohesion where division reigns supreme. State terrorism always needs a cementing doctrine that is religious or quasi-religious in the sense that it is above criticism, not only in the public space but preferably also in the hearts of the people.

The moral and political corruption of a growing number of leading functionaries raised a new dilemma. It transpired for Robespierre not just as a morally dangerous phenomenon but also as a potential political threat because he, correctly, believed that the nouveaux riches could easily forget their youthful enthusiasm and make a quick compromise with one or another form of restored monarchy. But the moral purifier needs a great supervisory eye that sees into the hearts and spots the seeds of corruption before they become public acts. In an atmosphere of institutionalized political paranoia, it is very difficult to decide where enthusiasm ends and hypocrisy begins. Like all prophets, Robespierre also identified himself with his newly found deity and was increasingly convinced that he had the capacity of seeing into human hearts. He might therefore have honestly believed in his mission to establish a new cult. He might have also assumed that the new cult would make the virtuous ones, who for ontological reasons are eternally in minority, capable of such insight. At the same time, acting as the "great supervisory eye," he deliberately manipulated the apparatus of the revolutionary government and the Convention. Fanaticism and cynicism mingled in this system of political fundamentalism.

For the Cult of the Supreme Being was the crowning act of a long-term strategy initiated by Robespierre almost from the very beginning of the dictatorship. Its ultimate end was the creation of strictly defined moral maxims for a political establishment by making moral prescriptions into binding legal decrees, which is precisely the definition of political fundamentalism.[47] This is why I believe, in contrast to both Mathiez and Aulard, that the new cult was neither an improvisation by Robespierre nor a simple rebaptism of the inchoate initiatives of the popular movement that had given to itself various ad hoc apellations. Rather, it was the final act of the long-term strategy growing out of Robespierre's deep philosophical and political dissatisfaction with the rationalizing trend of the Constituent Assembly. Aulard sums up, in my view correctly, the major change introduced in the speech of Floréal (which was in fact an amendment to the never-enacted Montagnard Constitution of 1793). The speech, which grounded the decree on the Supreme

Being, left no right for the citizen other than "the right to goodness," that is, a uniform behavior strictly defined by the Supreme Being and its *pontifex maximus*.[48] This is tantamount to the elimination of the liberal heritage of 1789 insofar as it no longer tolerates the diversity of political and moral behavior. The famous gesture, pinpointed by Robespierrist and anti-Robespierrist historians alike, of setting the allegorical statue of atheism on fire in the festivity of the Supreme Being was almost a quotation from the days of the Inquisition.

The second function of the new cult well reflects the carrot-and-stick nature of Robespierre's thought. On the one hand, the decree of the Convention by implication made religious skepticism punishable under the law. On the other hand, the new deity appeared in its prophet's own presentation as a utilitarian fiction: "[I]f the existence of God, if the immortality of the soul were but dreams, they would still be the finest of all the conceptions of human intelligence. . . . In the eyes of the legislator, truth is all that is useful and of practical good to the world." Mathiez then adds a highly revealing comment to these words: "Robespierre held to the idea of God; *but he did so because this idea has a social value.*"[49] The crucial question here reads as follows: What was the social value of the Supreme Being?

The inauguration of the Cult of the Supreme Being was meant to be the festivity of a covenant between the Supreme Being and the Republic of Virtue which, ironically, bore strong resemblances to a commercial contract with ironclad guarantees for the this-worldly partner. This combination of devotion and benefits had eminent pragmatic advantages. It provided the answer to the difficulties stemming from Robespierre's anthropological pessimism combined with political activism. Insofar as human beings, with the exception of a saintly minority, are irredeemably egoistic, the new religion can "imbue their hearts with virtues" if, and only if, it guarantees rewards for a virtuous life. There must be a mirror symmetry between "the only right to goodness" (which is, in actual fact, an imperative beyond appeal) and the absolute guarantee of the rewards of goodness, else the tyranny of goodness would become unbearable. The Supreme Being thus appeared as the god of distributive and retributive justice. What Foucault termed a "pastoral state" negotiated here a full circle: state-guaranteed rights and state-imposed penalties (actually, only one kind of penalty) appeared in a perfect metaphysical symmetry. The only loser was moral and political freedom.

The great political metaphysician solved a serious internal tension of his own vision of the world via the third function of the Cult of the Supreme Being. Put in the language of a later age that learned its lesson from him, the inauguration of the new cult meant the "end of prehistory," the onset of the "real history of humankind." Here is again his own testimony: "All has changed in the physical order; all must change in the moral and political order. One half of the world-revolution is already achieved, the other half has yet to be accomplished."[50] The term *world revolution* must not of course be interpreted in the sense of a proto-Comintern. It is common knowledge that Robespierre was a rabid nationalist and an avowed enemy of the revolutionary crusade proposed by the Gironde. However, the nationalist streak of his own thought posed a very serious problem for the statesman living in the dawn of a universalist era. Unlike Cromwell, whose shadow he constantly dreaded, Robespierre could not possibly regard his nation's revolution as a domestic affair. His new political religion seemed to have provided him with an answer to this problem as well. France, the domicile of the Republic of Virtue resting on the Cult of the Supreme Being now emerged in his vision as the country of the elect, as an eternal paradigm. Once the great example had been set, it was a matter of other peoples' virtue and intelligence to imitate it. Both national pride and universalist aspirations seemed to have been satisfied in one stroke:

> The French people appear to have outstripped the rest of the human race by two thousand years; one might even be tempted to regard them as a distinct species among the rest. . . . Yes, this delightful land which we inhabit, which nature favours with her caresses, is made to be the domain of liberty and happiness; this proud and sensitive people is truly born for glory and virtue. O my country, had fate caused me to be born in a foreign and distant land, I should have addressed to heaven my constant prayers for thy prosperity; I should have shed tears of emotion at the story of thy combats and thy virtues; my eager soul would have followed with ardent anxiety every movement of thy glorious Revolution; I should have envied the lot of thy citizens, I should have envied that of thy representatives.[51]

The Cult of the Supreme Being remained eternally buried under the debris of Thermidor. The European observers of the French Revolution, friends and foes alike, had enough of a task to interpret other aspects of its colossal heritage. This self-restraint seemed to be all the more appropriate since "the great teacher of the philosophy of state," as Hegel described Napoleon, for once untied the Gordian knot instead of cutting it. The paradigmatic solution of the problem, namely the *separation of church and state*, was first implemented by the Napoleonic concordat. But since the French Revolution could neither impose itself on Europe nor even consolidate itself on the domestic scene for almost a century, among its many unfulfilled promises, the one concerning secularization also remained an eternally postponed hope for much of the European world.

And this particular postponed expectation developed into a crucial political dilemma. For when people in sufficiently great numbers prove incapable of coping with the "alienness" of their self-created artifact, the free political state, they often take refuge in the sacralizing of the political. Our century, teeming with leftist and rightist scenarios of "redemptive politics," is almost a textbook case of these trends. All of these attest to the existence of very strong limits set to the great hope of the Enlightenment: the *absolute* secularization of the political. But none "proves" that the very trend is futile. For this writer, the answer to the dilemma is the difficult combination of stubbornly maintaining and expanding the process of political secularization and simultaneously deflating the exaggerated hopes invested into such efforts. This is the philosophical and political "moral" of the story of the Cult of the Supreme Being.

NOTES

1. See Augustin de Barruel, *Mémoires pour servir à l'histoire du jacobinisme*, on the influence attributed to philosophers, freemasons, and to the illuminati, on the revolution of France. Facsimile edition, trans. J. Walker (New York: Delmat, Scholars' Facsimiles and Reprints, 1974).

2. Pierre de la Gorce, *Histoire réligieuse de la Révolution Française* (Paris: Librairie Plon, 1919).

3. The classic version of the republican story has been recounted by Jules Michelet, *Histoire de la Révolution Française*, (Paris: Robert Laffont, 1978), 1: 308. Hamel, the paradigmatic Robespierrist of historiography, is much less generous to the antagonists of his idol.

4. See Jean Jaurès, *Histoire socialiste de la Révolution Française*, ed. Albert Soboul (Paris: Éditions Sociales, 1969); vol. 1, *La Constituante*, particularly the chapters on the confiscation of the land of the church and the Civil Constitution.

5. Good examples are John McManners, *The French Revolution and the Church* (New York and Evanston: Harper and Row, 1969); and Timothy Tackett, *Religion, Revolution and Regional Cultures in Eighteenth-Century France* (The Ecclesiastical Oath of 1791) (Princeton: Princeton University Press, 1986). Jaurès, McManners, and Tackett are included here in the same group only by virtue of their similarly atomistic readings of the church policies of the Revolution which, according to all three of them, contained some sound ideas as well as enormous blunders or injustices. Neither of these chronicles represents a holistic narrative of the conflict of the church and the Revolution.

6. Edgar Quinet, *Le christianisme et la Révolution Française* (Paris: Fayard, 1984).

7. An interesting characterization of *Le cercle social* can be found in Hans Maier, *Revolution und Kirche—Studien zur Frühgeschichte der christlichen Demokratie (1789–1901)* (Freiburg in Breisgau: Verlag Rombach, 1979), pp. 130–137.

8. Alphonse Aulard, *Le culte de la Raison et le culte de L'Être Suprême (1793–1794)*, *Essai Historique* (Paris: Felix Alcan, 1904), p. vi. In fact, Quinet made the explicit statement (*Le christianisme*, p. 173) that he was not a Protestant nor did he believe that France would or should become Protestant. However, one representative contemporary commentator, Novalis, indeed experimented with the equation of the radical climax of the Revolution with Protestantism: "Soll die Revolution die französische bleiben, wie die Reformation die lutherische war? *Soll der Protestantismus abermals widernatürlicherweise als revolutionäre Regierung fixiert werden?* . . . Historisch merkwürdig bleibt der Versuch jener grossen eisernen Maske, die unter dem Namen Robespierre in der

Religion den Mittelpunkt und die Kraft der Republik suchte" (emphasis added). "Die Christenheit oder Europa," in Novalis, *Werke*, ed. Ernesto Grassi (Munich: Rowohlts Klassiker, 1961), p. 47.

9. Quinet, *Le christianisme*, pp. 66–67, 71, 86.

10. Ibid., p. 102.

11. Ibid., pp. 103–106.

12. Ibid., pp. 230–231.

13. Maier, *Revolution und Kirche*, p. 124.

14. The major documents of this controversy are Aulard, *Le culte de la Raison et le culte de L'Être Suprème*; Alphonse Aulard, *Christianity and the French Revolution*, trans. Lady Frazer (Boston: Little, Brown, 1927); and the famous essay by Albert Mathiez on the Cult of the Supreme Being in *The Fall of Robespierre and Other Essays* (New York: Knopf, 1927). See also Albert Mathiez, "L'Église et la Révolution Française," *Revue des Cours et Conferences* 33, no. 1 (Paris, 1931–1932); and his *L'origine des cultes révolutionnaires* (Paris, 1904). A most recent work of questionable value, Pierre Pierrard, *L'Église et la Révolution* (Paris: Nouvelle Cité, 1988) takes sides against Mathiez and the later Aulard and, with an unsubstantiated reference to Solé's opinion, denies that the process of dechristianization had indeed the backing of wider strata of the populace; p. 97.

15. The most important modern research on rituals and ceremonies in the Revolution can be found in Mona Ozouf, *La fête révolutionnaire, 1789–1799* (Paris: Gallimard, 1976); and Jean Starobinski, *1789: Les emblêmes de la raison* (Paris: Flammarion, 1973). The paradigmatic work of historical sociology on the issue of the conflict of Revolution and Church is Charles Tilly, *The Vendée* (Cambridge: Harvard University Press, 1964). After his enormous research, the multidimensionality of the rebellion of Vendée can no longer be denied. But I still remain unconvinced by the main thesis that questions the centrality of the religious issue in the movement and reduces its role to that of an independent variable. The thesis could only be maintained if the analyst secured a "metaposition" for himself from which he could dismiss the explicitly stated central intent of the actors as "ideology" or self-delusion. But such a position is hermeneutically impossible.

16. A good example of the more recently prevailing lack of interest in the merit of this issue can be found in François Furet and Mona Ozouf, *Dictionnaire critique de la Révolution Française* (Paris: Flammarion, 1988), chap. "Dechristianisation."

17. Tackett, *Religion, Revolution and Regional Cultures*, pp. 7–8.

18. The complexity of the situation of the church on the eve of the Revolution is lucidly presented by Louis S. Greenbaum's unpretentious and important book: *Talleyrand, Statesman–Priest: The Agent-General of the Clergy and the Church of France at the End of the Old Regime* (Washington, D.C.: Catholic University of America Press, 1970).

19. The argument of the royal power, used as a threat rather than a blueprint for action, has been described by Greenbaum, *Talleyrand*, pp. 83, 88. The argument of the revolutionaries was summed up succinctly by Maier, *Revolution und Kirche*, p. 106.

20. The problem of *appel comme d'abus* is a widely discussed issue. A good description of the meaning and function of this legal term can be found in Robert Genestal, *Les origines de l'appel comme d'abus* (Paris, 1951).

21. For the key category of the necessary holiness (and duality) of the royal person,

see E. Kantorowicz, *The King's Two Bodies* (Princeton: Princeton University Press, 1957). Quinet, *Le christianisme*, pp. 214–216, and Maier, *Revolution und Kirche*, p. 80, add important considerations to the discussion of the issue.

22. The peculiarity of the team of revolutionary experts has been persistently emphasized in the literature. Already Michelet stressed the Jansenist convictions of Camus, *La Révolution Française*, 1: 311; de la Gorce made the allegation that Barnave's preeminent role as one of the first advocates for the confiscation of the wealth of the church had been motivated by his Protestantism, de la Gorce, *Histoire réligieuse*, 1: 142–143; both de la Gorce, *Histoire réligieuse*, 1: 201, and Tackett, *Religion, Revolution and Regional Culture*, p. 17, remark that Durand de Maillane, an expert on canon law, as well as Treilhard were, as leading members of the Ecclesiastic Committee of the Constituent Assembly, epitomes of the old tradition of *légistes*, the legal experts of court or parlements, who were traditional enemies of the church. The role played by Mirabeau, a professed libertine, and Talleyrand, a renegade, are common knowledge. Yet the problem was not their bias but their unique brand of reason.

23. My description of the situation of the church, concerning both its "parliamentarianism" and well-organized bureaucracy as well as its internal problems, relies on Greenbaum, *Talleyrand*, pp. 2, 3, 26, 27, 38, 58, 59.

24. An almost identical description, albeit a different characterization, of the Civil Constitution of the church, can be found in Tackett, *Religion, Revolution and Regional Culture*, pp. 8–16, and in de la Gorce, *Histoire réligieuse*, 1: 197–199.

25. Tackett, the most conscientious scholar of the church-related issues in the *cahiers de doléances*, gives an extremely illuminating statistical sample of 202 cahiers of the Third Estate, *Religion, Revolution and Regional Cultures*, p. 13. It is perfectly clear from this representative sample that the major grievances about the situation of the clergy felt by the members of the Third Estate were the issues of the tithes (47 percent demanded their total or partial abolition); the wish to acquire at least part of the church land (27 percent); the demand for the abolition of the *casuel* (47 percent); the demand for social mobility within the church, i.e., the opening of clerical posts to talent (44 percent); and the requirement that prelates fulfill their "social function" (40 percent). Although this was indeed strong support for the work of reform, it was at the same time no encouragement for extreme radicalism. In analyzing this problem, the methodological warning of the eminent historian, Henri Sée, about the "source value" of the cahiers of the clergy, "La rédaction et la valeur des cahiers de paroisse," *Revue Historique* 103 (1910): 292–306, should be heeded.

26. The statement is quoted in Michelet, *La Révolution Française*, vol. 1, 311.

27. The most detailed description of the naive proposal by Dom Gerle in the Constituent Assembly to declare Catholicism the national religion is to be found in de la Gorce, *Histoire réligieuse*, 1: 159–162.

28. On the question of "popular sovereignty" see K. D. Erdmann, *Volkssouveränität und Kirche. Studien über das Verhältnis von Staat und Religion in Frankreich vom der Generalstände bis zum Schisma* (Cologne, 1949).

29. For Arendt's remark, see *On Revolution* (New York: Viking Press, 1952), pp. 112–114.

30. Tony Judt analyzed more recently the change of the Catholic vote in *Le Marxisme et la gauche française* (Paris: Hachette, 1986), pp. 274–278.

31. John L. Talmon, *The Origins of Totalitarian Democracy* (London : Secker and Warburg, 1952), p. 21 and passim.

32. Treilhard's dictum is quoted in de la Gorce, *Histoire réligieuse*, 1: 224.

33. Ferenc Fehér, *The Frozen Revolution (An Essay on Jacobinism)* (Cambridge: Cambridge University Press, 1988), p. 74.

34. See Ozouf, *La fête révolutionnaire*; and Starobinsky, *1789*.

35. Anne Louise Germaine Staël-Holstein, *Des Circonstances actuelles qui peuvent terminer la Révolution et des principes qui doivent fonder la République en France* (Geneva: Droz, 1979), p. 227.

36. Ibid., 236–237.

37. Robespierre's words are quoted in Mathiez, "The Cult of the Supreme Being," in *The Fall of Robespierre*, pp. 100–101.

38. See the analysis of the allegedly aristocratic character of eighteenth-century materialism and atheism versus the "plebeian" idealism and moralization coupled with terrorism in Georg Lukács, "Der faschistisch verfälschte und der wahre Georg Büchner," in *Deutsche Realisten, Gesammelte Werke*, vol. 6 (Neuwied/Berlin: Luchterhand Verlag, 1968).

39. Mathiez, "The Cult of the Supreme Being," *The Fall of Robespierre*, pp. 86–89.

40. Robespierre's invective against Diderot quoted in Aulard, *Le culte*, p. 273.

41. Mathiez, "The Cult of the Supreme Being," *The Fall of Robespierre*.

42. Ibid., p. 89.

43. See Payan's extremely interesting interpretation in Aulard, *Le culte*, pp. 282–288.

44. François Furet has been emphasizing, both throughout his crucial *Thinking the French Revolution*, and more recently in a seminar given at New York University, 12 October 1988, this new attitude that he, rightly, attributes not to the Jacobins alone but to the Revolution as a whole.

45. Mathiez, "The Cult of the Supreme Being," *The Fall of Robespierre*, pp. 88–89, emphasis added.

46. The problem of freedom and happiness (rather: freedom versus happiness) has been recently analyzed by Agnes Heller in "Freedom and Happiness in Kant's Political Philosophy," in manuscript.

47. I have analyzed in *The Frozen Revolution*, pp. 61–62, the strangely mixed character of the draft of the (never-enacted) Constitution of 1793, which was a supreme law, that is, a legal document, and a binding oath in front of the Creator, that is, an irrevocable religious commitment, at the same time.

48. Quoted in Aulard, *Le culte*, p. 273.

49. Mathiez, "The Cult of the Supreme Being," in *The Fall of Robespierre*, pp. 100–101, emphasis added.

50. Ibid., p. 96.

51. Ibid., pp. 97–98. Reinhart Koselleck bases his theory—in *Futures Past (On the Semantics of Historical Time)* (Cambridge, Mass., and London: MIT Press, 1985), pp. 49–50—that every revolution carries the germs of world revolution in itself, despite its eventual nationalistic self-limitation, on precisely this speech of Robespierre.

PART THREE

The Ideological Legacy of the French Revolution

TEN

Practical Reason in the Revolution: Kant's Dialogue with the French Revolution

Ferenc Fehér

Was there a *genuine* dialogue, that is, a conversation of two parties turning toward each other, between Immanuel Kant and the actors of the French Revolution? Or is it only posterity that constructs reciprocity between merely symbolic interlocutors who were in fact simply in a relation of simultaneity? Decades after the French Revolution, representative commentators assumed a direct relationship between Kant's philosophy and the mainstream, sometimes even the extreme poles, of the revolutionary process. The irreverent yet profound parallel drawn by Heine between the two audacious petits bourgeois, Maximilien Robespierre, who challenged a king, and Immanuel Kant, who challenged God, is typical of this kind of understanding.[1] Marx, in an aperçu that was never further elaborated by him, termed Kant's philosophy the adequate German reaction to the French Revolution (a remark, by the way, which was not necessarily a compliment on the part of Marx).[2] But by now we know that the adequate reception in France of Kant's philosophy took place only decades after the Revolution.[3] It is an equally well-known fact that Kant, ever true to his life-style, never made the slightest effort, unlike Humboldt or August Wilhelm Schlegel, to visit the scene of the great event. Even less did he commit himself to an active engagement in the style of Georg Forster. As Hannah Arendt correctly remarked, Kant always remained in the position of the spectator.[4]

THE FIRST GREAT POLITICAL PHILOSOPHER OF MODERNITY

And yet, we can draw the unambiguous conclusion from the sparse facts at our disposal that some of the central actors of the Revolution not only heard vague rumors about the crucial significance of Kant's philosophy but even guessed that the Revolution, which in Robespierre's words intended to real-

201

ize the promises of philosophy, needed Kant's theory, or a confrontation with this theory, for its own special purposes. In letters written to a friend in 1794–1795, Abbé Grégoire, the actual head of the constitutional clergy and one of the earlier founding fathers of the important, socially and religiously radical *Le cercle social*, made inquiries about Kant's book on religion. (He obviously had in mind the *Religion Within Reason Alone*.) And he knew what he was looking for. Grégoire needed a theory that would serve as the grounding for his complex strategy of a Christian democracy which fought against the terrorism of the earlier periods of the Revolution, against the relapse pure and simple into the prerevolutionary hierarchic structure of the Gallican church (which was the end result of the Napoleonic concordat), and against the barely concealed atheism of the leaders of the French Republic between the tenth of Thermidor and the eighteenth of Brumaire. Grégoire correctly guessed that Kant's theory, banned in Prussia, could serve as the foundation of such a position. What he could not realize without actually reading the book was that for Kant even Christian democracy was an unacceptable degree of institutionalization of the "invisible church."[5]

Sieyès, who along with Condorcet was one of the greatest theoretical minds among the protagonists of the French revolutionary drama, expressed an even livelier interest in Kant's philosophy. When Wilhelm Humboldt visited Paris in 1798, Sieyès, then for a moment back again at the apogee of political power and gravely concerned with designing the proper constitution for the Revolution after so many constitutional crises, organized a colloquium for Humboldt in which Destutt de Tracy, Cabanis, and other *idéologues* participated. The purpose of the seminar was to get an authentic summary of Kant's philosophy from someone who seemed to be the adequate interpreter. When the semiofficial *Moniteur* published an enthusiastic review of Kant's book on perpetual peace in 1796, it characterized the German philosopher as a fellow republican. From this source alone Sieyès must have been aware that Kant not only had a general theory of knowledge and morals but also a political philosophy.[6] And despite the apparent fiasco of the encounter, the theoretical instinct of the great revolutionary statesman was correct again. Throughout his active career from the convocation of the Assembly of the Three Estates to the eighteenth of Brumaire, Sieyès had been constantly preoccupied with how best to establish the republican institutions. Their essence was for Sieyès, just as for Kant, not a matter of technical arrangement. Both of them were convinced that the appellation of the form of the state is secondary. What is of primary relevance for the Republic are the actual forms of the channels through which genuine power is exercised.

The most famous encounter between Kant and the theoretical–political actors of the Revolution was his public debate in 1798 with Benjamin Constant over the "supposed right of telling a lie motivated by philanthropy," as

Kant characterized Constant's position. It is almost never appreciated that this exchange had a political dimension as well as an ethical one. Constant intended, with his famous parallel between the liberty of the ancients and that of the moderns, the former illiberal, the latter liberal, to provide a theoretical framework for the Republic that could serve as a safeguard against both Jacobin terror and a (new or old) kind of personal power. Paradoxically, neither of the polemicists realized that they shared a common premise: the criticism of ancient democracies as illiberal establishments. For Constant, Kant's ethical rigorism was doubly suspect. He believed he detected in what he regarded as Kant's collapsing of the ethical dimension into legality the vestiges of a terrorisic moral rigor similar to the ruthless style of ancient city-states *and the "democratic" zeal of Robespierre,* which had just recently been overthrown in Thermidor but which could return any time. A moral rigor of this kind, Constant was convinced, gave no latitude for the individual's self-defense against merciless laws. Furthermore, Constant was deeply troubled by Kant's very example: our absolute moral duty, regardless of consequences, to truthfully answer the question of a prospective murderer who comes to our house to make inquiries into the whereabouts of an innocent victim. For who could not grasp immediately that Kant's example, wittingly or unwittingly, referred to a situation that had been typical of the Jacobin terror, its atmosphere of constant house searches and quick executions? Without discussing the merit of the issue, I would only state that of the two positions that clashed here, Constant's thesis represented the mainstream liberal, *habeas corpus* principle according to which one owes obligations only to such laws as have been (directly or indirectly) endorsed by him or by his representatives. Constant further contended that truthfulness, a moral duty, implied no legal obligations. But for Kant, in spite of certain important similarities between his theory and Constant's political philosophy, there was no difference between the rigor of moral and of legal obligations: both barred exceptions.[7]

The encounter of representative French revolutionary actors with Immanuel Kant's philosophy ended on a truly bizarre note. In 1801 Napoleon, then still nominally the first consul of the Republic, summoned Villers, the first French Kant expert. In his usually curt manner Napoleon assigned Villers to make a concise and comprehensible summary of the famous German theory within a short time. The result, which was predictable from the confrontation between the philosopher of perpetual peace and the founder of modern militarism, the thinker for whom the mere pragmatics of politics were worthless and the supreme *Realpolitiker,* was disastrous. Napoleon deleted Kant from his personal list of VIPs and publicly called him yet another *sciarlatano* in the style of Cagliostro.[8]

Although these representative examples perhaps prove that "the French Revolution" was ready and ripe for a dialogue with Kant's philosophy, there is no need for extensive demonstration of such a readiness on the part of Kant even though he referred explicitly and critically only once to a statesman of the revolution: Danton.[9] Such a demonstration is superfluous because, put simply, it was the French Revolution that activated the latent *political dimension of Kant's philosophy.* There could be no doubt whatsoever that in Kant's view, even prior to the French Revolution, the proper position of the philosophical faculty had been "on the left," as he was to put it later in *The Strife of the Faculties.* For this, it suffices to read "What Is Enlightenment?" But the new critical philosophy born in the Copernican turn had not extended its legislation to the public sphere proper before 1789.

However, the outbreak of the Revolution, this "crucial fact of nature," imposed the obligation on the philosopher to publicly draw the political conclusions from his critical philosophy. And Kant, who was often accused of "philistinism," lived up to this obligation to the full, albeit sometimes in a thinly veiled manner that never deceived the authorities.[10] Despite the enormous *general* theoretical results of the works written in the 1790s, *The Metaphysics of Morals, On the Common Saying, Religion Within Reason Alone, On Perpetual Peace,* and *The Strife of the Faculties* can be characterized as major works of modern *political* philosophy.

The reader who is familiar with the history of the French Revolution will find in these works a continuous philosophical commentary by Kant on almost all crucial junctures and decisions of revolutionary France. He was deeply concerned with the fundamental problem of the "legality" of a revolution, and, within the issue of legality, with the ways the Assembly of the Three Estates had transformed itself into a Constituent Assembly. He had a philosophical and highly critical opinion on the relationship between the king (as the repository of the executive power) and the Constituent Assembly, on the manner of practically suspending the king's executive power by the Assembly, and on the unification (which, Kant hoped, was only temporary) of the chief executive and the supreme legislative powers in one body. He had a deep and balanced opinion on the reform of the Gallican church, one that neither the revolutionaries nor the church dignitaries would have been happy with, but which had an important message for both contending factions. Everyone is familiar with his flat condemnation of the trial of Louis XVI which has never ceased to be the topic of heated debates up until today. Kant also had a passionate interest in the constitutional problems and the incessant constitutional crises of the Revolution.

In this dialogue of Kant's with the Revolution, which is not a mere aggregate of aperçus but which sprang from profound meditation on the problems posed by the Revolution *under the primacy of practical reason,* a completely modern type of political thought emerged. Immanuel Kant, and not Hegel, who forged a methodological axiom from this attitude, was the first great political philosopher of modernity. In marked contrast to most of his predecessors,

Kant did not design political–philosophical blueprints for future action from past models. Rather, through constant thought experiments, Kant transformed the present process understood as history into the raw material as well as a treasure trove of unresolved dilemmas for political philosophy. The Kantian attitude of the observer was not one of *au-dessus-de-la-mêlée*. Rather it was the stance of a new political philosophy and the end of the typical approach of political thought of the Enlightenment. Kant the spectator was far from impartial. But he contended that both the attitudes of a fully committed militant and that of the philosopher–king (one that he explicitly rejected and which was merely the obverse position of the king who reigns philosophically) were incompatible with a political philosophy under the primacy of practical reason.[11]

RES PUBLICA NOUMENON

The two problems firmly posited for investigation by Kant's political philosophy were, first, *the fact of the Revolution and its relationship to a new republican legal order as a dilemma* and, second, *the possible structure of the Republic.* Concerning the *characterization* of the "fact of the revolution," a surprising harmony prevailed between Kant and Robespierre. In the trial of the king, the lawyer of Arras tore to pieces the legal double-talk of his colleagues in the Convention with a single brutal gesture. Enough of the legal farce, he brusquely demanded. This is not a trial, you are not judges, Louis is not an accused at the bar. You are revolutionary statesmen making an emergency decision on behalf of the Revolution. Taking an emergency measure of this kind means, Robespierre added, that we temporarily return to the state of nature in the act of destroying our enemy.[12] Kant would have greatly appreciated (and perhaps he did) Robespierre's truthfulness, because this was precisely what Kant believed to be the truth about the fact of Revolution, and because truthfulness was an unconditional duty in his philosophy. With a brusqueness similar to Robespierre's, Kant stated in *On the Common Saying* that the revolution is *status naturalis*.[13]

But at this point, the philosopher–observer and the revolutionary politician (who was also an amateurish philosopher of history) radically parted ways. The recognition that the Revolution meant a (presumably temporary) relapse into the state of nature prescribed a single course of action for Robespierre: those who make a revolution have to apply revolutionary measures regardless of the costs. For Kant, the recognition of the "natural character of the fact of the revolution" generated a deep, sometimes tragic, but for posterity always stimulating dilemma. On the one hand, the Revolution, as our relapse in the state of nature, as a "natural event," appeared to him as a cataclysm with a Janus-face in the phenomenal world. One of its faces, the one appearing in *status naturalis*, was horrifying. However, the well-known dictum from *The Strife of the Faculties* shows us the smiling face of the same complex phenomenon. In this often-quoted place Kant was occupied in his usual manner with the problem of whether there is a single *factum brutum*, like the existence of mathematics for our faculty of knowledge or that of the moral law for our morality, that makes it possible to elaborate a *theory of progress*. And he found his fact in "this great public event," which, as a proof of the *progress in nature*, authorizes us to believe in the possibility of progress in the moral world.[14] For the Revolution had proven indisputably that there is something in our phenomenal nature which rebels against despotism and shows affinity with freedom.[15]

However, for Kant, unlike Robespierre, there was no simple transition from the natural to the moral–legal world, and he would have thrown away the maxim of Marat about "the tyranny of freedom" as a contemptible exercise in revolutionary Jesuitism. Even those who interpret Kant as a classic of liberal thought will find difficulties with his categorical denial of the right of a "lawful revolution" or rebellion. Indeed, resistance of any kind to a tyrannical authority, which is an accepted tenet of all liberal theories of government, is disallowed. This rejection of the theoretical possibility of a "lawful revolution" was repeated *ad nauseam* in his political writings of the 1790s.[16] Kant emphasized that even the authority of that paragon of liberal transitions, the "glorious revolution" of 1688, had been based on a lie. The "constitutional agreement" on which the British regime had been resting until his own days, Kant remarked, had conveniently forgotten about the rebellion, and thus the usurpation of power, which had brought the new order of things to pass.[17] If we add Kant's equally well-known proviso affirming the authority of the Revolution once it has consolidated itself into a legal order, an authority that is beyond appeal to the same extent as was its predecessor,[18] Kant appears either as a legal stickler or a thinker of paradoxes, which would have been for him a brutal insult. And I find the thesis of Kant's self-censorship, as a supposed solution of the puzzle, more of a slander than an explanation.[19] For Immanuel Kant could remain stubbornly silent when he was not able to speak what he regarded as truth.

Without being in agreement with Kant in the slightest, for I certainly do not believe that there is any moral–legal authority that can forbid people to rebel against tyranny, Kant's arguments seem to me neither inconsistent nor lacking in moral and political lessons. For Kant, the moral and legal worlds constituted a unity under the primacy of morality. Both were based on our freedom, and at the centerpoint of both there was duty, but in two different ways. Morality was the stricter domain because there our obligations were *internal*. Respect for the moral law, for the goal- and not just the means-character of the other, had to be the actor's sole motive for the recognition of his act as properly moral. Legality allowed for more latitude. Here the legislator was not concerned with the actor's motives, only with his unconditional compliance with the law. As a result of this unconditionality, Kant never ceased to emphasize the coercive (*Zwang*) character of even those laws that had been passed in the most free agreement. As long as they are valid, we are *subjected* to them, we are *subjects of the law*. Only if we observe them unconditionally, that is, without making exceptions, do we show respect for the (good) maxims. Only thus can we raise ourselves from the mere phenomenal–natural to the noumenal, the properly human, genuinely free level.

This in itself would not be an absolute argument against the Revolution as an act of disrupting the chain of legality. For a revolution could also be a constitutive act, one of establishing new and better laws. And Kant was perfectly aware of both the despotic character of most laws up to his time and of the possibility and promise held out by new republican laws qua the completion of our *ethisch–bürgerlich* existence.

Moreover, his conception did not exclude *absolutely, that is, for reasons of principle*, the possibility of a "lawful revolution." There are at least three scenarios for this unlikely event, each of them having a certain kind of historical plausibility. The first is the *abdication of the absolute prince on behalf of the "republic."* A strong argument can be made for Kant's interpretation of the transition in France from the Assembly of the Estates to the Constituent Assembly as the realization of this scenario. In terms of this version, Louis freely abdicated from his *reign* as absolute prince by the act of acquiescing to *rule* as a "caretaker sovereign," that is, the supreme executive. (This could be conceived of as a free decision by Louis despite the symbolic violent gesture of the masses, the storming of the Bastille, since he could have chosen, together with his brothers, the option of an immediate emigration.) A second scenario is the Posa–Philip story with a happy ending: the moral and political edification of the despotic ruler under the impact of the good advice given by a republican friend (where, it can be argued, entering into friendship, an equal and symmetrically reciprocal relationship with someone, is the prince's virtual starting point of self-reformation, his first "republican" act). And, in fact, this scenario was acted out in real life a few years later, in the court of Alexander I of Russia. But the fact is that the story in real life ended as negatively as in the theater. The difference was that in life it was also lacking in tragic grandeur. This result verified not only Schiller's *but Kant's own skepticism* toward the second possible Kantian scenario. For Kant invested incomparably more faith in public than private edification. A third, logical version of the "lawful revolution" was the possibility that an absolute prince, facing the overwhelming forces of a foreign invasion, turns to the populace and expects such miracles from the *citizens'* zeal as could not be expected from the subjects' devotion. On this basis, the prince would grant them some kind of a constitution, which is what happened under the "hundred days' rule" of Napoleon.

But skeptical as Kant always remained concerning our phenomenal nature, he foresaw at this point the more than latent possibility of a great and perhaps irretrievable historical catastrophe. In his *Anthropology*, he made a four-tiered typology of all possible human regimes that could be established after we had left the state of "wildness" tantamount to "independence from laws." This stage is confinement to the natural domain, a not yet properly human existence. The types are the following: anarchy (law and freedom without power); despotism (law and power without freedom); republic (a combined rule of power, law, and freedom); and finally barbarism (power qua violence without either law or freedom).[20] For Kant only two of these scenarios, the despotic, our long common past state of affairs, and the republican, our future and possible emancipation from tutelage, may have been the genuinely historic types of societal order. He was convinced that we could neither relapse into "wildness" (since we had long lost our innocent ignorance) nor lastingly live in anarchy.

But how about *barbarism?* According to my hypothesis, the lasting rule of power as permanent violence without laws and freedom suddenly appeared on Kant's historical horizon under the impact of the French revolutionary drama. He witnessed the consecutive waves of creating and then almost immediately bending or shelving laws, a process that would have generated the atmosphere of an operetta had it not been for the blood dripping from the actors. Kant saw enthusiasm publicly degrading itself into a pathological passion and solemn declarations about universal freedom linked with the immediate and flagrant violation of the liberties of whole human groups. He watched as the centrality of freedom was replaced with that of happiness (a change of principles that he particularly detested and from which he expected the worst possible outcome).[21] He heard the dithyrambs chanted collectively in praise of violence and the relapse in the state of nature which was confirmed by deliberately plunging revolutionary France into war. For Kant, this was the penultimate crime a free people could commit against itself and the rest of the world. The sight of all this filled Kant with the gloomy foreboding that the Revolution could destroy itself. This perspective was not excessively frightening for Kant since he believed that that "great public event," the fact of progress in nature, would never be forgotten.[22] What he dreaded most was the example set by the moral suicide of a nation that perpetuated lawlessness and raised the violation of the maxim to the rank of virtue. In Kant's terms this choosing of the evil maxim could uproot even the bases of freedom in itself and would offer the worst possible example for the world.

It was Kant's great disciple, Schiller, who, in his celebrated *Letters on the Aesthetic Education of Man*, almost simultaneously with the master's publicly raised doubts and fears, developed the radically modern category of barbarism as the pathology of our culture.[23] And Schiller only drew the conclusions from Kant's premises in his pathomorphology. The Revolution had failed,

Schiller concluded more apodictically than Kant himself would have spoken, because it had brought into the political arena not free men but the helots of our civilization. The demons of unsatisfied needs and the cultural cripples of the modern division of labor with their one-sided skills rushed on the scene to be endlessly manipulated by the demagogues. In Schiller's understanding, barbarism has nothing to do with the savagery of the primitives. It is a modern malaise, one that takes the refined form of pathological enthusiasm and feeds on evil maxims. Once the coercive force of law was removed for a single moment (here Schiller and Kant were on the same wavelength), there was a greater chance for our lasting and *premeditated* relapse into the "state of nature" than for the creation of the free republic. *And a lasting and premeditated relapse into the state of nature is tantamount to barbarism.* Hence Kant's inflexible verdict over every act of rebellion as high treason that deserves the ultimate penalty. Only when such an act is capable of organizing itself into the rule of law does it, by an unintended dialectic of history, deserve the same unquestionable authority as did its predecessors.

Those who grasp Kant's deep-seated anxiety about barbarism as the possible future of our civilization, an anxiety triggered by the scenes of the Revolution, will have a better understanding of what Marx called *die deutsche Misère* than did the German left of the 1840s, which coined the term and explained the phenomenon as the result of the "spinelessness" of the German bourgeoisie and of the philosophers who were supposed to represent this bourgeoisie.

On this basis, we can also better understand Kant's categorical condemnation of the trial of the king. Since I have set forth my views extensively in a debate with Michael Walzer, I will only briefly return to the issue.[24] For Kant, just as for Robespierre, the legal conviction of a king *for his past reign* was perfect nonsense and therefore, Kant added, a crime in the highest degree. (It was for him an even greater nonsense and a more monstrous crime in the case of a monarch who, after having reigned as an absolute prince, accepted to rule as the supreme executive.) Kant was of two minds even on the issue whether or not a monarch, forced into the status of a citizen, was morally and legally authorized to make attempts at regaining his former power. In this respect, his statements are contradictory, although he did not hesitate to condemn almost every attempt at a foreign intervention on the basis of *Völkerrecht*.[25] Moreover, Kant was, correctly, convinced that the Constituent Assembly had been usurping the king's supreme executive power, which was an additional reason for the monarch to resent his own undignified dependence.[26] Kant was sufficiently realistic to accept violent acts as *emergency measures* (particularly in the state of nature) under the condition that those perpetrating them accept their responsibility for the crimes committed. As long as the perpetrators paid their due to truthfulness, the abstract chance for the tyrannical moralist to mend his ways still existed. But once an act of murder was displayed publicly and proudly as supreme justice, *the people had chosen the evil maxim*, which was the most negative term in Kant's vocabulary.[27]

And yet, Heine's and Marx's diagnosis was correct, even if their explanation of the phenomenon remained one-sided: *die deutsche Misere* did exist. The price Kant had to pay in his political philosophy for his own extraordinary sensitivity toward the future dangers of modernity was blocking his own way to the much-longed-for realm of freedom, the republic, by *discounting popular action altogether*. Kant repeatedly asserted in his political writings of the 1790s that the hope for (republican) change can come only from the top, not from the bottom. In the main, what remained, despite Kant's own skepticism about the scenario, was the politics of *Don Carlos*. True enough, Kant added one important recommendation to his idea of "reform from above": the *thesis of the centrality and necessity of the public sphere*. Kant thoroughly condemned every kind of politics *based on a maxim that could not be made public*. He even made explicit what kind of politics he had in mind: that of open contempt by the absolute prince for the populace based on a repulsive misanthropy. This maxim secretly exists but cannot be made public because it would trigger rebellion, Kant asserted.[28] And although Kant's expectations concerning the "republican effects" of a free public sphere, especially concerning a *free press*, were legitimately high, they could not delete the marks of "German misery" from his work.

This limitation did not prevent Kant from stipulating the republic as at least a possible free future for humankind. The main issues of Kant's republican theory are the idea of a *res publica noumenon*; the centrality of the representative system; the relationship of powers to each other in the republic; and the character and prerogatives of the sovereign in its capacity of chief executive.

The *res publica noumenon* as a regulative idea[29] is much less abstract speculation than a *Realpolitiker* would assume. Had Sieyès been familiar with the problems behind it, he would have been thrilled by Kant's train of thought and would have found the German philosopher a thoroughly kindred spirit (as he had guessed in advance). Kant's major point here is *the distinction between republic and democracy*: the first was his regulative political idea, the second a profoundly problematic establishment. By way of explanation, Kant points to the only democracies he was familiar with (the American example apparently weighed very little for him): the ancient city democracies of Hellas. And in sharp contrast to the idealization of the ancients which was so typical for his age and his own generation, he found them repulsive rather than attractive models. Ancient city democracies, Kant averred, had either been despotic in themselves or they had ended up in despotism. They were not familiar with the idea and practice of *representation*, and therefore their political system was at the mercy of a constantly changing popular opinion as well as abandoned to outbursts of popular fury.[30]

The great originality of Kant's political philosophy consists not merely in being the first to make the distinction between republic (qua the regulative idea of the free state in modernity) and "democracy" (as the latter's first and highly imperfect form of appearance on the political scene).[31] Equally original was the other distinction logically following from the first, the distinction between the *form of government* and the *forms of power*.[32] This second distinction is normally attributed to Max Weber by the history of theory.

Kant's distinction was more than a terminological clarification. It was a profound conception that had literally grown out of his dialogue with the French Revolution. Similarly to Kant, two representative actors of the Revolution, Sieyès and Robespierre, had contended before and during the crisis of Varennes that the appellation of the state was, as Kant put it seven years later, a mere matter of letters. But they had different (implicit or explicit) considerations in making the distinction between forms of government and forms of power. For Robespierre, the criterion of a state of political affairs to qualify as genuinely republican was, irrespective of the appellation of the form of government, *le bonheur du peuple*. We know how passionately Kant opposed putting happiness, instead of freedom, at the center of republican considerations. Therefore, although his recommendation was in formal harmony with Robespierre's thesis, substantively they were on a collision course.

However, Sieyès's argument would have been very close to Kant's mind. Sieyès, like Kant, was preoccupied with the ways genuine political freedom could be achieved in large and complex national bodies. In his meditations he had returned, once again like Kant, to Aristotle's tripartite division of powers or forms of government (the two concepts remained undistinguished in Aristotle). From Sieyès's conception the same deeply ingrained suspicion of the direct rule of the *demos* transpired as from Kant's political philosophy. Sieyès too had, for reasons similar to those of Kant (namely, both rejected the idea of corporations within a "republic"), a thorough aversion for born-again aristocracies, meritocratic or commercial. This was one of the reasons why Sieyès, always a tacit and therefore surviving enemy of Jacobinism, never joined the Gironde. Despite these similarities, however, the distinction between the forms of government and the forms of power gained true theoretical lucidity and depth only in Kant's political philosophy.

It is common knowledge that, of the main revolutionary trends, both the Gironde and the *Montagne* deluded themselves into believing themselves to be either the born-again or the last Greeks and Romans in the modern theater of politics. For serious theoretical reasons, some of which have already been mentioned, Kant categorically refused to don the costume of the ancients. And in this refusal he was one with Sieyès, a completely modern and individualist political thinker, as well as with Constant, who made the first philosophical effort to distinguish the freedom of the ancients from that of the moderns. Their major reason for rejecting the ancient paradigm was their understanding of the Greek and, to a degree, even the Roman democracy as a direct rule (power) of the *demos* (or *plebs*) over the rest of the *civitas*. Sometimes this rule took legal forms. At other times, it was exercised through naked violence. But much too often it transpired as domination without general freedom. Sieyès, Constant, and Kant unanimously believed that freedom could be guaranteed by, and reside only in, a *legally organized authority* to which the *citoyens actifs* give their free consent but to which they are *equally subjected without exception*. However, we shall see that Kant, who happily went along with Sieyès and Constant as far as their thesis of a legal authority was concerned, parted ways with them when the question of *the moral foundations of the republic* was raised. In this case the ancient example became unexpectedly important for him.

The character and the function of the *supreme executive* was a source of great theoretical concern for Kant. His problem can be formulated in the following terms. To him, there seemed to be nothing sacred in the crucial *process of legislation* and therefore in the legislators themselves. They had the mandate of the people, and they had to do a job relying on reason, which was an exacting and complex but ultimately normal human task. But once the laws were passed and transferred to the supreme executive power whose function was their enforcement, the laws had to assume a *sacred character* in Kant's conception which demanded absolute obedience to them.

The sacred character of law, this product of human and this-worldly legislators, posed the following problem for Kant with regard to the supreme executive. If the person whose task is to enforce the sacred laws is a mere agent of the state, how can the sacred character of the laws be ascertained from such a prosaic figure? If he is more than an agent, what will distinguish him from the well-known figure of the prince? This dilemma, never resolved by Kant, caused a certain kind of terminological vacillation in his theory. For Kant, a critic of the term "popular sovereignty," the "sovereign" was identical with the chief executive. At times, Kant referred to this "sovereign" as "invisible," "the personified law," rather than as an agent. However, in discussing the conflict of Louis XVI with the Constituent Assembly and the usurpation of the executive power by the legislative, Kant treated "the sovereign" like an agent of the republic.[33] This minor inconsistency was solved by Kant, to the degree that the problem could be solved at all within the horizon of his age, by his theory of the role of *Vernunftsreligion* and the "invisible church" in the republic. But this issue cannot be addressed here.

POLITICS AND MORALS

Neither foes nor friends missed the *moralistic* character of Kant's dialogue with the French Revolution. His political theory indeed displayed the peregrinations of practical reason in the Revolution. In an immediate sense,

Kant's attention was focused *on the morality of the political actor.* Kant in fact elaborated a consistent theory of the relationship between politics and morals. *Politics without morals,* Kant contended, was based on the ugly vice of contempt for humans, and it internally bolstered the practice of despotism.

However, there is a perverse way of relating morals to politics, that of the "political moralist," a type that is worse than the mere political pragmatist or "political technocrat." Kant carefully lists the three evil maxims of the political moralist, the worst of which is "justify everything."[34] It can come as no surprise for the readers of Kant that the "political moralist" appeared in his typology as an infinitely worse type of the political actor than the (hypocritically or misanthropically) pragmatic one *precisely because of his evil maxims.* By contrast, *the moral politician* makes the moral law the maxim of his politics, and he sees his task as the reconciliation of *raison d'état* with the moral law as much as possible. His principles are practical reason and justice.[35]

Kant was fully aware of the enormous difficulty of reconciling the moral maxim with the practical exigencies of a given political task, the traps that lie in wait on the moral politican's thorny path. He even assumed that his favorite actor could at some point degrade himself into a *despotic moralist.* (And we can have hardly any doubt that he had in mind the Jacobin politician in general, perhaps even Robespierre in particular.)[36] A despotic moralist contaminates the political atmosphere around himself and becomes the founding father of a *despotic republic.* However, Kant assumed that the "moral politician" could mend his ways and return to the correct path. We are already familiar with the absolute Kantian precondition of this kind of moral reform: truthfulness even in the despotic, therefore evil act; *respect for the good maxim instead of choosing the evil maxim* in defense of an aberration. This is why Kant defended the right of Louis XVI against the Convention. This is why he demanded, to the point of absurdity, obedience to even despotic (republican or monarchic) laws. This is why, in an aside in his *Anthropology,* speaking of "political fantasy," he appreciated even the "fantasies" or the fiction of the high rank and equality of the people, which were solemnly announced by the French Convention and never taken seriously by those despotic legislators.[37] For it was the good maxim alone that stood between the republic and the abyss: the relapse into barbarism.

However, Kant was incomparably more concerned with the moral character of the republic than with the morality of its statesmen. To a degree, he was prepared to subscribe to the principle of the "moral politician" (despite the danger that the latter had the penchant to degrade into a despotic moralist): *the republic, Kant contended in unison with Robespierre, cannot exist without virtues.* And in the *formal* respect, Kant accepted the model of the ancient republics which he otherwise severely criticized as the unfree rule of *demos.*

At the same time, the two material principles Kant integrated into his "doctrine of virtue," one's obligation to one's own perfection and one's

obligation to the (morally approved) goals of others, were sufficiently up-
dated and *substantively defined* to represent the spirit of *modernity* in Kant's
moral and political philosophy. The first was the principle of physical and
materal *culture*, *Bildung* in the proper sense of the Goethe period, a principle
juxtaposed to our phenomenal existence, which, in Schiller's authentically
Kantian description, appeared as self-fragmentation and self-degradation.
The second substantive principle, one's obligation to the other's (morally
acceptable) goals, was the *principle of association*. This provided as much space
for "happiness" (or the social question) as possible within Kant's theory. For
Kant was not an ideologue of unlimited wealth. On the contrary, one can
infer from one of his remarks that he regarded extreme inequality as a serious
error (and "injustice") of the government.[38] He simply did not believe, here
in unison with Saint-Just's attitude toward economics, that positive legislation on happiness was possible. However, the introduction of the second
material principle, that of association, at least provided a public space within
the republic to address the issue of happiness, the celebrated social question.

One would find tremendous difficulties with a clear-cut classification of
Kant's political philosophy as consistently either liberal or radical. And this
is not meant as a criticism, rather as a compliment. The critique of political
reason, which was accomplished under the guidance of practical reason,
yielded a completely new, *dialogical* type of political theory whose issues
remain on the agenda of the present.

NOTES

1. Heinrich Heine, *Zur Geschichte der Religion und Philosophie in Deutschland*, in *Sämt-
liche Schriften* (München: Piper, 1971), 3: 594–596.

2. Karl Marx, "Das philosophische Manifest der historischen Rechtsschule," in
Karl Marx and Friedrich Engels, *Werke* (Berlin: Dietz-Verlag, 1958), 1: 80.

3. The best *philological* treatment of Kant's influence in France so far can be found
in Maximilien Vallois, *La formation de l'influence Kantienne en France* (Paris: Librairie
Felix Alcan, 1932). More can be found on this issue (but without a systematic historical analysis of Kant's impact on "the French ideology") in the following works: *La
philosophie politique de Kant* (Paris: PUF, 1962); A. Philonenko, *Théorie et praxis dans la
pensée morale de Kant et de Fichte* (Paris: Vrin, 1968); G. Vlachos, *La philosophie politique de
Kant* (Paris: PUF, 1962).

4. Hannah Arendt, *Lectures on Kant's Political Philosophy*, ed. Ronald Beiner (Chicago: University of Chicago Press, 1982). The analysis of Kant as a "spectator" can be
found on pp. 44–45. I am in perfect agreement with Arendt's dictum: "[T]he French
Revolution had awakened him . . . from his political slumber (as Hume had awakened
him in his youth from dogmatic slumber, and Rousseau had roused him in his man-
hood from moral slumber)" (p. 17). However, as will become clear from what follows,

I decidedly disagree with Arendt's opinion that "there is" a political philosophy in Kant, yet one which "does not exist" (i.e., has remained unwritten) (p. 31).

5. The reference to Grégoire's correspondence with Philippe-Jacob Müller, a professor at the University of Strassburg, is found in Vallois, *Formation*, p. 34. Kant's position on the crucial and hotly debated issue of the revolutionary reform of the church can be summed up in the following terms. The church has no right to complain about the confiscation of its wealth. This wealth had been based on "popular opinion" (*Volksmeinung*) which has now evidently changed. Corporations anyhow have no *raison d'être* in a republic (this argument was identical with the position of Sieyès): *Metaphysik der Sitten. Rechtslehre*, in Immanuel Kant, *Werke in Zwölf Bänden* (Frankfurt: Suhrkamp, 1956), 8: 444–445. Kant even went further. In the spirit of his own distinction between church (*Kirchenwesen*) and religion, the latter being a purely internal issue of the citizen, he recognized the state's legitimacy in reforming the organization of the church. However, he declared every intervention into religious beliefs by the state as negative acts "beneath the dignity of the state" (Kant, in *Werke*, 8: 447–448). So far, Grégoire would have enthusiastically subscribed to Kant's philosophy of religion.What he, a partisan of Catholic democracy, would not have been able to accept in Kant's position was the philosopher's very active hostility to the minimum institutionalization of religion and the "invisible church," the ethical community of believers. In *Die Religion innerhalb der blossen Vernunft*, in *Werke*, 8: 852–853, Kant declared, certainly not without a certain degree of Protestant bias, that *every form of the organization of* the church (papal absolutism and Catholic democracy *alike*) are forms of the same fetishistic religion, and, despite the name, forms of the same despotic rule. This was, by the way, in perfect harmony with Kant's general conception of democracy as an imperfect realization of *res publica noumenon*, about which I will say more later.

6. For the reference to the enthusiastic review of *Moniteur* as well as to Sieyès's interest in Kant's philosophy, see Arsenij Gulyga, *Immanuel Kant* (Frankfurt: Suhrkamp, 1983), p. 280.

7. For Kant's rejoinder to Constant's critique of his position in Constant's *Des réactions politiques* (Paris, 1797), see *Über ein vermeintes Recht aus Menschenliebe zu lügen*, in *Werke*, vol. 8.

8. On Napoleon's "encounter" with Kant and the unsuccessful attempt of the first French Kant expert, Charles Villers, to convert the first consul to Kant's philosophy, see Gulyga, *Immanuel Kant*, pp. 280–281. Vallois, *Formation*. pp. 51–124, gives a detailed characterization of Villers's interpretation of Kant. He briefly mentions Villers's "report" for Bonaparte titled "Philosophie de Kant, aperçu rapide des bases et de la direction de cette philosophie" (Paris, Fructidor An IX, 1801), in *Formation*, p. 57.

9. In *Über den Gemeinspruch: Das mag in der Theorie richtig sein, taugt aber nicht für die Praxis*, in *Werke*, 11: 159. Presumably, Kant polemicizes here against Danton in his capacity as minister of justice in the fall of 1792, and Danton's much too summary declaration of civil rights and properties as null and void in an emergency situation and in the absence of a factual contract.

10. More recently, André Tosel made efforts in his *Kant révolutionnaire (Droit et politique)* (Paris: PUF, 1988), to characterize Kant's political philosophy as a reaction to

the Revolution. Although I appreciate this methodological approach to the problem, I cannot accept Tosel's consistent attempts to "homogenize" Kant's political philosophy in the sign of Jacobinism.

11. "Dass Könige philosophieren, oder Philosophen Könige würden, ist nicht zu erwarten, aber auch nicht zu wünschen" (*Zum ewigen Frieden, Anhang*, in *Werke*, 11: 228).

12. See the characterization of Robespierre's unique position in Ferenc Fehér, *The Frozen Revolution* (Cambridge: Cambridge University Press, 1988), p. 107.

13. The state of rebellion is characterized by Kant as "Zustand einer völligen Gesetzlosigkeit (status naturalis), wo alles Recht aufhört, wenigstens Effekt zu haben," *Über den Gemeinspruch*, in *Werke*, 11: 158.

14. *Der Streit der Fakultäten*, in *Werke*, 11: 356–358.

15. Kant makes an explicit reference to the existence of "the drive of freedom" in his *Anthropologie*, in *Werke*, 12: 604.

16. Here are a few typical examples of Kant's categorical rejection of a "right to revolution" or rebellion: *Über den Gemeinspruch*, in *Werke*, 11: 154, 156, 158–159 (here Kant characterizes the leaders of the revolutions of Switzerland, the Netherlands, and England as *Staatsverbrecher*, "criminals against the state"); *Zum ewigen Frieden*, in *Werke*, 11: 245, 246; *Der Streit der Fakultäten*, in *Werke*, 11: 360 (fn.); *Metaphysik der Sitten. Rechtslehre*, in *Werke*, 8: 437, 438, 439.

17. *Über den Gemeinspruch*, in Werke, 11: 160.

18. *Metaphysik der Sitten. Rechtslehre*, in *Werke*, 8: 442.

19. A whole book has been dedicated to this not particularly convincing explanatory principle by D. Losurdo, *Autocensura e compromesso nel pensiero politico di Kant* (Naples, 1985).

20. *Anthropologie*, in *Werke*, 12: 686.

21. A detailed analysis of Kant's position concerning happiness is given in Agnes Heller's "Freedom and Happiness in Kant's Political Philosophy," manuscript.

22. The celebrated statement in *Der Streit der Fakultäten*, to which I have already referred (*Werke*, 11: 358), explicitly predicts the possibility of *the collapse of the Revolution under the burden of its own crimes*. At the same time, it considers the serious possibility of its resuming its work in a better "second edition."

23. Friedrich Schiller, *Letters on the Aesthetic Education of Man*, trans. Reginald Snell (New York: F. Ungar, 1965), pp. 34–35, 40–41.

24. Fehér, *Frozen Revolution*, pp. 97–112, "Revolutionary Justice." For Michael Walzer's rejoinder to my criticism, see his "The King's Trial and the Political Culture of the Revolution," in *The Political Culture of the French Revolution*, ed. Colin Lucas, vol. 2 (Oxford: Pergamon Press, 1988).

25. Kant's vacillation can be seen in the contradiction between his two major statements on the issue. In *Zum ewigen Frieden, Anhang*, in *Werke*, 11: 246, his position is the following: After the victory and the consolidation of a revolution, which had been by definition the violation of the (former) law but which in turn became legal authority, the monarch is bereft of the right (together with all other citizens) to rebel against the new authority because *it has now become law*. But it goes without saying that he cannot be punished now for his past reign *because he then had been law*. In *Metaphysik der Sitten. Rechtslehre*, in *Werke*, 8: 442–443, Kant's argument is more complex. The

logical and moral impossibility of punishing the former monarch for the past reign is of course further maintained. But at this point, Kant has doubts whether the ex-monarch has the right to rebel against those who had *unlawfully* overthrown his rule. Naturally, this is the ideal quotation for those who subscribe to the thesis of Kant's self-censorship. I am, however, convinced that the structure of the argument suggests even here that Kant was exclusively preoccupied with justice.

26. In *Metaphysik der Sitten*. *Rechtslehre*, in *Werke*, 8: 465, Kant for once spoke directly (and not only indirectly and hypothetically) about the French Revolution and (without mentioning his name) Louis XVI. He regarded Louis's concessions, which finally led to the fusion of the "sovereign" (the supreme executive) with the legislative power, as the king's tragic mistake. The (historically correct) description leaves no doubt as to Kant's understanding: the *sub rosa* unification of executive and legislative power in the hands of the Constituent Assembly was usurpation and despotic rule.

27. Kant's most comprehensive statement is the long footnote in *Metaphysik der Sitten*. *Rechtslehre*, in *Werke*, 8: 440–441, on the trials of Charles I and Louis XVI. It is worth mentioning that here Kant almost anticipated an argument more recently represented by Walzer, one of "political justice" in defense of the trials. In this regard, Walzer's new argument, as it appears in his paper published in *The Political Culture of the Revolution*, can be rendered, with a certain simplification, in the following way: They would have killed him anyway; *therefore*, it is better that they gave to the act the "form of law," which made it "political justice." Kant's sharp answer to this antici-pated train of thought was that the legal form had made the sham trial worse. *Notrecht* (emergency law or political justice) is a presumed, not a real principle of justice. *Necessitas non habet legem* (*Metaphysik der Sitten*. *Rechtslehre*, in *Werke*, 8: 343). Kant's major concern here and elsewhere was *the protection of the purity of the maxim of action*, which he regarded as the sole guarantee of a future return to republican legality.

28. For the principle of the obligatory public character of the *maxim* of politics, see *Zum ewigen Frieden, Anhang*, in *Werke*, 11: 244, 245. The principle which cannot be made public is described in *Der Streit der Fakultäten*, in *Werke*, 11: 359 (fn.).

29. The principle of *res publica noumenon* is formulated most unambiguously in *Der Streit der Fakultäten*, in *Werke*, 11: 364.

30. His aversion to the (potentially or actually) despotic character of the ancient city republics was expressed in the most explicit fashion in *Zum ewigen Frieden*, in *Werke*, 11: 206–208.

31. Ibid.

32. The terms are either *Form der Beherrschung* versus *Form der Regierung* or *Staatsform* versus *Regierungsart* (*Zum ewigen Frieden*, in *Werke*, 11: 206, 208). In both cases, the first term refers to the technical appellation of the state, the "form of government." The second term refers to the distribution of *powers*, the crucial ways in which power is exercised either despotically or in a republican manner.

33. *Über den Gemeinspruch*, in *Werke*, 11: 149 (fn.). Here Kant termed the head of the state (*Oberhaupt der Staatsverwaltung*) "the personified law." He emphasizes that the "sovereign" (the head of the state) is *not* an agent of the state. But in *Metaphysik der Sitten*. *Rechtslehre*, in *Werke*, 8: 435, Kant described the "regent" or the "prince," that is, the supreme executive power, *as an agent of the state*.

34. The three evil maxims are (1) *fac et excusa* (act and find excuses); (2) *si fecisti*

nega (if you did it, deny it); (3) *divide et impera: Zum ewigen Frieden, Anhang,* in *Werke,* 11: 236.

35. Ibid., p. 240.
36. Ibid., p. 234.
37. *Anthropologie,* in *Werke,* 12: 485.
38. *Metaphysik der Sitten. Tugendlehre,* in *Werke,* 8: 591.

ELEVEN

Hegel and the French Revolution: An Epitaph for Republicanism

Steven B. Smith

Today no one can seriously doubt that the concept of revolution is a central organizing assumption of political life. There are various reasons to explain the importance of this term and others associated with it. In the first place, the phenomenon of revolution is thought to embody processes of change, development, and growth. So deeply have these notions become embedded, not just in popular discourse but in the more sophisticated languages of the natural and social sciences, that it is difficult to imagine how we could even begin to think without them. Second, most of the contemporary world powers—America, France, Russia, China, not to mention a host of lesser nationalities—have all established themselves by announcing a revolutionary break with their prerevolutionary pasts. Whether one is for or against these revolutionary movements, they appear to be a feature of the modern political landscape which is not likely to go away.

For most social and political theorists, it was the French Revolution (and only later the Russian) that became the model by which to measure revolutionary change.[1] Two perspectives were typically adopted to explain this event. The first, proposed by Edmund Burke and later taken over by the "historical school," saw the Revolution as an attempt, motivated by misguided theory, to remake the world and human nature itself in accordance with its own vision of a just and humane society. In their efforts to establish a new republican order, the revolutionaries were led to rename months, abolish historical provinces, and establish new religious cults to worship abstract reason, none of which had any ties to previous French experience. Burke's *Reflections on the Revolution in France* is nothing if not an object lesson on how a dogmatic interpretation of natural rights and the social compact can leave little room for such things as prudence, compromise, and balance which are essential to the political. For Burke, all attempts to found constitutions *de novo* must be doomed to failure, and to the extent that such experiments are "metaphysically true" they must be "morally and politically false."[2]

The second perspective was announced originally by Alexis de Tocqueville in his classic study *The Ancien Régime and the French Revolution*. Although Tocqueville's analysis bears certain superficial resemblances with Burke, especially in his skepticism regarding abstract rationalism, a close reading of his text shows that he could not have been more different. Whereas Burke stressed the role of ideas or revolutionary ideology, Tocqueville was crucially concerned with the study of institutions and the emergence of the modern administrative state. Furthermore, whereas Burke emphasized the absolute novelty of the Revolution, accepting the claims of the revolutionaries at face value, Tocqueville tried to penetrate behind the rhetoric of the Revolution to the social and political crises that had occasioned it. The core idea of Tocqueville's history is the profound continuity between the Ancien Régime and the Revolution. Just as in *Democracy in America* Tocqueville showed that the process of democratization was not something new but had deep roots going back over 700 years to the heart of feudalism, so too in the *Ancien Régime* does he show how the policies of the Jacobins did no more than extend the growth of public power and the tendency toward administrative centralization which had been established as early as the reign of Louis XIV. "Even if [the Revolution] had not taken place," Tocqueville sagely remarked, "the old social structure would have been shattered everywhere sooner or later . . . the Revolution effected what in any case was bound to happen."[3] According to François Furet, a recent historian of the Revolution, the paradox of Tocqueville's analysis is that the French Revolution was already three-quarters over before it even began.[4]

In this chapter I want to suggest that Hegel provides us with another third perspective on the revolutionary experience. Hegel neither wants to emphasize the absolutely unprecedented character of the Revolution as did Burke, nor does he want to minimize its specificity by dissolving it into a kind of *longue durée* as did Tocqueville. Hegel wanted to celebrate the Revolution but only after it had been firmly located and hence ensnared within his own philosophy of history. Once he had done this, I suggest, it became possible to honor the memory of the Revolution precisely because and to the degree that it no longer represented a threat. Henceforth the French Revolution like the other great turning points of modern European history—the Protestant Reformation in Germany and to a lesser extent the beginnings of the Industrial Revolution in England—could be regarded not as isolated or discrete happenings but as part of a worldwide struggle aimed at the realization of freedom. It was Hegel's attempt ultimately to domesticate the Revolution by regarding it as a "moment," but only a moment in the collective *Bildung* of humanity, that constitutes in my opinion his unique contribution to the interpretation of the French Revolution.[5]

THE IMPULSE FROM PHILOSOPHY

"We should not therefore contradict the assertion," Hegel once wrote, "that the [French] Revolution received its first impulse from philosophy."[6] By philosophy in this context it is clear that Hegel is referring to that movement in modern thought that goes under the name of Enlightenment. Although modern scholars have debated whether the Enlightenment is to be understood as a one or a many, a period of skepticism or of dogmatism, the birth of secular humanism or the last gasp of an age of faith, it seems to me central to understand its aspiration as revolutionary in its essence. The Enlightenment set itself the ambitious task of liberating thought from the "kingdom of darkness" in order to make men into the masters and possessors of the world.

From its inception the Enlightenment thought of itself as initiating a total break with the past. This, at first sight, appears paradoxical since the concept of Revolution originally implied a return to first principles as indicated by the syllable *re-* in the Latin word *revolutio.*[7] For the Greeks and Romans, revolution was understood as part of a cyclical pattern of history in which birth, growth, decay, and regeneration were conceived along naturalistic lines. The Greek term *metabolé* was used to indicate either change or corruption, the inevitable fate that awaited all things.[8] In human affairs, just as in the cosmos, a few invariant forms followed the same irresistible force as the stars follow their paths in the heavens. This pattern constituted a revolution in the original lexical sense of circulation. Thus Plato's cycle of regime transformation in books 8 and 9 of the *Republic* was followed closely by Aristotle's theory of constitutional change in the *Politics.*[9] For Aristotle, who gave the classical conception of political change its canonical expression, there can be no such thing as a new beginning, for "practically everything has been discovered on many occasions—or rather an infinity of occasions—in the course of time."[10] The same cyclical pattern was taken up in the *Histories* of Polybius who uses the concept *anakuklosis politeion* to indicate the sempiternal recurrences into which human affairs are driven as if by nature. The cycle was a *physis*, a natural process, through which regimes were bound to pass unless by a stroke of good fortune they were able to escape this fate.[11]

The original meaning of the term *revolution*, then, implied a return to some previously occupied position and not an overturning of all that has gone before. At the outset of modernity Machiavelli could still speak of revolution as a *ridurre ai principii*, that is, the periodic revitalization of civic life that can only come through a return to its original principles.[12] In the same vein Hobbes could write of the events in England between 1649 and 1660 that "I have seen in this Revolution a circular motion of Sovereign Power."[13] And Locke in the famous nineteenth chapter of the protorevolutionary *Second Treatise of Government* could describe the "dissolution of government" as a return of the legislative power to its original hands. For Locke, as for Burke later, revolution properly signified a restoration of the original constitution, a retrieving of ancient liberties, so that he could call King William the "Great Restorer" and describe the "Glorious Revolution" of 1688 as glorious precisely because it lacked what in the modern sense we call revolutionary. Revolution meant for these thinkers the very opposite of the idea of "irreversible change" or "total change" with which the term later came to be associated.[14]

The concept of revolution made its way into modern European vocabularies through the language of literary criticism to describe the changes in fortune of a character from one state to another.[15] Its later use signified a process of development or acceleration toward new and therefore unpredictable states of affairs. Revolution in this sense implied a capacity for novelty and an openness to change that were often seen as the root of the modern Enlightenment. In the decades before and after 1789 the term was expanded by thinkers to apply to areas as diverse as law, morality, religion, economics, and politics. The author of the article on "Revolution" in the *Encyclopédie* could define the term rather blandly as "a considerable change in the government of a state."[16] But by 1772 Louis Sebastian Mercier could observe that "Tout est révolution dans ce monde,"[17] and Robespierre at the height of the French Revolution could announce: "Tout a changé dans l'ordre physique; et tout doit changer dans l'ordre moral et politique."[18] From then onward the term acquired overtones of an almost irresistible movement that would inaugurate a new era of human happiness in which autocracy would be exploded, superstition banished, and republican government established as the only political system rational in theory and tolerable in practice.[19]

Here, as in so many matters, German philosophy accurately depicted the mood of the times even while it failed to participate in the leading events.[20] Kant has rightly been called "the philosopher of the French Revolution" not only for his uncompromising insistence on the freedom and dignity of man but for his rejection of all authority that does not stem from man's own critical rationality.[21] According to Heinrich Heine, Kant was "the arch destroyer in the realm of ideas [who] far surpassed Robespierre in terrorism." In both Robespierre and Kant one finds "the same stubborn, keen, unpoetic, sober integrity . . . the same talent for suspicion." The only difference is that "the one directs his suspicion toward ideas and calls it criticism, while the other applies it to people and entitles it republican virtue." By denying legitimacy to everything that was merely customary or traditional, Kant, the deicide, completed the work only half-heartedly carried out by Robespierre, the regicide. Accordingly, the *Critique of Pure Reason* was "the sword with which deism was executed in Germany."[22]

Even allowing for some degree of poetic overstatement, Kant continually identified his philosophy with the Enlightenment and especially the events unfolding in France after 1789. In the Preface to the *Critique of Pure Reason* he identified his age as one of *Kritik* to which everything must submit. Henceforth nothing—neither politics nor religion—was to remain exempt from "the test of free and open examination."[23] Although Kant's views on the French Revolution constitute a study in themselves, his clear preference was for a policy of republican government at home combined with a federation of republics to govern international affairs abroad. By a republic Kant meant a form of government that requires the maximum degree of participation in the shaping of public decisions. Thus Kant could maintain that if we think of the commonwealth as a concept of pure reason "it may be called a Platonic *ideal* (*res publica noumenon*) which is not an empty figment of the imagination but the eternal norm for all civil constitutions"[24] or as he put it in the *Rechtslehre*, a republic is "the only enduring political constitution in which the law is autonomous and is not annexed by any particular person."[25]

The same attitude is evinced in Kant's last published work, "The Contest of Faculties" (1798), in which he claimed to find evidence of a moral tendency toward progress evinced in "an occurrence in our times":

> The revolution which we have seen taking place in our own times in a nation of gifted people may succeed, or it may fail. It may be so filled with misery and atrocities that no right-thinking man would ever decide to make the same experiment again at such a price, even if he could hope to carry it out successfully at the second attempt. But I maintain that this revolution has aroused in the hearts and desires of all spectators who are not themselves caught up in it a *sympathy* which borders almost on enthusiasm, although the very utterance of this sympathy was fraught with danger. It cannot therefore have been caused by anything other than a moral disposition within the human race.[26]

This event, the French Revolution, proved to Kant that moral factors did play a part in history, however small. This moral tendency could be discovered in the enthusiasm provoked by the spectacle of revolution. That Kant could descry the execution of Louis XVI as a sin worse than murder but still congratulate the principle of revolution by which that action was carried out tells us something about its power. From Kant onward the concept of revolution acquired an almost transcendental significance that later thinkers would transmute into an idea of historical inevitability. Starting with Kant but proceeding in an unbroken line from Hegel to Marx, from Lenin and Trotsky to Mao Zedong, revolution became a kind of sacred duty undertaken by selfless men acting to fulfill the conditions of reason and freedom.

REASON AND REVOLUTION

Hegel was perhaps the first great thinker to internalize revolution as the principle of political life.[27] Two passages taken from widely different periods of his life indicate the enduring grip of the French Revolution on his thought.

The first passage is taken from a letter to his friend Schelling written in 1796. Speaking of the Revolution's vindication of the "rights of man," Hegel goes on to say:

> I believe that there is no better sign of the times than the fact that humanity is being represented as worthy of dignity and esteem in itself. . . . The philosophers demonstrate this dignity, the people will learn to feel it; and they will no longer be content to demand their rights which have been reduced to dust, but will seize them, appropriate them. . . . Thanks to the propagation of ideas which demonstrate how things ought to be, the indolence of those who confer eternity on everything that exists is disappearing. The vitalizing power of ideas . . . will elevate the spirits and [men] will learn to devour these ideas.[28]

The second passage is taken from Hegel's lectures on the *Philosophy of History* written over twenty-five years later. From his chair of philosophy at the University of Berlin, Hegel, reflecting back on the experiences of the French Revolution, could still say:

> Never since the sun had stood in its firmament and the planets revolved around him had it been perceived that man's existence centers in his head, i.e., in thought. . . . Anaxagoras had been the first to say that *nous* governs the world; but not until now had man advanced to the recognition of the principle that thought ought to govern spiritual reality. This was accordingly a glorious mental dawn. All thinking beings shared in the jubilation of this epoch. Emotions of a lofty character stirred men's minds at that time; a spiritual enthusiasm thrilled through the world, as if the reconciliation between the divine and the secular was now first accomplished.[29]

These two passages tell us a great deal. First, they are striking evidence of Hegel's "idealism," by which I mean his passionate conviction that it is ideas that motivate men and shape history. The French Revolution was not the outcome of demographic changes in the French population or the desire for cheaper foodstuffs, but can be traced back directly to the ideas of the Enlightenment with its demand that society realize the conditions of reason and freedom. Hegel's description of the Revolution as a "glorious mental dawn" testifies to his celebration of the Revolution not as just another event in European history but as an apocalyptic "moment" in the destiny of humanity, its liberation from bondage and servitude.

At the same time, however, there is a second, deeper meaning to these passages concealed by the rosy optimism of the first. On this second view, although Hegel continued to regard the French Revolution, along with the Protestant Reformation and Kant's "Copernican Revolution" in epistemology, as one of the great watershed moments in modern history, he also saw it as a great moral and political tragedy. Like Burke, to whom he has often been compared, Hegel came to see the revolution as the harbinger of an era of "ideological" politics.[30] Unlike the older Aristotelian conception of politics as prudence (phronesis), which found a resonance in Burke's later appeals to tradition and history, these new advocates, ideologues, and "men of principle" (Prinzipienmänner) as Hegel derisively calls them, set themselves up as the engineers and architects of the new social order.[31] The revolutionaries, consequently, destroyed the fabric of traditional politics by appealing from the "is" to the "ought," from actually existing but imperfect regimes to the one naturally sanctioned social order. Whereas the older politics presented itself as a play of particular passions and interests, the new politics assumed a higher and therefore more doctrinaire bearing. "It is not private interest nor passion that desires gratification, but Reason, Justice, Liberty; and equipped with this title, the demand in question assumes a lofty bearing, and readily adopts a position not merely of discontent, but of open revolt against the actual conditions of the world."[32]

Hegel traces the tragic, even nihilistic, character of the French Revolution back to the philosophy of the Enlightenment that was its cause. At the core of the philosophy was a conception of human beings as possessors of certain natural or inalienable rights. According to the thinkers who first promulgated this theory, government has its origins in the rational desires of individuals to protect and defend their preexisting rights as human beings. This conception already signaled an important shift in the way we think about the legitimacy or justice of government. Prior to the seventeenth century, governments made no reference to rights as their standard of legitimacy. To the extent that rights existed at all, they were considered derivative from a person's obligation as a member of a particular family, estate, or political community.[33]

The idea of universal human rights that belonged to individuals as such was wholly an invention of modernity. This is not to say that human rights went unopposed, but by the end of the eighteenth century the doctrine of human rights had become the dominant strategy for justifying political institutions. Henceforth it would be impossible for regimes to legitimize themselves without some recognition of the rights of their subjects, which rights the regime was entrusted to protect and defend. Documents such as the American Declaration of Independence and the French Declaration of the Rights of Man and Citizen did no more than put the stamp of approval on what philosophers like Locke and Rousseau had already declared in such works as the *Second Treatise* and the *Social Contract*.[34]

Hegel believed that the problems of the French Revolution were caused by its attempt to instantiate the principles of natural rights developed by the philosophers of the Enlightenment. The problems with the philosophy of rights were threefold: they rested on (1) a methodologically faulty conception of the self or the subject of rights, (2) a politically faulty conception of the common good, and (3) a morally faulty conception of civic virtue. After examining each of these problems in turn, I want to turn in conclusion to a paradox in Hegel's own understanding of the role of revolutionary movements in history.

Hegel is well known for his attack on the theory of rights for promoting an "abstract" or unreal conception of the self as denuded of all cultural traits and characteristics. Natural-rights theorists from Hobbes to Kant (and, more recently, Rawls) typically claim to discover the most universal features of human beings by means of a kind of thought-experiment, hypothetically stripping or peeling away everything we have acquired through the influence of custom, history, and tradition in order to discover the prepolitical state of nature and the natural man lurking behind them. In an early essay on *Natural Law* Hegel attacked the "antisocialistic" character of these theories for denying the natural sociality of man and for "posit[ing] the being of the individual as the primary and supreme thing."[35] Such theories were static, lacking any sense of the dynamics of human history and the developmental structure of the moral personality. The self who is the subject of rights is not something "given" once and for all, but is a being in the making, that is, a creature with a history.

In rejecting the conception of the subject of natural rights, Hegel found it necessary to distinguish between two contending views. The first is the early modern school of Hobbes and Locke, which he designated as "empirical" or what today might be called naturalistic.[36] In describing these theorists as empirical he meant that they tried to derive human rights from certain purportedly natural or observable needs that all human beings have in the state of nature. These theorists envisaged a research agenda where rights could simply be read off of certain natural propensities like the desire for life or property. For Hobbes, perhaps the paradigm case of the empirical approach, the most basic need that all human beings have is the desire for self-preservation. Hobbes defines a right as "the liberty each man has to use his own power as he will himself to the preservation of his own nature."[37] And from the claim that each individual has a right to do what is necessary to preserve his own life, Hobbes adduces the duty to acknowledge the same right in others and to seek peace whenever others do so as well.

The second approach to natural rights Hegel calls "formal" and applies mainly to philosophies of the Rousseauean–Kantian type.[38] These theories are formal because the ground of right they seek is not by means of an extrapolation from material needs and wants. Rather, if rights are to be strictly universal they must be grounded in something that transcends our empirically limited desires. This something is the will, which is not the sort of thing one can discover through ordinary empirical or scientific investigation but which is more like an absolute presupposition that must hold if our talk of rights is to make sense. This approach to rights is similar to what Robert Nozick has recently called a transcendental argument in philosophy.[39] It begins with some empirical or factual premise and moves backward to deduce its conditions of possibility. With this transcendental turn in the argument, talk of rights takes on a significantly higher and more abstract level than it had attained in earlier thinkers. Rather than beginning with such mundane concerns as the desire for life or property, Rousseau and Kant typically speak of the right to self-determination or autonomy, the right to participate actively in making the law and not simply the right to be represented in council.

For reasons already alluded to, Hegel thought both of these methods were defective. Instead of setting out, as the empiricists do, by positing rights in some hypothetical state of nature or, as the formalists do, as part of the transcendental structure of consciousness, Hegel regarded rights as part of the dynamic structure of history. Rights claims are not static but are part of a long and arduous historical process leading men gradually, but inexorably, toward an awareness of their own freedom. By freedom is meant here not anything especially mysterious. Freedom, for Hegel, is a predicate not of individuals but of peoples or communities. Freedom is always realized within a particular institutional framework that, at a minimum, must contain such things as the rule of law, a market economy, and an impartial bureaucracy. These institutions are not just a precondition for but a dimension of freedom without which we cannot even begin to think of rights.

Rights are not, then, a gift of nature but are rooted in the prereflective customs and habits (Sitten) of a people. He confirms this point by a linguistic allusion to the Greek word for ethics, *ethos*, which he contrasts to "the newer systems of ethics [which] in making independence and individuality into a principle, cannot fail to expose the relation of these words."[40] The "newer systems of ethics" to which Hegel here alludes are, of course, the natural-rights theories that insist that all duties and obligations derive from the agent's will. The subject of rights is taken to be not any particular person but an *agent*, a term the very generality of which already stakes a claim. The claim that rights pertain to individuals as such is itself bound up with the dynamics of Western history, which in turn is closely related to the processes of modernization and development.[41] The fact that we think of ourselves not as bearers of particular social roles but as agents capable of acting autonomously is not for Hegel a natural condition but a historical accomplishment. Right means for him, approximately, the entire range of practical reason as proceeding from immanent rules embedded in historical circumstances. Just as there is no such thing as the autonomous individual outside the objective norms and rules of our situations, so is there no such thing as a right independent of all context and history.[42]

In identifying rights as part of the broader ethical life of a people, Hegel is returning to an older quasi-Aristotelian conception of a community as a structure of relations within which our moral powers can develop. The idea here is that rights are "situated" within the objective structure of communal norms and purposes so that "what is good and bad, right and wrong, are supplied by laws and customs of each, and there is no great difficulty in recognizing them."[43] Interestingly the theorist who comes closest to Hegel's perspective is not the dogmatic Rousseau but the more flexible Montesquieu who Hegel recommends as a model of judicial discretion. Thus in *L'esprit des lois* did Montesquieu seek to comprehend "both the higher relationships of constitutional law and the lower specifications of civil relationships down to wills, marriage laws, etc. from the character of the whole and its individuality."[44] The important methodological point Hegel is making is that rights are not prior to the community but are part of "the absolute ethical totality," which is "nothing other than a people."[45] In contemporary parlance, the right is not prior to but presupposes the good.

THE POLITICS OF VIRTUE

The French Revolution looked to Hegel, and to many of his generation, as an attempt to recreate the conditions for social and political harmony which not only the Ancien Régime but all of postclassical culture had torn asunder. The revolutionaries, acting out of a desire to bring the doctrines of the philosophers down to earth, directed themselves against all traces of transcendence and other-worldliness. To bring about this reconciliation of the rational and the real, the radicals like Robespierre sought to recreate the kind of consensus and public spiritedness evinced by the ancient polis. The polis experience, at least as theorized by Rousseau, was based on a devotion to the general will at the expense of private interests and elevated the virtue of the citizen over and above those of the private man or bourgeois. "This will is not," Hegel tells us, "the empty thought of will . . . a mere symbol of willing; it is concretely embodied universal will [allgemeiner Wille], the will of all individuals as such."[46]

The reference here to the universal will is clearly an allusion to Rousseau's *volonté générale* that is at the basis of the social contract. The general will is the source of freedom because it is the creation of all, and hence no one is coerced to do anything he has not agreed to do. Each individual participates in the creation of the general will and, in doing so, does no more than obey rules that he has set down for himself. Since there are no a priori limitations on what the general will may in fact will, it satisfies the individual's desire for freedom. The general will is not only the source of freedom but of security because its dictates must be universally and impartially applicable to all who have contracted. It is, then, the only possible source of right since its dictates accord with both the principles of freedom and those of equity.

Rousseau conceived the social contract, then, as the substitution of one type of freedom for another. Natural (or what we would call "negative") freedom, the freedom to do as one likes, is exchanged for rational liberty, the freedom to live by laws of one's own making. Our rights are the exclusive product of the general will, which must take the form of public civil law. But if we ask, What is it that this rational will wills?, What is the content of this will?, Rousseau can provide no satisfactory answer. There is the same kind of vacuity about the general will that Hegel thought he observed in Kant's Categorical Imperative except that it is more dangerous since Rousseau saw the general will as a public legal body. The general will is not universal in the Kantian sense, applicable to rational persons as such, but in the more limited sense of applicable to members of particular communities localized in time and place. The general will, Hegel writes in the *Philosophy of History*, is free when "it does not will anything alien, extrinsic, foreign to itself. . . but wills itself alone—wills the will."[47]

Hegel's reason for rejecting the Revolution's attempt to create the conditions necessary for the realization of the general will is precisely its lack of attention to the particularities of context and situation. Its abstractness and lack of content resulted in a "rage of destruction" that had "no inner significance or filling" anymore than "cutting off a head of cabbage or swallowing a draught of water." The claim that the general will is the only legitimate ground of society would not only abolish all existing institutions and hierarchies but would regard "all differences in talent and authority as being superseded." Nothing would be allowed to exist that is not a product of the general will. Even God, "the empty *être suprême*" of the radicals, is said to hover there "merely as an exhalation of stale gas." The culmination of the Revolution was, then, "the sheer horror of the negative" in which all the "determinate elements disappear with the disaster and ruin that overtakes the self in the state of absolute freedom."[48]

The argument being made here is that although the general will can abolish, it cannot create. It can destroy the Old Regime but cannot build a new one. The idea of the general will is that I am only free when I obey the laws that I have myself helped to create. But since the law is the outcome of a collective decision, it cannot be decided by me alone. If everyone is to be free, then everyone must at least participate in the decision-making process. There is no sense here as, say, with Hobbes of authorizing someone else to do the work. The idea of government by consent, what Hegel calls "a mere symbol of willing," is insufficient. Any halfway measure such as representative institutions would be a violation of my inalienable right to self-legislation. The result is to create a permanent and implacable opposition between the people and their government which will always appear to them as a corporate body, a "faction" interposing itself between them and the general will.

The problem with Rousseau's general will is that it remains too abstract to serve as an instrument for political reform. Indeed, its very abstractness, as I will show in a moment, makes it peculiarly susceptible to manipulation by political demagogues. The general will specifies a set of procedures by which valid laws can be achieved; it says nothing about what the character of those laws should be. Rousseau apparently thought that this procedural formalism alone was sufficient to prevent abuse but, as subsequent events were to show, his agnosticism about the ends and purposes of law was to prove dangerously open-ended.

The inability of the Revolution to create a cohesive republican community is not only related to an empty conception of the common good but to an equally vacuous notion of civic virtue. Following Rousseau, the revolutionaries saw the new French Republic as based on an austere, self-sacrificing conception of virtue in which private goals were ruthlessly subordinated to the pursuit of the public good. The chief task of the Revolution became the construction of a Republic of Virtue. The question the revolutionaries had to confront, then, was this: What guarantee does the man of virtue, the republican citizen, have that he is really acting for the public good? What are the guarantees against self-delusion and hypocrisy?

The only standard that the man of virtue can provide of his own moral goodness turned out ultimately to be his own self-certainty or sincerity. Sincerity thus became the essence of virtue. But herein lies the difficulty. For if sincerity is the only criterion of moral worth, then citizens must be judged not according to the outcome of their deeds but by their subjective convictions alone or the "law of the heart." The result of this purely subjective conception of virtue was to unleash a relentless search to unmask those hypocrites who pursue their own private ends under the guise of public spiritedness. As Hegel depicts it, the Reign of Terror was nothing more than the working out on the public stage of this obsessive concern with inner purity:

> Virtue is here a simple abstract principle and distinguishes the citizens into two classes only—those who are favorably disposed and those who are not. But disposition can only be recognized and judged of by disposition. Suspicion therefore is in the ascendant; but virtue, as soon as it becomes liable to suspicion, is already condemned. . . . Robespierre set up the principle of virtue as supreme, and it may be said that with this man virtue was an earnest matter. Virtue and Terror are the order of the day; for Subjective Virtue, whose sway is based on disposition only, brings with it the most fearful tyranny. It exercises its power without legal formalities, and the punishment it inflicts is equally simple—Death.[49]

One might, of course, wonder, why hypocrisy should be responsible for such a wave of violence and fanaticism. Hannah Arendt has argued that the desire to root out hypocrisy stems from the Revolution's own "favored simile" of itself as tearing the mask, the persona, off a corrupt French society to expose behind it the uncorrupted natural man. For a theorist like Arendt for whom politics is, literally, a kind of "play acting" where actors become the roles and legal personae that they assume, this search for the natural or authentic man behind the mask is bound to be destructive.[50]

According to Arendt, the tragedy of the French (and later the Russian) Revolution stems from what could be called the fallacy of misplaced compassion. Just as Rousseau had seen compassion as the source of all morality, so did Robespierre and Saint-Just regard virtue as the ability to identify oneself immediately with the immense poverty and suffering of the majority of the French people. Compassion, which Rousseau had regarded as the capacity to enter into the suffering of another fellow creature, was turned into a more diffuse sense of pity that meant (in Arendt's terms) "to be sorry without being touched in the flesh."[51] Virtue thus becomes a purely subjective capacity to sympathize with the plight of an abstract other, whether that be the *malheureux* or the "wretched of the earth." Arendt traces the degeneration of the Revolution into despotism and terror back to this unusual capacity for moral sensitivity:

> [E]ven if Robespierre had been motivated by the passion of compassion, his compassion would have become pity when he brought it out into the open where he could no longer direct it toward specific suffering and focus it on particular persons. What had perhaps been genuine passion turned into the boundlessness of an emotion that seemed to respond only too well to the boundless suffering of the multitude in their sheer overwhelming numbers. By the same token, he lost the capacity to establish and hold fast to rapports with persons in their singularity; the ocean of suffering around him and the turbulent sea of emotion within him...drowned all specific considerations, the considerations of friendship no less than considerations of statecraft and principle.[52]

The result of Robespierre's Republic of Virtue was to create a regime motivated by precisely the kind of "pious cruelty" that political realists like Machiavelli had warned against. For Arendt, as for Hegel, the greatest cruelties in history have been committed out of an excessive idealism and devotion to causes. This was certainly true during the French Revolution where a Reign of Terror was established to purge the nation of all those "enemies of the people" suspected of harboring impure thoughts. The Revolution became self-devouring when those men, like the members of the Committee of Public Safety, entrusted with the oversight of the common good, came to regard even their own motives as suspect. Under these circumstances the temptations to suspect and then denounce one's neighbors, friends, and associates became irresistible.

Hegel's critique of the French Revolution should be seen, then, as an epitaph for republicanism. The language of republicanism, as Montesquieu had demonstrated before him, belongs ineluctably to the past. The failure of the Revolution to create anything faintly resembling the Greek polis or the Roman res publica stemmed from its utter lack of connectedness to the present. In its original form republicanism was animated by the goals of political comradeship, fraternity, and communal solidarity. But as the two greatest republican theorists of modernity, Machiavelli and Rousseau, acknowledged, these virtues could also be narrow, particularistic, and intolerant. Valuing public freedom above all else, republicanism was led to act with a kind of punitive zeal against all those who fail or refuse to participate in the corporate project. This zeal is in turn aggravated by a quasi-religious ethos that exalts courage, self-sacrifice, and military glory above all other endeavors. The attempt to recreate republicanism today is not just politically irresponsible; it is historically false.[53]

THE REVOLUTIONARY HERO

There is, finally, a paradox in Hegel's treatment of the French Revolution. The paradox is that while the Revolution was reprehensible for the murder, violence, bloodshed, and terror it created, it was still regarded by Hegel as a "progressive" force in history, moving humanity closer to a certain desirable goal, namely, freedom.[54] Nowhere does this paradox emerge more clearly than in Hegel's treatment of the revolutionary hero.

Hegel's concept of the revolutionary hero is the person responsible for large-scale social and political change. What interested him in particular was the discrepancy between the subjective intentions of individual revolutionary actors and the objective consequences of their deeds. In a series of brilliant analyses Hegel shows how individuals—Alexander, Caesar, Luther, and Napoleon are his typical examples—were often unaware of the larger import of their actions. Thus what Caesar thought he was doing in crossing the Rubicon was one thing. The influence that this action had not only in his own time but on later history is something entirely different and was no part of his conscious intention. This is the famous Hegelian doctrine of the "cunning of reason" whereby whatever individuals may have subjectively intended, the actual import of their deeds was and could not but be unknown to them.[55]

Hegel appears to praise the revolutionary hero, often *malgré lui*, for helping to advance the cause of human freedom. Hence he is typically more concerned to forgive the revolutionary his sins than with sympathizing with the victims of his heroics. Although Hegel may never actually say that the ends justify the means, he recognizes that progress toward freedom is not achieved blamelessly. Thus in an early work on "The German Constitution" Hegel singles out Machiavelli's *Il Principe* not for holding up "a golden mirror for an ambitious oppressor" but for showing his fellow countrymen how to make a revolution. When one reads Machiavelli's work as Hegel recommends, not as "a compendium of moral and political principles applicable indifferently to any and every situation, i.e., to none" but as a response to "the centuries before . . . and the history of his own time," one will see him less as a teacher of evil than as a teacher of popular liberty. Although many of the actions recommended by Machiavelli would be "criminal" if carried out by private citizens, Hegel maintains that if such actions are in the service of state-building rather than personal advantage one gains "a totally new complexion on the procedure of the prince." Machiavelli's work is in this respect "a great testimony to his age and to his own belief that the fate of a people . . . can be averted by genius." Unfortunately, Hegel concludes, "Machiavelli's voice has died away without effect."[56]

This last statement proved altogether unwarranted. Even as Hegel was putting the final touches on this essay, his call for a German Theseus found resonance in the deeds of Napoleon who was busy putting the Florentine's plans into effect. Although Napoleon, this "world soul" as Hegel called him, is never mentioned by name in the *Phenomenology*, Hegel's writings are replete with oblique references to him. In his Jena lectures on the *Philosophy of Mind*, for instance, he is clearly casting Napoleon into the role of a Machiavellian prince or a Rousseauist legislator who founds a state by a sheer act of will. "All states are founded," he says, "by the sublime acts of great men. . . . Theseus founded the Athenian state; also in this way during the French Revolution a terrible power held the state generally. This power is not despotism but tyranny, pure terrifying power."[57]

Even as he lauds the revolutionary founders of the state for providing the conditions for freedom, Hegel recognizes that their actions are rarely received so benignly by their own people. In this way was "Theseus repaid with ingratitude" and "Richelieu and others with hatred for their acts of violence."[58] This might be called history's revenge upon the hero. They are overthrown not because their actions are intrinsically evil but because they have become superfluous. Thus Hegel remarks of Robespierre that "power abandoned him because necessity abandoned him and so he was violently overthrown."[59] Once their ends are accomplished, their services are no longer needed. In the language of the later *Philosophy of History*, such men merely "fall off like empty hulls from the kernel."[60]

It is sometimes remarked that Hegel saw himself as the German Machiavelli trying to do for his time what Machiavelli had done for Italy.[61] This comparison is apt as far as it goes, but herein lies the difference. Although Machiavelli did not live to see the realization of his plans for national liberation, Hegel regarded Napoleon's goal of a fully unified Europe as already well under way. If Machiavelli was a kind of revolutionary John the Baptist, Napoleon was Hegel's messiah. Of course, the extent of Hegel's Bonapartism has been a subject of considerable controversy among Hegel's principle interpreters. For Alexandre Kojève, the Napoleonic Empire makes possible for the first time in history the universal recognition of the right to equal freedom and dignity. Only in the "universal and homogeneous state" that Napoleon brought into being can man be fully and completely "satisfied," for only here has the revolutionary struggle for recognition been brought to an end. But when the foundation for the state has been laid, the work of the architect is made redundant. Like the original Theseus, Napoleon, the modern tyrant, is fated to disappear from the scene he helped to create. Strictly speaking, it is not Napoleon but Hegel who comes at the end, for he alone can put into conceptual form what Napoleon did.[62]

But here lies the paradox. Hegel praises Napoleon as the agent of a historical mission of which he (Napoleon) was only dimly aware. But how is such praise merited if it is achieved at the cost of thousands and even millions of innocent lives? Moral praise or approbation is generally reserved for persons whom we deem to have acted on good reasons or with good intentions. At least since Kant the role of intention or the "good will" is thought to play a crucial part in moral evaluation. But Hegel is prepared to award praise to persons who, through no intention of their own, produced consequences that merely happen to be beneficial. The preferred form of moral justification, then, is a kind of consequentialism where even great criminals can be considered praiseworthy if good consequences are seen to follow from their actions. Clearly, then, revolutionary figures are justified in riding roughshod over conventional moral constraints so long as their actions are deemed beneficial in the long run.

The chief problem with Hegel's philosophy of history is practical, not theoretical. If one believes that what one ought to do is what contributes most to the greatest amount of total freedom, then there are no clear limits on how one can treat existing persons in order to realize that goal. Until that end is reached all actions, however cruel they may seem, can be justified against the standard of a generic humanity raised to the level of an implacable judge, jury, and executioner. History becomes, then, a kind of secularized theodicy in which present evils are explained and even justified in terms of the good consequences they will ultimately cause to bring about. Indeed, the history of the twentieth century has been replete with tyrants from Stalin to Hitler to Pol Pot who have excused their crimes on the grounds of their contribution to some future well-being. This kind of moral justification appears as nothing so much as a set of IOUs issued against an indefinite future.

It must be said that Hegel's own position is ambiguous regarding the completion or end of world history. His thought fluctuates between two poles: one which emphasizes the transient and dialectical character of all being, and another that depicts the ultimate consummation or realization of freedom at the end of history. It is well known—or at least often believed— that Hegel thought he lived at the end of history, at that "absolute moment" in historical time when the philosophical demand for freedom and its political realization had at last been accomplished. No longer would it be necessary to think of freedom as an abstract ideal that continually recedes before us; freedom instead would be something fully and adequately embodied in the institutions and practices of the modern European state. Such a state would provide the grounds for the final "reconciliation" between reason and reality. Only at the end of history, "when philosophy paints its grey in grey," will the owl of Minerva come home to roost.

Yet even on Hegel's own account another possibility suggests itself. Even leaving aside his remark that America is "the country of the future," he cannot altogether rule out future animadversions of the spirit.[63] If Hegel was right to say that philosophy is not simply about history but is something that takes place in history, "its own time apprehended in thoughts," then there is no way, strictly speaking, to know that we stand at the end of history. To know this would require the ability to get outside of history, to see it, as it were, from a God's-eye view. But this is precisely what Hegel says we cannot do. On his own account man is the historical animal par excellence. Since there is no way to escape from history, there is no way of knowing whether, or if, it has at last come to an end.

Nevertheless, the result of Hegel's philosophy of history has not been to restrain the revolutionary spirit but to liberate, unwittingly, a kind of political messianism that promises to deliver humanity not from any particular evil but from evil in general. It is not any particular order of society but the human condition itself that must be transformed. For this kind of eschatology, the end is not brought about by a superintending providence operating outside of history but through conscious human will and activity working in and through history. Consequently, it is never enough to wait patiently for the end; it is necessary to force the end, to act as if the end were already immanent in our deeds. Thus there is an implicit social activism concealed here which encourages revolutionary militants to initiate the terrors that must precede the end of history. Political messianism may be born out of frustration and even rage against existing political realities, but it is in the end forced to turn against politics as such. The dream of an end of history, like the biblical end of days, is predicated on the destruction of the world as we know it, and most of the people in it.[64]

CONCLUSION

If Hegel's views on revolution can be faulted it is for turning what was originally a messianic and eschatological vision into a theory of history and human progress. There is, of course, a vigorous literature debating Hegel's appropriation of the messianic theme. For some, notably Karl Lowith, his views on the end of history represent a "secularized" eschatology, whereas for others, like Hans Blumenberg, the very idea of a secularized eschatology is a contradiction in terms. Whereas eschatological thinking speaks of a final judgment breaking into history from the outside, the idea of progress to which Hegel is attached seeks possibilities at work within or immanent in history. Far from being identical in function, the idea of progress originally set itself over against eschatological expectations brought about through divine intervention. Progress has little to do with millennial faith in a transcendent deity but much to do with "human self-assertion" and the desire to take control over one's own destiny. The Hegelian (and later Marxist) construction of an end of history is not a *Heilsgeschichte* that sees divinity breaking into history from the outside but is the outcome of purely immanent developments that can be either hastened or retarded by human activity.[65]

It should go without saying that Hegel was not a terrorist and should not be saddled with the tyrannical moralisms of both the left and the right. He even, arguably, sought to dampen the revolutionary spirit of his age by showing history to be a "slaughterbench" where heroic individuals invariably come to grief. Nevertheless, Hegel's ideas about the progressive character of revolutionary movements clearly resonate with certain of our leading beliefs about progress and modernization. Whereas the ancient Greeks spoke of revolutions as part of an endless cycle of nature doomed to eternal repetition over time, one of the hallmarks of modernity has been the belief that we are capable of breaking out of this cycle and creating something new. Certainly, the scientific, industrial, and political revolutions of the modern age have been thought of as evidence that humankind is awakening from its dogmatic slumber and rolling back the forces of ignorance and superstition. If we understand the Enlightenment to mean the ultimate triumph of reason over unreason, then it would seem that the Hegelian belief in the emergence of reason and freedom in history represents the culmination of the Enlightenment.

In the face of the experiences of the twentieth century it is difficult to retain anything of the Enlightenment's faith in history as the story of man's secular redemption. The Enlightenment's belief that advances in our scientific and technological rationality can bring about a "better world" has been all but relegated to the status of one of the self-consoling mythologies of the age. At the very least the belief that further advances in history will lead to the amelioration of human suffering has been massively contradicted by the experiences of Auschwitz and the Gulag. The chief task facing political theory today must be to keep alive some sense of the primacy of human rights and the dignity of the individual while resisting the temptations of a dynamic, teleological philosophy of history.

NOTES

1. For some works in the comparative study of revolution, see Crane Brinton, *Anatomy of Revolution* (New York: Vintage, 1965); Isaac Deutscher, "The French Revolution and the Russian Revolution: Some Suggestive Analogies," *World Politics* 4 (1952): 493–514; Theda Skocpol, *States and Social Revolutions: A Comparative Analysis of*

France, Russia, China (Cambridge: Cambridge University Press, 1979). For a withering attack on the French–Russian analogy, see François Furet, *Interpreting the French Revolution*, trans. Elborg Forster (Cambridge: Cambridge University Press, 1981), chap. 1 entitled "The Revolution Is Over."

2. Edmund Burke, *Reflections on the Revolution in France* (Harmondsworth: Penguin, 1984), p. 153.

3. Alexis de Tocqueville, *The Old Regime and the French Revolution*, trans. Stuart Gilbert (New York: Doubleday, 1955), p. 20.

4. The best study of Tocqueville's history, to my knowledge, is Furet, *Interpreting the French Revolution*, pp. 132–163; see also Melvin Richter, "Tocqueville's Contributions to the Theory of Revolution," *Revolution*, ed. C. J. Friedrich (New York: Atherton, 1966), pp. 75–121.

5. See Steven B. Smith, *Hegel's Critique of Liberalism: Rights in Context* (Chicago: University of Chicago Press, 1989).

6. G. W. F. Hegel, *The Philosophy of History*, trans. J. Sibree (New York: Dover, 1956), p. 446.

7. Reinhart Koselleck, "Historical Criteria of the Modern Concept of Revolution," *Futures Past: On the Semantics of Historical Time*, trans. Keith Tribe (Cambridge: MIT Press, 1985), p. 42; Hannah Arendt, *On Revolution* (New York: Viking, 1965), pp. 35–36.

8. See Pauly-Wissowa-Kroll, eds., *Real-Encyclopedie der classischen Altertumswissenschaft* (Stuttgart: J. B. Metzlersche, 1932), 30: 1313–1316.

9. Plato, *Republic*, 8: 544c; Aristotle, *Politics* 5: 1316a 1 ff.

10. Aristotle, *Politics* 7: 1329b 25–30.

11. Polybius, *Histories* 6: 7–12; for a useful discussion see Robert D. Cumming, *Human Nature and History* (Chicago: University of Chicago Press, 1969), 1: 95–97, 149–151.

12. Machiavelli, *Il Principe e Discorsi* (Milan: Feltrinelli, 1983), pp. 379–384.

13. Thomas Hobbes, *Behemoth: Or The Long Parliament*, ed. F. Tönnies, 2d ed. (London: F. Cass, 1969), p. 204.

14. Peter Burke, "Renaissance, Reformation, Revolution," *Niedergang: Studien zu einem geschichtlichen Thema*, eds. Reinhart Koselleck and Karlheinz Stierle (Stuttgart: Cotta, 1980), pp. 144–145.

15. R. G. Collingwood, *The New Leviathan* (Oxford: Clarendon Press, 1942), pp. 199–200.

16. M. Diderot and M. d'Alembert, eds., *Encyclopédie ou Dictionnaire Raisonné des Sciences, des Arts, et des Métiers*, 3d ed. (Geneva: J. L. Pellet, 1778–1779), 29: 97.

17. Koselleck, "Historical Criteria of the Modern Concept of Revolution," p. 45.

18. Arendt, *On Revolution*, p. 39.

19. Collingwood, *The New Leviathan*, pp. 201–202.

20. See Karl Marx, "Contribution to the Critique of Hegel's Philosophy of Right: Introduction," in *Early Writings*, trans. T. B. Bottomore (London: C. A. Watts, 1963), pp. 51–52.

21. Immanuel Kant, "What Is Enlightenment?" in *Political Writings*, trans. H. B. Nisbet, ed. Hans Reiss (Cambridge: Cambridge University Press, 1970), p. 54.

22. Heinrich, Heine, "The History of Religion and Philosophy in Germany," in *The Romantic School and Other Essays*, eds. Jost Hermand and Robert C. Holub (New York: Continuum, 1985), pp. 203–204.

23. Immanuel Kant, *Critique of Pure Reason*, trans. Norman K. Smith (New York: Saint Martin's, 1965), p. 9.

24. Kant, "The Contest of Faculties," p. 187.

25. Immanuel Kant, *The Metaphysical Elements of Justice*, trans. John Ladd (Indianapolis: Bobbs-Merrill, 1965), p. 112.

26. Kant, "The Contest of Faculties," p. 182.

27. The most useful discussions are Joachim Ritter, *Hegel und die Französische Revolution* (Frankfurt: Suhrkamp, 1965); Jürgen Habermas, "Hegel's Critique of the French Revolution," in *Theory and Practice*, trans. John Viertel (Boston: Beacon Press, 1974), pp. 121–141; see also Herbert Marcuse, *Reason and Revolution: Hegel and the Rise of Social Theory* (Boston: Beacon Press, 1955); Georg Lukács, *The Young Hegel: Studies in the Relations Between Dialectics and Economics*, trans. Rodney Livingstone (Cambridge: MIT Press, 1975); see also Smith, *Hegel's Critique of Liberalism*, pp. 85–97.

28. G. W. F. Hegel, *Briefe von und an Hegel*, ed. J. Hoffmeister (Hamburg: F. Meiner, 1952–1954), 1: 24.

29. Hegel, *Philosophy of History*, p. 447.

30. See J. F. Sutter, "Burke, Hegel, and the French Revolution," in *Hegel's Political Philosophy: Problems and Perspectives*, ed. Z. A. Pelczynski (Cambridge: Cambridge University Press, 1971), pp. 52–72.

31. Hegel, *Philosophy of History*, p. 451; see also his essay on "The English Reform Bill," in *Political Writings*, trans. T. M. Knox (Oxford: Clarendon Press, 1964), pp. 325–326.

32. Hegel, *Philosophy of History*, p. 35.

33. For the corporate basis of rights in premodern Europe, see Otto Gierke, *Natural Law and the Theory of Society 1500–1800*, trans. Ernest Barker (Boston: Beacon Press, 1957).

34. For useful discussions see Leo Strauss, *Natural Right and History* (Chicago: University of Chicago Press, 1953), chaps. 5–6; see also Dieter Henrich, "The Contexts of Autonomy: Some Presuppositions of the Comprehensibility of Human Rights," *Daedalus* (Fall 1982): 255–277.

35. G. W. F. Hegel, *Natural Law*, trans. T. M. Knox (Philadelphia: University of Pennsylvania Press, 1975), p. 70.

36. Ibid., pp. 59 ff.

37. Thomas Hobbes, *Leviathan*, ed. Michael Oakeshott (London: Macmillan, 1962), p. 103.

38. Hegel, *Natural Law*, pp. 70 ff.

39. Robert Nozick, *Anarchy, State, and Utopia* (Oxford: Blackwell, 1974), pp. 261–262.

40. Hegel, *Natural Law*, p. 112.

41. See Ferdinand Tönnies, *Community and Association*, trans. C. Loomis (London: Routledge & Kegan Paul, 1955); Sir Henry Maine, *The Ancient Law* (Tucson: University of Arizona Press, 1986).

42. See G. W. F. Hegel, *Philosophy of Right*, trans. T. M. Knox (Oxford: Clarendon Press, 1967), p. 233, par. 33A: "In speaking of Right [Recht] . . . we mean not merely what is generally meant by civil law, but also morality, ethical life, and world-history."

43. G. W. F. Hegel, *Lectures on the Philosophy of World History: Introduction*, trans.

H. B. Nisbet (Cambridge: Cambridge University Press, 1975), p. 80.

44. Hegel, *Natural Law*, p. 128.

45. Ibid., p. 92.

46. G. W. F. Hegel, *Phenomenology of Mind*, trans. J. B. Baille (London: George Allen & Unwin, 1971), pp. 600–601.

47. Hegel, *Philosophy of History*, p. 442.

48. Hegel, *Phenomenology*, pp. 602, 604, 605.

49. Hegel, *Philosophy of History*, pp. 450–451.

50. Arendt, *On Revolution*, pp. 91–104.

51. Ibid., p. 80.

52. Ibid., p. 85.

53. For some works advocating the revival of republicanism, see J. G. A. Pocock, *The Machiavellian Moment: Florentine Political Thought and the Atlantic Republican Tradition* (Princeton: Pinceton University Press, 1975); William M. Sullivan, *Reconstructing Public Philosophy* (Berkeley, Los Angeles, London: University of California Press, 1982); for a relentless critique of the alleged civic republican influences on American politics, see John Diggins, *The Lost Soul of American Politics: Virtue, Self-Interest, and the Foundations of Liberalism* (Chicago: University of Chicago Press, 1984).

54. Hegel, *World History*, p. 54: "World history is the progress of the consciousness of freedom."

55. Ibid., p. 89; see also Hegel, *Science of Logic*, trans. A. V. Miller (London: George Allen & Unwin, 1969), pp. 746–747.

56. Hegel, *Political Writings*, pp. 220, 221, 222–223.

57. G. W. F. Hegel, *Jenaer Realphilosophie. Vorlesungsmanuskripte zur Philosophie der Natur und des Geistes von 1805–1806*, ed. J. Hoffmeister (Hamburg: F. Meiner, 1969), p. 246.

58. Hegel, *Political Writings*, p. 241.

59. Hegel, *Jenaer Realphilosophie*, pp. 247–248.

60. Hegel, *World History*, p. 85.

61. Shlomo Avineri, *Hegel: Theory of the Modern State* (Cambridge: Cambridge University Press, 1972), pp. 60–61.

62. Alexandre Kojève, *Introduction à la lecture de Hegel*, ed. Raymond Queneau (Paris: Gallimard, 1947), pp. 95, 97, 153–154, 194–195.

63. Hegel, *World History*, p. 170.

64. For the religious roots of messianism, see Norman Cohen, *The Pursuit of the Millenium: Revolutionary Millenarians and Mystical Anarchists of the Middle Ages* (New York: Oxford University Press, 1970); Gershom Scholem, *The Messianic Idea in Judaism* (New York: Schocken, 1971); Michael Walzer, *Exodus and Revolution* (New York: Basic Books, 1985); for some of the secular uses to which these millenarian ideas have been put see Jacob Talmon, *The Origins of Totalitarian Democracy* (New York: Praeger, 1960); Bernard Yack, *The Longing for Total Revolution* (Princeton: Princeton University Press, 1986).

65. Karl Löwith, *Meaning in History: The Theological Implications of the Philosophy of History* (Chicago: University of Chicago Press, 1962); Hans Blumenberg, *The Legitimacy of the Modern Age*, trans. Robert M. Wallace (Cambridge: MIT Press, 1983); for a comprehensive bibliography of some of the recent work on this debate, see the *Annals of Scholarship* 5 (1987): 97–106.

TWELVE

Alexis de Tocqueville and the Legacy of the French Revolution

Harvey Mitchell

It must not be forgotten that the author who wishes to be understood is obliged to carry all his ideas to their utmost theoretical conclusions, and often to the limits of the false and impracticable; for if it is necessary sometimes to depart in action from the rules of logic, such is not the case in discourse, and a man finds it almost as difficult to be inconsistent in his language as to be consistent in his actions. (Tocqueville, *De la démocratie en Amérique*)[1]

In my lifetime, I have already heard it said four times that the new society, such as the Revolution made it, had finally found its natural and permanent state, when succeeding events proved this to be mistaken. (Tocqueville, "Réflexions diverses")[2]

Alexis de Tocqueville's observations on authorial concern for consistency are to be found in the Introduction to the first volume of *Democracy in America*. His disillusion with the prognostications heralding the end of the French Revolution comes close to the end of his fragmentary notes on its actual events, for which he failed to work out a satisfactory conceptual framework. His stance on the two problems raised in the epigraphs may be seen as an instance in his work of an underlying search for continuity. It was in 1850 that he said he was prepared to put his trust in "a freely ranging judgment on our modern societies and forecast of their probable future . . . which I can only find in writing history . . . [and] [i]t is only the long drama of the French Revolution that provides such a period."[3]

Thus for more than half his life, he was driven to seek consistency in his accounts of human actions that must by their very nature forever remain inconsistent: writers seemingly accomplished this feat with some ease, for almost without thinking about it, they imposed the language of logic upon and offered explanations for the actions they described. There is no reference

in Tocqueville's thoughts on the question of the writer's unconscious repro-
duction of the language of prevailing discourses, but there is every reason to
believe that he assumed that the writer works within it, constructing theories
of human action in accordance with it, investing them with the appearance of
unassailability, and also running the risk of becoming a prisoner of his own
constructs. A circular relation is created between the interpreting discourse
and the interpreted object, in the course of which the author loses sight of his
historical particularity. Tocqueville's sense of irony, his taste for the paradoxical, his cunning recovery of silent and stubborn human ambiguities,
attest to his awareness of the problem. He accepted it as a challenge more
consciously, he believed, than most of the *gens de lettres* of his own day, and set
out to bind human unpredictability and structural trends in a tightly constructed interpretation. In many respects, *L'Ancien Régime et la Révolution* was
just such a book, and he took enormous pride in its magisterial and econom-
ical perspective, for which he devised a rhetoric of necessary change and
equally necessary continuity. But he did not believe that he had succeeded in
creating the best kind of balance. He spent the last three years of his life
pondering how he could make a breakthrough to the Revolution itself, and he
perhaps also wondered if he had lived up to Montesquieu's book on the
greatness and decline of the Romans, which he held up to himself as a model
for his own work, because of his belief that it had overcome the problems of
"mixing. . . history, properly speaking, with philosophical history."[4]

At yet another level, he played with the idea that if sound grounds could
be established for reducing the role of probability in human affairs, coherence
would constitute less of a problem, inasmuch as human actions would not be
as subject to the power of the contingent; but he came to believe that individuals could only come to terms with the mysteries of probability, never
master them, just as he accepted the sense of incompleteness in his unsatisfied yearning for certainty.[5] This was matched by his resignation, amounting
to stoicism, that both the mysteries of the unknown and the unknowability
of truth could be borne by a faith in human power to sense the good.[6]
Taste for this kind of enquiry may be seen as a pervasive theme in his emo-
tional being and was expressed in his intellectual life in his project to interpret the Great Revolution as the starting point of a modern struggle between
impersonal forces and liberty. He was unwilling, as he wrote to the former
Restoration deputy, Royer-Collard, one of the more outstanding critics of its
politics, to believe in human decline in the face of the counterevidence of
human progress in so many areas of life.[7] He was consequently unwilling to
settle for a seemingly coherent account of the revolutions of the past which
would distort the nature of the struggle for liberty in an uncertain universe.
In daring to reach a less false account of it, he exposed himself to enormous
anxieties. To this will to comprehend the sources and outcome of the Revolution must be added his doubts in finding an understanding audience.[8] The

responses to his work never quite lived up to his own search for the polyvalent meanings of the Revolution. Hence his disappointment that he had not been understood never left him.

At the center of his interpretation of the French Revolution—whose history he believed was just as likely to escape finality as an author's quest for consistency, a truth destined to remain for him a permanent source of frustration—were the problems of continuity and determinateness, two of his favorite leitmotifs, which arose both from his study of politics and society and his own political and existential preferences. That the last might constitute an intrusion in his métier as historian he never concealed, but he felt confident that there was no necessary conflict between a work of historical enquiry and a teleological account of human affairs. The Revolution carried with it certain aspects of the past; the historian must try to embody them in a coherent interpretation; and, since Tocqueville did not belong to a nonexistent fraternity of historians entirely detached from politics, but to the tradition of men in politics who wrote about the past to locate themselves in the present, he also thought that an essential aspect of his life as a public writer was to discern how significant features of a society's past might point to others in the future, as yet hidden. Persons who were cognizant of the power of impersonal forces were in a better position to distinguish real from false choices and had some chance to shape their worlds.

Tocqueville saw the problem of the French Revolution as exposing the tensions between determinateness and choice, and continuity and change, not only within each of these dual pairs but between them. He saw the two dualities as the principal variants of human history in which they dovetailed, informed, and bore upon each other but were not easily, because they were not transparently, reconcilable. Thus he remained constantly poised on the edge of tentativeness when he spoke about modern liberty as the most likely casualty of democratic revolutions, expecting that his fears might indeed become realities but hoping that individuals and events might conspire to achieve the opposite. This thought remained with him forever. He took it up, for example, when he made a distinction between the stances of historians in different ages. Historians in aristocratic periods centered their explanations around the actions of great personages; historians in democratic times tended to rob human beings of their power and transfer it to great forces external to themselves—to necessities. Neither were right: the first, because they sacrificed what was concealed and of long duration to the momentary voices of the present; the second, because it was necessary "to raise the faculties of men, not to complete their prostration."[9] Tocqueville's stance was self-consciously aristocratic in a democratic age which heightened his desire to rescue the individual voice from necessities.

Liberty, from this heroic but melancholy stance, consisted in the exercise of options within contexts of varying opacity made up of layer on layer of customs, mores, moral systems, opinions, and language,[10] which cling to human beings most tenaciously when they mistakenly believe that they are fully aware of them and think they are able to soar above them, only to find that their imaginations have taken them too far. This is why he inveighed against the Enlightenment men of letters whom he could not forgive for dreaming about and encouraging "une société imaginaire."[11] That is why, in addition, Tocqueville's philosophy of history embodies an indignant protest against the notion that popular revolutions are planned. They are "desired rather than premeditated," and those who claim to be their leaders are simply borne along by the wind that takes them into unknown countries.[12] He mocked Lamartine's criticism that he had written about the Revolution as an accident. Rather, as he put it, the Revolution was "the great transformation of the whole of European society, achieved through violence, but prepared and necessarily heralded by the work of centuries."[13] Revolutions happen, and have a quality of determinateness that ought to check human beings who presume to act with a full knowledge of their surroundings. Conceding the presence of determinateness apparently was not the same as hard determinism, for the first did not amount to a capitulation to a "chain of fatality . . . suppress[ing] men from . . . history," as he had remarked earlier in his *Souvenirs*. Human beings, however, are equally mistaken, he said, when they beckon to a concept like chance to help them out of the tangle of the inexplicable; chance was a primitive code word for their ignorance, since there is nothing that is not prepared beforehand. Thus *sheer* chance is not only less interesting, it loses its power to defy the "natural law" and, hence, must shed its arbitrariness when it is seen, as Tocqueville did, as an integral part of multicausal explanation. Though he left unclear the nature of his position on design in the cosmos and in history, as we shall see later he was overwhelmed by the "surprise" of the Revolution. He was therefore not at all disposed to discount as inconsequential the precise moment when events took a particular turn, or when individuals acted in unexpected fashion. In retrospect, as soon as the unexpected is experienced and thought about in the present, it always mocks individuals with reminders from the past, yet continues to tantalize them with the notion that the past will not totally shape the present. Of course, the fantasy that they could start afresh in utopian fashion would always be hard to dispel, even if the realities of their previous "institutions, cast of minds and . . . state of morals" would catch them up and presumably set them right.[14] But if he was wary of utopian visions, he was far from unreceptive to the element of free choice. His mind was not set on condemning the past as an incubus on the present. He wanted to understand the role of human diversity in shaping it in order to avoid illusions about the future. Thus for Tocqueville the French Revolution had heavy paradoxical meanings. They were structured in humankind itself. The analogs of self and society could, he believed, capture civic reality; but that was not the same as claiming that it could be caught by reducing the complexities of civic reality to personal biography.

THE REVOLUTION AS CONTRADICTION

Tocqueville's interpretation of the Great Revolution found its way into his writings before the 1856 publication of *L'Ancien Régime*, but it cannot be treated satisfactorily without recognizing that it owed its genesis, not only to *Democracy in America*, but especially to his *Souvenirs*. His search for an unwavering, relatively stable reference point in himself, to be attained by finding an exit from his personal "labyrinth,"[15] reached an acute stage as he began to ponder the significance of the 1848 Revolution and its aftermath. He confronted his own *daimons* and the *daimons* of the Great Revolution in his "secret" *Souvenirs*, which he began to write at the age of forty-five, claiming that thoughts not subject to public scrutiny were the only ones free from dissimulation. Thus, he argued that if he could be true to himself, he could be true to his subject. For him there could be no questioning the intersubjectivity of such entities as the public and private, the social and personal. They were, he believed, threatened by the development of a government that, in its omniscience, would isolate persons and effectively destroy both their private and their public lives.[16] So in choosing an "unmoved" point in himself, he was not claiming that the points external to himself were subordinate to his will, but only that the world of self and others outside it were in a constant state of flux, and that individuals have no choice but to adopt a metaphysical fixity to make possible an interpretation of the empirical world. The maneuver was a heuristic device not to challenge but to confirm "the chain of history, so that [he could] the more easily attach to it the thread of [his] personal recollections."[17] Just as the 1830 Revolution released the energies that created *Democracy in America*, so 1848 was a turning point for Tocqueville. It forced him to bring into sharper relief the links he had already been making between the Great Revolution and the emergence of democracy.

When the second volume of *Democracy in America* appeared in 1840, he had been, if not completely, yet fairly, confident in his analysis of the trajectory of democratic revolution. He plotted it in general terms as a succession of psychosocial stages. In its first stage, enormous energies fueled by boundless ambition are released, bringing to dizzying heights of power groups of men competing with one another and inspiring others waiting in the wings to make the best of the general confusion caused by changes in laws and customs. The power shifts continue for some time after the consummation of the Revolution and take place in an atmosphere in which people cannot respond outside their former contexts of behavior. The second stage is a compound of recollection and a sense of instability, each stimulating further ambitions, while opportunities for satisfying them diminish rapidly. The last stage is reached with the complete disappearance of the privileged class of the aristocracy, the onset of political amnesia (the blotting out of the memory of the general and specific political struggles), and the restoration of order when the adaptation of desires to available means is reasserted: "the needs, the ideas, and the feelings of men cohere once again; men achieve a new stable level in society, and democratic society is finally established."[18]

Tocqueville's anatomization of the Great Revolution and its 1830 aftermath was, he came to believe, incomplete, because, with the coming of the 1848 Revolution, he saw that what had begun in 1787–1789 had not reached its end. He needed to move into the realm of self-absorption to recognize or rationalize his weaknesses and errors in the Orleanist Chamber of Deputies, to purge himself of them, and to deny his parliamentary colleagues' accusations of underhandedness and slyness. By these means, he overcame his pain; he found that he could, as he phrased it, take pride in his "pride" as a man, politician, and author. He wanted to think that the approval of others was not the source of his pride, which he compared with the restlessness and disquiet of the mind itself.[19] He was preparing himself for his return to the writer's loneliness soothed by the writer's superior stance,[20] the only center for a "sincere"[21] interpretation of the Great Revolution that had been leaving its marks in his imagination for a quarter-century, but which he and others after 1830 had mistakenly thought they had been able to assemble into a coherent whole. Not until he could "re-collect" himself[22] could he begin to *recollect*—this time, he hoped, more accurately—more of the wholeness of the Great Revolution, in order to reach some understanding of why the actors of 1848 had appropriated from it what suited them and discarded the rest. The only result of pillaging rather than understanding the past was the creation of a wholly new set of false recollections. "The terrifying originality of the facts remained concealed from them," because the enormous powers of unreliable memories, the fictionalization and the theatricalization of the past, hid it from their view. Thus they were hard at work in "acting the French Revolution, rather than continuing it."[23] Acting out could also mean playing at being revolutionaries and, indeed, Tocqueville's evocations of the theater to describe the actions of the politicians support such a view.

The 1848 revolutionaries were in part stuck in a scenario from the past; in fluctuating degrees, and in a chaos of fluttering poses, they were prisoners of its signs and behavioral practices.[24] Tocqueville characterized the dilemma of the subject or the self in the familiar terms of self-interest and lack of distance preventing him from seeing himself as he is; the "views, interests, ideas, tastes and instincts that have guided [the self's] actions; the network of little foot-paths which are little known even by those who use them," wove the intricate network of a veil or a screen.[25] He wanted to use the power of the past, rather than bury it in personal lives and social settings, in order to grasp something even more difficult. It he could emerge from the maze with a heightened understanding of where he had been, he could help rescue his countrymen from their *labyrinth*—a term that he had already used in his *Democracy*[26]—tell them where they had been, where they were likely to be going, and prepare them for the democratic future. But he did not want to slip into the naive belief that the past automatically teaches human beings much about the present, especially when "old pictures...[are] forced into new frames."[27] He also wanted to convince readers that the best lesson history could offer was that it never repeats itself despite the propensity human beings have to repeat themselves. He began with an acerbic observation on historians:

> I started to review the history of the last sixty years, and I smiled bitterly when I thought of the illusions formed at the conclusion of each period in this long revolution; the theories on which these illusions had been nourished; the erudite dreams of our historians, and all the ingenious and deceptive systems by the aid of which attempts were made to explain a present which was still dimly seen, and a future which was not seen at all.[28]

He then moved on to speak in even less-flattering tones about the politics of revolution. In his brilliant use of the metaphors of the theatre of the grotesque and comic to describe the events of February, May, and June, and later, in drawing his portrait of Louis Napoleon, the new democratic despot whose model for his assumption of power was the first Napoleon, he was trying to warn Frenchmen not to mistake illusory for real change. Shifting his focus to England about a year after he completed his *Souvenirs*, he used similar language in telling Nassau William Senior that revolutions inevitably lead to masquerades.[29] If the Great Revolution was to be saved from the burlesque into which the majority of its heirs had dragged it—the irony was that they believed they were being faithful to it—its real nature had to be revealed. This could not be done by fashioning a discourse of mutilation—cutting the Revolution from its roots in the Old Regime—nor by indulging in a cynical one dwelling on how it was being travestied—a sure sign of a partial understanding of its causes, and thus a failure to reply to its hidden cues for individuals to engage in choice. If Tocqueville had been an advocate of simple and stark continuity, his commitment to political liberty in a democratic age would have been a species of playacting more perverse than the political acting he deplored: a heavily constrained notion of liberty could only support belief in deep and irreversible social structures. To be sure, fissures and faults, located deep in human archaeology, were always at work, but if they created new resting places it was not without the help of human agency. A reverse advocacy of discontinuity, with implications of radically new directions, would have trivialized his project, since exercising liberty would have been as effortless as wearing comfortable clothes. The issue for Tocqueville was thus not reducible to a discourse on the relative merits of continuity and discontinuity as instruments of historical explanation. The Great Revolution had to be seen rather as an epicenter from which continuing shocks continued to radiate. In it inhered, as it were, the continuity with the past, and it was itself the very source of the change subverting it, with determinateness and choice engaged in a ceaseless dialectic. Tocqueville was playing on a subtle but vital difference when he spoke of the 1848 revolutionaries as "acting the French Revolution, rather than continuing it."[30] If the differences were obscured, historical continuity would be reduced in the long run to continual reenactments of a single scenario and not be seen for what it is—a *continuation* of a series or a succession of stages that had begun in France's prerevolutionary past, with the Great Revolution marking a partial embodiment of an obedience to ancient social and political impulses, as well as a harbinger of a new age. If Tocqueville's project is interpreted in the first sense, then change cannot figure in his philosophy of history; if, in the second, it is never far from it.

Tocqueville did not take either path unequivocally. His opening remarks in *L'Ancien Régime* about unintended consequences may be seen as a compromise, but they remained the basis of one of his abiding intellectual principles; he transformed it into a powerful image focused on the blindness of politicians, who, in their mutual challenges for place and power, actually think that intentions and results are unambiguously related, because, as he put it at one point, they fail to note that "the kite . . . flies by the antagonistic action of the wind and the cord."[31] The end of an action is not necessarily to be found in its intention. The net effect of the Great Revolution is to be sought as much in the unexpected tensions that create it as in those that it creates. Unintended consequences are in any case as important as, or indeed constitute, the paradox that the revolutionaries "used the debris of the old society to construct the edifice of the new."[32] This could be taken both as a silent rebuke to and as an endorsement of Edmund Burke, whom Tocqueville elsewhere criticized as blind to the abuses of the Old Regime and to the grandeur of the revolutionary image of renewal;[33] and it may appear to place Tocqueville on the side of those who see change as mere froth on the tides of an implacable history. Unlike Burke who tended to see change as an inversion or a perversion of a universal natural order but employed legalistic and utilitarian arguments against it, Tocqueville tried to remove himself from these remnants of an older theodicy and from the seductions of utilitarianism. Nor did he see change as part of providential design, as did Joseph de Maistre,[34] Louis de Bonald,[35] and even Mallet du Pan:[36] the first was literal minded and vengeful; the second saw the turmoil of the Revolution as part of an expiatory plan; the much more sober Mallet preferred to speak of a less personal "force des choses." Tocqueville used some of the providential vocabulary, drained it of its conventional religious referents, and substituted for them a far more distant and unknown divine presence, which almost amounted to a divine absence from human affairs. He therefore ultimately deprived providence of consequentialism, which is its marrow. He tried to be indifferent, as his thoughts on certainty and probability show, to rigorist notions of determinism. In most instances, he envisaged change as the instrument by which long-term trends asserted themselves more clearly and strenuously, shedding the encumbrances of obsolete practices sanctioned by conventional legal practices.

The reverse side of this notion of change, as Tocqueville saw it, was that the exalted ideals that animated the early revolutionaries were delivered a cruel and decisive blow. Whether or not he borrowed the notion of the Revolution as monster from Burke, he called it a creature of diseased minds, a "virus,"[37] but he thought of it as creator as well. The Revolution was both the symbol and devourer of the highest values. Its greatest legacy for Tocqueville was that it was both the child and mother of modern liberty. Nonetheless the temptation to devalue it seemed to be an older and more persistent psychic drive. He was not forgetting the liberties that he believed were once part of the corporate structure of the Old Regime and that had been crushed by the state as it assumed its modern shape and imposed itself over civil society. But he was more concerned about a new and modern liberty that had to find its appropriate political setting. The Revolution as contradiction lived as a reality in Tocqueville's mind so much so that he celebrated 1789 as "that period of [naive] inexperience, but also a time of generosity, enthusiasm, heroic courage, lofty courage and [a sense] of grandeur, a time of deathless memory to which the thoughts of men will turn with admiration and respect long after those who have seen it, as well as we ourselves have vanished."[38] It was in 1789 that Frenchmen were confident enough to believe that they could be equal and free at the same time. The years leading up to 1789, Tocqueville had hinted earlier, however, represented just such time. In that period between the silencing of the imagination characteristic of caste societies and the isolation and "torpor" of a society of conforming equals, "new ideas suddenly change[d] the face of the world."[39] As momentous as such periods in history are, Tocqueville would not let go of his more pessimistic view that liberty vanishes when admiration for absolute government feeds on the contempt human beings feel for their neighbors.[40] Tocqueville was once again giving voice to the dangers he had detected twenty years earlier in democratic societies—in which equality and tyranny were likely to coexist—of inflating the benefits of private comfort to the detriment of good citizenship.

The Revolution was thus a paradox. Because Tocqueville could not settle the question of the determinateness of the past, apart from his belief that the "unknown force"[41] at work in the destruction of aristocratic society could only have been regulated or slowed down by human agents with practical wisdom, the Revolution had been a promise yet perhaps also an unintentional trap. However, he did not draw out the full import of the paradox. He did not write the planned history of the "vicissitudes of that long revolution." His first aim had been to develop the motif that he had set out in 1836 in his *État social et politique de la France avant et depuis 1789*, which John Stuart Mill translated and published in the *London and Westminster Review*. In the *État*, he took care to say that the revolutionaries had been shaped by the old order and remained recognizable under the superficial change.[42] But, as he put it to Henry Reeve twenty years later, what the Revolution had truly accomplished and what its "violent labors" against the Old Regime had brought to birth that was truly new, were necessarily distinguishable. "But that [such a work] would lead me too far," he added.[43] As he grew older, his doubts about his capacity to explore these tensions increased and reveal how much he was troubled both by the common perception that the Revolution was a total break with the past and by his conviction that this was much too shallow an explanation.

Tocqueville's image of the cataclysmic and unpredictable force of the Great Revolution figured in his lexicon as a perplexing instance of the uncertain effect of human action in history, with the result that it threatened existence with meaninglessness. In the tropes of others closer to the Revolution in time, either as participants or observers, its unfolding caught them in its embrace, inflaming passion, rarely cautioning distance. In spite of his declarations of "disinterestedness," his aim to be "strictly precise,"[44] and his pride in his patient archival research, his adoption of a strategy of detachment was tinged with a degree of self-doubt, but he never quite grasped its roots, possibly because he saw nothing contradictory in passionately avowing his political beliefs while denying that they constituted a species of prejudice, since he could not conceive of it as inimical to or obstructive of his great love for and his need to defend liberty. He wanted to possess the secret of the event and the idea, to capture them, as it were, as they occurred, were thought, or were uttered—to find them in the grid of the Revolution in its actuality. The challenge threw him into a state of perplexity, inducing a state of vertigo.[45] He deeply sensed that he could not achieve the feat of penetrating to the raw reality of persons and movements; that at best his history would be a work of pale representation, but he wanted desperately that it should be more "true" than the work of others. He saw himself as a philosopher–historian and instructor to the future; by appealing to a "superaddressee"—I am borrowing Bakhtin's conception of the writer's ideal audience[46]—he thought he would be able to release the discrete mysteries of the French Revolution as well as reveal the general laws of revolution in their largest sense. But his project was to be accomplished, he promised himself, by resolutely setting himself apart from historians who claimed "mathematical exactness" in speaking about human affairs,[47] only to fall victim, as politicians and kings were prone, when they thought they were avoiding the mistakes of their predecessors, to errors of their own.

Tocqueville honestly acknowledged that his pose in the *Souvenirs* paled to nothingness in the light of the power of the events of 1848 upon which, in repose, he was reflecting.[48] And those events, he said, almost immediately assumed a mimetic character. Tocqueville treated the revolutionaries of 1848 as unconscious parodists of 1789, who just as unconsciously contributed to a comic view of the past; the comic was history's revenge; it offered the consolation of laughter; in Tocqueville's scale of values it was ironic laughter; it was the other side of history that is usually thought to have only a serious dimension. Thus the comic did not conceal the nature of human history but was instead a way to a fuller knowledge of it.[49] Are we justified in concluding that in Tocqueville's view the men of 1848 were merely replaying an old script in their floundering uses of the radical rhetoric of 1789, and were unable to devise a new one that would take them and France beyond it? This makes sense if we recall his belief that the 1848 actors did not continue what 1789 had begun. Such an insight nevertheless left Tocqueville with a feeling of deep unease. Could he articulate how what he admired in 1789 might be continued and bring an end to the Revolution, some sixty years after it had shaken the world, without reconstituting the realities of the immense varieties of the conflicts and their participants preceding and during the Revolution? His contemporaries, whose every weakness he caught in verbal caricatures worthy of Daumier, were, he thought, fair game; but they were safely locked away in his "secret" memoirs of the 1848 Revolution, although the fact that he could not keep the *Souvenirs* completely secret, as his correspondence with some of his friends shows, proves how much his call upon his inner self was determined by his need to make sense of the Revolution, and that he could not begin to do so without reemerging from his solitude.[50] Would he be able to expose the flaws and extol the deeds of the principal actors of the Great Revolution, the "real" but dead actors, those whose actions and whose party labels the politicians and enthusiasts of 1848 ingested so greedily? Would the "real" actors be any more real than their imitators? In theory, the answer could be yes, since, in Tocqueville's framework, they represented a genuine break with the past and their conduct constituted a foundational act. This question, however, he could not confidently confront, though he knew how important it was to open the question of the role of key actors. It was their impotence, volatility, fear, and self-interest that he observed. They were overwhelmed by momentary confidence and longer-term bafflement.[51] He was more comfortable moving around the long antecedents and the long-term effects of the Revolution, despite his conviction that human beings cannot be absolved from and in fact contribute to the making of their own history, whether for good or ill, and should therefore be a proper subject of historical enquiry. The utterances of the men of 1789 could not be more opaque than the impermeability of the institutions, including language, under which they lived and which had originally shaped them together as a community, which tied them together by invisible bonds and bound them to a more and more remote past. They had to be transparent in some mythic beginning—in the years leading up to 1789, and in 1789 itself—the brief period in which modern liberty for Tocqueville came to life and which came to serve as a constant reminder of what people could accomplish. But, as we shall see, even such a privileged moment did not elicit from him a prolonged interpretation of the leading actors either at the outset of or during the Revolution.

"LE MAL RÉVOLUTIONNAIRE"

Tocqueville feared being swallowed up in an ocean of materials, and he swam away from its undertow by subordinating the actors to his theory that the choice made in favor of liberty was blown off course—more—that the totality of human actions, rather than persons, took on a pathological character, for which he invented the locution, "le mal révolutionnaire." Imprecise though it was, it may best be understood as an inversion of the will that amounted to a kind of illness or impoverishment of the spirit. Images of disease, sickness, defective organs, and the need to dissect them to find causes were meant to expose the sources of the Old Regime's defects.[52] That was one path to understanding. Physiological metaphors for political breakdown were commonplace before Tocqueville's time. So were metaphors of unsettled and "unnatural" states of mind for deviant political and social action. He made use of both, but his language suggests that, although he found plausible explanations for the violence of the Revolution, he was more perplexed by revolutionary mentality than by the breakdown of entrenched polities. It should be noted that he did not integrate these as part of a single dynamic process. He could write with comparative ease about the signs of a complacent and dying social order and a well-intentioned but ineffective, inept, and often mendacious administration, but he found "le mal révolutionnaire," which followed the breakdown of the Old Regime, too intractable a subject. From the context with which he surrounded the phrase, it is safe to say he meant the successively more violent stages of the Revolution itself. Le mal révolutionnaire, he seemed to be arguing, was synonymous with revolutionary government, which was illegitimate, although he did not say how, except by suggesting it was due to the excesses of democracy itself. The newness of democratic equality led to scenes of brutality and inhumanity. The violence, which he contrasted with the benign nature of democratic theory, possessed a virulent quality that grew out of the very texture of the lives of oppressed people and need not therefore be surprising. Le mal révolutionnaire was also more importantly a kind of philosophy and theory of action; the likelihood was that, even when it exhausted itself along with the concrete particularities giving rise to and created by revolutionary society, it would not disappear but would remain as a permanent, if shadowy, human passion. It had always been at, or the Revolution had brought it to, the surface of human experience; and it was repeatable.[53] We cannot know whether he thought the mal révolutionnaire was a fall or an original flaw, since he seems to have been unable to choose between these two explanations. Thus he could scarcely have found it a simple matter to speak of individual responsibility, and he retreated to the notion that, if anything, the "mal" manifested itself and could best be represented as an example of a profound break with the past, which, in its turn, descended into incoherence and error.[54]

The development of such incoherence—the revolutionary disease—may have been given, he was suggesting, its impetus and rationale by the pamphleteers who were especially prominent in 1788–1789. Tocqueville's notes reveal a fairly close inspection of several of their ideas; there is no evidence that he ever looked at the later, more revolutionary papers and pamphlets. The earlier ones were produced by men whose ideas, he claimed accurately, constituted more than just a transition point between the old and the new political discourses. The outlines and often the substance of their ideas were already, if not fully in every case, establishing a lexicon of revolutionary challenge. The prime example was Sieyès, whose pamphlet, *Qu'est ce que le Tiers-Etat*, Tocqueville described as a veritable *cri de guerre*—"a specimen of the violence and the radicalism of opinion, even before the struggles that are said to have provoked violence and radicalism." In doing so, it was the germinal expression of the Revolution ("le plus congénital de la Révolution"). In his call for full-scale war against the ancient social and legal structures of France and the absolute and unlimited triumph of his theories, without due regard for their practical effect, Tocqueville sounded a note of outrage and wonder at the breathtaking presumption that could ignore the cultural and political heritage of an ancient civilization and reduce politics to the mechanical counting of heads.[55]

Two crucial points emerge from his analysis of Sieyès's powerful and decisive pamphlet, which he resumed and expanded in his evaluations of pamphlets written by Mounier,[56] Barnave,[57] Brissot,[58] Rabaud-Saint-Etienne,[59] and Péthion.[60] The first was their animus against the idea of favoring the united action of the legal orders and social ranks, exemplified by the decision of the three Estates at Vizille in the province of Dauphiné to remain a single body.[61] The second was the almost total repudiation of Montesquieu's constitutionalism, which Tocqueville said was distorted by the pamphleteers who saw it as a screen to promote the special interests of the privileged. All of them were too blinded by their aversion for the Old Regime to grasp the benefits of a gradual readjustment of the balance of political forces in the monarchy.

For example, Mounier's great error was to allow himself to be carried away by the bizarre notion that a bicameral assembly was to be avoided because only a unicameral one could effect the changes France required. Only after they were introduced did Mounier feel secure enough to entrust the nation to a divided assembly. Such a formula, which placed the political future of the nation at the mercy of a single class or a single party, Tocqueville complained, was "excellent indeed for making a revolution, but hardly the one to bring an end to it at the right time." The obliteration of all the features of an orderly society in these circumstances degraded liberty, and equality, left on its own, simply became another name for servitude.[62] Such a process in Tocqueville's eyes was a striking demonstration of how the powers of centralization were strengthened. Mounier's precise aim, he said, was not to support centralization, but he supported the steps that led to it[63] ("Il ne veut pas précisément la centralization, mais ce qui y conduit"). This instance of unintentional consequences was once again the reward of false premises.

Barnave, too, had originally spoken out against innovation, when the monarchy dared to invade the rights of the magistrates in 1788. He did so, Tocqueville observed with approval, in the spirit of Montesquieu's detestation and fear of despotism. Tocqueville marveled at Barnave's youthful appeals for a union of all classes and interests, his praise of the "illustrious families" of France that protected the monarchy with their blood, and his "sincere" appeals to natural equality and democracy; and although Tocqueville wondered about the prospects of a permanent union of all the forces ranged against the despotic state, he conceded that such a union had reached the limits of the possible.[64]

Thus, though he kept coming back to the theme of united action, noting that the future Girondin, Brissot, had appealed for caution, conciliation, and harmony, he acknowledged that Brissot's opposition to the exclusivity of the first two orders was his major and most decisive argument. As a result of his stay in the United States, he had become convinced that a Convention was a necessary step toward the remaking of the political map of France. For Tocqueville this was a truly revolutionary idea. Whether or not Brissot's text justifies Tocqueville's reading of it, Tocqueville derived a certain pleasure from and accorded his respect for Brissot's understanding of the conservative nature of the American political experience. As proof, Tocqueville mentioned the American decision to adopt a bicameral legislature. He may also have been recalling his praise of the makers of the American Constitution. Recognition of the utility of American practices was much more desirable in Tocqueville's opinion than the views of the "worst imitators" who had "taken from the United States the abstract principles of their constitution without having felt the need of applying them conservatively which had been achieved in America."[65]

From Brissot Tocqueville went on to consider Rabaud-Saint-Etienne who, he dryly observed, took four years to discover that he was tired of acting the part of the tyrant and was executed for admitting that he was mistaken for thinking that the regime of privileges was more to be feared than royal power. Rabaud's sudden insight, Tocqueville could not resist adding, was a good case of human intelligence knowing too late that it was liberty that needed support; instead, the mind had mistakenly turned its energies to equality.[66] But there was more in Tocqueville's interpretation of the desire shown by all the pamphleteers to move swiftly against any political ploy to retain any semblance of traditional representation. What choices did they have, Tocqueville finally asked himself? Almost none since, in their desire to end privilege, they were unable, because of the profound political differences between France and England, to adopt the English political model to enable them to reduce and limit rather than abolish what had to be ended.[67] Similarly his notes on a pamphlet attributed to Pétion show how he continued to perceive that the revolutionary discourse was moving further and further away from Montesquieu's ideas and that, although liberty was not foresaken, the "final word of the Revolution" came to be "let us try to be free by becoming equal, but it is a hundred times better to cease to be free than to remain or to become unequal."[68]

The revolutionaries who then came into their own were "men who carried audacity to the point of sheer insanity, for whom no innovation was surprising, no scruple could act to restrain, and who would never hesitate to execute an action." Tocqueville was again sounding the theme of equality, the hunger for which had become so overwhelming that it was elevated above and displaced for all practical purposes everything else that the actors of 1789 were bringing to political consciousness in their desire to regenerate France. Those who were responsible for the deflection were not, however, "new beings," nor "the isolated and ephemeral creation of a single moment, destined to disappear with it. They had rather formed a new race of men that endured and gained ground throughout the civilized world, everywhere preserving the same features, the same passions, and the same character. They were already here when we were born, and they are still with us."[69]

Humanitarianism and generosity, two of the noblest features of the Enlightenment, had been blighted by an inhuman revolution.[70] Le mal révolutionnaire had produced murderous effects and was always ready to be summoned up from the depths of human experience. On what grounds was he making these ominous claims? In part, he was calling on Burke's outrage at the climate of revolutionary suspicion of all established opinion. But he was more interested in exposing the origins and consequences of popular opinion. He did so delicately but devastatingly. He was far from denying the connection between ideas and actual events; but he refused to extend to the extreme actions of Year II a footing in solid ideas. At best, those actions and the ideology inspiring them constituted the revolutionary degradation of political ideas and conduct. He had little regard for most of the men of letters of the Old Regime, whom he mistakenly represented as misunderstanding the nature of politics, and who assumed, so to speak, the role of an unofficial public opposition, but did so irresponsibly by producing streams of impractical ideas.[71] At the same time, he made a distinction between abstract ideas and popular expressions of opinion. To the first he conferred a kind of dignity by conceding the good intentions of their theorists, while condemning the savage practices of the uneducated, unlettered, and disorderly elements in society, who took control of and shaped the violent phases of the Revolution. The humanitarians who were trying to transform political culture had no way of controlling their intellectual products, as the latter began to attract a mass audience.[72] In *Democracy*, he had already dissected the power of public opinion; in *L'Ancien Régime*, he adverted to the processes by which public opinion achieved its force in the political and cultural structures of monarchical France. In democracies, he noted in his earlier work, opinion truly came into its own as mistress of the world, because equality erased trust among private men but enhanced their faith in the infallibility of public judgment.[73] In the French Revolution, books were used by the populace, including the peasantry, to satisfy their "lust for revenge."[74] This led to the inevitable deterioration of opinion, as it descended downward to the people from the literary figures and self-styled philosophers.[75] Tocqueville's intention was to make the link between his earlier belief that the ubiquitous nature of public opinion in democratic nations stifled the critical mind and his later belief that nothing could resist its tyranny in revolutionary times. As if to underline this point, he expressed envy for the way in which the English upper classes had made a revolution in 1688 and carefully controlled it by ensuring that it did not pass into the hands of the people. Not so the National Assembly, which had wavered in its resolution. It failed to pass Lally-Tollendal's "timid" motion of 22 July 1789, urging popular moderation, and thus transferred sovereignty to the people of Paris.[76]

Tocqueville saw in the democratic revolution a single but agonistic event that tore its principal actors apart: for him it was indeed the specter haunting Europe, but it was also the creator of a new society. He may have departed from the full import of his original assertion that democratic peoples must "secure the new benefits which equality may offer them . . . [and] to strive to achieve that species of greatness and happiness which is our own,"[77] but he did not doubt even then that were the descent of democracy into democratic despotism to become more and more irreversible, it would be because human beings were wrong to believe it right but were still willing to satisfy their inclination to simplify rather than diversify the means to reach their greatness.[78] However, he questioned his own pessimism when he opposed Arthur de Gobineau's racial theories. He contrasted the "illness" of the revolutionary belief in total self-transformation with the "illness" of the postrevolutionary belief in the futility of will and virtue, and rejected both such expectations and such nihilism.[79]

The theme of continuity that has so enthralled readers of Tocqueville has blinded them to what he regarded as new in the Great Revolution and its echoes in the nineteeth century and after. He did not intend to support, nor may he be read retrospectively as doing so, the claim that the Terror foreshadowed the broad outlines and experiences of the *univers concentrationnaire* of the twentieth century. So respectful was he of the unique rather than the uniform circumstances of events that he distinguished the 1793 Terror that "still preserved in its crimes a certain hypocrisy of forms and honesty missing" from Louis Napoleon's repressive policies that were sending thousands of unfortunate victims into exile without trial.[80] He made the same point after 1856 when he described the "perfected atrocities" characteristic of the Directory, that is, the deportations to Guiana of journalists and politicians, the imprisonment of priests, the forced loans, the confiscations, and the law of hostages, which were, he said, much more cruel than any of the laws of 1793 and were not necessarily consequent on them.[81]

His general remarks on the Terror are couched in language he had consistently used. His conviction that the majority's loss of its rights and willing acquiescence in its own exploitation by tyrannical minorities recalls Montesquieu's conviction that individuals have a profound propensity for subjection. What had to be painted, Tocqueville promised in his notes, was the state of the revolutionary mind by means of which the majority rendered the tyranny of the minority possible. He admired Mallet du Pan's *Mémoires* for adverting to an explanation of the Terror that bordered on his own concerns. It was a powerful force that he said came close to organizing disorganization and uniting the forces of despotism and anarchy, and which was, he agreed with Mallet, not a singularly French but a European phenomenon, one of the most "active and contagious diseases of the human mind."[82] Quite early on, in the first volume of his *Democracy*, he noted that any legislative body, such as the French Convention, which had usurped the role of government, was destined to self-destruction because, while its power was subject to shifts in the popular will, it tyrannized society in the name of that will, by claiming a false identity with it. Its vigor was thus an artifice, subject to imminent disclosure.[83] The insight is reminiscent of Montesquieu's depiction of the operations and ultimate impotence of despotism.[84] Something like the overthrow of the despotism of the legislative power, Tocqueville intimated, must have begun but was not completed at Thermidor. By the end of his life, he was satisfied that he had discerned the contours of the new democratic despotism. He had shifted his concern from the powers concentrated in the legislative body to those in the clenched fist of the executive power.[85] The study of the Revolution's inflation of the popular will strengthened his conviction that it was the key to popular subjection.

It is not at all certain that he was prepared to entrust liberty to the bourgeoisie of his own day, who were hardly the same as they were at the beginning of the Great Revolution.[86] He was less interested in embarking on an analysis of their newer sources of wealth than in commenting on the development of their power and their total inwardness. They had undergone a sea change in two generations. Tocqueville was once again reflecting on the ironies and paradoxes of unintended consequences. By triumphing in 1789 and after, the bourgeoisie ended the unity of opposition to the crown. That union had captivated Tocqueville's admiration because it symbolized a willingness for self-sacrifice. By contrast, 1830 was the triumph of selfishness—it gave the bourgeoisie the chance to establish their full identity and their hegemonic power to demonstrate how they would utilize it. Tocqueville excoriated their abuses of power over the next eighteen years, noting disdainfully that they were enduring ignominies in 1848 similar to those suffered by the nobility whom they had displaced. The new governing class, "through its indifference, its selfishness and its vices," proved "incapable and unworthy of governing the country."[87] Just as he inveighed against the old aristocracy for its exclusiveness, he turned against a similar shortcoming in the bourgeoisie of his own time but found that, despite their common defect, one difference between them was striking, perhaps decisive. The middle class was far from being a homogeneous body. It expanded and contracted, it bordered on other classes, and, for this reason, was hard to locate, define, or attack, even if it tried to retain its exclusivity.[88] Indeed, it was liable to greater vulnerability than the aristocracy and would, in the light of 1848, be forced to face the fact that property was no longer shielded by the system of odious privileges that had been abolished in the Great Revolution, and was therefore more directly open to attack.[89]

Tocqueville just as determinedly ridiculed what he thought were the illusions of the socialist sects. There could be no question of entrusting them with the defense of liberty. But we should not forget that he adverted to the existence in the eighteenth century of conflicting views of political economy,[90] calling into question the paramountcy of private property. He thus helped to bring to consciousness the question of how the desire to free the market from legal restraints, traditional conventions and customs, and the power of the state triumphed over the challenges to a market society and had become the established dogma of the discourse of political economy. Tocqueville's reactions to the observed effects of the new political economy, rather than to its growing but by no means assured status as a body of noncontingent truths, were far from positive. Although he admitted that the growth of the modern economy conferred technological benefits, and although he affirmed that commerce prepared individuals for freedom,[91] he had, long before his work on the Revolution, believed it necessary to look at the "concealed relationship between . . . liberty and commerce." From his examination, he drew the conclusion that freedom in its largest sense gave birth to commerce.[92] Indeed, he was in some important ways more sympathetic to some of the dying moral principles that underlay a premodern economy, while denying at the same time that they had any final purchase in a world that was being instructed by its leading political economists not to confuse commerce and ethics. In *Democracy*, his views on individualism and jeremiads against the effects of economic success and well-being on the prospects of personal political liberty made up his testament to the ultimate vacuity of restless ambition in a world that had ended endemic scarcity and had enthusiastically embraced material gratification as a goal, while investing with intense passion the power that such self-concentration gave to people in a democratic society to act in the name of but almost invariably against civic responsibility. It was as if he were saying that in some inexplicable way the relationship between modern political economy and liberty had been distorted—that commerce, the child of liberty, might in due course strangle its parent, rather than preserve it, and thus help to smother civic responsibility whose leading principle was liberty.

His conviction was not without its sense of desperation, and the problem was how to overcome or at least to mitigate it. As is often the case in interpreting Tocqueville's thought, what he failed to integrate into his deft crafting of his consistent view of the past holds the key to the question. When in *Democracy* he charted the development of equality in America and in France, the two societies in which forms of democracy had been reached by different routes—one without, the other with violent revolutionary struggle—he saw equality not only as a legal and political reality, but also as a desirable condition for expanding economic capabilities in the eyes of those who yearned for it. One may therefore read *L'Ancien Régime* in a state of forgetfulness of the immensely significant role Tocqueville gave in his *Souvenirs* to the bourgeoisie's defense of property in the prelude to and aftermath of 1848, in the course of which, as we saw, he took a much harder line against the nonpropertied majority. If we remain forgetful, we may also overlook the extent to which he had seen the 1830 Revolution as a license for the bourgeoisie to plunder society. He castigated them for not taking care to see how their apotheosis of and seduction by wealth would generate bitter social conflict. And after 1848, he predicted darkly that fate decreed alternations between license and oppression, rather than a regulated and stable system of liberty.

Tocqueville thought about liberty's and history's elusiveness as a positive inducement to human beings to see them both as reminders of their fragile hold on life's meaning. The only liberty that mattered was the liberty that allowed human beings to obey the laws they themselves enacted, provided the nations of which they were part made a proper use of it.[93] He valued "the stable, regulated liberty, restrained by religion, custom and the law" about which he spoke in his *Souvenirs*,[94] and not the unregulated liberty that led to the undoing of the "authentic" liberty he believed was one of the great unclaimed legacies of the Enlightenment.[95] It is therefore an error to think that Tocqueville would have been ready to concede that in democracies "the new sense of equality, society and humanity [could] only be reconciled with liberty on condition that it never be realized." This conclusion is reached on the grounds that actualization would see human beings "slipping into the imaginary which would effect a split between the reign of opinion and the reign of power, between the reign of science and men who are subjugated."[96] Tocqueville, it is true, warned against this. The revolutionaries, he complained, had moved recklessly into an embrace of their own artifice, "une société imaginaire," and had produced a disaster. Instructive for Tocqueville in his understanding of the Revolution was that it provided additional evidence of the fragility of modern liberty. In *Democracy*, he had spoken about the practical measures he believed necessary to strengthen liberty. But after 1848, after writing *L'Ancien Régime*, and during the last three years of his life as he reflected further about the events of the Revolution, he could not resist coming back to those moments before and during the earliest stages of the Revolution when a rare moment had united all classes. That is the only meaning that may be given to his belief that 1789 would remain enigmatic so long as human beings were caught in the tangle of reliving, rather than continuing, what it had begun. He had set out to escape from the labyrinth of the past, constructed a coherent view of it to instruct his fellow creatures to avoid its deepest recesses, and invented his own imaginary future to keep the image of liberty alive.

NOTES

1. Alexis de Tocqueville, *De la démocratie en Amérique* (Paris, 1951), 1, pt. 1 : 13–14/ pt. 1 : 17; citations henceforth will appear as *DA*. The numbers following the slash indicate references to the translation, *Democracy in America*, 2 vols. (New York: Vintage, 1945). Whenever I believed my translations gave a more accurate rendering of the original text, I have used them. The reference is to the full edition, *Oeuvres complètes*, J. P. Mayer, ed., *Oeuvres, papiers et correspondance d'Alexis de Tocqueville* (Paris: Gallimard, 1951–), hereafter *OC*.

2. Alexis de Tocqueville, "Réflexions diverses," in *L'Ancien Régime et la Révolution* (Paris: Gallimard, 1952–1953), 2, pt. 1 : 343. Citations henceforth will appear as *AR*. References to the page numbers in *The Old Regime and the French Revolution* (New York: Doubleday Anchor Books, 1955), trans. Stuart Gilbert, will appear following the slash in the parentheses. I have again altered the translations where I saw fit. Translations from the second volume are my own.

3. Tocqueville to Kergorlay, 15 December 1850, *OC: Correspondance d'Alexis de Tocqueville et de Louis de Kergorlay* (Paris: Gallimard, 1977), 13, pt. 2: 229–234.

4. Ibid.

5. Kergorlay to Tocqueville, 6 January 1838, 13, pt. 1: 119–124; Tocqueville to Royer-Collard, 6 April 1838, 15 September 1843, *OC: Correspondance d'Alexis de Tocqueville et de Pierre-Paul Royer-Collard* (Paris: Gallimard, 1970), 11: 59, 114–116.

6. Tocqueville to Corcelle, 1 August 1850, *OC: Correspondance d'Alexis de Tocqueville et de Francisque de Corcelle* (Paris: Gallimard, 1983), 15, pt. 2: 227–230.

7. Tocqueville to Royer-Collard, 15 September 1843, *OC: Correspondance d'Alexis de Tocqueville et de Pierre-Paul Royer-Collard* (Paris: Gallimard, 1970), 11: 114–116.

8. Tocqueville to Henry Reeve, 6 February 1856, *OC: Correspondance d'Alexis de Tocqueville et de Henry Reeve* (Paris, 1954), 6, pt. 1: 160–61.

9. *DA*, 1, pt. 2: 90–92/90–93.

10. *DA*, 1, pt. 1: 289, 300/301, 310.

11. *AR*, 2, pt 1: 199/146. See H. Mitchell, "Political Mirage or Reality? Political Freedom from Old Regime to Revolution," *Journal of Modern History* 60 (1988): 28–54. Gustave de Beaumont, Tocqueville's friend who was reading the proofs of *L'Ancien Régime*, pressed him for a fuller explanation, since in all countries, he wrote, writers are often far removed from practical affairs. Tocqueville replied that in France they not only had no practical involvement but had no idea of what actually went on in government. Their ignorance was due to the absence of political liberty; in free countries, by contrast, they somehow have an instinct for it without taking part in it. See Tocqueville to Beaumont, 24 April 1856, *OC: Correspondance d'Alexis de Tocqueville et de Gustave de Beaumont* (Paris: Gallimard, 1967), 8, pt. 3: 395.

12. *S*, 57/34–35. *OC: Souvenirs* (Paris: Gallimard, 1964), 12, 57/34–35. Citations henceforth will appear as *S*. Page references following the slash are to *The Recollections of Alexis de Tocqueville*, trans. A. T. de Mattos (New York: Meridian Books, 1959).

13. Tocqueville to Ampère, 21 October 1856, *OC: Correspondance d'Alexis de Tocqueville et de Jean-Jacques Ampère* (Paris: Gallimard, 1970), 11: 351.

14. *S*, 84/64.

15. *S*, 2/87.

16. *AR*, 1, pt. 1: 74/xii.

17. *S*, 47/21.

18. *DA*, 1, pt. 1: 250–251/256–257.

19. *S*, 104/90.

20. Cf. G. A. Kelly, "Parnassian Liberalism in Nineteenth-Century France: Tocqueville, Renan, Flaubert," *History of Political Thought* 8 (1987): esp. 479–486.

21. *S*, 29, 102/1, 87.

22. *S*, 30/2.

23. *S*, 74/54.

24. Cf. the richly suggestive essay by I. M. Lotman, "The Decembrist in Daily Life (Everyday Behaviour as a Historical–Psychological Category)," *The Semiotics of Russian Cultural History: Essays by I. M. Lotman, L. Ia. Ginsburg and B. A. Uspenskii*, eds. A. D. Nahkimovsky and A. S. Nahkimovsky (New York: Cornell University Press, 1985), pp. 95–149. "The contemporary observer would see the everyday behavior of the Decembrists as theatrical, that is to say, directed toward a *spectator*. But to say that

behavior is *theatrical* does not imply that it is insincere or reprehensible in any way"
(p. 105).

25. *S*, 107/87.

26. *DA*, 1, pt. 1: 90/pt. 2: 91.

27. *S*, 59/37.

28. *S*, 87/68.

29. Tocqueville to Nassau William Senior, 13 November 1852, *Correspondence and Conversations of Alexis de Tocqueville with Nassau William Senior from 1834 to 1859*, ed. M. C. M. Simpson, 2 vols. (London, 1872), 2: 31–32.

30. *S*, 74/54.

31. *S*, 50/26.

32. *AR*, 2, pt. 1: 69/vii.

33. *AR*, 1(2): 338–342. Tocqueville was reading Burke's *Reflections on the Revolution in France* (1790) with marked attention.

34. J. de Maistre's two major works are *Considérations sur la France* (1797) and *Essai sur le principe générateur des constitutions politiques et des autres institutions humaines* (1809).

35. L. de Bonald's early work (1796) was his *Théorie du pouvoir politique et religieux*. He also wrote *Législation primitive* (1802), and his *Démonstration philosophique du principe constitutif de la société* was published in 1830.

36. See Mallet du Pan, *Mémoires et correspondance pour servir à l'histoire de la Révolution française*, ed. A. Sayous (Paris, 1851).

37. Tocqueville to Kergorlay, 16 May 1858, *OC: Correspondance d'Alexis de Tocqueville et de Louis de Kergorlay* (Paris: Gallimard, 1977), 13, pt. 2: 337–338.

38. *AR*, 2, pt. 1: 247/208.

39. *DA*, 1, pt. 2: 266, n. 1/274, n. 1.

40. *AR*, 2, pt. 1: 76/xv.

41. *AR*, 2, pt. 1: 73/xii.

42. *État* in *AR*, 2, pt. 1: 65; cf. *AR*, 2, pt. 1: 72/10.

43. Tocqueville to Henry Reeve, 5 February 1856, *OC: Correspondance d'Alexis de Tocqueville et de Henry Reeve* (Paris: Gallimard, 1954), 6: 161.

44. *AR*, 2, pt. 1: 73/xii.

45. Tocqueville to Freslon, 20 September 1856, cited in A. Jardin, *Alexis de Tocqueville 1805–1859* (Paris: Hachette, 1984), p. 486.

46. M. M. Bakhtin, *Speech Genres and Other Late Essays*, trans. V. W. McGee (Austin: University of Texas Press, 1986), p. 126.

47. *S*, 84/64.

48. *S*, 85–86/66–67.

49. L. Shiner argues that Tocqueville's carnavelesque treatment of the 1848 revolutionaries and politicians undermines any serious intent he might have had. I would claim that Tocqueville's growing pessimism and relentless attempt to extract answers from a recalcitrant past could be relieved only by the use of irony and of the comic, but he meant those devices to put his serious intentions into bold relief. See Shiner's "Writing and Political Carnival in Tocqueville's *Recollections*," *History and Theory* 25 (1986): 17–32.

50. Tocqueville to Kergorlay, December 15, 1850, *OC: Correspondance d'Alexis de Tocqueville et de Louis de Kergorlay* (Paris, 1977), 13, pt. 2: 229.

51. *AR*, 2, pt. 2: 175–176, 192–193.

52. *AR*, 2, pt. 1: 73/xii.

53. *AR*, 2, pt. 2: 368–369.

54. For a discussion of some of these problems, see G. Canguilhem, *On the Normal and the Pathological*, trans. C. R. Fawcett (Dordrecht, Boston, and London: D. Reidel Publishing Company, 1978), pp. 171–175. Another perspective is to be found in J. Elster's theory that illusions (or imaginaries) occur when "both the external situation and the internal processing . . . come into play. . . . [O]ne could also speculate, though I would be more sceptical as to the value of the outcome, that differences in social origin generate differences in the internal apparatus and thus in the liability to illusions (keeping the external situation constant)." See J. Elster, "Belief, Bias and Ideology," in *Relativity and Relativism*, eds. M. Hollis and S. Lukes (Cambridge, Mass.: MIT Press, 1982), p. 137.

55. *AR*, 2, pt. 2: 139–147.

56. I am following the editors of *L'Ancien Régime et la Révolution* in the *OC* in the citation of Mounier's work consulted by Tocqueville: M: Mounier, *Nouvelles observations sur les Etats généraux de France* (1789). This will also be the case for succeeding citations.

57. The editors do not provide a reference to Barnave's brochure. Tocqueville's own notes refer to its title as *Contre les édits du 8 mai et le rétablissement des parlements* (1788).

58. J.-P. Brissot de Warville, *Plan de conduite pour les députés du peuple aux Etats généraux de 1789* (1789).

59. Rabaud-Saint-Etienne, *Considération sur les intérêts du tiers état par un propriétaire foncier* (1788).

60. Pétion, *Avis aux Français sur le salut de la patrie* (1788). I have retained the original Orthography for Pétion.

61. *AR*, 2, pt. 2: 75–78, 145.

62. *AR*, 2, pt. 2: 150–151.

63. *AR*, 2, pt. 2: 148.

64. *AR*, 2, pt. 2: 153–154.

65. *AR*, 2, pt. 2: 155–157; and *DA*, 1, pt. 1: 208–209/214.

66. *AR*, 2, pt. 2: 160.

67. *AR*, 2, pt. 2: 158–163.

68. *AR*, 2, pt. 2: 168–169.

69. *AR*, 2, pt. 1: 208/157.

70. *AR*, 2, pt. 1: 246/206.

71. For a corrective, see K. M. Baker, "On the Problem of the Ideological Origins of the French Revolution," in *Modern European Intellectual History*, eds. D. LaCapra and S. L. Kaplan (Ithaca, N. Y., and London: Cornell University Press, 1982), pp. 197–219.

72. *AR*, 2, pt. 1: 246/207.

73. *DA*, 1, pt. 2: 18/11.

74. *AR*, 2, pt. 1: 246/207.

75. *AR*, 2, pt. 1: 196/142. If Tocqueville could not formulate the means of tracing the unexpected expressions of revolutionary ideas and practices from their presumed

theoretical foundations expounded by the writers who evoked "uns société imaginaire," Augustin Cochin simply gave body to Tocqueville's general observations but eschewed altogether any consideration of the theory/practice problematic. Cf. F. Furet, *Interpreting the French Revolution*, trans. E. Forster (Cambridge: Cambridge University Press, 1981), pp. 164–204, esp. 203–204. Also note P. Ricoeur's rejection of Furet's idea that we may be led back from Cochin to Tocqueville. Ricoeur writes, "No conceptual reconstruction will ever be able to make the continuity with the *ancien régime* pass by way of the rise to power of an imaginary order experienced as a break and as an origin." See P. Ricoeur, *Time and Narrative*, trans. K. McLaughlin and D. Pellauer (Chicago and London: University of Chicago Press, 1984), 1: 221–224. On the generation of an expanded public opinion looking for a wider public space before the Revolution, see K. M. Baker, "Politics and Public Opinion Under the Old Regime: Some Reflections," in *Press and Politics in Pre-Revolutionary France*, eds. J. R. Censer and J. D. Popkin (Berkeley, Los Angeles, London: University of California Press, 1987), pp. 204–246.

76. *AR*, 2, pt. 2: 188.

77. *DA*, 1, pt. 2: 338/352.

78. *DA*, 1, pt. 2: 347/386–387.

79. Tocqueville to Gobineau, 20 December 1853, *OC: Correspondance d'Alexis de Tocqueville et d'Arthur de Gobineau* (Paris: Gallimard, 1959), 9: 201–204.

80. Tocqueville to Henry Reeve, 9 January 1852, *OC: Correspondance d'Alexis de Tocqueville et de Henry Reeve* (Paris: Gallimard, 1954), 6: 132.

81. *AR*, 2, pt. 2: 270.

82. *AR*, 2, pt. 2: 227–228.

83. *DA*, 1, pt. 1: 89/92.

84. Montesquieu, *De l'Esprit des Lois*, in *Oeuvres complètes*, ed. R. Caillois (Paris: Gallimard, 1951), 1: 396–407.

85. *AR*, 2, pt. 2: 320–322.

86. See A. Kahan, "Tocqueville's Two Revolutions," *Journal of the History of Ideas* 46 (1985): 585–596 for a consideration of Tocqueville's treatment of the bourgeoisie in his volume of notes.

87. *S*, 39/13.

88. *S*, 63, 94/41, 77.

89. *S*, 36–37/10–11.

90. *AR*, 2, pt. 1: 213–214/164; pt. 2: 128–129.

91. *DA*, 1, pt. 2: 268/261.

92. Alexis de Tocqueville, *Voyages en Angleterre, Irlande, Suisse et Algérie* (Paris: Gallimard, 1958), *OC*, 5, pt. 2: 90–92.

93. *AR*, 2, pt. 1: 75/xv.

94. *S*, 86/88.

95. *AR*, 2, pt. 2: 132.

96. C. Lefort, "Reversibility," *Telos* 63 (1985): 116.

THIRTEEN

Transformations in the Historiography of the Revolution

François Furet

Translated by Brian Singer

I

The French Revolution was first interpreted in terms of class struggle, before Marx, by the liberal historians of the Restoration. The mechanics of Marx's explanation of history would remain similar, though the outcome and actors were different. He continues with the idea of class conflict but extends it to the proletariat and bourgeoisie, and turns their conflict into the last act in the history of human alienation, since the proletariat is said to bear within itself the end of class society. But this new "end of history" does not prevent him from interpreting, like his bourgeois predecessors, the causes of the French Revolution in terms of the middle class ascendancy—an ascendancy slowly achieved at a social level in the last centuries of the Ancien Régime and crystallized in 1789 when the bourgeoisie came to political power.[1]

The problem with this sort of interpretation, even before Marx, is its inability to account for the modes by which power is taken and held: for it analyzes the contents of the revolutionary event, not its forms, and still less its duration. This can be illustrated by a brief look at the French liberals. Guizot, for example, works out in great detail the idea of the historical rise of the middle class, tied to the entire march of civilization. He examines its economic dimension: the growth of production and consumption, the progress of the market, the rise in living standards, the wealth of the cities and the extravagance of the wealthy; its social dimension: the increased role of the middle class that, freed from feudal domination with the increasing emancipation of the Communes, had become central to the construction of national unity; its moral dimension: the conquest of individual autonomy, both in relation to God (Protestantism) and the City (citizenship as the individual's participation in human history); and lastly its political dimension: the constitution (or reconstitution) of law and the public sphere—which had been fragmented under feudalism and reincarnated by the monarchy in the name of the nation. *Civilization*—a term that Guizot took from the eighteenth century to express less a state than a process, that by which European society becomes "civil"—encompasses at one and the same time the growth of the economy and liberty, the progress of the individual and administrative unity, the Reformation and the nation–state. Its secular dismantling of the feudal system culminated with 1789, which finally allowed modern society and its deus ex machina, the middle class, to appear in the full light of history. "When periodizing revolutions," he notes in his lessons of 1820–1821, "one must begin with the day they burst forth—it is the only precise date one can assign them. They do not, however, take place within such a time framework. The tremors that one terms 'revolution,' are less a symptom of what is beginning than the declaration of what has happened."[2]

But the problem now becomes how to explain the frenzied course of events after 1789. For if the Revolution expressed a necessity of history, a history that had been all but realized prior to it, then it is the revolutionary event itself, its "shadows" and "tempests," to use Guizot's revealing vocabulary, that becomes opaque. And this for two reasons: first, the event displays a strange discrepancy between its rationale, that is, the ensemble of causes that brought it about, and its course, which would lead to its excesses. Instead of establishing representative government, which was to crown and complement the new society, the Revolution followed an erratic trajectory that placed it in conflict with its own principles—since neither Robespierrism nor Bonapartism are compatible with liberty. Second, the uncontrollable character of that trajectory suggests that the middle class, though supposedly victorious in 1789, did not really control its course. There was something truly anarchic about the Revolution of 1789, more powerful than any individual or class strategy, something that would swallow up all of its actors and for a long time render impossible the formation of a stable government. But as Guizot never wrote on the French Revolution itself, he left neither an in-depth analysis of the revolutionary course of events as such, nor a commentary on the difficulties involved in conceptualizing the necessity of 1789 along with all the seemingly contingent events it inaugurated.

These same difficulties can be found in Mignet, himself an author of a history of the Revolution,[3] but one who was no less convinced of the necessity of revolutions in general, and of that of 1789 in particular. As with Guizot, he viewed 1789 as having been completed prior to its actual occurrence. "All the Estates General did was to decree a Revolution that had already been completed." It was, therefore, irreversible. Still, it had traversed tumultuous periods, which appeared incompatible with the seemingly self-evident character with which it had first been greeted. Nonetheless, this same chaotic movement was "almost inevitable" (Introduction, p. 4). In order to demonstrate this claim, Mignet does not have recourse to a "ruse of reason" type of reasoning but resorts instead to a series of interconnected actions deliberately intended by the actors themselves. If the Revolution was necessarily so long, bloody, and complex, despite being inscribed in what preceded it, it was because it had such powerful enemies who reoriented its direction. In their struggle against the Revolution, these enemies provoked the passions of its most extreme partisans. Thus, following the middle-class revolution, there was the people's revolution of 1792, and then, once the nation was saved, the pendulum swung back with the Thermidorian reaction. If there was indeed something necessary about the course of the revolutionary events, it was of a secondary order, deduced from the primary necessity that gave birth to modern society under the guidance of the middle class.

Thus Mignet saves his philosophical reading of the revolutionary events at the cost of logical inconsistencies. The year 1789 was inevitable, an event prepared beforehand by the entire evolution of the Ancien Régime; yet it provoked tremendously hostile reactions on the part of individuals and classes with enough strength and freedom of action to oppose it. The "second revolution," that of 1792, made by the "multitudes" against the middle class, does not possess the dignity of the first, since it did not correspond to any larger necessity of history. It could not, by definition, create institutions or laws since its violence was entirely defensive; and yet it too was inevitable, if only temporarily, as a provisional line of defense for the first revolution. In this manner the determinist interpretation is able to encompass all the detours of revolutionary politics in the name of a grand design, as in Joseph de Maistre,[4] though in a completely different sense. Even those struggles most closely tied to personal rivalries draw their raison d'être from the two provisional ends of the Revolution, to destroy the Ancien Régime *and* push back the enemy, in order to restore it to its normal course, its original social base and project, the establishment of the rule of law. The dictatorship was a parenthesis necessary for the establishment of liberty; the rule of the people was the necessary instrument of middle-class government. What appears as the most improvised is still determined by social groups, in accord with the Revolution's nature.

Marx read Mignet's *History*, along with all the literature on the subject, during his one-year stay in Paris in 1844. But his understanding of the French Revolution remained indebted to the *Phenomenology* and the *Philosophy of Right*.[5] Hegel had elaborated his theory of the state *via* a critique of the Revolution, and Marx, in his turn, criticized the Hegelian philosophy of right by turning its theory of the state upside down—without, however, losing sight of the French Revolution, the privileged and almost obsessive example of the period. For Hegel the state lies atop society, as the supreme substance of that history which is to close the characteristically modern gulf between the public and private spheres and realize man's liberty. With Marx, the young Marx of 1843–1844, the opposite holds true: civil society has primacy over the state. And modernity is characterized above all else by a market society—with the extension of market relations throughout the spheres of production and distribution, and the removal of all obstacles to economic activities—and by the private individual, a monad enclosed in his work, interests, calculations, and pleasures, separated from his fellow man and indifferent to the community and its concerns.

Now, 1789 was a product of this modernity. In effect, with the French Revolution bourgeois society appeared in its nudity, liberated from its feudal chains. After Guizot and Mignet, Marx also provided a social interpretation of 1789, if in modified terms. He too claimed that the bourgeoisie, which had already mastered society, crowned its domination by seizing political power. And in this regard, the bourgeoisie established a representative democratic state, the successor to absolute monarchy. That is to say it established a public sphere that appears autonomous—radically separating the political from the societal realm—but which remains dependent. This state appears autonomous because its representative character expresses the separation of society from the state, and its democratic character (its universality) expresses the abstract equality of the citizen relative to the individual's real situation in civil society. This autonomy, however, is a lie: the state is merely the communitarian mask for a social reality marked by private individualism; a simple alibi that provides the illusion of equality in an inegalitarian world. The separate individuals of modern civil society have alienated themselves within the imaginary community of the state.

This dialectic between the social and political realms provided Marx not just with a general interpretation of the Revolution but with elements for charting its course. As an exemplary expression of modern politics, the French Revolution disclosed with exceptional clarity what Marx called "the state's idealism." This was the significance of 1789, but even more so of 1793 and the Jacobin dictatorship, during which period the revolutionary spirit was revealed in its most radical form. But in this unequal contest, where the social man was the real basis of the imaginary, political man, civil society ended up recovering what the Revolution had temporarily usurped. If 1793 had been the apogee of the citizen's emancipation, Thermidor 1794 was its truth. Yet the revenge of the real on the idea was short lived, since it was followed by the Bonapartist dictatorship. For although Napoleon certainly takes bourgeois interests into account—he was, after all, responsible for the Civil Code, the true social foundation of the postrevolutionary world—he imposed on the bourgeoisie a dictatorial state that had other interests, that had its own ends, and was indeed itself its own end. In this sense, Napoleon reinvented the Terror even as he gave it a different content, that of conquest instead of virtue. The imperial dictatorship was an administrative version of the Terror, achieved at the cost of a change in objective. Here Marx returned to a theme dear to liberal historiography: the elaboration of a relation between Robespierrism and Bonapartism in terms of the state's domination of society.

But as a result, he too ran into the problem common to every social interpretation of the Revolution, that posed by the multiplicity of political forms. It may be easy to conceptualize the transition from 1789 to 1793 (from the constitutional monarchy to the Republic) in terms of the radicalization of men and ideas, but how does one explain the fact that the government established in Thermidor 94—this time a truly bourgeois regime—would also slide out of control and end up in 1799 in a new version of the absolutist state? The first Bonaparte already raised the same difficulty for the young Marx that the second Bonaparte raised for the mature Marx: that of a state established by the bourgeoisie and partially in its service, yet independent of it. Both bourgeois and nonbourgeois—what did Robespierre represent? and what does Napoleon represent? Although the mature Marx never returned to the Revolution as systematically as in his "youthful" writings, it is not hard to see from his writings on the Second French Republic and the rise of the second Bonaparte that he had never resolved the enigma already present in his analysis of 1789 in *The Jewish Question* or *The Holy Family*. If the "illusion" of the modern state is simply a mystification by which the bourgeoisie disguises its undivided class rule, why was there this seemingly endless series of revolutions and coups d'état, all presumably in the service of this same power? Marx is most promising when, as in the *Eighteenth Brumaire of Louis-Napoleon Bonaparte*, he reintroduces the idea of the state's independence relative to society. But he never followed through with this idea, as suggested to him by France's history. For it was constantly being eclipsed by the opposite idea: the state as an instrument of the dominant class and as such tied to the latter's fortunes—triumphant in its rise, condemned during its decline. The prisoner of a determinist philosophy not unlike that of the liberals, Marx found himself in the same impasse for having interpreted France's political history in terms of the development of its civil society and economy.

Perhaps this impasse prevented Marx from writing the history of the Convention about which he dreamed during his youth, but it did not stop his successors. For the historiography of the French Revolution during the twentieth century has been dominated in most European universities, beginning with the Sorbonne, by the Russian Revolution of 1917 and Leninism. The first appeared, at the time, to constitute the social revolution prophesied by Marx, which was to follow France's political revolution. Once power was consolidated, the prediction appeared to be confirmed, and the Russian revolution was situated in an almost natural line of succession with 1789—and all the more plausibly as the Russian Bolsheviks did not cease to claim the Jacobins as their predecessors. As for Leninism, that most subjectivist variant of Marxism, it enabled a glorification of the disruptive, creative, and

almost demiurgical aspect of the concept of revolution, not just as a privileged form of action, but as its only valid form—at the expense of a concern
for the objective conditions behind the historical events.

This explains two features of the Leninist interpretation of 1789 which
push Marx's analysis in a leftward direction. Marx had always upheld the
idea, developed by the French historians of the Restoration, that the absolute
monarchy's power was autonomous relative to society, the arbiter between
the nobility and Third Estate; but twentieth-century "Marxist" historiography[6] sees the absolutist state as aristocratic, governing in the interests of a
formerly feudal class that still retained its social dominance. This claim cannot be found in Marx and is a projection onto the past of Leninism's intransigence relative to the class content of the modern capitalist state—the instrument of monopoly capital, whatever its "formal" procedures. And this claim
changes the Marxist interpretation of the French Revolution, since for Marx
eighteenth-century French society was already largely bourgeois.

At once the French Revolution no longer appears the same. If it still remains, in the last analysis, a product of capitalist development, in its Leninist
version it now appears borne by a twofold necessity; for it also had to overturn and uproot an aristocratic society and a state that would defend themselves tooth and nail. In this domain as in others, Leninism privileges the
voluntarist side of Marxism. More than simply the advent of the bourgeoisie,
the French Revolution appears as the epic drama by which the bourgeoisie
revealed and created itself, as a succession of regimes punctuated by violent
acts in which the bourgeoisie struggled with and triumphed over a formidable counterrevolution. In contrast to Marx, the Leninist historian of the
Revolution celebrates the course of the Revolution more than its results. This
explains the greater emphasis placed on 1793 than 1789, and the preference
for the Jacobins over the Constituents, to say nothing of the Thermidorians.
With the men of 1793, the historian who admires October 1917 finds himself
on familiar ground, since the Soviet experience also illustrated the necessity
of dictatorship and Terror. He shares with the Jacobins and Bolsheviks the
belief that revolutionary action can and must change society: the very same
belief that Marx had analyzed as characteristic of the political illusion that
the social revolution was to have buried and overcome.

The superimposition of the image of the Russian on the French Revolution gave rise to new and original works of research and erudition, most
notably with regard to the study of the popular classes and their actions
during the latter part of the eighteenth century. At the same time, however,
it inevitably deepened the problems presented by the social interpretation
of the revolutionary events since Mignet and Marx had written in the
nineteenth century. Both had already found it extremely difficult to conceptualize the Revolution's character in relation to its course. If the bourgeois
revolution culminated in what is nonbourgeois (and "anticipates" the rev-

olution to come), why call it bourgeois? But here the contradiction, which inheres in Marxism, between historical necessity and subjective voluntarism, is taken to extremes. On the one hand, it is incarnated in two collective actors who had contradictory interests but were harnessed to the same historical mission. And on the other hand, the bourgeoisie, though it had reached maturity, continuously demonstrated its inability to realize the task to which it had been assigned. In effect, the bourgeois government of 1789 proved the least stable of governments, since it cleared the way for state forms that the bourgeoisie did not control, such as the dictatorship of Year II and Bonaparte's despotism.

II

In the last thirty years the whole of the social interpretation of the French Revolution has progressively unraveled—not just in its Marxist form but also in its earlier, classically bourgeois and liberal form, as it first appeared with the historians of the Restoration. The Marxist version, it is true, had weakened the explanatory value of this interpretation by associating the idea of the bourgeoisie with precise historical conditions, like the prior victory of a capitalist economy. And the leftish, Leninist version of Marxism rendered the concept of the bourgeois revolution even more problematic by superimposing 1917 on 1789 and glorifying the dictatorship of Year II, the Revolution's most voluntarist episode. As a result, the social interpretation of the Revolution has continuously lost its relevance with the addition of specific, supplementary characteristics imputed to its necessity.

This point can be clarified by an examination of precisely these conditions, this time by going back over the course of the history, while considering the Leninist, the simply Marxist, and the original, liberal–bourgeois interpretations respectively.

In the case of Marxism–Leninism, the problem is to situate the Revolution's least bourgeois period—characterized by the provisional domination of the sans-culottes, a state-controlled economy, and a terrorist dictatorship directed not just against the aristocracy of birth, but of wealth as well—within the overall necessity of the Revolution's bourgeois nature. Why was the bourgeoisie's political ascendancy accompanied by episodes that are its negation? The contradiction is all the more difficult to resolve as greater emphasis is placed on the Revolution's unfolding than its results and, in particular, on the dictatorship of 1793 that supposedly "anticipates" the conditions of the revolution to come, that of 1917. In this version, what is appreciated above all else is the revolutionary character of 1789, rather than its bourgeois character. And it is difficult, when celebrating the rupture between democracy and the law, and the inability of the men and principles of 1789 to establish durable political institutions, to uphold the bourgeois nature of the Revolution as one's central interpretative thread. In order to do so one must resort to the idea of an aristocratic counterrevolution that forced the bourgeoisie into an alliance with the people and led to the extended use of violence. But the reasoning here proves circular, for resistance to the Revolution, which was almost nonexistent in 1789, was in fact conditioned by the Revolution's radicalism and cannot be explained in terms of class interests.

Now it is true that one does not find this hypervoluntarist conception in Marx. He insisted on the objective factors that led to 1789 and, in particular, the maturity of the French bourgeoisie as the socially dominant class prior to its conquest of power. But as Marx linked this social dominance with that of the capitalist economy, he led the historian before another impasse, one that was underscored in the 1960s by the English historian, Alfred Cobban:[7] at the end of the eighteenth century, the French economy, being based largely on agricultural production and a multiplicity of small rural plots, was not capitalist, as can be seen if compared to the English economy of the same period. And the bourgeoisie of 1789—the bourgeoisie that, for example, filled the Third Estate's seats in the Estates-General or, a little later, the administration of the departments—was not a capitalist bourgeoisie. If it included a certain number of shopkeepers and merchants (but practically no "manufacturers"), its vast majority was composed of legal practitioners—lawyers, judges, prosecutors—an entire world that owed more to French absolutism and the state-bureaucratized society of the Ancien Régime than to the "Manchester" spirit. Furthermore, if one judges the French Revolution not by its actors but by its objective results, one cannot speak of it in terms of capitalism; for the French economy remained more than ever, if compared with England, of a preindustrial type. The Revolution and the Empire democratized the bureaucratic and military values of the old French society, giving the people access to a domain once reserved for the aristocracy. Far from having transformed these national values, the revolutionary period gave them new roots.

If one must hold on to the idea of a bourgeois revolution, then it would be better to endow that revolution with that indeterminacy which it had for the Restoration historians, and make it the tip of a much larger movement, designated somewhat vaguely as the progress of "civilization." From this perspective one can delimit a series of long-term conditions of 1789, such as the quantitative growth of the economy, the progress of communications and exchanges, the decline in mortality rates, improvements to the domestic and urban environments, and the modernization–unification of the kingdom by state action—all things with which the men of the eighteenth century were very much concerned. The French Revolution was a child of growth and not of stagnation. But the historian gains nothing by making the bourgeoisie alone responsible for such progress, since he cannot situate the bourgeoisie, at the end of a long historical process, as the sole actor or beneficiary of the

Revolution. And so the historian finds himself having to renounce the idea that there exists, for the explanation of 1789, some royal road around which all the causal series could be arranged, and whose centerline would be formed by the bourgeoisie, the central actor in the development of civil society.

Now, such a renunciation need not detract from the Revolution's historical dignity—on the contrary. By ceasing to be the product of a class, it appears all the more as at the origins of modernity. Indeed, one is now in a position to rediscover the role attributed to it, for better or worse, by its most perceptive witnesses—Sieyès, Benjamin Constant, Burke, Kant, Fichte, and Hegel: that of bringing forth a world of autonomous individuals, entrusted with reconstructing the City on the basis of their free wills. The latter is not a specifically bourgeois project, since it continues to define the efforts of even those who seek to go beyond the bourgeois horizon, according to socialist doctrine. It encompasses all the attempts undertaken since 1789 to form a political community out of the atomized social universe of the modern individual. In this sense, both the bourgeois universe and the socialist claim to succeed the latter are its progeny. And it remains our point of departure for understanding what separates us from the Ancien Régime, whatever our views relative to the future of modern society. In other words, for today's historian the enigma of 1789 remains intact: it constitutes both a rupture and an origin. It remains our principle figure of historical discontinuity and cannot be domesticated within the terms of the short- or long-term domination of a class, in accord with some preassigned future.

By uncoupling 1789 from the bourgeoisie, one rediscovers something of the mysterious indeterminacy of these celebrated events. One gives the historical actors back their freedom of action—actors who wanted above all to be free, that is, to be able to transform the course of history by an act of will. And the best indicator that this liberty has been restored is the importance given to the Revolution's political dimension, that is, to the way the actors themselves thought and expressed what they were doing. The names they assigned to things are the best signs of the passions they experienced. When a period is obsessed with its political divisions, to the point of using them to define a radical rupture with the past and create a completely new language relative to man and society, it hardly seems reasonable to reduce the period to the advent of an economic form. The French Revolution was, above all else, a laboratory of modern politics. It offers an exceptional wealth and complexity of political materials, as well as many intelligent actors and penetrating commentators. In order to approach its true historical reality, one must give up viewing history as though people in the past were submerged in an opacity that only the historian (or philosopher) can illuminate. One must return to what in history was explicit, which, in the case of the French Revolution, is to be found in its political history, as marked out by an extremely important historico–philosophical tradition. The latter is as old as the Revolution itself (for it begins with, for example, Sieyès or Burke[8]), moves beyond France's frontiers (since German philosophy provides a fundamental contribution), and is enriched throughout the nineteenth century, notably as a result of the French intelligentsia's obsessive relation with—and consequently, its intellectual enthrallment to—the last ten years of the preceding century.

In truth, the French Revolution is so vast an event, and so rich and deep, that it has become central to an analysis of the specificity of modern democracy in relation to the ancient world, as well as to the nation–state assembled by the absolutist monarchy. This line of investigation did not begin post factum but during the Revolution itself, and by its own actors. For example, an examination of the parliamentary debates at the beginning of the Revolution—in the year 1789—reveal that the great figures of the Constituent Assembly were aware of and discussed at length the problems they would have to face: the relation between what was designated as a "revolution" and the preceding centuries, the complexity of the articulation between the rights of man and positive law, the inalienable character of the people's sovereignty and the indispensability of delegating it, the organization of the sovereign into different powers, the compatibility of the legislative power of the sovereign Assembly with the derivative executive power retained by the formerly absolute monarch, and so forth. We have not ceased to pose the same questions in the very terms they were conceptualized by the actors and their contemporaries—and as such, they remain questions basic to our own time. Now all these debates soon converged onto a single, obsessive theme, that of "ending the Revolution"—which twentieth-century historiography has dismissed as due merely to reactionary fears, when it concerns a central problem of modern politics with which we are still very much occupied.

The same applies to what, a little later, was called the "Terror." The Thermidorians, or at least certain of them, were more subtle analysts of the phenomenon than Mathiez or Soboul,[9] even though they specialized in this period. Benjamin Constant, in particular, had an infinitely richer line of questioning than Mathiez.[10] Of course Constant "knew" fewer of the details, but the questions posed by the young Swiss Thermidorian, beginning the year after Robespierre's fall, are far more interesting than those of the communist historian more than a century later. One more proof, amongst so many others, that neither chronological distance nor archival research suffice to guarantee any gains in comprehension, when these supposed advantages are accompanied by a decline in the substantiality of the hypothesis or in the quality of the minds. In many regards, the task of today's historian is to rewrite the Revolution's history within the lines of questioning elaborated by the nineteenth century, but with the enriched documentation bequeathed by the twentieth century.

In this rediscovery of the importance of politics—and of the nineteenth century—a particular place must be reserved for Alexis de Tocqueville, an author who remains essential, at least for the French historian. If, as I believe, the French Revolution was truly what it claimed to be, namely, the empirical form by which the world of free and equal individuals appeared historically, then Tocqueville was probably the person who studied the implications of this epoch-making project with the greatest persistency. He considered the latter in its deepest sense, for "democracy" in his intellectual system does not designate a type of political regime, nor even a state of society, but the condition of modern man, required to view his fellow citizens as his equals. True, Tocqueville saw the victory of democratic principles as the product of a providential design, and thus as the very meaning of universal history. But in his eyes democracy can be subject to very different destinies, since equality can just as easily give rise to the citizen's liberty as the state's despotism.

Now the French Revolution illustrates both possibilities. In 1789 the entire nation rallied against despotism to give birth to democracy, since aristocratic liberty combined with democratic liberty to render the revolutionary explosion governable within the framework of free institutions. But what then followed, with the legislative and the Convention, provided a glimpse of the potential, in the new world of individual equality, for an infinitely more comprehensive despotism than the power of the former absolutist kings. Moreover, the French Revolution only ended with the establishment of a new absolute monarchy, which recreated in an infinitely more authoritarian and centralized form, the administrative state of the Ancien Régime. What Tocqueville sought to discover was the secret link that ties the egalitarian individualism of modern democracy to the tentacular expansion of the centralized state. As he did not have time to write his projected volume on the French Revolution proper, we will never know how he would have analyzed its history in detail; but at least it is possible to know how, with regard to its philosophical foundations, he viewed the question of the drift toward despotism.

By contrast, as regards the other fundamental problem posed by the Revolution, that of its radicality, or in different terms, that of the origins of its rationalist voluntarism, Tocqueville left us his *L'Ancien Régime*.[11] The entire book is devoted to answering the following question: How can one explain the nonhistorical character of the Revolution, its rejection of the past and its abstract constructivism, in terms of what preceded it? He responds by citing two tendencies operating in the Ancien Régime, and which formed its very substance. On the one hand, the absolute monarchy's destruction of aristocratic society and every political tradition of liberty. On the other hand, the elaboration of a philosophy of the "tabula rasa," which one can already find preformed in Turgot and Condorcet at the height of their power and influence in 1774–1776. The Ancien Régime gave democratic radicalism both an instrument for the total subversion of authority, through the centralized state, and an education in such subversion, through the citizens' alienation in a world of pure ideas. As such, *L'Ancien Régime* was not so much a preface to the Revolution or repertory of its origins, than a first revolution predating that of 1789. There lay a tradition concealed behind the rejection of tradition, which would weigh on the Revolution's course and lead to a rediscovery of the centralized state, in a far more perfect version than under the former kings.

One can, moreover, imagine Tocqueville's analysis of the hidden continuity between absolutism and the Revolution being enriched by extending it to the national political imaginary. The monarchy had developed its power as an incarnation of the nation, as the head of a political body conceived of as immemorial, constitutive of social life (l'être ensemble), and as represented by the king of France—"represented" in the earlier sense of the term, that is, as identical to what it reproduced (reproduit à l'identique). It is this totality that the Revolution smashed, on the one hand, by breaking up the organicist society of bodies into free individuals, and on the other, by separating the nation from the king. Now the deputies had to "incarnate" the nation, but from within an atomized society. A difficult task in the best of cases— particularly when undertaken for the first time—but in this case almost impossible, since it was a matter of joining the radical individualism of 1789 with a no less radically unitary conception of the nation.

This can be seen, for example, during the first great constitutional debate of 1789, at the end of August/beginning of September, when the deputies were organizing the transfer of the king's absolute sovereignty to the people—a transfer that began on the seventeenth of June when the assembly of the Third Estate rebaptized itself as, simply, the "National Assembly," and thereby carried out the first, most basic act of the Revolution. In this fundamental debate, the right wing of the revolutionary camp, the first moderates of the Revolution, pleaded for sovereignty in the English manner, with a king and parliament composed of two chambers. But the idea of tying the Revolution to the national past by sharing power between the old monarchy and the new national representation proved impossible for two reasons. First, the "monarchists" were appealing to a tradition and monarchy that did not exist, or no longer existed, if it ever had even the beginnings of an existence in the French past. And then the attempt to "restore" this monarchy, accompanied by a second chamber that would have revived the phantom of aristocratic power after two centuries of absolutist rule, appeared all the more unreal given the radical condemnation as "feudal" of a principle that threatened to survive the absolute monarchy after having preceded it.

In this sense, the radical camp had a more traditionalist understanding than the moderate party: it appropriated the sovereignty developed by absolutism, while the monarchists sought to reinvent it in a form it never had. The radicals gave the Constituent Assembly the sovereign power to reconstruct the political body. But the peremptory affirmation of chronological discontinuity on the part of the patriotic party, which gave new meaning to the word *revolution*, was inseparable from the reappropriation of a conception of political sovereignty that owed its character to absolutism. The people took the place of the king, but the place remained the same. In effect, pure democracy had replaced absolute monarchy. And just as the earlier conception had left no room for anything but the monarch, the new sovereign power could not consent to anything that was not of the people or its "representatives." As such, the idea of the Ancien Régime being formed in August–September 1789 implied the symbolic and practical overturning of the throne and was proclaimed as such by a large majority of the Constituents, despite being masked by the king's new position as the nation's first functionary.

In this way one can, without referring to the history of ideas or the confrontation of social classes, cast new light on the radical character possessed by the Revolution since the beginning, when the counterrevolution did not yet have a social base or any real force. The Ancien Régime and the Revolution formed a couple, radically disjointed yet inseparable.

At this point I do not want to illustrate by further examples how one might renew the history of the Revolution, conceptualized in terms of both the actors' freedom of action and their situational constraints. Indeed, the latter enables one to give them back their extraordinary historical initiative, while simultaneously restoring the Revolution to the historical continuity with which it wanted to break so passionately. By following both these paths the historian can understand the tremendous collective overinvestment in politics that marked the revolutionary years, the difficulties in taming its explosive force, and its latent messianism. The demonstration of the inconsistencies of the social interpretation of 1789 has liberated political analysis from the tutelage of the economic infrastructure, and returned to the center of historical interest the enigma identified by the most penetrating minds of the revolutionary era: How can one form a body of people out of modern individuals, who define themselves by what separates them? The opposition between political and social rights which has fascinated so many generations of commentators is itself simply a variant of this same question, which the Revolution posed at first triumphantly, then tragically.

After almost a hundred years of a historiography obsessed with going beyond the French Revolution—or what amounts to the same, with the limits of the latter—we are now, by contrast, in the midst of rediscovering that the problems posed by the French events of 1789 still form the substance of our present political civilization. I am tempted to stress this point today more than ever, during this *fin de siècle*, when the bankruptcy of all the attempts to resolve the contradictions of the era of free individuals appears so

clearly. And when the evidence suggests, now more than ever, that democracy's dynamics are based on the idea of a political body formed of individual wills and pledged to guarantee and constantly extend individual rights.
In this sense we still remain within the world of 1789, and with the
problems posed during that celebrated year by an Assembly that had been
convoked for other purposes, but which still speaks to us today as if it
were only yesterday.

NOTES

1. The most classical analysis can be found in Guizot's lectures given at the
Sorbonne in 1828–1829. See François Guizot, *Histoire de la Civilisation en Europe* (Paris,
1928), partially reprinted in *Historical Essays and Lectures* (Chicago: University of Chicago Press, 1972).

2. François Guizot, *Essais sur l'histoire de France*, 2d ed. (Paris, 1824), p. 16.

3. F.-A. Mignet, Introduction, *Historie de la Révolution française, de 1789 jusqu'en 1814*
(Paris, 1824).

4. Joseph de Maistre, *Considérations sur la France* (1797).

5. I have written at length on this matter in *Marx et la Révolution française* (Paris:
Flammarion, 1986), translated into English as *Marx and the French Revolution* (Chicago:
University of Chicago Press, 1989).

6. One finds the aristocratic class content of the absolutist state scattered throughout twentieth-century Marxist historiography. For example: Boris Porshnev, *Les
soulèvements populaires en France de 1623 à 1648* (Paris: SEVPEN, 1963), translated from
the Russian: Louis Althusser, *Montesquieu, la politique et l'histoire* (Paris: PUF, 1959);
Perry Anderson, *Lineages of the Absolutist State* (London: New Left Books, 1974).

7. Alfred Cobban, *The Social Interpretation of the French Revolution* (Cambridge: Cambridge University Press, 1964).

8. For example with Emmanuel Sieyès, *Essais sur les privilèges* (Fall 1788) and
Qu'est-ce que le Tiers-Etat? (January 1989), or Edmund Burke, *Reflections on the Revolution
in France* (November 1790).

9. I am thinking in particular of the books of Albert Mathiez dedicated to Robespierre and his role in the Terror. For example, *Robespierre terroriste* (Paris: La renaissance du livre, 1921) or *Autour de Robespierre* (Paris: Poyot, 1926).

10. Benjamin Constant, *De la force du gouvernement actuel et de la nécessité de s'y rallier*
(Paris, 1795), recently republished with a Preface by P. Raynaud in the *Collection
Champs* (Paris: Flammarion, 1989).

11. Alexis de Tocqueville, *L'Ancien Régime et la Révolution* (Paris, 1856).

INDEX

Designer:	U.C. Press Staff
Compositor:	Asco Trade Typesetting Ltd.
Text:	10/12 Baskerville
Display:	Baskerville
Printer:	Maple-Vail Book Manufacturing Group
Binder:	Maple-Vail Book Manufacturing Group